KEYS TO THE BEYOND

SUNY series in Western Esoteric Traditions

David Appelbaum, editor

KEYS TO THE BEYOND

*Frithjof Schuon's Cross-Traditional
Language of Transcendence*

PATRICK LAUDE

Cover: *Apparition of the Buffalo Calf Maiden* (1959). This painting by Frithjof Schuon represents the coming of the holy Pte San Win, "White-Buffalo-Calf-Woman," to the Lakota people, bringing to them the sacred pipe. The original painting is 10 by 24 inches. © Schuon Estate.

Published by State University of New York Press, Albany

© 2020 State University of New York

All rights reserved

No part of this book may be used or reproduced in any manner whatsoever without written permission. No part of this book may be stored in a retrieval system or transmitted in any form or by any means including electronic, electrostatic, magnetic tape, mechanical, photocopying, recording, or otherwise without the prior permission in writing of the publisher.

For information, contact State University of New York Press, Albany, NY
www.sunypress.edu

Library of Congress Cataloging-in-Publication Data

Names: Laude, Patrick, 1958– author.
Title: Keys to the beyond : Frithjof Schuon's cross-traditional language of transcendence / Patrick Laude.
Description: Albany : State University of New York, 2020. | Series: SUNY series in Western esoteric traditions | Includes bibliographical references and index.
Identifiers: LCCN 2019055788 (print) | LCCN 2019055789 (ebook) | ISBN 9781438478999 (hardcover : alk. paper) | ISBN 9781438478982 (pbk. : alk. paper) | ISBN 9781438479002 (ebook)
Subjects: LCSH: Absolute, The. | Schuon, Frithjof, 1907–1998—Criticism and interpretation. | Metaphysics. | Spiritual life. | Religion—Philosophy.
Classification: LCC BD416 .L38 2020 (print) | LCC BD416 (ebook) | DDC 200.92—dc23
LC record available at https://lccn.loc.gov/2019055788
LC ebook record available at https://lccn.loc.gov/2019055789

10 9 8 7 6 5 4 3 2 1

In Memoriam Sharlyn Romaine

"These days I have made a painting showing the White Buffalo Calf Woman bringing the Pipe to the Indians. One may wonder why I made this painting, or others, and why I have been so involved with American Indians (. . .) (. . .) These paintings and their contents are obviously explained by my position at the crossroads of traditional worlds, and this position itself is explained by the cyclic moment in which we live."

—Frithjof Schuon, letter to Martin Lings, November 20, 1958

Contents

Acknowledgments	ix
Introduction	1
1 *Ātman*, *Māyā* and the Relatively Absolute	27
2 The Avatāric Mystery	53
3 *Upāya*: Religion as Relatively Absolute	95
4 The Nature of Things and the Human Margin	123
5 Trinitarian Metaphysics	153
6 Necessary Sufism and the Archetype of Islam	187
7 The Divine Feminine	237
8 The *Yin-Yang* Perspective and Visual Metaphysics	265
9 The "Tantric" Spiritualization of Sexuality	295
10 Esoteric Ecumenism	323
Conclusion	351
Bibliography of the Works of Frithjof Schuon	363
Bibliography	367
Index	375

Acknowledgments

My deep gratitude goes to John Paraskevopoulos and Harry Oldmeadow for their thorough reading of the manuscript.

I am also thankful to André Gomez, Jean-Pierre Lafouge and Reza Shah-Kazemi for their insightful criticism and suggestions regarding several passages of this book.

My sincere thanks to Daniela Boccassini and Carlo Saccone, editors of *Quaderni di Studi Indo-Mediterranei*, for their permission to reproduce sections from chapter 2 that were included in *Quaderni di Studi Indo-Mediterranei*, vol. 10: "Oikosophia: Dall'intelligenza del cuore all'ecofilosofia," edited by Daniela Boccassini (*Mimesis*, 2017): 285–306.

Finally, many thanks to Michael and Joseph Fitzgerald and the Schuon Estate for kindly providing a reproduction of Frithjof Schuon's painting and granting permission to reproduce it on the cover of this book.

Introduction

In his seminal book *Sufism and Taoism*, Toshihiko Izutsu (1914–1993) called for a cross-cultural meta-philosophy that might provide rigorous intellectual tools for comparative studies of Western and Eastern metaphysical traditions. Izutsu referred to Henry Corbin's notion of a "dialogue in meta-history" to express the wish that "meta-historical dialogues, conducted methodically, will eventually be crystallised into a *philosophia perennis* in the fullest sense of the term."[1] This *philosophia perennis* would be nothing less than a conceptual synthesis of the world's wisdom traditions that, without claiming to supersede their respective doctrinal integrity, could function as a philosophical and theological *lingua franca* in a globalized world. The current project takes stock of this intellectual challenge and proposes to make a contribution toward this goal. In other words, it takes the fact of intellectual globalization as a starting point and a motivating factor for the elaboration of a philosophical metalanguage, a *philosophia perennis*. This philosophical *lingua* may function as an enlightening instrument of hermeneutics and theoretical exposition, while engaging a wide spectrum of metaphysical teachings from East and West. The current questions and challenges surrounding cross-civilizational relations makes the need for such a contribution particularly compelling and one that is likely to attract broader attention.

The expression *philosophia perennis* can be traced back to the sixteenth century. It is found, for the first time, in the treatise *De philosophia perenni* (1540) by the Italian humanist Agustino Steuco. Although the term appeared during the Renaissance, the idea of a perennial wisdom that is

---

1. Toshihiko Izutsu, *Sufism and Taoism: A Comparative Study of Key Philosophical Concepts* (Berkeley: University of California Press, 1983), 469.

common to mankind has ancient and medieval roots.[2] It is only in the twentieth century, with the seminal figures of René Guénon (1886–1951) and Ananda K. Coomaraswamy (1877–1947), that a cohesive school of thought emerged centered on the idea of a universal core wisdom underlying all religious traditions. Many prominent scholars have followed in the wake of these two pioneers, beginning with Frithjof Schuon himself, and a number of reliable studies are now available that address the perennialist *Weltanschauung*.[3]

In the English-speaking world, the idea of a *Philosophia perennis*—or a *Sophia perennis*—has been popularized by the works of Aldous Huxley (1894–1963) and Huston Smith (1919–2016). There is no doubt that Huxley's *The Perennial Philosophy*, first published in 1945, became the best-known contribution to the idea that a core metaphysical truth lies at the heart of religions and their wisdom traditions, both Eastern and Western. Moreover, Huxley's exposition was not limited to metaphysics; it also encompassed psychology in the classical sense of a "science of the soul" and a corresponding ethics understood as disciplines that enabled recognition of the "transcendent ground of all being."[4] The "immemorial and universal" wisdom presented by Huxley corresponds, in essence, to the central teaching of the so-called perennialist school. In fact, many popular and scholarly essays on perennialism routinely associate the name of Huxley with perennialism. However, it must be noted that several perennialist authors, such as Gai Eaton and Kenneth Oldmeadow, have questioned this association by arguing that some of Huxley's positions, far from being representative of the perennialists' traditionalist outlook, reflect

---

2. Cf. C. Schmitt, "Perennial Philosophy: Steuco to Leibniz," *Journal of the History of Ideas* 27 (1966): 506.

3. Let us mention but a few among the most comprehensive: Seyyed Hossein Nasr's *Knowledge and the Sacred* (Albany: State University of New York Press, 1989), Kenneth Oldmeadow's *Traditionalism—Religion in the Light of the Perennial Philosophy* (Colombo, Sri Lanka: Sri Lanka Institute of Traditional Studies, 2000), and, from a more historical point of view, Setareh Houman's *From the Philosophia Perennis to American Perennialism* (Chicago: Kazi Publications, 2014).

4. "*Philosophia Perennis* . . . [is] the metaphysic that recognizes a divine Reality substantial to the world of things and lives and minds; the psychology that finds in the soul something similar to, or even identical with, divine Reality; the ethic that laces man's final end in the knowledge of the immanent and transcendent Ground of all being—the thing is immemorial and universal." Aldous Huxley, *The Perennial Philosophy* (New York: Harper Perennial, 2009), vii.

a thoroughly modernist perspective. These critiques have included, among other traits, an excessively idiosyncratic choice of sources, an intellectualist and modern bias against ritual and ceremonial life, as well as some underlying compromises with the scientific outlook.[5] A symptom of some of these flaws is already apparent on the second page of Huxley's book. After after having acknowledged that the nature of Reality is "such that it cannot be directly and immediately apprehended except by those who have chosen to fulfil certain conditions, making themselves loving, pure in heart, and poor in spirit," the author raises the question of knowing why this is so, and opines that "it is just one of those facts which we have to accept, whether we like them or not and however implausible and unlikely they may seem."[6] Spiritual literature is replete with the idea that only the empty can be filled and only the humble can be elevated, a principle of metaphysical limpidity that led Meister Eckhart to write that "to be empty of all created things is to be full of God, and to be full of created things is to be empty of God."[7] Huxley takes as an implausible mystery a consequence of the metaphysical evidence of the relationship between the Real and the unreal. More generally, it could be argued that one of the main issues at stake in Huxley's work is the status of the core universal wisdom he postulated in relation to the diversity of religious and traditional teachings and practices. This is, needless to say, a complex and subtle question but there is little doubt that Huxley's outlook on the matter is significantly divergent in several major ways from the perennialist perspective. Huxley's is characterized, in this respect, by two tendencies. The first consists in all-too-often abstracting the ideas and themes of the *Philosophia perennis* from their textual connections and traditional contexts. The second—in some ways related to the first—consists in overemphasizing the effects of human limitations in discerning religious matters. It is not the purpose of this work to investigate Huxley's writings with these objections in mind. It is more pertinent to note, for our current purpose, that Huxley's version of the *Philosophia perennis* can easily be confused (by too hasty a reading) with certain aspects of Schuon's own viewpoint,

---

5. See Oldmeadow, *Traditionalism*, 158.
6. Huxley, *The Perennial Philosophy*, viii.
7. Meister Eckhart, *The Essential Sermons, Commentaries, Treatises and Defense* (Mahwah, NJ: Paulist Press, 1981), 288.

as will readily become apparent in a following chapter, "The Nature of Things and the Human Margin."

Huston Smith, by contrast with Huxley, presents us with an outlook that is a direct tributary of the perennialist worldview as articulated by Guénon, Coomaraswamy, and Schuon. Smith was particularly indebted to Schuon, whom he repeatedly praised in superlative terms.[8] In fact, Smith's works may be approached, to a large extent, as academic permutations of major themes in Schuon's works. There is no doubt, however, that Smith's formulation has distinct flavors of its own. His best-seller, *The World's Religions*, is implicitly informed by a recognition of the spiritual efficacy of each religious tradition that he considers in this work. His subsequent book, *Forgotten Truth*, is also primarily a defense of "The Common Vision of the World's Religions" (to cite the work's subtitle) beyond the diversity of their exclusive forms. What is most remarkable about Smith's reflection on religions, however, is that it proceeds from outward multiplicity to inward unity, with each religious tradition drawing him into its own harmonic coherence and spiritual allure: "When I discovered Hinduism and saw its beauty and profundity, I intended to practice it, a faithful devotee, forever. But then when I encountered Buddhism and later Islam, and was dazzled by their heady possibilities, I had to try them on for size. They fit."[9] In that sense, Smith's works invite contemporary readers to consider the principles of the perennialist outlook. A dominant view today is that the reality of confessional diversity constitutes an *a priori* refutation of any kind of absolute religious claim. The historical, theological, and ritual multiplicity of faiths is usually taken as evidence for relativism. Smith, on the other hand, regards this diversity of religious phenomena as suggestive of the universality found in spiritual experience and the ontological principles that it entails. Thus, in contrast to Schuon, Smith sees this transcendent unity not as an *a priori* intuition but as the outcome of a lengthy process of study and acquaintance: "Twenty years before it [i.e., *Forgotten Truth*]

---

8. "In Japan, I gave a brilliant lecture on Shintoism. I simply parroted what the book's author, someone named Frithjof Schuon, had said. Later in India, I chanced upon another volume by this Schuon called *Language of the Self*, which I thought equally brilliant. Still later, I found Schuon's *Understanding Islam* to be the best introduction to the subject and his *Transcendent Unity of Religions* one of the best spiritual books I ever read." Huston Smith, with Jeffery Paine, *Tales of Wonder—Adventures Chasing the Divine* (New York: HarperCollins, 2009), 144.

9. Smith, *Tales of Wonder*, 113.

was published in 1976, I wrote *The World's Religions* . . . which presented the major traditions in their individuality and variety. It took me two decades to see how they converge."¹⁰ In this, as in several other regards, Smith's intellectual contribution might adequately be characterized as an attempt at formulating the basic principles of the Perennial Philosophy from within the epistemological and cultural strictures of modernity and its postmodern aftermath. Thus, it should come as no surprise that a critique of the scientistic outlook occupies a prominent place in Smith's work. In *Forgotten Truth*, he tells his readers that he once enthusiastically "jostled to join . . . [the] ranks" of thinkers convinced that "scientists' achievements were so impressive, their marching orders so exhilarating."¹¹ Thus, Smith's intellectual development placed him in a particularly suitable position to address the concerns and objections of a wide array of contemporary readers. It could even be argued that the main thrust of Smith's approach lies in its capacity to introduce traditional principles in a conceptual framework that is readily accessible to modern minds, particularly in North America. It goes without saying that any work being written today, whether perennialist or not, must also address the needs and limitations of a diverse contemporary audience. This is what Schuon meant when he wrote, in the preface to his *Understanding Islam*: "What is needed in our time . . . is to provide some people with keys fashioned afresh—keys no better than the old ones but merely more elaborated and reflective—in order to help them rediscover the truths written in an eternal script in the very substance of the spirit."¹² This being acknowledged, it must be added that most perennialist writings do not take the *de facto* epistemological and cultural norms of modern mankind as their starting point. Or, if they do so, it is only by way of clearing the ground through scathing critiques of the modern *Weltanschauung* in their expositions of the *Sophia Perennis*.

As a final remark, it bears mentioning that Huston Smith's contribution is also explicitly bound up with the experiential and, indeed, experimental aspects of humanity's psycho-spiritual odyssey. This aspect of his work echoes some of Huxley's endeavors, and it is no

---

10. Huston Smith, *Forgotten Truth—The Common Vision of the World's Religions* (New York: HarperCollins, 1992), v.
11. Smith, *Forgotten Truth*, 7.
12. Schuon, *Understanding Islam* (Bloomington, IN: World Wisdom, 2011), xvii.

coincidence that Smith first came in contact with the author of *Brave New World* in the context of their common interest in the effects of entheogens.[13] Both authors wanted to give metaphysics an experimental confirmation through an exploration of the so-called "doors of perceptions" and the modifications of consciousness afforded by psychedelic drugs. While not necessarily denying the principle of the need for grace and spiritual guidance within a traditional path, these explorations stand in sharp contrast to the stern reservations of some major scholars of religion, like D. T. Suzuki, for instance, who unambiguously stated that "the world induced by LSD is false or unreal."[14] This also conforms to Schuon's uncompromising views on the matter when he stresses the incompatibility between genuine spiritual intention and the "profanations" entailed by the "purposes of experiment" and "tangible results."[15]

Although Izutsu's call for a *philosophia perennis* originated from a sense of need, and therefore lack, there is no doubt that, when considering the development of religious metaphysics in the last five decades, important steps toward the crystallization of such a *philosophia* can be identified. Among other possible considerations, one cannot but be struck, in reviewing

---

13. "Huxley, when I knew him, ranked as one of the giants of twentieth-century literature. His visionary experiences with mescaline led me to use entheogens to advance one rung—forgive the wordplay—*higher* on the Great Chain of Being." Smith, *Tales of Wonder*, 172.

14. "*The true man* refers not to a man in the ordinary sense. Rather it points to the subject or the 'master' of all that is experienced—the very reason for man being truly himself. It is also the *mind* in its deepest sense, or mind activity. It has no tangible form of its own, yet it penetratingly reaches every corner of the universe; it sees with our eyes, hears with our ears, walks with our feet, and grasps with our hand. . . . What religion demands of us is this *true man*. What use is there in sitting back and regarding objective visions which, however beautiful they may seem, are unreal; a doll is lifeless, after all. Only *the true man*, full of vim and vigor, will do. The world induced by LSD is false or unreal. Victims of doting Zen teachers and addicts of one kind or another—how the place swarms with such people—like those fish stretched out in the fish market, no sign of life at all." D. T. Suzuki, "Religion and Drugs," in *Selected Works of D. T. Suzuki Volume III* (University of California Press: Berkeley, 2016), 238.

15. "Purity of intention, as expressed and confirmed by such a vow, embraces the fundamental virtues of the soul; obviously it precludes the spiritual means from being employed for a purpose beneath the level of its own content, such as the pursuit of extraordinary powers, or the wish to be famous and admired, or the secret satisfaction of a sense of superiority; purity of intention likewise precludes this means from being used for purposes of experiment or for the sake of tangible results or other profanations of this sort." Schuon, *Treasures of Buddhism* (New Delhi: Smriti Book, 1993), 161.

the field of comparative religion, by the still hardly recognized—at least in academia—but deeply determining influence of the philosopher of religion, Frithjof Schuon. His works have been praised as eminent expressions of the kind of *philosophia perennis* Izutsu was calling for. In over two dozen books written during a period of sixty years, Schuon established himself as the principal spokesman of the intellectual current sometimes referred to in English speaking countries as perennialism. Even though they are largely independent of the usual academic channels of diffusion and protocols, his works have inspired a significant number of highly positive responses among scholars in Europe, North America, and Asia. His celebrated *The Transcendent Unity of Religions*, first published in French in 1948 and then in English in 1953, has become a classic. This book, like Schuon's other works, embraces a wide spectrum of traditional material, from Hindu and Christian concepts to Islamic and Buddhist symbols. It is proposed, therefore, that Schuon's opus be given due consideration and priority when considering the possibility of a contemporary perennial philosophy.

Given the uncommonly synthetic and richly cross-civilizational character of Schuon's contribution, one may wonder why his works have not received a wider and deeper recognition in academia. There are a number of reasons for this, most of which have been addressed by James Cutsinger in the introduction to his most recent work on Schuon.[16] One of the main stumbling blocks in the academic reception of Schuon has been that most of his key concepts are given inflections of meaning that do not always strictly abide by the normative sense they may have acquired in their traditions of origin. Schuon borrows a number of terms from specific religious or theological traditions while expanding their semantic scope beyond the strict confines of their respective confessional definitions. He has thereby forged a metaphysical vocabulary that is both steeped in tradition and arguably "post-modern," as it were, in its supra-confessional outreach. These recurrent terms of Schuon's technical vocabulary, from *upāya* and *yin-yang* to "quintessential Sufism" and "vertical Trinity," deserve close attention because they are profoundly indicative of a certain way of understanding the function and limits of conceptual expression in metaphysics and spirituality. In other words, these terms are keys in the sense that their import is primarily functional or instrumental. They are conceptual hints or allusions to higher realities and not conventional

---

16. James Cutsinger, *The Splendor of the Truth* (Albany: State University of New York Press, 2012).

philosophical notions. In fact, one of Schuon's main concerns has been to debunk the epistemological pretensions of philosophical totalization or the rational exhaustion of Reality.[17] In the phrase "keys to the Beyond," the latter word refers not only to the inexhaustibility and ineffability of the Ultimate but also to the intellectual, spiritual, and hermeneutic shift toward the universal that is inherent in metaphysical expression as understood by Schuon. The main objective and focus of the following chapters is to develop some of the full implications of these key terms both by delving into their specific traditional denotations and by exploring their universal connotations in Schuon's universe of meaning. Such a task is particularly timely when both hardened and increasingly formal and ideological religious identities on the one hand, and skepticism or hostility toward religious traditions on the other, are gaining ground and increasingly clashing with each other.

While a growing number of books and essays[18] have been devoted to Schuon in the last decade, most of them center on biographical con-

---

17. "The desire to enclose universal Reality in an exclusive and exhaustive 'explanation' brings with it a permanent disequilibrium due to the interferences of Māyā; moreover it is just this disequilibrium and this anxiety that are the life of modern philosophy." Schuon, *Light on the Ancient Worlds* (Bloomington, IN: World Wisdom, 2006), 77.

18. James Cutsinger's *Advice to the Serious Seeker: Meditation on the Teaching of Frithjof Schuon* (Albany: State University of New York Press, 1997) is an introduction to Schuon's teachings written from the dialogical point of view of a professor of religious studies addressing the intellectual challenges of students in search of transcendent meaning. The exposition of Schuon's ideas is developed through a series of philosophical and spiritual clues appropriate to students' needs. This pedagogical approach allows for an engaging meditation on some of the major themes of Schuon's works. This book is therefore an accessible introduction to the works of Schuon, which does not presuppose any prior familiarity with them or an extensive background in religious studies. It is specifically written with undergraduate students and a general audience in mind. Jean-Baptiste Aymard and Patrick Laude's *Frithjof Schuon: Life and Teachings* (Albany, NY: State University of New York, 2001) is a more conventional introduction to Schuon's life and works. It comprises four chapters, the first two of which, authored by Aymard, sketch an intellectual biography, while the last two, penned by Laude, scrutinize some of the central and challenging dimensions of Schuon's work, namely the notion of "esoterism" and the meaning and implications of his "spiritual aesthetics." This book, by contrast with Cutsinger's, presupposes a solid background in comparative religion and some prior exposure to Schuon's work. Michael Fitzgerald's *Frithjof Schuon: Messenger of the Sophia Perennis* (Bloomington, IN: World Wisdom, 2010) is the most comprehensive biography of Frithjof Schuon to date. It includes a wealth of quotations from Schuon's writings, including many excerpts from correspondence and unpublished materials. Harry Oldmeadow's *Frithjof Schuon and the Perennial Philosophy* (Bloomington, IN:

siderations or provide syntheses of his work as a whole, whereas very few academic studies have approached Schuon from contemporary critical perspectives. The present book does not delve into biographical data. Other books and essays have done so in different contexts and with various intents. At any rate, it is taken for granted that the study of a metaphysical and spiritual output does not require, in itself, any familiarity with the life of its author. The distinctive feature of this book lies elsewhere: it approaches Schuon's perspective through its cross-traditional conceptual vocabulary. This may be deemed a unique and effective approach not only for understanding Schuon's work, but also for articulating elements of a coherent "metalanguage"[19] that may open the way to a rigorous and

---

World Wisdom, 2010) is a comprehensive introduction to Schuon's works. It provides a clear, rigorous, synthetic, and richly referenced overview of Schuon's intellectual and spiritual perspective. It was conceived by the author and the publisher as a companion volume to Fitzgerald's biography. It situates Schuon within the context of the perennial philosophy in the twentieth century. James Cutsinger's *The Splendor of the Truth* is an anthology of some of the most important chapters and essays written by Schuon. The book contains a substantial and thoughtful opening devised to introduce the works of Schuon to the specific concerns of scholars of religious studies. It is, in a sense, a scholarly case for the academic study of Schuon and for a wider and deeper consideration of his work within university research agendas and curricula. It must be added that all of the above were written by scholars whose own intellectual perspectives is indebted to Schuon, hence the suspicion and critique raised by some other scholars that the biographical dimensions of these works amount to "hagiography." Other works have taken diversely critical or skeptical stances vis-à-vis Schuon both as an author and as a spiritual figure. These works include a chapter from Mark Sedgwick's *Against the Modern World* (Oxford: Oxford University Press, 2009), a section of Andrew Rawlisson's *The Book of Enlightened Masters: Western Teachers in Eastern Traditions* (Chicago: Open Court, 1998), passages from Arthur Versluis's comprehensive study of American esoteric currents, *American Gurus: From Transcendentalism to New Age Religion* (Oxford: Oxford University Press, 2014), and Patrick Riggenberg's *Diversité et unité des religions chez René Guénon et Frithjof Schuon* (Paris: L'Harmattan, 2010). These studies differ in many ways, in both scope and intent, but they tend to converge in either suggesting or assessing that Schuon's perspective entails a breaking away from traditional norms and orthodoxy. These evaluations associate what they consider to be suspicious or worrisome doctrinal developments with unconventional aspects of Schuon's biography, such as his affinity with "primordial nudity." Thus, within such hermeneutic perspectives, particular biographical elements gleaned in various private documents are interpreted as reflecting, or perhaps even inspiring, doctrinal positions deemed problematical. Finally, a thorough examination of Frithjof Schuon's life and thought can be found in Setareh Houman's *From the Philosophia Perennis to American Perennialism* (Chicago: Kazi, 2014).

19. The term "metalanguage" is not used here as implying a deficiency of language, in any of its traditional forms, in conveying adequate notions of the Transcendent. It

fruitful comparative treatment of metaphysical traditions, East and West. In doing so, this study may contribute to the growing field of cross-religious and trans-religious hermeneutics and understanding, thus facilitating their application to distinct intellectual and spiritual traditions. Thus, the perspective afforded by this approach may not only provide keys for a further understanding of one of the most important religious philosophers of our time, but it also makes a contribution to the development of a cross-religious lexicon that may function as an effective metalanguage in the study of comparative religion and mysticism.

To this end, the following chapters serve as an introduction to Schuon's work, in the sense that they provide readers with an examination of some of the fundamental tenets of his perspective, through the analysis of such key ideas as the "relatively absolute," "esoteric ecumenism," or the "metaphysical transparency of phenomena."[20] However, it must be acknowledged that short of some prior degree of acquaintance with Schuon's work, most readers are likely to encounter conceptual challenges due to the density and, at times, technicity of Schuon's doctrinal idiom. As a result, the following chapters might arguably be most helpful to those who have already entered Schuon's conceptual world through exposure to one or more of his books. Our hope is that such, and other, readers may find intellectual benefit in a discussion of key concepts that bring together the various dimensions of Schuon's work and, therefore, highlight its organic unity. Such might be the case, in particular, for those who, engaged in the academic study of religions, may find it difficult to situate Schuon's uncustomary syntheses in relation to more academically analytic works on specific religious traditions. Thus, the pages of this book are not exclusively focused on Schuon's work but offer, in addition, elements of theological contextualization of its key terms, as well insights into the ways they may both differ from and relate to their respective religious sources of inspiration.

---

simply denotes a form of "supra-traditional" language that both fully recognizes the validity of religious concepts and makes use of their ability to enlighten metaphysical and spiritual realities beyond the usual scope of their original traditional context.

20. Harry Oldmeadow's *Frithjof Schuon and the Perennial Philosophy* is a more synthetic and systematic introduction to Schuon's works than the current book. It is also more pedagogically structured and meets all the demands of a substantial, reliable, and accessible introductory work.

The Christian theologian Jean Borella has characterized Schuon's approach and mode of expression as "spherical,"[21] no doubt by contrast with more linear modalities of metaphysical expression. Besides its connotations of density, this suggestion of circularity implies that, in Schuon's writings, the whole circumference of intellectual, traditional, and spiritual considerations is relative to a meaningful center that is in itself inexpressible. It may also imply that the dialectical circumference is symbolically connected to the center through strikingly perceptive conceptual and verbal crystallizations that create intellective pathways of access to it. Inasmuch as these essentially metaphysical formulations provide the basic architecture of Schuon's thought, the current book could well serve as an introduction to his opus, facilitated, in particular, by an extensive selection of quotations from his works. From a slightly different point of view, a number of passages from the following chapters could be considered as ways of unpacking the densely concentrated substance of Schuon's writings. Furthermore, some of the considerations presented in this study could even be understood as meditative unfoldings and prolongations of Schuon's own insights. This manner of proceeding echoes Titus Burckhardt's characterization of meditation: "Normally, meditation proceeds with a circular motion. It starts from an essential idea, developing its diverse application in order, in the end, to reintegrate them in the initial truth which thus acquires for the intelligence that has reflected on it a more immediate and a richer actuality."[22]

The very focus of this book—the notion of a metalanguage that issues from traditional idioms but also transcends them—raises fundamental questions concerning the legitimacy of any inflection or displacement of traditional meanings. Is not the Schuonian redefinition of some traditional terms problematic from the perspective of the integrity of intellectual and spiritual forms within the respective traditions? This issue, or objection, is moreover inseparable from the question of the epistemological status of Schuon's metalanguage, and of his perspective in general; thus the difficulties and challenges raised by some critics of Schuon's writings with

---

21. "We would readily call it [Schuon's style] 'spherical' because he instills the maximum meaning into the minimum of words." Quoted from *Etudes Traditionelles* (Paris: January-March 1982) in Aymard and Laude, *Frithjof Schuon—Life and Teachings*, 49.

22. Titus Burckhardt, *Introduction to Sufi Doctrine* (Bloomington, IN: World Wisdom, 2008), 95.

regard to the claimed universality of their scope.[23] Schuon has himself expressed, especially in his poetry, the extent to which his experiences and personal sensibilities have shaped his perception of the world. So what meaning should we ascribe to objectivity and universality, and should we deem them incompatible with subjectivity and particularity? On some level, it is all too obvious that existential and cultural experiences help to fashion one's representation and expression of Reality. The Intellect, as Schuon understands it, is in itself free from any subjective and particular determinations, but its actualization is not extrinsically independent of its context, no more than the expression of its insights is exempt from linguistic, cultural, and personal predispositions. The intellective, although Divine in its essence, is embedded in the human, and the latter cannot but color the former. This is in itself not incompatible with intellectual objectivity and the ability to consider aspects of, and points of view on, Reality. What matters most, in this respect, is the objective receptivity of the human subject and the scope of one's contemplation, two conditions that make it possible to displace oneself, as it were. This being said, there is no question that Schuon's doctrinal elaborations are, partly, a tributary of the historical, intellectual, and cultural contexts in which they arose. To begin with, the very notions of *sophia perennis* and *religio perennis* could not but be reformulated in the context of an increasingly globalized world, one in which a wider access to a broadening array of experiences and interactions have raised unprecedented questions and called for new syntheses. The development of these notions benefitted, moreover, from a wider and deeper access to traditional sources that had been hitherto difficult of access or simply unavailable. While the historicist bent of contemporary scholarship has led many experts to treat circumstantial contexts as determining the ideological content of a given body of works, the perennialist perspective conceives of the intellectual vision as informing

---

23. Patrick Ringgenberg, in particular, has questioned the validity of Schuon's concepts of universality and objectivity, and opined that subjective and cultural determinations have actually shaped his outlook. As illustrative instances of such determinations, Ringgenberg points out that Schuon's artistic sensibility reveals subjective preferences and affinities that he sees as demonstrating the impossibility of attaining an "objective" and "universal" outlook. Ringgenberg, *Diversité et unité des religions chez René Guénon et Frithjof Schuon*, 325.

the contextual data, the latter being available as a kind of material that is merely contingent on the intellectual crystallization of the teachings.[24]

Modern and postmodern paradigms are perhaps entirely based on a repudiation of the notion of objectivity in light of subjectivist relativism and the end of the so-called grand narratives of meaning being the order of the day. The intellectual thrust of Schuon's work stands in clear opposition to such views. It starts from the premise that relativism, in whatever domain and in whatever mode it may manifest, suffers from an inherent self-contradiction. In other words, claims that reject the very notion of objectivity undermine their own validity insofar as they assert the truth of relativism. In Schuon's words, the relativistic "assertion nullifies itself if it is true and by nullifying itself logically proves thereby that it is false; its initial absurdity lies in the implicit claim to be unique in escaping, as if by enchantment, from a relativity that is declared to be the only possibility."[25]

One of the most powerful expressions, in our times, of the relativistic tendency manifests in what Paul Ricoeur coined a "hermeneutic of suspicion."[26] This type of critical interpretation aims at debunking the pretense of objectivity that it sees as masking unconscious presuppositions and unavowed biases that are themselves indicative of implicit or unconscious ideological determinations. By contrast, the "hermeneutic of recollection" aims at unveiling or recovering the meanings thought to be inherent in the text. The critical questioning of the very possibility

---

24. To take but one example, the fact that Schuon appears to have come into contact with the works of the Śaivite sage Abhinavagupta—with which he shares some deep affinities—at a later stage in his life, and probably too late to integrate them into in his own books, does not in itself lessen the scope and relevance of his insights on Tantric inspiration. Schuon mentions Abhinavagupta several times in his late German poetry: "*Wenn du in Māyās Spiel das Wahre siehst: In einem Weib, in Dingen der Natur—Sagt Abhinavagupta—zeigt sich Gott In dieser Form; die Form ist Ātmā nur. Kein Götzendienst ist dies; nein, tiefes Sehen; Buchstabenglaube kann es nicht verstehen.*" *Adastra–Stella Maris* (Sottens, Switzerland: Les Sept Fèches, 2001), 184. "When thou seest the True in *Māyā*'s play: In woman, or in the beauty of Nature, Then—says Abhinavagupta—it is God Who shows Himself in forms; the form is none other than Ātmā. This is not idolatry, but deep insight; Those who cling to the letter cannot understand." Schuon, *Adastra & Stella Maris* (Bloomington, IN: World Wisdom, 2003), 191.

25. Schuon, *Logic and Transcendence* (Bloomington, IN: World Wisdom, 2009), 6.

26. Paul Ricoeur, *Freud and Philosophy: An Essay on Interpretation* (New Haven, CT: Yale University Press, 1970).

of objectivity is therefore based, in the first type of hermeneutic, on the hidden and not on the evident; the subjective assumptions and preferences that are perceived as underlying—and undermining—the explicit or implicit claims of objectivity. The subjective is a synonym, here, of the reality that underpins the works below the surface of the objective meaning. The two are fundamentally distinct, indeed often opposed. Unveiling the subjective strata of meaning amounts, therefore, to laying suspicion upon the objective literality of the work, thereby laying bare the realities of interest and power that it disguises. In this view of things, claims of objectivity and universality must alert the critical analyst to the underlying determination of particular subjective assumptions. In other words, there is an intrinsic discrepancy between the objective and the subjective, the universal and the particular, the former being the ideological veil of the latter. Such an understanding may be thought to preclude the very possibility of an epistemological compatibility of the particular sphere of the subjective and the universal realm of the objective, the latter being none other than the illusive projection of realities of power and interest. Schuon's view, by contrast, reflects the traditional schema of two levels of epistemological reality that are, in a way, incommensurate and yet parallel in another sense and, therefore, ought not to conflict in their respective purviews. There is no need for the individual subject to hide or deny its particularity in its own sphere of affinity since this particularity does not in itself infringe upon the intellective recognition of principles. In other words, objectivity and universality do not have to carry the implication of a radical epistemological invalidity due to the subjective sphere of the individual. The latter may veil or prolong the former in proportion to one's intellectual receptivity and moral disinterestedness or lack thereof.

The previous considerations on the objective dimension of reality must lead us to further elucidate what constitutes its ultimate constituents in Schuon's work. This is the realm of metaphysics. This word does not refer here to the Greek etymological meaning of *meta ta physika*, the domain that lies beyond physical reality. It is not even to be taken as a synonym of ontology, or the science of "being as being," as it is often understood in philosophical discourse. In Schuon's lexicon, metaphysics is best characterized in contradistinction with the realm of "theology" and "ontology." "Theology" focuses on God, in the ordinary sense of the term, that is as Creator, Revealer, and Savior. Thus, the adjective "theological" is, in Schuon's books, a quasi-equivalent of "ontological," since God is referred to by Schuon as Being. God is Being, and a discourse on God, that is theology, is none other than a discourse on Being, that is, ontology. In Schuon's perspective, theology relates, therefore, to God *qua* Being as the first determination of the Divine Essence, which is also the first cause of the manifold existents. The Divine Essence in itself is in no way determinate; it *is* beyond all determinations. The first determination, which can be capitalized as Determination, since it is the source and paradigm of all further determinations, lies "below" the Essence as such. As Being, it constitutes the ontological degree of Reality. By contrast, metaphysics pertains to the super-ontological realm, or to Beyond-Being, the Essence, and can be best characterized, therefore, by paradoxical expressions: it is the science of the limitless and the knowledge of the unknowable.[27]

Such paradoxes call into question ordinary concepts of knowledge, and invite us to pay attention to another question of terminology, that which is implied by Schuon's use of the word gnosis. This term is fraught with difficulties for both historical and polemical reasons. The Greek term refers literally to knowledge, but the history of the word has been associated with Ancient Gnosticist schools and churches, a fact that has contributed to obscure its meaning. Generally speaking, gnosis refers to a type of spiritual knowledge by identification that is experiential and not simply theoretical. It is also widely contrasted with faith and involves, for its proponents, an epistemological and soteriological superiority over the latter. Finally, and correlatively to the previous characters, it entails the principle that true knowledge is both divine and immanent to the human being. All the aforementioned aspects of gnosis lead it to be vehemently rejected by ordinary religious belief on account of their apparent incompatibility with the realities of faith and grace. Schuon's view, by contrast, is that gnosis constitutes in fact the perfection of faith, or the actualization of its intellective core. Moreover, Schuon contemplates gnosis as a kind of immanent and "supernaturally natural" grace that does not divinize humans *qua* humans, but rather highlights the most elevated meaning of human theomorphism. In

---

27. "Now, can Metaphysics as we understand it be defined? No, for to define is always to limit, and what is under consideration is, in and of itself, truly and absolutely limitless and thus cannot be confined to any formula or any system whatsoever. Metaphysics might be partially characterized, for example, by saying that it is the knowledge of universal principles, but this is not a definition in the proper sense and in any case only conveys a vague notion." René Guénon, *Studies in Hinduism* (Hillsdale, NY: Sophia Perennis, 2001), 89.

this view of things, to be fully human means to realize that which is most deeply embedded in mankind, the immanent imprint of Divinity.

In Schuon's view of gnosis, intellective selfhood, being transcendent, must be distinguished from our personal subjectivity; that is, the former determines the contents and modalities of the latter in a universalizing manner, but it cannot be identified with it *tale quale*. Schuon's considerations on the *avatāra* provide most helpful keys in this regard as developed more fully in a chapter of this book. This is a basic gnostic insight that Schuon shares with many traditional metaphysicians and mystics. In several passages of his work, Schuon has made the point that objectivity does not amount to a de-humanization, and even less so to the disappearance, or illegitimacy, of personal subjectivity.[28] Schuon's metaphysics may be universal—and thus consonant with other esoteric idioms—in its doctrinal substance, as the chapters of this book seek to demonstrate, while also being legitimately personal in its delineation, emphases, and modes of expression. The doctrinal core of Schuon's metaphysical exposition lies in envisaging non-dual Reality under an indefinite number of aspects and vantage points. Its dimension of universality pertains to the receptivity of the Intellect to these aspects and points of view on the basis of its inherent recognition of the absoluteness and infinity of the Ultimate. Humanly speaking, though, universality does not entail an exhaustive grasp of all aspects of the Real, nor does objectivity signify a total identification of the individual *qua* individual with the Intellect. The limitations of the individual being are intrinsic to its definition as "individual," but they do not in themselves constitute an obstacle to the objective recognition of the virtually unlimited aspects of the Real. While this awareness must entail a kind of death to distorting biases,[29] it is in no way incompatible with preferences inherent to our individual and formal affinities.[30] In his first book, Schuon contrasts the dogmatic

---

28. "This liberty or this objectivity will never be manifested by a dehumanization of the human on the pretext of metaphysical sublimity, for transcendent Truth puts each thing in its place and does not mix levels. Supreme wisdom is in complete solidarity with holy childhood." Schuon, *Esoterism as Principle and as Way* (Bedfont, Middlesex: Perennial Books, 1981), 233.

29. "We have written in one of our books that to be objective is to die a little, unless one is a pneumatic, in which case one is dead by nature, and in that extinction finds one's life." Schuon, *To Have a Center* (Bloomington, IN: World Wisdom, 2015), 41.

30. This duality appears in the Christian teaching of the two natures: "Christ, as the living form of God, would have to display in his humanity supernatural prerogatives

conception with the metaphysical outlook by comparing the former to "a view that supposes the immobility of the seeing subject" and the latter to "the sum of all possible views of the object in question, views that presuppose in the subject a power of displacement or an ability to alter his viewpoint, hence a certain mode of identity with the dimensions of space."[31] This analogy implies the virtual unlimitedness of the metaphysical perspective. It also points to its freedom *vis-à-vis* the static one-sidedness of religious theology, as suggestively expressed by Schuon's placement of John 3:8 as an epigraph to his first published work: "The wind blowest where it listeth, and thou hearest the sound thereof, but canst not tell whence it cometh, and whither it goeth."[32] In other words, what lies at the foundation of intellective objectivity is not the individual as such but its power of displacement in response to the diversity of aspects and points of view. In two very different spiritual contexts, Ibn 'Arabī and Simone Weil provided parallel symbolic expressions of the universality and objectivity that is the horizon of Schuon's work. For Ibn 'Arabī, the summit of human perfection is the "station of no station" (*maqām lā maqām* or *maqām lā muqām*), in conformity with a mystical meaning of the Qur'ānic admonition "there is no stand (*muqām*) for you, therefore turn back [or return] (*fa-arji'ū*)" (33:13). While ordinary religious consciousness is characterized by the affirmation of God (i.e., as a stand or station), which is manifested in one's belief inasmuch as his denial is also reflected in other beliefs, the gnostic—or supreme "knower by God"—"transcends this tragedy of an excluded, denied God . . . [and] knows, or rather, he sees, that there is nothing in the universe that is not a place of epiphany."[33] Thus, Ibn 'Arabī evokes the infinity of the "voyage

---

that it would be vain to enumerate, while, being incontestably human, he would have certain limitations as is proven by the incident of the fig tree, whose sterility he did not discern from afar." Schuon, *Form and Substance in the Religions* (Bloomington, IN: World Wisdom, 2002), 202.

31. Schuon, *The Transcendent Unity of Religions* (Wheaton, IL: Theosophical Publishing House, 1984), 5.

32. *De l'unité transcendente des religions* was indeed Schuon's first book in French, a language that was to become his primary means of exposition. However, Schuon had already published *Leitgedangen zur Urbesinnung* in 1935 with Orell Füssli Verlag in Zürich.

33. Claude Addas, *Ibn 'Arabī—The Voyage of No Return* (Cambridge: Islamic Texts Society, 2000), 98-99.

in God,"[34] the infinity of His theophanies, and also the limitations of the particular stations that call for an unending spiritual motion from one to the next. This is akin to Schuon's "speculative" point of view that amounts to a perfect inner receptivity to virtually all aspects and viewpoints. As for Simone Weil, she provides her readers with a most penetrating distinction between the consideration that flows from subjective attachment and the pure contemplation of the object[35] that is utter receptivity "in waiting." Here the symbolic function of spatial motion is prolonged and heightened by "temporal motion," whereby objective reality is revealed by being purified from the superimposition of attachments that constitute so many ego-centered stases. The capacity for objectivity is intrinsically connected to what Weil refers to as the "sense of the relation," as expressed for instance in the following passage: "We have to see things in their right relationship and ourselves, including the purposes we bear within us, as one of the terms of that relationship."[36] The sense of the relation is therefore none other than the intellectual and spiritual ability to take account of aspects and points of view.

While one may recognize the reality of objectivity, hence virtual universality, resulting from a contemplative receptivity to the wealth of manifestations of the Real, the question may arise of the legitimacy of apprehending and using doctrinal teachings outside their strictly traditional framework of linguistic and cultural reference. Such concerns lead, in particular, to the further question of knowing whether the recognition of a metaphysical or spiritual reality necessarily presupposes a familiarity with its linguistic medium and its cultural or civilizational context. In

---

34. "The other group, containing once more God's elite, are made to voyage in Him—the passive form of the verb *safara* is used to show that they do not undertake this voyage relying on their own rational powers but allow themselves to be guided by God to His Presence." Ibn 'Arabī, *The Secrets of Voyaging*, translated by Angela Jaffray (Oxford: Anqa Publishing, 2015), 175.

35. "Application of this rule for the discrimination between the real and the illusory. In our sense perceptions, if we are not sure of what we see we change our position while looking, and what is real becomes evident. In the inner life, time takes the place of space. With time we are altered, and, if as we change we keep our gaze directed towards the same thing, in the end illusions are scattered and the real becomes visible. This is on condition that the attention be a looking and not an attachment." Simone Weil, *Gravity and Grace* (London: Routledge, 2003), 120.

36. *The Notebooks of Simone Weil*, translated by Arthur Wills (London: Routledge, 2004), 334.

an unpublished letter from 1928,[37] Schuon contends that the knowledge of a language does not facilitate per se the understanding of an idea expressed through its linguistic channel, no more than the ignorance of this same language necessarily prevents one from grasping the same idea. Furthermore, the content of the expression transcends the expression itself to the extent that the expression is truly symbolic and its referent therefore conceptually ungraspable independently of the symbolizing form. The perspective enunciated by Schuon is particularly relevant when the incommensurability between the metaphysical or spiritual reality and its formal means of conveyance is the most evident. Thus, in the context of a discussion on the German translation of the *Tao Te Ching*, Schuon remarks that, in the case of spiritual writings endowed with a depth of meaning akin to that of the *Tao Te Ching*, "one cannot learn to understand them by the fact of reading them, one must, as it were, understand them before approaching them." Furthermore, Schuon notes that it would be of little importance if he were not to know the meaning of certain words, or even to be unable to mentally conceptualize particular statements. These two remarks relativize, without mooting, the significance of the exactitude of a translation and, by the same token, that of the understanding of the original language of expression. What this means, in effect, is that a knowledge of Chinese, even if it be outstanding, in no way guarantees access to the intellectual or spiritual essence of the *Tao Te Ching*, while ignorance of the language is not, in itself, incompatible with such an understanding, provided that the human consciousness that approaches it conforms to its intended meaning.

The aforementioned remarks are of the utmost importance in providing an entry into the epistemology that governs Schuon's works, one that he shares with esoteric teachings from East and West. This epistemology is not analytic and *a posteriori* but synthetic and *a priori*. What is meant by these terms, echoing Kant's terminology but lending to it a radically different meaning than the one envisaged by the "sage of Königsberg," is a distinction between a discursive and deductive concept of knowledge and one that may be best defined as intuitive and anamnestic. The former stems from an analytical grasp of the meaning inherent in concepts and the words that convey them. To understand means to extract meaning, as it were, from terms and notions. By contrast, Schuon's epistemology—which may be termed Platonic in a broad

---

37. Letter of January 2, 1928. Quoted with the permission of the Schuon estate.

sense—sees the act of understanding as presupposing a prior knowledge of the object that is understood, whereby concepts and terms are only occasional means of actualization. In other words, one can know only that which one already knows, often without knowing that one knows it. It follows from the premise of this epistemology that understanding does not, and cannot, depend upon a literal grasp of conceptual terms. Meanings, of course, are immanent to a text, but they can be accessed, as the case may be, with minimal support from the text. The text is a symbol and not merely a discursive repository.

The foregoing remarks legitimize the epistemological practice of using traditional notions with a degree of freedom vis-à-vis their long-established roots and contexts. Needless to say, serious concerns about this approach are likely to be raised by representatives of the various traditions as well as from the academic world. One possible way of tackling this critical question is by considering the relationship between formal expression, meaning, and Reality as elucidated through basic semiotical categories. In this regard, it has been proposed that one may envisage three principal ways of "making sense": the syntagmatic, the paradigmatic, and the symbolic.[38] The syntagmatic meaning derives from a kind of horizontal relation between the terms of a sequence. What is emphasized here is the way in which the meaning of a given term is dependent on its relationship with what precedes and follows it. Thus, there is a traditional syntax, as it were, that is integral to any religious universe of meaning. How we understand the Book differs, for instance, in Christianity and Islam according to its sequential position in a tradition's economy. As for the paradigmatic meaning, it refers to vertical alternatives as opposed to the horizontal elements of a sequence, that is, they are viewed as "brothers" rather than "neighbors."[39] For instance, the meaning of the Book in Islam is derived by way of contrast from the perspective of the Word made flesh in Christianity notwithstanding their shared sacred framework. As for the symbolic meaning, it is predicated on an ontological correspondence, or even consubstantiality, between the signifier and the signified, with the latter, however, remaining transcendent to the limitations of the former, while being conceptually unfathomable independently of it. Schuon's understanding of the meaning of metaphysical and spiritual expression

---

38. Roland Barthes, *Critical Essays* (Evanston, IL: Northwestern University Press, 1972), 210.

39. Barthes, *Critical Essays*, 207.

evidences deep kinship with the symbolic kind which postulates both a continuum, whereby the signifier is none other than the signified, disclosing the full depth of its content, and a discontinuity that results from the formal limitation of the symbol. By contrast with symbolic meaning, the syntagmatic and paradigmatic types cannot possibly attain speculative unlimitedness since they depend upon finite determinations through the mediation of neighbors or brothers. The syntagmatic, for its part, presents a clear affinity with literalism. It is the type of meaning for which the signified cannot be freed from the chain of signifiers and is thus rendered most restricted in its scope. As for the paradigmatic, it proceeds through meaningful differentiation. It is therefore akin to rational delimitation, to clear and distinct delineations that separate paradigmatic alternatives. Theology, inasmuch as it is a rational exercise in conceptual formalization, is susceptible to following the paradigmatic way. The distinction between "Substances" and "Persons," for instance, has contributed to driving trinitarian theology in diverging directions.

What the syntagmatic and paradigmatic meanings have in common is their intrinsic relationality. It is through relations of sequence and difference that signs are, in such contexts, meaningful. The symbol, by contrast, is not relational as such, since it points to a unity of being. A proper understanding of a symbol does not result from discursive connections or rational distinctions. It amounts to penetrating the depths of its inner reality. By contrast with the syntagmatic and the paradigmatic, the symbolic meaning is synthetic and intuitive. In other words, it encompasses autonomy and depth in that it is most detached from a merely analytical treatment of terms. It represents a meaningful totality that is independent of anything but its symbolic referent, which is also in a sense its ontological ground. In a similar line of inquiry, Gilbert Durand has distinguished the sign, the allegory, and the symbol by observing that it is the symbolic correspondence alone which ensures that both the signifier and the signified are virtually unlimited. While the sign involves an "indicative equivalence" that is largely arbitrary and the allegory amounts to a "translation," the symbol may be best understood as an "epiphany."[40] With the symbol, there is an openness on both sides of the signification. On the one hand, there is a plurivocity to the symbol: that is, the same symbol may refer to an indefinite number of realities or levels of reality. On the other hand, the

---

40. Gilbert Durand, *L'imagination symbolique* (Paris: Quadrige/PUF, 1964), 19.

reality that is symbolized can also be conveyed by a virtually unlimited range of symbolic signifiers. In other words, the symbol may refer to different aspects of Reality, while the latter may also be envisaged through a variety of symbolic points of view. This virtual illimitation also applies to the metaphysical idea conceived and experienced as a speculative symbol; it can refer to a number of realities while, conversely, the same reality may be referenced through an indefinite array of symbolic ideas.

Metaphysical ideas are rarely assigned a symbolic status, however, and this is so inasmuch as the symbolic tends to be exclusively associated with the graphic and auditory realms. This is also largely a result of restricting ideas to the status of mental representations. Nevertheless, to the extent that it is connected to metaphysical realities, the speculative idea is also a kind of symbol, one that communicates something of its ontological referent. This means that it is both more and less than an ordinary concept. It is "more" insofar as its adequateness conveys an intuition of its metaphysical content, but it is "less" to the extent that its meditation also involves an awareness of formal contingency and its inability to exhaust Reality. The symbol is both different from that which it symbolizes and—more truly—none other than it. However, this identity is not akin to a mere formal correspondence, like a word would translate another word. It is more comparable to a formal crystallization that conveys the very reality of that which lies beyond, or below, its own form. Thus, contact with a form is accidentally necessary in order to establish meaning, but the latter is, in principle, independent of that contact, since it may occur through different symbolic instances. In light of these reflections, one may draw a distinction between two kinds of literality. There is a sacramental literality, as it were, whereby the presence of a meaning inheres in the form itself in a way that is preconceptual (i.e., Śaktic, to use a Śaivite term), and there exists another type of literality that is, by contrast, strictly conceptual and, therefore, much more indirect. By and large, the central terms of Schuon's metalanguage are akin to the former, hence their mobility and universality. It must be noted, moreover, that this type of symbolic understanding and practice is far from being uncommon in Asian spiritual contexts, where the fluidity of concepts and symbols are recognized as pedagogical boons. For instance, some modern Hindu sages such as Ramana Maharshi have made use of biblical concepts and passages to illustrate their non-dual teachings. Commenting upon the scriptural statement "I am that I am," Ramana Maharshi refers to God's naming of Himself in the Bible as the best definition of *Ātman*.⁴¹ And yet, it is unlikely that most Jewish and Christian theologians would recognize their own conceptual and religious framework in this non-dual interpretation of Exodus 3:14.

This work comprises ten chapters. The first four highlight the centrality of certain notions that assist in the discernment between absoluteness and relativity that lies at the core of Schuon's perspective and language. The latter is primarily couched in Advaitin terms, and this is the focus of the first chapter. Schuon's metaphysical idiom is akin to the non-dualistic Hindu tradition of *Advaita Vedānta*, as embodied in the works of Shankarāchārya (788–820). The two concepts of *Ātman* (Divine Self) and *Māyā* (Universal Appearance) lie at the heart of Schuon's account of this perspective. Although these notions are normative in *Advaita*, as principles of discrimination between Reality and illusion, Schuon makes use of them in a way that involves some significant inflections of meaning. Among the latter, the manner in which Schuon, by contrast with Shankara, distinguishes between different degrees of *Māyā* is particularly important in understanding his contemplation of the qualitative diversity of phenomena. These distinctions allow him to ground ethics and aesthetics in an arguably much more nuanced way than most of his Advaitin sources. The second chapter is centered on the notion of the *avatāra* considered as Schuon's paradigm for the manifestation and presence of the Absolute within the relative. It is widely known that, in the Hindu tradition, *avatāras* are divine descents. The term refers to the incarnation of diverse divine agencies for the purpose of teaching or restoring the cosmic order. The *avatāra* manifests the enigma of an apparent conjunction between the Divine and the human. Schuon makes use of this concept as a key for exploring the paradoxes and complexities of the religious problem inherent in humanizing the Divine and divinizing the human, a major stumbling block in the theological dialogue between Christians and Muslims. The

---

41. "Each one wants to know the Self. What kind of help does one require to know oneself? People want to see the Self as something new. But it is eternal and remains the same all along. They desire to see it as a blazing light, etc. How can it be so? It is not light, not darkness. It is only as it is. It cannot be defined. The best definition is 'I am that I AM.' . . . It is only Being, but different from the real and unreal; it is Knowledge, but different from knowledge and ignorance. How can it be defined at all? It is simply *Being*." Ramana Maharshi, *Talks with Ramana Maharshi* (Carlsbad, CA: Inner Directions, 2001), 86.

third chapter provides an examination of the Buddhist notion of *upāya*, most often translated as "skillful means." This notion is central in Schuon's opus as it suggests ways in which the relative, or intrinsically relative spiritual means, can provide ways of access to the Absolute within religious traditions. In Buddhism, it refers to the didactic medium through which the truths taught by the Buddha are transmitted. These means are provisional, in the sense that they do not and cannot convey the ultimate truth, being only formal ways to orient individuals according to their particular needs, qualifications, and circumstances. Schuon extends the scope of this notion to religions in general, thereby stressing the twofold nature of religions as absolute and relative, ultimate and provisional. The fourth chapter consists of a study of two key notions: the "nature of things" and the "human margin." This discussion refers to the interplay of absoluteness and relativity within the field of religion, highlighting as it does the complex relationship between the necessary as a reflection of the Absolute and the contingent that is inherent in human relativities. This distinction suggests the ways in which the all-too-human, and problematic, dimensions of religion can be situated, contextualized, and largely neutralized through discerning their limitations.

The fifth and sixth chapters are characterized by a more exclusive consideration of principles and phenomena pertaining respectively to two specific traditions, namely Christianity and Islam. The common focus of these two chapters is the manner in which absoluteness and relativity intersect, and are sometimes abusively conflated, in the fields of theology and spirituality. The fifth chapter looks at the ways in which Schuon formulates the notion of the Trinity in metaphysical terms. His writings include a significant number of passages devoted to a profoundly metaphysical interpretation of the Christian Trinity. In this respect, Schuon is primarily concerned with critiquing mainstream Christian theological views of the Trinity, which he perceives as unsatisfactorily equating the relative aspect of divine relationships with the unconditioned realm of the Absolute. This critique leads him to propose alternative understandings of the Trinity that both alleviate the aforementioned concerns and articulate a universalized version of the Divine Tri-Unity. As for the sixth chapter, it delves into Schuon's "reconstruction" of Sufism on the basis of his distinction between "quintessential" and "average" Sufism, and his parallel delineation of its "necessary" and "possible" manifestations. "Necessary Sufism" is the type of spirituality that intrinsically derives from the very tenets and key practices of the Islamic religion. This "necessary" Sufism culminates in "quintessential Sufism," which is none other than the metaphysical substrate of Islam and the spiritual core of its practices. These distinctions lead Schuon to demonstrate not only the Islamic nature of Sufism but also the ambiguities and perplexing paradoxes that have plagued its historical development.

The next three chapters of the book address different aspects of the principle of universal complementarity—primarily exemplified by the polarity of the feminine and masculine—and the ways in which it furnishes access to ultimate Unity. The seventh chapter is devoted to Divine Femininity. Schuon's works include two full chapters and a considerable number of passages devoted to the Virgin Mother. These writings are based on Christian and Islamic sources, and they provide, in a sense, a Marian bridge between these two religions. Schuon's Mariology, however, goes beyond the world of Abrahamic monotheism and leads one to consider the meaning of the Divine Feminine within a wider metaphysical framework that includes figures such as the Hindu *Shakti* and the Buddhist *Tara*. The eighth chapter delves into the implications of the *Yin-Yang* polarity in Schuon's works. These two Chinese cosmological concepts have been popularized in a number of Western cultural settings. In Chinese classical thought, they refer to the alternating and complementary duality that weaves the very texture of the universe. Schuon universalizes the meaning and function of these two key cosmological principles by making use of them as epistemological keys to understanding the paradoxes of the relationships between Unity and diversity in both the Divine Order and the creaturely realm. Finally, the ninth chapter considers the masculine-feminine complementarity from the vantage point of sexual symbolism. Schuon makes use of spiritual categories drawn from Asian traditions that capitalize on the positive and potentially liberating content of sexuality. The generic term *Tantrism*, with all its uncertainties and ambiguities, can be taken to refer—among other aspects—to spiritual paths that take sexuality as a central manifestation of the creative energy of the Infinite. These paths highlight and advocate a number of concepts and practices that facilitate the process of spiritual realization and integration. In Hindu mythology, the figures of Śiva and Krishna epitomize the various aspects of spiritualized eroticism. Here again, Schuon is primarily interested in extracting the universal sap of such teachings beyond the specific confines of their traditional forms, so that he may elucidate, for example, aspects of the "tantric" inspiration found in certain monotheistic prophets and sages.

The final chapter takes the question of ecumenism as its central concern. While Schuon's concept of the "transcendent unity of religions" has been understood by many as the main focus of his work, it is suggested here that it is only a relatively extrinsic aspect of his perspective. At any rate, Schuon's concept of "esoteric ecumenism" challenges the ordinary presuppositions and limitations of studies in comparative religion and interfaith engagement. The notion of esoteric ecumenism implies going beyond the formal theological teachings of particular religions so as to engage with their metaphysical core. This type of ecumenism aims to transcend the well-meaning platitudes that characterize many instances of interfaith dialogue. It suggests both a convergence of the deepest spiritual intuitions and a lucid awareness of the formal differences among religions, along with their causes and limitations. The term esoteric does not refer here to a secret and hardly accessible doctrine but to an inner and essential core, the recognition of which is indispensible for an integral reading of religious forms, their common "stratosphere" and their diverse "atmospheres."

1
Ātman, Māyā and the Relatively Absolute

One of the notable features of Schuon's works is a recurrent recognition of the eminence of Advaita Vedānta teachings, specifically as expounded by Shankara, in terms of metaphysical depth, synthesis, and directness. Schuon hailed from the Christian world of the Bible and loved the cosmic liturgy of the Roman Church. He was also intimate with the esoteric tradition of Islam and deeply sensitive to the spiritual vibrations of Buddhist "forms of Emptiness"; furthermore, he experienced profound kinship with the spiritual world of North American shamanism. Nevertheless, there is no question that Schuon considered Shankarian Advaita as the most direct expression of Reality. He actually refers to it as to the peak of spiritual intellectuality: "India presents, with the Śaivite and Shankarian Vedānta, the summit of the *philosophia perennis*."[1] In wondering why this is so, one finds an answer in Schuon's oft-repeated basic ternary delineation of his perspective as metaphysical discernment between the Real and the unreal, concentration upon the Real and conformity to the Real. Metaphysical discernment is the primary axis of Schuon's work as it is, analogously, the principle method of *Advaita* as the way to realize *Brahman*. In fact, *Advaita* includes metaphysical discernment as the first qualification for the path of non-duality as taught, for instance, in Shankara's *Commentary on the Brahma-Sutrā*.[2] It is arguably this emphasis on discernment that

---

1. Schuon, *The Eye of the Heart* (Bloomington, IN: World Wisdom, 1997), 70.
2. "The aspirant must possess the native ability to discern between what is real and what is only apparently real, between truth that is timeless and events that are time-

differentiates Advaita and Schuon's perspectives from other Indian teachings such as the Buddhist notion of "co-dependent origination" and the Kashmiri Śaivite account of metaphysical unfolding through the syzygy *Śiva-Śakti*. Although the latter, like all traditional mystical and theosophical teachings, imply and even assert a metaphysical distinction between the Ultimate and the non-Ultimate, they do not take the discrimination between the two as a starting point in their doctrinal exposition. Nāgārjuna's priority, for instance, lies in a fundamental and systematic critique of substantial causality so that the way may be cleared to highlight the metaphysics of Emptiness inherent in the teachings of co-dependent arising. In this way, Buddhist thought, without excluding discriminative metaphysics, tends to avoid substantializing phenomena and reifying the Absolute, through an analytical method of epistemological decomposition, an approach adopted by most Buddhist ways. As for Abhinavagupta's outlook, and that of Kashmiri Śaivism in general, it is not as purely discriminative as Shankara's but tends to emphasize the transformative nature of the inherently free, liberating, and creative power of Paramaśiva. Here, discrimination might even be equated with an epistemological stasis, inasmuch as it may be suspected of failing to avail itself of the universally creative and transformative immanence of *Śiva-Śakti*. Needless to say, both Buddhist and Kashmiri Śaivite teachings cannot but involve instances of metaphysical discernment between the Ultimate and the non-Ultimate, although they do not take this discernment as the starting point of their perspective.

In addition to giving primacy to discernment, what distinguishes Advaita Vedānta from metaphysically equivalent teachings, such as those we have just mentioned, is the relative directness and synthetic conciseness of its core philosophical doctrine, notwithstanding the dialectical and conceptual complexity of its argumentative developments. This is, primarily, due to the way the Advaita Vedāntin perspective revolves around the two central notions of *Ātman* and *Māyā*—that is, Reality and Appearance—or their metaphysical and functional equivalents. *Ātman* is none other than the subjective dimension of *Brahman*, the Ultimate Reality, while "in the writings of Śamkara and in those of post-Śamkara Advaitins, the terms *Māyā* and *avidyā* ('ignorance') come to be used interchangeably, with *avidyā* actually taking precedence over *Māyā* in the explanation of bondage

---

bound. He must, in short, have the ability to discriminate (*viveka*) between the spiritual and the superficial." Eliot Deutsch, *Advaita Vedānta: A Philosophical Reconstruction* (Honolulu: University of Hawaii Press, 1973), 105. Deutsch's comment is based on *Brahmasūtrabhāṣya*, I, 1, 1.

and freedom."[3] Another recurring term that is intrinsically connected to *avidyā* is *adhyāsa*, the superimposition upon Reality; in other words, the epistemological cause of ignorance and, therefore, the source of *Māyā*. At any rate, all other notions can be considered to be related, in one way or another, to the two key concepts of *Ātman* and *Māyā*, which encompass the whole field of being and existence. All things are encompassed by *Ātman* and *Māyā*, even though it is truer to state that everything is ultimately reducible to *Ātman* or *Brahman*, since it alone *is* in a real sense.[4] *Ātman* is the Real envisaged as "Self," without attaching to the latter the notion of the duality of subject and object, since the Self lies beyond all dualities and subsumes all multiplicity; it is none other than the Supreme *Brahman*, the Absolute, which the Hindu tradition contemplates as *Sat*, *Cit*, and *Ānanda* (Being, Consciousness, and Bliss), without these terms being reducible to qualities or attributes as such, since they do not delimit or determine *Ātman* in any manner.

The ontological and epistemological primacy of *Ātman* is, no doubt, the hallmark of Advaita Vedānta among contemplative paths. Divine Selfhood, therefore, is always ontologically, epistemologically, and methodically paramount. The operative aspect of this priority appears fully when considering that Advaitin *jñāna* begins with the Unity of the Divine Self. This is because the Subject precedes the Object, so to speak, insofar as consciousness entails and, in a sense encompasses, being. In this respect, Schuon provides his readers with an understanding of *jñāna* and *bhakti* that illuminates the aforementioned primacy of the Self in Advaita Vedānta. By contrast with the latter, which is intrinsically metaphysical, *bhakti* is the way of religion, the path founded on the relationship between the human soul and God. A human being, inasmuch as he or she is a *bhakta*,[5] begins the spiritual path with the axiomatic recognition

---

3. Deutsch, *Advaita Vedānta*, 33.

4. This is why, ultimately, L. Thomas O'Neil proposes to refer to Shankara's doctrine as *Brahmavāda* rather than *Māyāvāda*: "It is true that *Māyā* holds an important place within the epistemological and metaphysical frame of the Advaita but we must not turn the term *Māyā* into an ontological one except in a very special sense. . . . Perhaps then it would be best to refrain from the description of Śankara's Advaita as *Māyāvāda* and say rather that Advaita can be termed *Advaitavāda* or *Brahmavāda*." L. Thomas O'Neil, *Māyā in Śankara: Measuring the Immeasurable* (New Delhi: Molilal Banarsidass, 1980), 193.

5. This distinction is necessary, according to Schuon, insofar as the "individual portion" of the human subjectivity is necessarily "relational" and, therefore, intrinsically engaged in a form of *bhakti*: "To say 'man' is to say *bhakta*, and to say 'spirit' is to say *jñānin*;

of a duality between the subject and the Divine Object. *Bhakti-yoga* may lead to a mode of extinction whereby the human lover, through mystical union, attains unity with the Divine Beloved, albeit "asymptotically," as it were. Nevertheless, its indomitable foundation is one characterized by the loving relationship of a human subject with a Divine Object of Love. Love presupposes the presence of two, even though it may reduce these two to One through its transformative alchemy. By contrast, Schuon asserts that the way of knowledge is intrinsically the way of Unity inasmuch as the starting point is not the relationship between mankind and God, but the One Divine "I" that is the essence of all realities. This is the reason why the path of knowledge most often appears as static, even sterile, from the perspective of Love. *Jñana* is not dynamic in the sense that it merely consists in actualizing a recognition of what is and has always been. The Self cannot be proven or presented like an object since, as Shankara puts it, "the relation of identity with It has not to be directly established, for it is already there."[6] *Jñana* proceeds, therefore, through a combination of objectifying false identifications and merging with the Essence. The ego and its contents are treated as objects, which means that they are apprehended as foreign to the true Selfhood that is ultimately revealed as the only Reality. From one point of view, the *jñanic* path is an objectifying de-identification from the envelopes with which the subject is mis-identified; from another vantage point, it is a de-objectifying identification with the Self that dwells beyond the polarity of subject and object.

 Ātman is traditionally related to the notion of spirit and to the Indo-European etymon that refers to breathing. Many traditions associate spirit and breath, and Schuon extends this symbolism to its metaphysical source, thereby associating *Ātman* with the "breathing out" of the world. Sufism, notably in the thought of Ibn ʿArabī, makes use of a similar symbolism with the notion of the "Breath of the Compassionate" (*nafas-ar-rahmān*), which refers to the creation of the universe. Interestingly, Schuon refers to *Māyā* as being breathed out by *Ātman*: "*Māyā* is the

---

human nature is so to speak woven of these two neighbouring but incommensurable dimensions. There is certainly a *bhakti* without *jñana*, but there is no *jñana* without *bhakti*." Schuon, *Esoterism as Principle and as Way* (Bedford, Middlesex: Perennial Books, 1981), 22.

6. *Brhadāranyaka Upanisadbhāsya*, IV, iv, 20, in Sudhakshina Rangaswami, ed., *The Roots of Vedānta: Selections from Sankara's Writings* (Gurgaon: Penguin Books India, 2012), 173.

breath of *Ātman*; *Ātman* 'breathes' through *Māyā*. *Māyā* is the air breathed by *Ātman*, and this air is a quality of His own Infinitude."[7] Besides the evocation of the oneness of Being that this symbolism obviously entails, a further implication of the analogy lies in that the Infinite "needs" the air of *Māyā* to remain "alive" as Infinite: in other words, the universe unfolds from a necessary dimension of the Principle without which the Principle would not be the Principle.

As intimated above, one of the most important characteristics of Advaita Vedānta lies in the ultimate conjunction of its ontology and epistemology. Both *Ātman* and *Māyā* can be approached from either point of view. Thus, Shankara considers *Māyā* as an ontological power emanating from the Divine Lord,[8] originally a kind of divine "magic" through which the Lord may manifest himself to mankind, as well as a principle of delusion that lies at the foundation of a false identification with the *jīva* and the body, thus preventing one from realizing the Self.[9] The first understanding derives from the *Veda* and refers to a magical and creative power of the gods.[10] It has been suggested, in this connection, that the "theistic connotations of the word were relatively strong in Shankara's mind."[11] But *Māyā* is also the outcome of ignorance and stems therefore

---

7. "This breathing—apart from its inner or substantial prefigurations—is extrinsic, in the manner of our breathing here on earth, where a link is made between the inward, the living body, and the outward, the surrounding air. The Universe proceeds from God and returns to Him; hence the cosmic cycles governing the microcosm as well as the macrocosm." Rangaswami, 15–16.

8. "*Avidya* ('Nescience') or *Maya*, called also the 'Undifferentiated,' is the power of the Lord. She is without beginning, is made up of the three *Gunas* and is superior to the effects (as their cause). She is to be inferred by one of clear intellect only from the effects She produces. It is She who brings forth this whole universe." Śaṅkarācārya, *Vivekachudamani of Shri Shankaracharya*, Swami Madhavananda (Kolkata: Advaita Ashrama, 1966), 108.

9. "Perfect discrimination brought on by direct realisation distinguishes the true nature of the subject from that of the object, and breaks the bond of delusion created by *Maya*; and there is no more transmigration for one who has been freed from this." *Vivekachudamani*, 136.

10. "In every figure he hath been the mode: this is his only form for us to look on. Indra moves multiform by his illusions." *Rig Veda*, Vi, 47:18. G. Ch. Narang, *Message of the Vedas* (Lahore: New Book Society, 1946), 65.

11. *A Shankara Source Book, Volume 1: Shankara on the Absolute*, compiled and translated by A. J. Alston (London: Shanti Sadan, 2004), 35.

from a misperception of Reality. In this epistemological sense, *Ātman* and *Māyā* can be approached either objectively as Reality and Appearance or subjectively as Selfhood and the superimpositions on it. However, the second perspective is more akin to a specifically Advaitin point of view since the Absolute is Subject "before" being Object—at least to the extent that such a distinction may be drawn when referring to the Reality that transcends the polarity of subject-object—and since objectification comes in the way of realizing *Ātman*. When the Absolute Reality is envisaged as ultimate and all-encompassing Selfhood, then Appearance can only proceed from what Advaita refers to as a limiting adjunct or superimposition (*upādhi*) upon the true Self. In fact, this term, with its correlate of ignorance, *avidyā*, appears more frequently in Shankara's work than *Māyā* itself. In Indian logic and philosophy the term *upādhi* conveys the ideas of limitation (particularization of the object of knowledge), imposition (an external projection upon an object), and covering or veiling (an obstruction or obscuration). These three connotations are quite rich in meaning and most relevant to the non-dualistic view of Reality. In fact, by contrast, the dualistic metaphysics of Madhva, the main proponent of Dvaita (or dualist) Vedānta is centered on the aspect of limitation while denying the reality of veiling.[12] From an Advaitin point of view, while it is valid to state that ignorance is a limitation of the Self in the sense that it "makes the Self appear as limited"[13]—hence the theory of *avaccheda-vāda* that considers the *jīva* as a limitation of *Ātman* (although this limitation has no reality in itself)—it must be added that it pertains to the illusory *upādhi*, which means that it cannot be considered to be a real difference that one could recognize as preexisting. *Upādhi*, in an Advaitin sense, does not refer to a limitation itself as much as it does to a projection of the limitation of the body or the *jīva*, the individual self, upon the true or universal Self. Therefore, it entails a false identification and thus a covering of the Self. The *upādhi* is a superimposition of difference upon That which is intrinsically

---

12. Thus, in reference to Madhva's *Upādhi Khandana*, B. N. Krishnamurti Sharma writes that "the function of an *Upādhi* is to place in bold relief an existing difference not readily perceived and 'not to create a non-existing difference.'" *History of the Dvaita School of Vedānta and its Literature* (New Delhi: Motilal Barnarsidass, 1960), 140.

13. Shankara states: "The nature of ignorance proves to be this: it represents that which is infinite as finite; presents things other than the Self that are non-existent; and makes the Self appear as limited." *Brhadāranyaka Upanisadbhāsya*, IV.iii.20, *Roots of Vedānta*, 87.

non-difference. Typically, of course, the dualist argument against Advaita consists in asserting that *upādhi*, as the source of ignorance, cannot be accounted for without ascribing the latter to the absolute *Brahman* itself, lest its origination—in this perspective—remain unintelligible. Now this argument is sometimes thought to be buttressed by the Advaitin recognition that *Māyā* is without beginning, giving it a seemingly parallel reality to Brahman that appears to contradict its non-dualistic outlook. However, it can be argued that the epistemological outlook of Advaita Vedānta leads it to set aside the onto-cosmogonic dimension of *Māyā* as relativity, since the latter is exclusively envisaged from the point of view of its illusory character as an obstacle to a recognition of *Ātman*. In other words, the epistemological problem of ignorance, the recognition of which constitutes the starting point of the way of *jñana*, envisages Appearance as a covering or negation of Reality, although it does not exclude considering it, at times, as proceeding from it *qua Brahman*. All the same, there is no doubt that, for Shankara, *Māyā* is essentially connected to *avidyā* or ignorance, to the point of being identified with it. This point of view does not exclude that *Māyā* or, rather, certain of its dimensions or degrees, may lead to *Ātman* or facilitate its realization—and necessarily so since the guru is, implicitly, *a priori* a part of *Māyā*, although this aspect is not the primary focus of Shankara's attention. In other terms, Shankara normally considers *Māyā* as the all-encompassing principle of obscuration rather than as being endowed with the discrete qualities it assumes in its incessant unfolding. Advaita envisions *Māyā* from the point of view of *Ātman*, if one may say so, and not from the standpoint of its own degrees or aspects of relativity as *Māyā*, even though it recognizes the composition of *Māyā* from the three cosmological *gunas*. As Eliot Deutsch has observed: "Creation may be considered a positive activity of Brahman only from the . . . empirical point of view; only to the extent that we are subject to *Māyā*, *avidyā*, and are engaged in the activities of *adhyāsa*."[14] In fact, *Advaita* does not even treat the ontological account of *Māyā* as a production of *Brahman* as real, since the realization of the latter annuls the very question of creation.

Accordingly, the Advaitin approach to *Māyā* does not necessarily do justice to the full semantic scope of the term. When Ananda Coomaraswamy proposed to translate *Māyā* by "Divine Art," he was referring to the Upanishadic implications of the term. It must be recognized, first of all,

---

14. Deutsch, *Advaita Vedānta*, 41.

that direct references to the notion of *Māyā* in the Upanishads are quite rare, being largely restricted to the *Svetāsvatara Upanishad* and the *Maitrī Upanishad*. Although there is no universal consensus as to the etymology of the word *Māyā* as found in these Upanishads, several interpretations have been propounded that refer to various dimensions and aspects of *Māyā*. Notions of power and wisdom, associated with creation and a capacity to "measure" reality, form an initial cluster of references in which the positive side of *Māyā* is stressed. This "measure" refers to relativity and form, the principal constituents of *Māyā*: measure is always limited as it delineates exclusive formal realities. However, as L. Thomas O'Neil has emphasized, this also means that, in Advaita, *Māyā* is a measure of That which is immeasurable, *Brahman*. In other words, *Māyā* presupposes *Brahman* or *Ātman*, and it functions as a measure of *Brahman* in the sense that it inherently falls short of this reality and thus points to it.[15] Its power is associated with the idea of projection, magic, and illusion, suggesting negative connotations of delusion, although this is not necessarily so since magic may also signify the power of the *Brahman* to produce in general. Thus, the *Svetāsvatara Upanishad* refers to the Lord as *māyin*, or productive of *Māyā*, with some translations emphasizing the magic power of the act of creation, others its wisdom and imagination, while others, again, stress its projection of illusion.[16] Without entering into the details of the various arguments regarding the scriptural intent behind the Upanishadic worldview, it is clear that *Māyā* refers to a divine power of projection and formation, and that this artful, magical, or imaginal production may be considered either positively, as expressing Divine creation and manifes-

---

15. "This is so because *Māyā* acts as the measuring out of phenomena so that Brahman remains. . . . Within the structures of epistemology and metaphysics *Māyā* can never be 'illusion' because it maintains its reality as a kind of 'measure' as long as one is still within the name-form complex. . . . *Māyā* is provisional forever but not eternal. It is the measure of distinction between Brahman with and Brahman without distinction." O'Neil, *Māyā in Śankara*, 202.

16. "*Māyā* is a power that, being derived from a certain uncommon knowledge, can be used either for good or for bad purposes; thus it is an intelligent power or a cunning shrewdness. This power appears to be detachable from the one to whom it belongs, so that it may be used for different purposes, both good and bad. It has indeed both a personal and a cosmic character. No wonder that, since powers tend to corrupt, even this greatest power of the Gods is corrupt not only in its usage by them but also in the very concept of its meaning, so that later on *Māyā* came to mean the power of deception and delusion." Raimon Panikkar, *Hinduism, Part 1: The Vedic Experience* (New York: Orbis Books, 2016), 508–9.

tation, or negatively, as a principle of epistemological entanglement and deceptive illusion. In fact, the very notion of magic itself can be taken auspiciously or inauspiciously, which suggests that creative manifestation can be the bearer of Reality or the dispenser of illusion.

According to the *Svetāsvatara Upanishad*, the Divine Reality, including in its non-dual Essence, is intrinsically associated with its power of production, that is, *Māyā*, while the microcosmic and epistemological effects of this production are evidently negative, in that they involve a misidentification of the Brahman with the individual self, the *jīva*. Thus, the Upanishad teaches that "Brahman projects the universe through the power of Its *Māyā*. Again, in that universe Brahman as the *jīva* is entangled through *Māyā*" (4:9). In other passages from the same Upanishad, what appears, at first, to be an unintended entanglement resulting in ignorance is envisaged as an intentional covering on the part of Brahman Himself: "May the non-dual Lord who, by the power of His *Māyā*, covered Himself, like a spider, with threads drawn from primal matter, merge us in Brahman!" (6:10). The image of the spider, which is also to be found in the *Maitrī Upanishad*, is all the more significant in that it brings together the positive and the negative aspects of *Māyā*. On the one hand, *Māyā* is consubstantial with *Brahman*, being drawn from the same non-dual Essence; on the other, *Māyā* is the means by which the Divine conceals itself, thereby giving rise to ignorance. It is worth noting that the intention of the Upanishadic prayer, cited above, is none other than the reunion of the *jīva* with the *Ātman*. Although this is not explicitly stated in the verse, it could be assumed that the very same power which effects the concealment of Brahman may be reversed, through *jñanic* realization, to reveal the potential of the *jñana* to merge with the One as non-dual Reality, since the thread that makes this possible is none other than an aspect of the spider.

While Advaita Vedānta, being primarily concerned with the problem of the origin of ignorance, focuses mostly—but in no way exclusively—on the concealing and delusive power of *Māyā*, other streams of Hindu gnosis take into account both the positive and negative aspects of the onto-cosmic deployment of *Māyā*. Kashmiri Śaivism, for example, explicitly sees the stream of manifestation as being endowed with reality and salvific power. Thus, in Śaivism, the power of projection inherent in *Śiva-Śakti* is seen as the supreme onto-cosmogonic principle in its own right. In this view of things, *Māyā* is integral to the *Śaktic* unfolding of the Absolute.

It could be argued that, notwithstanding Schuon's profound affinity with Advaita Vedānta, his perspective on universal relativity may be deemed to come closer, in several significant respects, to that of Śaivism. Nevertheless, the modalities of his metaphysical exposition remain profoundly different from the latter, the analytic and methodical complexities of which contrast with Schuon's more synthetic and essentializing style. In this sense, therefore, Schuon's perspective reflects a Tantric or Śaivite inflection of Advaita.

The substance of our previous remarks may be crystallized in what is arguably the most explicit and significant passage on *Māyā* to be found in Schuon's works: "*Māyā* is not only 'universal illusion,' but also 'divine play'. It is the great theophany, the 'unveiling' of God 'in Himself and by Himself' as the Sufis would say. *Māyā* is like a magic fabric woven from a warp that veils and a weft that unveils; a quasi incomprehensible intermediary between the finite and the Infinite—at least from our point of view as creatures—it has all the shimmering ambiguity appropriate to its half-cosmic, half-divine nature."[17] Let us note that the mention of Sufism in this passage echoes the suggestion, to be found elsewhere in Schuon's work, that notwithstanding the metaphysical eminence of *Advaita*, Sufi theosophy might be considered to be more explicit than the latter with respect to its accounting for the cause of manifestation itself. The key, in this respect, is what could be called the revelation of God to Himself, through Self-unveilings that make it possible for the Absolute to know itself, not only as pure Selfhood, but also through the detour of the subject-object relationship. It is to be remembered, in this regard, that the Sufi outlook shares in the Qur'ānic perspective on the relationship between God, creation, and mankind; one that must make metaphysical sense of the central injunction, incumbent upon the whole of creation—but particularly upon mankind—to worship the One. By contrast, it could be deemed that *Advaita*'s relative silence on the onto-cosmological why of *Māyā*, aside from its being connected to the epistemological thrust of its perspective, stems from the fact that any positive finality attached to *Māyā* would, from an Advaitin perspective, undermine the exclusive discernment that opens the way to the recognition of the only Self. Be that as it may, it is remarkable that Schuon's aforementioned definition of *Māyā* primarily highlights its dual nature, a duality that entails a lack of intelligibility but also, and above all, a capacity to reveal the Ultimate. While the term play is reminiscent of the vocabulary of Hindu *bhakti*, the divine *līlā* being the sport that has no other why than its own rev-

---

17. Schuon, *Light on the Ancient Worlds* (Bloomington, IN: World Wisdom, 2006), 75.

eling, the most significant symbolic analogy is no doubt that of a shimmering or iridescent fabric which both veils and unveils that which lies beyond it.

It is quite clear that Schuon's approach involves, with regard to its Shankarian reference, a shift from the epistemological to the ontological; a shift that results, overall, in a much more positive evaluation of *Māyā*. The following passage bears witness to this undeniable inflection: "*Māyā*, illusion or the 'Divine Art' which expresses *Ātman* according to indefinitely varied modes—and of which *avidyā*, the ignorance which conceals *Ātman*, is the purely negative aspect—proceeds mysteriously from *Ātman* Itself, in the sense that *Māyā* is a necessary consequence of *Ātman*'s infinity. Shankara expresses this by saying that *Māyā* is without beginning."[18] Schuon is quite aware of the fact that the Shankarian exposition of the relationship between *Ātman* and *Māyā* is not set in terms of the infinity of the former, but he does suggest nevertheless that Shankara cannot but encounter an aspect of this principle, albeit through the paradoxical epistemological detour of the beginninglessness of *Māyā*, root of ignorance. Thus Shankara associates the beginninglessness of *Māyā* with the eternity of the cycle of *samsāra*.[19] Since it is impossible to refer to a beginning of *Māyā* without seeming to attribute ignorance to *Ātman*, it is unavoidable that *Māyā* be given a sort of co-perpetuity in relation to *Ātman*, at least from the point of view of its origination. *Māyā*'s beginninglessness is like the mark of its intrinsic relationality with *Ātman*, so to speak, which is a way of signifying that ignorance is the ever-originated shadow of knowledge, just like the relative is the unending projection of the Absolute by virtue of the latter's intrinsic infinitude. On the other hand, the absoluteness of *Ātman*, its sole and exclusive Reality, must express itself in a way that would prevent *Māyā* from being endless, thus somewhat Absolute in its own way. Thus, Schuon writes: "The earthly *Māyā* frees itself through man, for each separate liberation is something absolute which, from a certain point of view, achieves Liberation as such."[20] In other words, while *Māyā*

---

18. Schuon, *Language of the Self* (Bloomington, IN: World Wisdom, 2003), 24.

19. "The illusion (*Māyā*) of *samsāra* having existed in time without beginning, they say that this tree of *samsāra* is eternal; for it rests, as is well known, on a continuous series of births, which is without beginning or end, and is therefore eternal." *Bhagavad Gītā Bhāsya*, XV, 4, *Roots of Vedānta*, 322.

20. Schuon, *Form and Substance in the Religions* (Bloomington, IN: World Wisdom, 2002), 40.

betrays the infinitude of *Ātman* through its beginninglessness, it expresses the Absolute by freeing itself in vanishing before *Ātman*.

Therefore, even though it takes from Shankara's view of *Māyā* the principle of epistemological scission, the notion of *Māyā* is given a much more ambivalent, and indeed ultimately positive, turn in Schuon's writings, in a way that echoes the Upanishadic denotations of the term. As we have seen, if Advaita considers *Māyā* as illusion, it is by virtue of a more epistemological rather than ontological standpoint. *Māyā* is the reality that prevents the recognition of the Self. It is a principle of obscuration. Thus, *Māyā* is generally not considered from the point of view of ontology since it is—after all—only an appearance that has to be dispelled, like a rope that is mistaken for a snake. As appearance, *Māyā* masks Reality but it is not approached as a means to reach the latter. However, Advaita, as shown in Shankara's work, emphasizes the reality of the guru and the traditional means of spiritual education, not to mention the Goddess[21]—all expressive, in one way or another, of "*Ātman* in *Māyā*" as a necessary means of realizing *Ātman*. Schuon's point of view on this matter is not different from Shankara's, although it may be considered to provide an original synthesis of Upanishadic views, Advaitin principles, and Śaivite insights.

The first function of *Māyā* is, for Schuon, separation and splitting or a dividing into two, *dédoublement*.[22] *Māyā* is the principle of duality whereby the Essential Non-Duality, which is by definition beyond the duality of subject and object, is broken down—albeit in illusory mode—and gives way to relativity and multiplicity. So it would appear that this separation and split is a negative tendency, and it is undoubtedly so considering that it involves a distancing from the Principle which is pure Reality. However, Schuon couches the matter in a way that is ultimately more positive than negative. This appears, most interestingly, in the following observation: "[Separation] the goal of which is the production of a plane of manifestation for the two consecutive functions, Radiation and Reverberation, to which correspond motion and form."[23] *Māyā* is not Radiation and

---

21. "Oh! Daughter of the Mountain, how can we describe your incomparable chin, which resembles the handle of a mirror, touched in affection with the finger-tip by your father, the Snowy Mountain and lifted again and again by your Lord, desirous of drinking your lips." Śaṅkarācārya, *Saundaryalaharī*, translated by V. K. Subramanian (New Delhi: Motilal Banarsidass, 2011), 35.

22. Schuon, *Form and Substance in the Religions*, 37.

23. Schuon, *Form and Substance in the Religions*, 37.

Reverberation but the very condition for the onto-cosmological affirmation of the Divine Principle through these two existential modes. *Māyā* has a positive finality that is a productive goal; it is not simply a mysterious veil covering Reality from our eyes—although it is also undoubtedly such from the point of view of the epistemological scission that it entails—but a power of projection that creates the very condition for the possibility of a manifestation of the Fullness of the Absolute in diverse and contrasted modes. Schuon compares it to a metaphysical Space in which Radiation and Reverberation can unfold.[24] In other words, separation is not an end in itself but a metaphysical detour that can be taken in a positive way, analogous to the Augustinian *felix culpa*, even though it is not a Divine Reality as such. It is notable that the word *separation* is not capitalized by Schuon, although the words *Radiation* and *Reverberation* are. Only the latter are, in a sense, Divine Aspects whereas separation is nothing but a function of *Māyā*.

Furthermore, both Radiation and Reverberation entail negative concomitances and effects. Radiation involves an increasing distance from the Principle. As such it spreads out, so to speak, between the Infinitude as inexhaustible wealth of Being—the ultimate principle of manifestation—and a nothingness that it never reaches. Thus Radiation involves a kind of gradual loss of being. As a whole, it could be said that Radiation is a good, or a degree of the Good, that necessarily entails evil, or absence of the good. But even this lack may appear as the external dimension of the Good. It is the dimension of continuity that prevails in this case since Radiation necessarily implies That which radiates, without which it would be impossible to speak of Radiation at all. However, this continuity also presupposes discontinuity in the sense that Radiation, perforce, entails a kind of going out or flowing forth away from the Origin. Similarly, but in a reverse sense, Reverberation implies a discontinuity between That which is reverberated and the reverberating reality that emerges. A distinction, or distance, between the Good and other than the Good is necessary for the Former to be echoed, or mirrored, in the latter.

Aside from the two principles of Radiation and Reverberation that it makes possible, *Māyā*'s "nature could be defined with the help of various terms, such as Relativity, Contingency, Separativity, Objectification, Differentiation, Exteriorization, and others still; even the term Revelation

---

24. *Māyā* is the container, not the contents: "She is the principle of projection or the container." Schuon, *Form and Substance in the Religions*, 37.

could be appropriately applied here in an altogether fundamental and general sense."[25] *Māyā* is Relativity in relation to the Absolute, since it is other than the Absolute. It means that *Māyā* is neither necessary—at least in its modes—nor free or independent, since its reality depends upon the non-recognition of *Ātman* and thus, ultimately, upon *Ātman* itself. The latter means that *Māyā* is also Contingency. The Separativity of *Māyā* is connected to its power of Reverberation, which entails distance between That which is reverberated and the reverberation itself. *Māyā* is therefore the principle of Otherness on all levels of Reality. This is the meaning of *Māyā*, in Schuon's lexicon, that comes the closest to the Śaivite *Śakti*. By contrast, there is no Separativity in *Ātman*, or in the pure Absolute, since any separation entails difference and therefore relativity, in one way or another. This Separativity involves, by definition, Differentiation, or the difference between the two terms that are separated. Moreover, Objectification is the central aspect of Separativity, since it refers to the very differentiation that lies at the core of the dualistic perspective that is inherently connected to *Māyā*; that is, the distinction between a subject and an object. When Shankara refers to *Māyā* as superimposition upon *Ātman*, he is alluding to this very power of objectification. *Ātman*, by contrast, is pure Subject, in the sense that it is pure Consciousness without an object—no reality being "outside" of the Subject—which means that any veritable relationship between subject and object is thereby annulled. Furthermore, *Māyā* as Exteriorization is none other than this ontological and epistemological scission, whereas, by contrast, *Ātman* is essentially pure Inwardness. As for the identification of *Māyā* as Revelation, it should not be construed in the sense intended by monotheistic religions, but in the Sufi sense of a Self-Unveiling of the Divine Essence. As we have already intimated, this particular perspective on *Māyā* is by and large foreign to Advaita Vedānta. Although the Sufi understanding comes closer to the point of view of Kashmiri Śaivism, it does not match the vision of the latter since, metaphysically, the Śaivite perspective tends to approach—*a priori*—the Śaktic projection of *Śiva* as a Veiling and a Binding rather than as an Unveiling and an Unbinding, although it conceives of the energy immanent in the former as the principle that makes it possible to unbind and unveil.

---

25. Schuon, *Form and Substance in the Religions*, 32.

In consonance with the Śaivite understanding of *Śakti*, Schuon's metaphysical exposition of the dual function of *Māyā* is most often connected to the metaphysical status of the feminine. Since another chapter of this work fully engages the question of Divine Femininity, we will confine our current remarks to some of the more relevant implications of this notion. The connection between *Māyā* and Femininity relates, at least symbolically, to the etymological interpretation that makes the word *Māyā* akin to *mā*, or mother, a root that points to the association of *Māyā* with the feminine as creative and productive, which is attested by its Hindu attribution to Lakshmi and the reference to the mother of the Buddha, Queen *Māyā*. As Mahalakshmi or Mahashakti, *Māyā* is intrinsically connected to the Infinite, this dimension of the Ultimate that is the Divine Womb, as it were, of the onto-cosmogonic manifestation. In this regard, one of the most powerful aspects of Schuon's work is what could be called a metaphysical rehabilitation of *Māyā* as qualitative projection of the outpouring essence of the Infinite. For Schuon, *Māyā* is indeed—in its highest and truest reality—the Divine Feminine itself and, as such, untouched by the impurities of the relative as separation, ignorance, evil, and suffering. While femininity refers to a power of creation or manifestation that is ambivalent—since it is by definition both identical to, and different from, the masculine source of its unfolding—the Feminine *in divinis* is untainted by this ambivalence, which pertains only to the cosmic strata of its extrinsic manifestations. It must be noted, in this regard, that Schuon clearly identifies the Divine *Māyā* with the Mystery of Mary when he writes that Mary cannot but be a Hypostasis since she is "'Spouse' of the God-Radiation and 'Mother' of the God-Image."[26] Thus, the Marian Mystery is, in its highest aspect, the Infinite Space opened for Radiation and Reverberation.

Three significant insights, from Schuon's *Form and Substance in the Religions*, express quite suggestively the various functions of *Māyā* as a feminine reality. They refer, respectively, to *Māyā*'s relationship with the Good, with evil and with liberation from evil. The first statement sounds *prima facie* as a kind of cross-religious *koān*: "God has created the world out of Love, thus through *Māyā*."[27] This is quite far from the reputation of *Māyā*, in the Vedānta, as seductive. The root of manifestation in God is

---

26. Schuon, *Form and Substance in the Religions*, 38.
27. Schuon, *Form and Substance in the Religions*, 41.

none other than *Māyā* as Love; that is, as Infinite gift of Self and embracing reintegration into the Self. Creation out of Love, or by *Māyā*, is therefore like an attempt at injecting Being into nothingness, so to speak, through Radiation and Reverberation. The reality of Love in God—or the reality of God as Love—is situated in his "bipolarisation in Radiation and Image—in function of *Māyā*." Without wishing to delve into the implications of these crucial remarks for Trinitarian metaphysics—which are discussed in a later chapter specifically devoted to the Trinity—it suffices to say that the Divine Reality is Love inasmuch as it is Infinitude and, therefore, Radiation and Reverberation by virtue of this Infinitude, i.e., sameness in otherness and otherness in sameness. In a sense, the Christian concept of Divine Love is like a *bhaktic* allusion to this mystery of *Māyā*—its unconditional and unfathomable dimensions being functional substitutes for *Māyā*'s creative and redemptive power as well as for its ambiguity. However, Schuon's second statement reveals the relativity of this ambiguity by specifying that "it is not the Divine *Māyā* that produces directly privative phenomena, for She bewails these from behind Her veil."[28] As indicated above, *Māyā* refers to incommensurable realities, from the Infinite Space of the Essence to the subversive figments of illusion, a principle that Śaivism expresses through its distinction between Divine Śakti, which is indissociable from Śiva, and innumerable Śaktic centers of energy that spin the world. The Divine *Māyā* is not directly responsible for the negative occurrences of manifestation, that is, phenomena that are as many partial or total negations of the Divine Qualities and archetypes (and which are the necessary ransom of existentiation), thus representing a distance from God. "Bewailing"—a suggestive allusion to the *mater dolorosa*—therefore symbolizes the transcendence of the Divine Reality and the separation that it experiences in relation to the manifested order. This "bewailing" also means compassion for a finite and imperfect realm that cannot be saved on its own relative terms, but only by virtue of the Absolute, and therefore not without sacrifice and suffering. Since separation can never be absolute, however, the weeping must eventually give way to the joy of deliverance: "The earthly *Māyā* frees itself through man, for each particular liberation is something absolute which, from a certain point of view, achieves Liberation as such."[29] Paraphrasing Schuon's terms, it could be

---

28. Schuon, *Form and Substance in the Religions*, 38.
29. Schuon, *Form and Substance in the Religions*, 40.

said that *Ātman* has hidden itself within *Māyā* so that *Māyā* can, in turn, reveal *Ātman*. The Upanishads do teach that this hiding place lies within the heart of man, for the principle that *Māyā* frees herself through man also means that man can free himself through *Māyā*.

It is significant that Schuon includes *Māyā* among the fundamental concepts that distinguish most clearly the esoteric outlook from the exoteric religious point of view. Most of the *aporiae* inherent to theology flow, in his view, from an exoteric incapacity to integrate the perspective of *Māyā* conceived as metaphysical Relativity. Moreover, if one relates *Māyā* to the two other distinctive notions of esoterism, namely Beyond-Being and the Intellect, one realizes that they are intrinsically connected to one another and constitute an onto-epistemological triad. Simply put, Beyond-Being is That which is not *Māyā* or That which lies beyond *Māyā*. As for the Intellect, it is the organ which, in the human being, makes it possible for the latter to know *Māyā*, which amounts to realizing its non-reality. The Intellect is "the Real within appearance" that reveals appearance to be other than the Real, thereby unveiling the exclusive reality of the Real.

Why is *Māyā* absent from exoteric perspectives and how is this absence manifested in their understanding of the spiritual dimension? The answer must be that the exoteric perspective, that is, the ordinary religious perspective, is characterized by its exclusiveness and its incapacity to take into account a variety of perspectives. The religious vision is one-sided because it is primarily concerned with absolutizing the particular view that it teaches as the precondition for salvation. Its perspective is that of the individual, and the individual *qua* individual cannot consider all the aspects of the Object since its scope is necessarily limited. The only way in which the individual can contemplate a diversity of aspects—thus opening itself to the latter—is by changing "location" by way of a spiritual "motion." However, the religious outlook precludes such a motion since it identifies the Absolute with a single object of faith that becomes invested with the totality of the former. *Māyā*, in Schuon's view, is precisely the reality that accounts for the diversity of aspects of the Real, seeing as this diversity results from the principle of relativity that it encapsulates. To be aware of *Māyā* means being cognisant of the ontological modulations of the Real. Now, from an exoteric perspective, a sensitivity to those modulations—if it were possible for the exoteric mentality to conceive of it—would be understood as a form of religious relativism that is destructive of true faith. The exoteric mentality cannot envisage the legitimacy of standpoints other than its own without relativizing the latter in a way that undermines its spiritual efficacy.

The "relationship" between Beyond-Being and *Māyā*—being understood that the former cannot actually enter into any real relationship since it is the One without a second—reveals a major metaphysical consequence in the distinction that it casts between the Absolute in itself and the "relatively Absolute." The latter is also referred to by Schuon as *"Māyā in divinis,"* thus indicating that there is a Divine Relativity; a paradoxical concept that the sense of the Absolute inherent to exoteric religious faith cannot accommodate. The "relatively Absolute" is the Absolute inasmuch as it relates to other-than-the-Absolute, particularly mankind. Inasmuch as the exoteric standpoint is, by definition, limited to this relationship and its perspective is that of "individual interest," it cannot truly envisage Beyond-Being, which by definition lies beyond any relationship. Similarly, the notion of the Intellect is foreign to the exoteric perspective, precisely because being Divine in its source and supra-individual in its operations, the Intellect, in mankind, is that which can transcend the polarity of subject and the object, thereby affirming the Unity of the Real. To discern the reality of *Māyā* would amount, for the exoteric point of view, to recognizing the Intellect as the organ that transcends Relativity, including the Divine-human relationship.

How does *Māyā* arise? Advaita Vedānta and Śaivism offer different responses to this question. Advaitin teachings assert that *Māyā* ranges "from the god Brahma to the blade of grass." In other words, *Māyā* encompasses the whole range of relativity that forms the realm of qualified reality. To be qualified means to be endowed with *gunas*—the cosmic qualities of *sattva, rajas* and *tamas*—the combination of which constitutes the texture of the manifest universe. However, qualities also refer to the meta-cosmic domain, as indicated by the concept of *Saguna Brahman* (the Absolute with "qualities"), in contrast to *Nirguna Brahman* (the "unqualified" Absolute). One of the most striking characteristics of the Advaitin *Māyā* is that it includes, at its summit, *Saguna Brahman*—the Relative *in divinis*—which Schuon also sees as the First Determination of the Principle, that is, Being. In the Advaita worldview, God is the supreme *Māyā* insofar as the reality of God presupposes that of existence and, therefore, the reality of "other-than-the-Principle." God is, in a sense, relative to creation without being contingent upon it.

The point of view of Kashmiri Śaivism differs in that it refers to *Māyā* as the ontological principle, or *tattva*, that initiates the realm of *bhedābheda* or "difference within non-difference." This signifies that *Māyā* is situated at the summit of the domain that lies between non-difference (*abheda*) and difference (*bheda*). Thus, *Māyā* is the sixth *tattva*, following the five highest ontological degrees that modulate the various stages of the germination of difference within non-difference through the unfolding of *Śiva-Śakti*.[30] Considering the cascading effect of the *tattvas* downstream, *Māyā* is the first of seven *tattvas* that facilitate the descent into difference and, as such, constitutes the first "filter" in the stream of Divine radiation. Occupying the highest degree within the intermediary ontological range, *Māyā* can be identified with the first principle of obscuration, but also with that critical point within difference that gives access to non-difference.

Considering the respective metaphysical delineations proposed by the two Hindu perspectives, one cannot but be struck by the fact that Advaita is exclusive and immediate, as it were, while Kashmiri Śaivism is inclusive and gradual. As a consequence, while the Advaitin *Māyā* is like an embracing totality that holds the entire range of existence under the spell of superimposition and ignorance, the Śaivite *Māyā* is akin to an ontological turning point that may lead downward or upward, depending on one's degree of awareness of the Unconditioned. It also means that the function and qualities assigned to *Māyā* are much more ambivalent in Kashmiri Śaivism than they are in Advaita Vedānta. It is important to note that *Māyā* is situated, in each case, on two different levels. In Advaita, as we have seen, *Māyā* begins on the level of Ishwara, the personal God, or *Brahman Saguna*. Ishwara is relative in relation to *Ātman*, being its determination or its reflection.[31] In Kashmiri Śaivism, by contrast, *Māyā* appears only below the level of the five highest *tattvas*. On the sixth level, "*Māyā tattva* begins its play. From this stage onward, there is *aśuddhādhvan* or the order in which the real nature of the Divine is concealed. All this happens because of *Māyā* and its *kañcukas*. *Māyā* is derived from the root *mā*, 'to measure out': 'That which makes experience measurable or limited, severs "This" from "I" and "I" from "This," and excludes things from one another, is *Māyā*.' "[32] *Śiva, Śakti, Sadāśiva, Īshvāra*, and *Suddha Vidyā*—the five supreme "cascades"—belong to the realm of non-difference

---

30. Abhinavagupta's *MahāMāyā tattva* is characterized by Jaideva Singh as marked by the "shrinkage of *abheda* (non-difference) and appearance of *bheda* (difference)." Abhinavagupta, *Parā-triśikā-Vivarana: The Secret of Tantric Mysticism*, translated by Jaideva Singh (New Delhi: Motilal Banarsidass, 1996), 127.

31. "The reflected consciousness of the Self (Ātman) is called Ishwara, and Ishwara reflected through the thinking faculty is called jiva." Suri Nagamma, *Letters from Sri Ramanasramam* (Tiruvannamalai, India: Sri Ramanasramam, 2014), 298.

32. Ksemarāja, *The Doctrine of Recognition: A Translation of Prathyabhijñāhrdayam*, translated by Jaideva Singh (Albany: State University of New York Press, 1990), 13.

and purity. They are merely internal differentiations within the fold of absolute Śiva-Consciousness, but they do not entail actual difference or separation. In a sense, they are not without analogies to the Christian Trinity, at least insofar as the latter entails both a Unity of Essence and modes of relationship within the Essence. However, compared to normative Christian Trinitarian theology, Śaivite metaphysics remains subordinationist in that it preserves and highlights the ultimate sovereignty of Śiva. This is in contrast to mainstream Christian theology that is averse to recognizing a similar subordination with regard to the relationship between the three Persons of the Trinity.[33] In the Śaivite system, the five supreme *tattvas* may be understood both as "degrees" and "modes," to make use of Schuon's terminology. On the one hand, they range over a cascading axis of determinations, with Śiva enthroned at the summit as pure Sovereignty and Freedom. On the other hand, they may be considered as different modes of Śiva-Consciousness, manifesting various emphases on unconditionedness, awareness, subjectivity, objectivity, and the equilibrium between them. It is as if the focus of consciousness were moved from one region of non-dual Reality to another. A very important conclusion to draw from the preceding distinctions is that Śakti as such cannot be identified with Māyā. In fact, Śakti pertains to the internal life of the Absolute Śiva, in which it crystallizes awareness or *vimarśa*. Although it must be conceived as the site of a "de-doubling"—the seed of the onto-cosmogonic unfolding—it is not, as such, a principle of "covering" (*kañcukas*) or ignorance. The five supreme *tattvas* simply encompass a kind of "Pleroma" that provides an "archetypal" foundation for the complexities of the world of difference and the network of its subject-object relationships. Śiva, Śakti, SadāŚiva, Īśvāra, and Suddha Vidyā "articulate" and "synthesize" the various modes and degrees of inclusive non-duality.

Making use of Schuon's technical metaphysical vocabulary, one could suggest that Advaita emphasizes—*a priori*—the dimension of absoluteness pertaining to the Principle, whereas Śaivism dwells on its dimension of infinitude. The Absolute is exclusively "one" and utterly independent from the relative. Inasmuch as it dispels *Māyā* in order to reveal the sole reality of

---

33. This is mostly true for the "immanent" Trinity, or the Trinity *in divinis*, but less so with regard to the so-called "economic" Trinity, since in this case the initiative of the Generation, Incarnation, and Redemption cannot but appear to lie, ultimately, with the Father.

Ātman, Advaita may be deemed to be "absolutist." By contrast, the Infinite is inclusive and therefore more "compatible" with a consideration of degrees of reality unfolding from the All-Possibility. In Schuonian metaphysics, there is no question of an ontological hierarchy between the Absolute and the Infinite, since—*qua* Absolute—the Ultimate is, *ipso facto*, also Infinite. Reality being a metaphysical space, as it were, it must be "measurable" in different ways: absoluteness is one way of "measuring" it while infinitude and perfection comprise other manners of doing so. It goes without saying that the analogy is only partial since a metaphysical dimension is in no way limited by other dimensions or by the "measure" that it entails.

As suggested above, Schuon offers a compelling and harmonious approach to understanding Advaita and Śaivism. His view, most surely, is consonant with the perspective of Advaita inasmuch as its starting point is the notion of discernment (*viveka*) between the Reality of *Ātman* as the Absolute and the appearance of *Māyā*. But it also has a striking affinity with the Śaivite concept of the Ultimate as the infinite freedom of Śiva, a freedom that encompasses the whole of existence within the fold of its intrinsic creativity.[34] When Schuon writes that the Absolute is—*ipso facto*—also the Infinite, he means that the Necessity and Independence of the Absolute is the other side of its infinite Freedom. In other words, since nothing can "constrain" the Absolute, nothing is able to be "exterior" to it. The lack of constraints entails an absence of limits and this exclusiveness calls for a corresponding inclusiveness as its "internal dimension," to use Schuon's own expression. This is another way of saying that the Necessary (the Absolute) includes the Possible (the Infinite), without which it would be bound and therefore, in a way, relative to what would bind it. The Infinite is, in that sense, the source or principle of the Relative and it prevents, as such, the latter from being absolutized, since it keeps it within the ambit, so to speak, of the Absolute. In the conjunction of the Absolute and the Infinite, the Absolute comes always first, not because there is a hierarchy of dimensions—these being on the same horizontal plane of the Essence or Beyond-Being—but simply because exclusiveness must precede inclusiveness when the Ultimate is envisaged from a human point of view. This is another way of saying that immanence cannot be apprehended independently from transcendence.

---

34. This leaves aside the historical question of a likely influence of Śaivism on some schools of post-Shankaran *Advaita*, which is not directly relevant to the present analysis.

This "combination" of Advaita and Śaivism appears in the way Schuon makes a distinction not only between *Ātman* and *Māyā* but also between a higher *Māyā* and a lower *Māyā*, with the latter echoing the ontological gradation found in the Śaivite *tattvas*. Furthermore, Schuon distinguishes not only Divine *Māyā* from cosmic *Māyā*, but also supra-formal *Māyā* from formal *Māyā*. The first refers to the Personal God inasmuch as He is "*Māyā* in *Ātman*" or the prefiguration of the relative in the Absolute. The second is manifestation as distinct from the Divine Principle. The third pertains to Divine and celestial realities "below" the level of the Essence. As for the fourth, it encompasses psychic and physical realities and is, as such, the degree of crystallization found in evil and all oppositions, that is, "coagulating magic, separative and individualizing and thus possibly subversive."[35] While differing significantly from Schuon's account of the degrees of *Māyā*, the Śaivite *tattvas*—thirty-six in number—are considered as spreading over three ranges: *abheda* (or non-difference), *bhedābheda* (difference-in-non-difference), and *bheda* (difference). The necessity of these three phases reflects the necessity of non-dualism, in the sense that any duality must be resolved through a third reality. This, by and large, is the function of *bhedābheda*. Without the latter, not only would the relationship between difference and non-difference, duality and non-duality, be unthinkable, but the very realization of the former from within the latter would remain impossible. It is instructive that Schuon has referred to this metaphysical resolution of duality and non-duality through the symbol of the spiral that incorporates both the dimension of discontinuity in the concentric circles and the aspect of continuity through the radii. The spiral is analogous to the realm of *bhedābheda* inasmuch as it reflects both the difference and the non-difference that run through the universe. Schuon echoes, *mutatis mutandis*, the Śaivite triplicity of *abheda*, *bhedābheda*, and *bheda* when he contemplates the three respective realities of *Ātman*, higher *Māyā* ("liberating" *Māyā*), and lower *Māyā*. The former emancipates by "unveiling" the Absolute Reality of *Ātman*, whereas the latter imprisons within the realm of appearances. Accordingly, Schuon's notion of higher *Māyā* is akin to *bhedābheda*, since it pertains to unity-in-distinction, like the reflection of *Ātman* within *Māyā*.

Māyā is marked by ambiguity by virtue of it not being *Ātman*. Ambiguity resides in the fact that *Māyā* is, in Shankara's own terms, nei-

---

35. Schuon, *Form and Substance in the Religions*, 36.

ther real nor unreal.[36] While the negative aspect of *Māyā* flows from the fact that it is not *Ātman*, its positive side is founded on its being none other than *Ātman*. Lest this duality be mistaken for a kind of symmetry, Schuon observes that *Māyā*, as Existence, remains unaffected by the impurities and evil inherent in its lower ranges. In other words, it could be said that *Māyā* is "more" *Ātman* than it is other-than-*Ātman*, as it is obvious that any kind of separation is "quite relative."[37] Separation is indeed "relative" to ignorance inasmuch as "other-than-*Ātman*" is only real from the standpoint of ignorance. Far from engaging in pseudo-mystical forays, Shankara does not deny the validity and existence of the world inasmuch as it is experienced from the point of view of "other-than-*Ātman*": the scriptural vantage point of identity is not incompatible, for him, with the conventional outlook of difference.[38] As a consequence, the question of the relationship between *Ātman* and *Māyā* can be envisaged either by considering the various degrees of exteriorization that the latter entails, or simply from the vantage point of its very ambivalence, irrespective of these degrees. Needless to say, the two standpoints are connected in the sense that the "transparency" of *Māyā*, or its liberating face, appears in an increasingly clear light as we ascend the ontological levels of its unfolding while, conversely, its opacity and alienating function are all the more prominent as we reach the lowest phases of the existentiating process. However, even on the lowest level of its manifestations, *Māyā* remains none other than *Ātman* and may therefore give access, in principle, to a recognition

---

36. "She is neither existent nor non-existent nor partaking of both characters; neither same nor different nor both; neither composed of parts nor an indivisible whole nor both. She is most wonderful and cannot be described in words." Śaṅkarācārya, *Vivekachudamani*, 40.

37. "This ambiguity [of *Māyā*], which is quite relative and far from being symmetrical, in no wise tarnishes *Māyā*." Schuon, *Form and Substance in the Religions*, 36.

38. "We do not maintain the existence of things different from Brahman in the state when the highest truth has been definitively known, as the srutis say, 'One only without a second,' and 'Without interior or exterior'; nor do we deny, for the ignorant, the validity of actions with their factors and results when the relative world of name and form exists. Therefore scriptural or conventional outlook depends entirely on knowledge or ignorance. Hence there is no apprehension of a contradiction between them. In fact, all schools must admit the existence or non-existence of the phenomenal world according as it is viewed from the relative or absolute standpoints." *Brhadāraṇyaka Upaniṣadbhāṣya*, III, v.1, *Roots of Vedānta*, 108.

of the latter since it is none other than *Ātman*, and since knowledge can therefore spring forth from any place and at any time by virtue of the unicity of the Real. This is best illustrated by Schuon's assertion (in his essay "Seeing God Everywhere")[39] that the Principle is "recognizable" or "visible" even in evil phenomena, since any phenomenon, including one most lacking in positive qualities, bears witness to the Essence by virtue of its mere existence, which is "absolutely" other than nothingness. This can be inferred from Meister Eckhart's paradoxical statement regarding atheists: "The more they blaspheme God, the more they praise Him."

The problem of nothingness and its status is closely related to this remark, in the sense that there must be in *Māyā* something that "resists" *Ātman*, and must be the trace of this illusory resistance. Thus, Schuon refers to nothingness as the "sin" of *Māyā*, the word being taken here in the sense of an inherent principle of fall and subversion. In this regard, *Māyā* is characterized by its tendency toward nothingness, but quite obviously a nothingness that is asymptotic and thus never reached given it possesses no true reality. The only "absolute" difference between *Māyā* and *Ātman* is that the former includes within its fold "something" that is not—and "absolutely" not in the sense of nothingness—or which can only be so on a conceptual level, like a shadow of the Intellect. The idea of nothingness, which has been so prevalent in modern and post-modern philosophy, indicates the "possibility of impossibility," to use a recurring expression in Schuon's lexicon. It is the lowest inverted reflection of the Absolute, which cannot be without being nothing.

The most significant consequence of these considerations is that Schuon's treatment of *Māyā* differs from the typical Advaitin dismissal of *Māyā* as appearance. It does this through a more explicit integration of that which, in *Māyā*, reflects Reality and the intrinsic contents of *Ātman*. Advaita teaches that the Self is *Sat, Cit,* and *Ānanda*, but it does not *a priori* contemplate the cosmic reflections of these dimensions as a means of recognizing *Ātman*. It tends to speak in terms of scriptural keys and subjective qualifications or predispositions for Self-realization, rather than specifically emphasizing the contemplative virtuality of the cosmic traces of *Ātman*. Aside from a similar focus on seeking deliverance, Advaita tends to view *Māyā* more as Reverberation than as Radiation, to use Schuon's terms, whereas the latter way of seeing is arguably more akin to

---

39. Schuon, Gnosis: *Divine Wisdom* (Bloomington, IN: World Wisdom, 2006), 88.

the vantage point of Kashmiri Śaivism. Reverberation can be conceived, from a certain point of view, as an Image of Reality that "covers" its full actualization, and the appearance of which must be dispelled so that the "original" Reality can be uncovered. The Advaitin notion of "*koshas*," or sheaths, of *Ātman* corresponds to this way of looking at the matter. This is the perspective of "form" rather than that of "energy." By contrast, the principle of Radiation involves an exteriorizing energy that, when redirected in a centripetal way, can be used as means of interiorization, by virtue of the continuity that binds all degrees and modes of Reality. This is, by and large, the perspective of Kashmiri Śaivism. By distilling and integrating the message of both schools, Schuon outlines a perspective characterized by an equilibrium between transcendence and immanence, to the extent that this polarity can remain valid. It must be stressed, however, that the ontological dimension of *Māyā*, its degrees and aspects, must be "re-dis-covered," as it were, in its epistemological dimension. In other words, what matters ultimately is not what *Māyā* is, or what kind of *Māyā* is considered, but only the way in which *Māyā* is contemplated and therefore dispelled as *Māyā*: "It is not a question of what an aspect of the Divine expresses, good or bad but, rather, a question of the man who can or cannot make use of such expression. Thus people are not idolaters because of their symbols—they can be so only through the disposition of their minds. He who puts his faith in appearances, serves idols, but he who believes in the spiritual, or rather, has knowledge of the spiritual, serves Truth—whether or not he uses a symbol to meditate, and whatever kind of symbol it may be."[40] *Māyā* is indeed a superimposition on *Ātman* but it is truly *Ātman* for those who contemplate it from, and within, *Ātman*.

All Hindu non-dual perspectives agree that the Supreme is Being and Consciousness. The two dimensions are indissociable in the One, and it is only through *Māyā* that a fissure is opened up that separates them from each other, albeit to various degrees. By combining and integrating these two dimensions and their corresponding perspectives, Schuon opens the way to a consideration of the diverse aspects of the Object, or Being, and the multiple points of view of Consciousness, or refractions of the one Subject. He also makes it possible for the perspective of Advaitin *jñana*, centered as it is on the Divine Self, to be couched in an ontological-cosmological idiom that bridges the gap between the language of Divine creation, or

---

40. Schuon, *Primordial Meditation: Contemplating the Real* (London: The Matheson Trust, 2015), 48.

manifestation, and that of Self-realization, without invalidating the former. This is not to say, of course, that this connection between the two languages cannot be found in the Hindu tradition itself, as has already been suggested—particularly in the discussion of *jñana* and *bhakti*. However, the fact that Schuon could make use of the subjective notion of *Ātman* to refer to the objective principle of creation shows that his perspective lies at the intersection of different traditional languages, suggesting both the relativity of religious terminology and the transcendence of the Ultimate Reality vis-à-vis any metaphysical syntax. This double consideration is central to Schuon's esoteric perspective, since it provides a metaphysical framework and the epistemological tools to make sense of multiplicity within Unity and Unity within multiplicity. Thus the concept of *Māyā* enables access to multiple paths for approaching *Ātman* while allowing one to account for the universality of metaphysics. It thereby provides a necessary key for the supra-confessional recognition of That which lies at the convergence of the plurality of paths.[41]

---

41. That a historical Advaitin, starting with Shankara, may not have opened such a line of understanding is an altogether different question, one quite independent of Schuon's situation and outlook, and may be accounted for, at least in part, by historical contexts and traditional determinations. There is a kind of self-sufficiency of traditional perspectives that makes them unlikely to delve into extrinsic areas of commonalities.

2

The Avatāric Mystery

The perspective of gnosis is fundamentally non-dualistic, a feature that clearly differentiates it from any conventional religious outlook, which tends to be dualistic because it is practically predicated upon the "subjectively absolute" reality of worship. By contrast, in the various forms of traditional metaphysics—whether they are associated with a religious universe or not—Reality, in the ultimate sense, does not admit of any scission or division, being fundamentally characterized by a unity of Essence. In other words, the Principle cannot but be one and this unity is necessarily exclusive of any duality, or multiplicity, lest the latter be unduly absolutized, resulting in the metaphysical "heresy" of positing two Absolutes. Notwithstanding this emphasis on Unity, gnostic perspectives have also tended to be receptive to the world of multiplicity that they consider as "not unreal," on its own level of reality, and often as a key to the recovery, or the recognition, of Unity. In the words of Seyyed Hossein Nasr: "Although the goal of sacred knowledge is the knowledge of the Sacred as such, that is, of that Reality which lies beyond all cosmic manifestation, there is always that stage of the gathering of the scattered leaves of the book of the universe, to paraphrase Dante, before journeying beyond it."[1] Whether one understands these two stages diachronically, or simply paradigmatically and therefore synchronically, there is no doubt that they correspond to two distinct and complementary dimensions of spiritual reality. Non-dualism, in that sense, is not a reductionist monism

---

1. Seyyed Hossein Nasr, *Knowledge and the Sacred* (Albany: State University of New York Press, 1989), 189.

of the kind Hegel mockingly compared to "the night in which all cows are black"[2] but, on the contrary, a "multi-stratified"[3] metaphysics of essential Unity. In other words, the Unity or Non-Duality that metaphysics recognizes is not an absolute negation of multiplicity but an essential integration of the latter into the former. It therefore presupposes an ability to consider levels of Reality, which allow one to recognize Unity within multiplicity and multiplicity within Unity. This non-dual and multistratified view of Reality lies at the foundation of an understanding of perfection as a synthetic realization of multiplicity reflecting the One within the many, and opening a way of return to, and reintegration into, the former.

When considering the realm of multiplicity that is our natural and immediate field of existence, manifestation can be symbolized as the unfolding of the Pythagorean tetradic triangle or *Tetraktys* (1 + 2 + 3 + 4 = 10), through unity and the first three numbers. In this sense, ten is the number of the manifested, or realized, perfection. It is the perfect unfolding of unity. In his commentaries on the *Tetraktys*, René Guénon emphasizes the centrality of the number 10 in the unfolding of manifestation by "showing the relationship that unites the denary directly with the quaternary,"[4] the latter standing, as the second even number, for manifestation itself. This is seen in how the *Tetraktys* includes four rows and its basis consists of four points. Guénon notes that four is, therefore, the number that marks the entrance into the realm of cosmology, the science of the manifested cosmos. Three, by contrast, is a metacosmic number, hence its numerous associations, throughout traditions, with intra-divine differentiations, such as the Christian Trinity or the Hindu *Trimūrti*. The

---

2. "To pit this single assertion, that 'in the Absolute all is one,' against the organised whole of determinate and complete knowledge, or of knowledge which at least aims at and demands complete development—to give out its Absolute as the night in which, as we say, all cows are black—that is the very *naïveté* of emptiness of knowledge." G.W.F. Hegel, *The Phenomenology of Mind*, translated by J. B. Baillie, volume 1 (New York: Routledge, 2014), 15.

3. This pertinent adjective was first used by Toshihiko Izutsu in reference to the Taoist and Sufi metaphysics of Ibn ʿArabī and Chuang-tzu: "Existence or Reality as 'experienced' on supra-sensible levels reveals itself as of a multistratified structure." *Sufism and Taoism: A Comparative Study of Key Philosophical Concepts* (Berkeley: University of California Press, 1983), 479.

4. René Guénon, *Symbols of Sacred Science* (Sophia Perennis: Hillsdale, NY, 2004), 101.

demarcating line passing between three and four, as referring respectively to the Divine realm and cosmic manifestation, is also expressed by Lao-tzu's metaphysical account in the forty-second chapter of the *Tao Te Ching*: "Tao gives birth to one, one to two, two to three, and three to the ten thousand things." Thus, four is implicitly the first numerical principle of the "ten thousand things" of manifestation that is itself a multiple of ten. While four symbolizes the initiation of manifestation, ten represents the totality—or the perfection of the process of its manifestation—that involves all hypostatic numbers from one to four, from principal non-manifestation to manifestation itself. Henceforth, the *Tetraktys* can be considered as the perfect realization of unity in multiplicity; first, metaphysically, and then cosmically. Analogically, in Kabbalah, the *Sephirot* or Divine degrees and aspects are ten in number, the tenth being *Malchut*, the final degree of the Divine that completes, or achieves, the process of Divine emanation. This degree is connected to the *Shekhinah*, the Divine Presence in the cosmos, which is a prelude to creation and sanctifies it.[5] Here also, the denary is the total and perfect unfolding of Divine Unity. Finally, the fact that in Hindu teachings the *avatāras* of Vishnu are ten in number is symbolically significant in suggesting the ways in which the potential amplitude of Divine Unity is developed, as it were, through and in the denary. Thus, the association of the number ten with the *avatāra* or incarnation points to the perfect articulation of Unity and multiplicity that is inherent to the Man-God.

Even though the notion of *avatāra* is clearly associated with the Hindu outlook, and its unsurpassed capacity to worship the Divine in and through everything (particularly through the human), it is also a key to understanding—from a supra-confessional point of view—some of the most central and universal metaphysical and religious issues pertaining to the relationship between the human and the Divine. The human perfection, to which we have made allusions earlier, raises the question of the extent to which, and the ways in which, the human and the Divine may intersect, integrate, coalesce, or even unite in the figure of the saintly

---

5. Hence the relationship of the *Shekhinah* with nuptial and creative symbolism: "The earthly union between man and woman . . . was taken as a symbolic reference to the heavenly marriage. These themes were combined with the mystical symbolism identifying Bride, Sabbath, and *Shekhinah*." Gershom Scholem, *On the Kabbalah and Its Symbolism* (New York: Schocken Books, 1969), 140.

soul, the *guru*, the prophet or the sage. In this respect, Frithjof Schuon, through his recurrent and supra-confessional use of the term *avatāra*, has opened the way to a meta-religious understanding of the meaning of this paradoxical, and in many ways puzzling, encounter between the human and the Divine. Consistent with the aforementioned metaphysical principles, the notion of the *avatāra* is actually central in Schuon's metaphysics and spirituality, since it is situated at a crucial point of articulation between the Divine realm of non-manifestation and the domain of manifestation, between the Divine and the human, while being interconnected with a number of essential dimensions of spirituality. This is so inasmuch as the notion of the *avatāra* is approached, as it is by Schuon, as expressing the direct *reflection* of Unity in multiplicity, or that of God in the cosmos. When he writes about the "mystery" of the *avatāra*, Schuon refers to an encounter between incommensurable realities. Needless to say, the term "reflection" fails to encompass the whole range of meaning and modalities of this encounter, which is also a kind of coincidence of opposites. The acceptations and limits of the word "reflection" need to be examined further, since, first of all, it may be understood in ways that emphasize continuity or, on the contrary, entail an unbridgeable distance. As we have indicated above, the concept of *avatāra* is definitely integral to the Hindu tradition in which it highlights both the very strong immanentist bent of the tradition as a whole. God is present everywhere and in everything,[6] and the significance of the human being endowed with Divine status, the *jīvan-mukta* or the *satguru*, is cardinal in the spiritual economy of Hindu life. All great "masters of being," or *satgurus*, are considered, in the *sanātana dharma*, as avatāric beings, and the Hindu religious sensibility readily vibrates to the dimension of transforming grace that is inherent in the sage and the saint. The term *avatāra* refers technically to a divine "descent." In this traditional context, it pertains more specifically to the ways in which gods—particularly, but not exclusively, Vishnu—take human or animal forms; potentially, in fact, any natural or supernatural form to restore the *dharma*, or the order of creation, when there is need to

---

6. "The pot is a God. The winnowing fan is a God. The stone in the street is a God. The comb is a God. The bowstring is also a God. The bushel is a God and the spouted cup is a God. Gods, gods, there are so many there's no place left for a foot. There is only one God. He is our Lord of the Meeting Rivers." Basavanna, *Speaking of Śiva*, translated with an introduction by A. K. Ramanujan (Baltimore: Penguin Books, 1973), 84.

respond to cosmic disequilibrium so as to reinstate the norm. In essence, therefore, the *avatāra* is a cosmic and soteriological manifestation of the metaphysical Principle, one that is called for by virtue of the need to restore the cosmos to a state of balance.[7]

The concept of Divine manifestation, or theophany, encompasses a very wide array of acceptations, and it is in this breadth that lies both the possibility of a universalization of the phenomenon of the *avatāra* and the need for distinctions with regard to the span of its contextual meanings. The widest characterization of the *avatāra* as "cosmic and soteriological

---

7. Considering the diversity of avatāric phenomena, Schuon provides an elementary classification of their modes. He distinguishes major *avatāras* and minor *avatāras*—or complete or partial incarnations—on the one hand, and solar and lunar avatāric manifestations on the other. As we have indicated earlier, the Hindu tradition tends to associate avatāric phenomena primarily with Vishnu, and only secondarily or marginally with other gods such as Śiva. The distinction between major and minor *avatāras* is to be found among the incarnations of Vishnu, sometimes considered as being thirty-nine in total, of which only ten are considered as major. In the context of this distinction, which pertains to the cosmic scope of the function and influence of respective *avatāras*, it is not unimportant to note that Schuon attributes the preponderance of Visnuite *avatāras* to the fact that the tradition associates this god with the function of conserving and ordering the cosmos, by contrast with Brahma's creative thrust and Śiva's transformative vocation. Probably the most famous expression of this Visnuite function appears in the *Bhagavad Gītā*, in the words of Krishna, himself the avatāric "spokesman" of Vishnu: "Whenever a decrease of righteousness (*dharmasya*) exists, Arjuna, and there is a rising up of unrighteousness (*adharmasya*), then I manifest Myself (*ātmānam*)": *The Bhagavad Gītā*, 4.7, translated by Winthrop Sargeant (Albany: State University of New York Press, 1994), 207. The distinction between "solar" and "lunar," which is independent from the first distinction, appears to refer to the lesser or greater totality of the function of the *avatāra* within the framework of a particular tradition. The solar *avatāra* is a founder or revealer when he is major, and a central revivifier, like Saint Francis, for instance, when he is minor. The lunar *avatāra*, as his symbolic qualifier indicates, prolongs the light of the tradition without marking a new beginning as such. Moreover, Schuon does not restrict the function of *avatāras* to religious figures only, since what is at stake is less the metaphysical message itself than the cosmic mission. Thus, he attributes to Alexander and Caesar an avatāric function in terms of creating a "historical and cosmic order" within which religion may appear and finds its providential sector of diffusion: "There is a providential relationship—with regard to the area of expansion and preparation of the environment—between Caesar and Christianity on the one hand and between Alexander and Islam on the other; Caesar is mentioned in the Gospels and Alexander in the Koran. This shows that the mission of the minor and lunar *Avatāra* can be situated on the political plane—but on a very vast scale—without implying a properly spiritual Message." Schuon, *Stations of Wisdom* (Bloomington, IN: World Wisdom Books, 1995), nn. 22, 87.

manifestation of the Principle" allows one to understand the way Schuon can universalize the meaning of this Hindu concept to refer to the manifested intersection of the Divine and the human in general, and its various modalities in particular. In principle, the term could even refer to any mode of Divine manifestation inasmuch as it denotes a descent although, in fact, the term is exclusively associated by Schuon with the Man-God, given that he refers to other analogous manifestations as theophanies. Even though Schuon is obviously aware of the fact that some religious and spiritual economies, preeminently those of Judaism and Islam, do not include—and indeed exclude—the notion of a Divine manifestation in and through human agencies, his point of view, as elsewhere in his work, pertains to what he calls the "nature of things" rather than to a particular religious economy. This means that he takes into consideration phenomena that are bound to occur in all religious climates by virtue of the nature of the Divine, the human and the relationship between the two. In other words, given that the Divine Reality, essentially, both underlies the universe and is infinite in its possibilities, it cannot but manifest itself (in various contexts in or through the human state) among other forms. Moreover, since this state is the one that, in our universe, represents for religious traditions the central and total locus of access to the Ultimate, it appears likely, not to say necessary, that it would become, in some instances, the theophanic site disclosing the highest Reality. In other words, the centrality of the relationship between the Divine and the human makes it, a priori, a privileged channel for manifesting the former. However, the ways in which such manifestation is understood and related to vary greatly, in conformity with the theological perspectives of the respective traditions.

In Hinduism, the *avatāra* necessarily refers to a god, as implied by the idea of a descent. Diana Eck has actually translated *avatāra* by "crossing down," which she reads as the counterpart of the upward direction of the *tīrtha* or "sanctuary."[8] Another related verbal root connotes "crossing over,"

---

8. "The *tīrthas* are primarily associated with the great acts and appearances of the gods and the heroes of Indian myth and legend. As a threshold between heaven and earth, the *tīrtha* is not only a place for the 'upward' crossings of people's prayers and rites, it is also a place for the 'downward' crossings of the gods. These divine 'descents' are the well-known *avatāras* of the Hindu tradition. Indeed, the words *tīrtha* and *avatāra* come from related verbal roots: tṛ, 'to cross over,' and avatṛ, 'to cross down.' One might say that the *avatāras* descend, opening the doors of the *tīrthas* so that men and women may ascend in their rites and prayers. The appearance of the Divine in this world is what Mircea Eliade has called hierophany, the 'showing forth' of

THE AVATĀRIC MYSTERY | 59

thereby suggesting an affinity with the Buddhist *tathāgata*, the "one who has thus gone." In a similar sense, Guénon translates *avatāra* as "downward crossing,"⁹ which clearly indicates a passing to this lower side of reality, a divine "transgression" as it were, which is the Divine counterpart of the human *tathāgata*, the "one who has thus gone," or the "one who has thus come."¹⁰ We will come back to this fruitful distinction in the context of our discussion of Buddhism; in particular, to the ways (also relevant to other traditions) in which this may be understood as referring both to a motion and to a passing beyond any motion since, like the *tathāgata*, the *avatāra* is, at the same time, descending into existence while remaining essentially Divine. At any rate, the notion of the descent of a god raises two main questions: first, the very possibility or reality of a divine descent and, second, that of the plurality of divine agencies, as implied by the words "a god." It is evident that these religions that exclude the possibility of a divine descent in human form by virtue of their insistence on Divine transcendence, and those that exclude any divine plurality, cannot be compatible, at least in their formal creed, with the idea of the *avatāra* as understood in Hinduism. The theological perspective of Islam is clearly incompatible, for example, with the notion of a Divine descent into the human realm and the cosmos. In fact, this incompatibility is arguably enshrined in the tradition as the most central character of this religion, as it stands opposed to any kind of divinization of the human, the cosmos, or any creaturely being, that could give rise to idolatry. The notion of *shirk*, diversely translated as association, idolatry, or polytheism, epitomizes this essential component of Islam. The religion brought by the Prophet Muhammad can be primarily characterized as a way of restoring pure monotheism, which means that all mediating theophanic realities are kept under the rubric of *āyāt*, or "signs" of God, being understood that these signs are either natural or induced by God's grace but cannot be understood, construed exoterically, as divine manifestations, although some Sufi readings do reach this type of understanding. The elements of beauty and order in nature, the verses of scriptures and the miraculous

---

the gods. In India it is clear that the gods have shown forth in thousands of places, some known and famous throughout India and some visited only by people from the immediately surrounding districts." Diana Eck, *Banaras City of Light* (Princeton, NJ: Princeton University Press, 1982), 35.

9. René Guénon, *Sacred Symbols*, 333.

10. Depending on whether one reads it as *tathā-gata* or *tathā-āgata*.

works of prophets, among other phenomena, point to the reality of *Allāh*, but they are not ordinarily considered as instances of Divine Reality as such. Similarly, the angelic realities are always distinct from God, being creaturely modes of knowing God that cannot be confused with Him and that are even able, as in the case of Iblis, to rebel against the Divine Order. From a historical and theological perspective, this is connected, of course, to the function of Islam as a protestation against Arab pagan polytheism. Therefore, in the world of Islam, the literal absence of an *avatāra* reveals a kind of void between the human smallness and the Divine Majesty. In other religious climates, this void would be filled, precisely, by the *avatāra*.

There is, however, another way to envisage the matter that is not theological but metaphysical. Through this distinction, we are referring to the difference between a perspective focused on God as personal Being and His relationship with His creation and another one which, without excluding the reality and legitimacy of the latter on its own level, is centered on the Absolute as such, that is, as being both exclusive and inclusive of the relative realm. Schuon refers to this way of understanding the Muslim creed in several places of his work, and we would like to focus on one of the most directly significant as demonstrated in his classic work, *Understanding Islam*. This, it must be stressed, is only one of the many possible expressions of the metaphysical idea at stake. It is expressed in the most important terms of the religious idiom of Islam, since it flows from the profession of faith specific to this tradition—the first half of the testimony of faith or the first *shahādah*. The *shahādah* is comprised of two halves, the first referring primarily to God—"there is no god but God"—and the second to His Prophet Muhammad—"Muhammad is the Prophet of God." Schuon makes the point that whereas the first *shahādah* is metaphysically crystal-clear, the second, while enunciating—on the surface—a very plain component of the Islamic creed, is more mysterious in its depth of meaning. The first *shahādah* refers to God as One, which is understood theologically as a numerical reality and, metaphysically, as an ontological unicity. In other words, it means either or both; namely, that there is one god as opposed to two, three or many, and that this one God is the only Reality there is, since anything else is not truly so; that is, in the way God is, as indicated in the Qur'ānic verse "Everything perishes but the Face of God" (28:88) Now, the second *shahādah*—*Muhammadun rasūlu-Llāh*—is, on close attention, a much more complex matter. First of all, distinctly from the first, it refers to a relational reality: Muhammad *is the Messenger of* God. Of course, one could argue that the first *shahādah* is relational as well, since it includes both god, *ilāh*, and God, *Allāh*, but this is actually not the case. While it is plain that the first testimony includes two terms, that is *Allāh* and *ilāh*, it does not state anything about their relationship as such. All it tells us is that one of the terms *is* while the second *is not*, or is not without the first, or is not in the sense in which the first is. Now the second testimony expresses a much more subtle truth. It informs us of the particular reality of the Prophet and, by extension, all prophets, and in fact all realities that partake in any analogous kind of ontological status. The difficulty has to do, precisely, with *this kind* of reality. By contrast, regarding the reality referred to in the first testimony, which is of a luminous evidence and cannot be subrated in any way, the one which is envisaged by the second testimony reveals layers of complexity, precisely because it relates two realities that appear to be, on the surface, unrelatable, that is, the Absolute and the relative. This means that, mystically or morally, it relates the transcendent God and a finite human being, a relationship that is an unfathomable mystery for human understanding, and a sort of metaphysical enigma since it establishes a correspondence between the Absolute, which is unconditioned and therefore in a sense unrelatable, and the relative, which being by definition conditioned cannot be related to the Absolute without appearing to introduce into the latter a conditioning element. Obviously, such a perplexing aspect of the second *shahādah* is not the way in which it is commonly understood. On a plainly confessional level, the statement simply means that a man, Muhammad, was the messenger of God. On an esoteric or metaphysical level, however, the ontological status of the Prophet amounts to a question, since it appears to associate the conditioned and the Unconditioned, the relative and the Absolute. In other words, even though this association cannot be understood in the sense of *shirk*, which would imply two absolutes, so to speak, it still inscribes the reality of man onto God and that of God onto man; and this inscription is crystallized in the word *rasūl*, that mediates, as it were, between Muhammad and *Allāh*. The question of the *avatāra*, as envisaged by Schuon, lies at this very juncture.

As we have already suggested, by virtue of being situated at the point of contact of two seemingly incommensurable realities, the *avatāra* highlights a perplexing enigma. This enigma is exoterically intractable because exoterism cannot but be one-sidedly expedient, which means that it cannot account for the complexities of the various facets of Reality and for the various vantage points from which it can be approached. It draws its power of persuasion and psycho-social mobilization, as well as its moral and practical effectiveness, from the literal one-dimensionality of its message, which does not mean—needless to say—that the message itself is one-dimensional. Such a complex and subtle account, which would allow for the possibility of shifting from one given point of view to another, and is hardly compatible with apostolic zeal, would impede the creed's ability to be universally diffused. In other words, the creed cannot do justice to all aspects and vantage points without losing its main convincing power of inspiration, that is, its exclusiveness, at least from a collective point of view.

Considering matters from a standpoint that is independent from any particularist and confessional outlook, and in an esoteric ellipse that amounts to a sort of universalization of the Christian lexicon, Schuon does not shun from making use of the expression "Man-God" to refer to the *avatāra*. Although this expression applies literally to the case of Christ in Christianity as true man and true God, while corresponding generically, as we will see, to the archetype of the *avatāra* such as is understood by Schuon, it needs be further analyzed and qualified when applied to other religious traditions. With Schuon, the meaning of the Christian Incarnation is summarized in the oft-quoted patristic formula "God became man so that man may become God," and it is, as such, that it provides a universal framework for understanding the cycle of salvation in each and every religious faith. However, the general structure of this cycle does not account, in itself, for the specificity with which it is modulated in the respective traditions. As Schuon himself expresses it, for some—and it is so, for instance, for Muslims with regard to the Prophet of Islam—the "Man-God" is like an opening onto heaven whereas, for others (and the case of Hindus is paramount in this respect), it is comparable to a descent of the Divine itself. In the first case, what is envisaged is a human being in, and through, whom the Divine manifests and opens a way of access to transcendence, leaving aside the question of how we may understand the mode of this opening manifestation. In the second case, we have a personal aspect or face of the Divine Reality assuming a human form. The first type of conception remains, largely, a tributary of the emphasis on transcendence and, consequently, tends to stress the human aspect of the *avatāra*. In fact, as we have already mentioned, the very notions of the *avatāra* and Man-God remain altogether foreign to the climate of religions like Islam, as well as Judaism, precisely because of the seemingly absolute gap between the human and the Divine that they highlight. It is only incidentally, and within the context of esoteric schools of thought and spiritual currents, that the divine roots of the divine man are recognized, or taken into account, but always with the kind of precautions that befit the religious climate of Abrahamic monotheism, the primary intent of which is to parry any kind of human idolatry and worship of the human. In the case of Islam, some authenticated and canonical prophetic utterances allude to the uncreated dimension of prophethood, and the Prophet himself inasmuch as he is identified with it. One of the most striking occurrences, in this respect, is that of the prophetic tradition "I was a prophet when Adam was between spirit and body."[11] Although the general economy of the Islamic tradition makes it impossible for most commentators to draw the most consistent conclusions from this statement, it is in itself a direct testimony to the fact that the metaphysical reality of the Prophet entails an element of uncreatedness, in whichever way one may be able to understand it. Besides this metaphysical dimension of the matter, Muslim devotion to the Prophet takes account, in its own way, of the universal and transcendent dimension of his person in extolling his excellence among humans and the privilege of his early purification.[12] Schuon takes these traditional indications, the amplitude of the function of the Prophet, and the nature of his spiritual mission as foundations for his claim that Muhammad can be considered as a greater *avatāra* who "passively receives the Message that God 'causes to descend.'"[13]

Be that as it may, the symbol of the opening, as also that of the door, is particularly well suited to convey the upward direction of the religious gaze, and the character of mere human intermediary that corresponds to

---

11. Quoted by al-Hākim, *Spiritual Teachings of the Prophet*, edited by Tayeb Chouiref (Louisville: Fons Vitae, 2011), 206. Interestingly, other traditions relate that the Prophet was the first creature, which is literally at odds with the idea that Adam was the first human. This ambiguity is enough to suggest the semi-divine and semi-human dimension of the Prophet from the point of view of his inner prophetic reality.

12. "According to the traditional account, two angels cleft open the chest of the infant Mohammed and cleansed him, with snow, of the 'original sin' that appeared in the form of a black stain on his heart. Mohammed, like Mary, or like the 'human nature' of Jesus, is not therefore an ordinary man. That is why it is said that 'Mohammed is (simply) a man, not as an (ordinary) man, but in the manner of a jewel among (common) stones' (*Muhammadun basharun lā kal-bashari bal huwa kal-yaquti baynal-hajar*)." Schuon, *The Transcendent Unity of Religions* (Wheaton, IL: The Theosophical Publishing House, 1993), 122.

13. Schuon, *Christianity/Islam: Perspectives on Esoteric Ecumenism* (Bloomington, IN: World Wisdom, 2008), 71.

the Islamic *avatāra*. The opening shows the way of, or to, the heavens. It opens a perspective on the sky and makes it present, as it were, or at least accessible, but without ever abolishing the distinction between indoors and outdoors, terrestrial immanence and Divine transcendence. Even though the sky is accessible through a window, and is even somehow identified with it subjectively—from within a vision—it remains, nevertheless, situated beyond the frame of a window and, therefore, radically different from it. Let us note, as a significant illustration of those points, that in Islam the Prophet ascended during his nocturnal mystical journey, the *mi'rāj*, whereas the Qur'ān is considered a descent (*tanzīl*). The Book is no doubt less susceptible of becoming an object of idolatry than a man, in the context of Abrahamic monotheism, since in it, to use Schuon's terminology, it is the element of Truth, rather than that of Presence, that predominates. Being metaphysical in its foundation, and theological in most of its canonical expressions, Truth remains abstract, as it were, whereas Presence involves elements of spiritual "concreteness" and terrestrial manifestation that make it susceptible to being worshipped. In such a perspective, as we will later elaborate, the esoteric concept-image of reflection is replaced with that of divine inherence, which would be deemed, from an Islamic point of view, to be an incarnation or *hulūl*. The Islamic perspective rejects any sense of dwelling of the Divine in the human, although it does not necessarily exclude some notion of Divine appearance, as already implied in the Divine Name *az-Zāhir*, the "Exterior" or the "Manifest." Revealingly so, the general tendency among Islamic scholars has been to understand the evidence of God, not as a theophanic disclosure but as a manifestation directed toward a human deciphering. Ghazālī, for instance, understands this Name as referring to God being manifest to human intelligence.[14] It is therefore not God who is manifest, in a sense, but His existence. Consequently, this rational view of God's manifestness amounts to recognizing that there is nothing that does not bear witness to God. The nature of this witnessing is not, therefore, understood in terms of God's Presence but rather in terms of His creative Power, through its effects. Creatures bear witness that God is their Creator. It is only with some Sufis that

---

14. "(Certainly it is that) God Most High is hidden if He is sought through the perception of the (five) senses and the treasure house of the imagination, but He is manifest [*az-Zāhir*] if sought through the treasure house of the imagination and its reasoning faculties." Ghazālī, *Ninety-Nine Names of God in Islam*, translated by Robert Charles Stade (Ibadan: Daystar Press, 1970), 110.

the meaning of *az-Zāhir* (and the verb *zahara*) goes beyond this indirect meaning. In Ibn 'Atā Allāh's *Hikam*, for example, we can read that God "*Zahara bi-kulli shay'in, Zahara fi kulli shay'in, Zahara li-kulli shay'in,*" which means that God Himself "appears with everything, in everything and to everything."[15] In this view of things, however, the most manifest is also the principle of hiddenness, a point that Ghazālī also makes plain—through his analogy of light—when referring to "the One who is concealed from mankind by His light, the One who is hidden from them by the degree of His manifestness!"[16] Thus, transcendence reasserts its rights, as it were, within immanence itself.

If we turn to the image of descent, as applied to the Man-God, by contrast, there is obviously a sense of downward movement and, therefore, an emphasis on immanence. This is typically the Hindu point of view. In this perspective, it is a particular aspect of the Divine Reality, in the form of a god, which manifests itself in the very garb of mankind, or sometimes even in animal form. It is clear that while it is the human aspect that predominates in the Abrahamic type of theomorphic anthropology, it is the divine dimension that is dominant in the Hindu perspective. The latter is characterized by the multiple transformations and vicissitudes of the god, and even by his transfiguration or amplification to cosmic proportions, as is clearly the case with Krishna appearing to Arjuna (in the *Bhagavad Gītā*) in the form of the universal and cosmic Lord of the World, *viśvarūpa*.[17] In this sense, the world itself *is* God.

Whereas the Islamic religious archetype, to make use of Schuon's expression, insists on the human aspect of the *avatāra* and the Hindu archetype, by contrast, highlights its divine aspect, Christianity presents us with a third type of avataric pattern: first, because the divine descent is central to the spiritual economy of the entire tradition, and has therefore a much greater bearing on its economy, being indeed its very source and

---

15. *Al-Hikam*, trans. Danner, 26.
16. Ghazālī, trans. Stade, 110.
17. "I see You everywhere, infinite in form,
    With many arms, stomachs, mouths, eyes;
    I see neither end, nor middle nor yet the beginning of You,
    O Lord of all, Whose form is the universe."

The Bhagavad Gītā, trans. Sargeant (Albany: State University of New York Press, 1994), 468.

raison d'être; and, second, because this centrality is expressed through the dogmatic tenet that Christ is, and indeed has to be, both human and divine, which means that neither of the two natures must lose its identity and prerogatives at the expense of the other. The Christ is true man and true God. The Incarnation—and we need here to capitalize the word both in order to follow conventional usage and to indicate its unicity in Christian theology—does not obliterate the human nature of Christ. Does this mean that the term human is therefore to be taken in a purely generic way, or rather in a radically distinct manner that precludes the view of any human ordinariness on the part of Jesus? For Schuon, it is clear that if Christ is human, he is so in a way that is archetypical, in the sense of being the "Son of Man." This very term appears many times in the Old Testament to refer to humankind, but its use in the New Testament refers to a perfection that transcends the purely terrestrial manifestations of the human, since it applies to Christ. It is precisely this archetypical character, crystallized by the expression "Son of Man," that distinguishes it from ordinary manifestations of humanity. This is the consideration that leads Schuon to assert that Christ is not human in the purely ordinary sense of the term; that is to say in the manner of an ordinary human individual. Unquestionably, the Man-God is an individual, one who is different from other individuals. The attributes of this individuality make it participant in a psychic "particularization analogous to what in ordinary mortals we call 'desire.'"[18] The expression "what . . . we call 'desire'" in ordinary human beings already indicates, however, a single term referring to two vastly different realities, implying thereby a transmutation of the natural that is not without analogy with a change in substance. Notwithstanding this, the individuality assumed by the Word through its incarnation in the flesh must entail some limitations by definition, but these limitations are those of relativity itself,[19] and they are therefore obviously not incompatible with spiritual and moral perfection. So, even though the limitations of the individual have a different meaning in the Man-God, his humanity

---

18. Schuon, *The Eye of the Heart* (Bloomington, IN: World Wisdom, 1997), 104.

19. This dimension of relativity is, according to Schuon, inscribed in the name *Jesus*, as distinct from the universality of Christ: "'Jesus'—like 'Gotama' and like 'Mohammed'—indicates the limited and relative aspect of the manifestation of the Spirit, and signifies the support of this manifestation; 'Christ'—like 'Buddha' and 'Rasūl Allāh'—indicates the Universal Reality of this same manifestation, that is to say the Word as such." *The Transcendent Unity of Religions*, 92.

cannot be understood in a purely generic way. The truth lies half-way, so to speak, in the sense that, in his case, the Universal penetrates the individual to such an extent that one cannot speak of an ordinary human: "It is the very substance of the individuality which, in the divine man, is transmuted by the Real Presence."[20] For Schuon, it is not plausible that the individuality of Jesus be, in every way, comparable to that of other human beings. However, this distinction is not to be understood with respect to the individuality as such, or to the consciousness of the natural human ego but, rather, in regard to the fact that, in the Man-God, the individual self "which he possesses—in the same way he possesses his physical body—cannot be an obstacle to him."[21] This is a way of suggesting that the individuality is, in this case, "penetrated and determined by the Universal." One can distinguish, therefore, in the Man-God, three different degrees of selfhood, as it were. The first is the individuality as such; the second is the divine individuality as totally unhampered by subjective limitations and its being perfectly informed by the Universal, i.e., the Spirit; and the third is the Supreme Identity of the Essential Self. In an ordinary human being, the self is identified with the first of these layers whereas the subjectivity of the Man-God oscillates, so to speak, between the second and the third dimensions. We can see, through these various remarks, how the encounter between the human and the Divine places us in a context that defies usual and conventional categories, and therefore functions, at least virtually, as a kind of Zen *koān*, a perplexing enigma that contains a potential illumination. As James Cutsinger suggestively puts it: "The mystery of the two natures is a wonder indeed, and it would be foolish to think that one might give it a conclusive or definitive explanation or discern the full range of its meaning."[22]

The case of the Buddha is analogous to that of Christ in the sense that the human individuality of Siddharta Gautama and the universality of Buddhahood have to be both distinct and conjoined, none being exclusive of the other. Siddharta is the Buddha in a way that is not without analogy to the manner in which Jesus is the Christ, as indicated by the distinction, in him, between the "individual name" and the title referring to his

---

20. Schuon, *The Eye of the Heart*, 105.
21. Schuon, *The Eye of the Heart*, 105.
22. James S. Cutsinger, "The Mystery of the Two Natures," *Sophia: Journal of Traditional Studies* 4, no. 2 (1998): 106.

universal function. In the same way, the nature of Christ is universal, or archetypical—in the sense of being divine—the reality of the Buddha is primarily universal since it is none other than the nature of Awakening, or the nature of Reality as such; i.e., the Buddha-nature or the "nature of things," as Schuon would put it. However, like Jesus, the Buddha Siddharta is also undoubtedly an individual, an Indian prince whose story is considered by the tradition as historically grounded, paradigmatic, and a pedagogical tool in tracing the way to Buddhahood.

The fact that Buddhism is, essentially, non-theistic, and thus appears to preclude the idea of a "Divine descent," should not prevent one from identifying a number of central features of its teachings that are akin to the most universal implications of the *avatāra*. Thus, the doctrine of the three bodies of the Buddha (*trikāya*) constitutes the closest approximation to an avatāric doctrine in the context of Buddhism. It allows us to distinguish, at any rate, between Universal Reality, which is the *Dharmakāya*, and an individual and physical manifestation, the *Nirmāṇakāya*, in addition to the *Sambhogakāya*, the body of "enjoyment" or "reward" that refers to the celestial reality of the Buddha. Schuon refers to this teaching in several passages because it provides him with a structure that is applicable to a plurality of traditional contexts. He refers to it as to "the doctrine of the three 'hypostases' of the Blessed One: the *Dhārmakāya* (the 'universal body') is the Essence, Beyond-Being; the *Sambhogakāya* (the 'body of felicity') is the 'heavenly Form,' the 'divine Personification; the *Nirmāṇakāya* (the 'body of metamorphosis') is the human manifestation of the Buddha."[23] On this basis, Schuon considers the Buddha-nature on three levels: as Essence, Determination, and Manifestation, or as Beyond-Being, Being, and Existence. This threefold understanding echoes, to some extent, the three degrees of the Christic reality that we have sketched above.

In Theravāda Buddhism, according to Guang Xing, *dharmakāya* simply refers to the teachings of the Buddha and therefore—indirectly—to the essence of the reality to which these teachings refer. In Mahāyāna, however, the *Dharmakāya* becomes more directly ontological in scope, being conceived as none other—in its metaphysical essence—than "the principle of the universe, [which] does not bring together causes and conditions, as it neither arises nor disappears."[24] At this juncture, the *Dharmakāya* is

---

23. Schuon, *Treasures of Buddhism* (Bloomington, IN: World Wisdom, 1993), 156–57.
24. Guang Xing, *The Concept of the Buddha: Its Evolution from Early Buddhism to the Trikāya Theory* (London: Routledge, 2005), 84.

therefore identical to the Ultimate Truth. It becomes synonymous with the Absolute, as is plain from the consideration that the *Dharma*, understood as interdependent co-origination or as Buddha-nature, exists independently from whether or not any Buddha arises in the world: "Whether the Buddhas arise or not, the *Dhamma* exists from all eternity."[25] Inasmuch as the Buddha is identified with co-dependent origination, the *Dharma* is his very nature, his *kāya*. It is therefore taught, consistently, that the *Dharmakāya* is the reality of the Buddha that is not subject to perishing. However, only the Mahāyāna draws direct ontological conclusions from this identification by referring to a Buddha-nature, or *tathatā*, the "Suchness" of things. As for the third "body" of the Buddha, the *Sambhogakāya*, its concept appears to develop at a later stage,[26] and it is clearly related to the concept of the *bodhisattva*'s advent, both inasmuch as the latter accumulates merits through his "sacrificial work" for the emancipation of all beings, and insofar as he epitomizes the "enjoyment" of the reward of celestial grace. However, the *Nirmānakāya* is evidently the most relevant to our investigation, since it refers to the human "envelope" of the Buddha and, therefore, raises the question of the relationship between the Absolute and human relativity. The *Nirmānakāya* is the manifested reality of Buddhahood that "displays various acts such as birth, enlightenment and *parinirvāna* for the sake of sentient beings."[27] It does so as a manifestation of compassion to all beings, as if the nirvānic Reality were consenting to enter the samsāric flow in order to save beings from bondage.

In keeping with the avatāric sense of an encounter between incommensurate realities, there is no question that the realization of Buddhahood constitutes a kind of coincidence or "union"—although the term carries misleading connotations in such a non-theistic and non-dualistic context—of the first and third "bodies": "He who sees the *Dhamma* (*dharmakāyo*) sees me, he who sees me sees the *Dhamma*."[28] Now, this "union" is not conceived in the manner of an incarnation descending from above but as the realization, or actualization, of Reality in and through the very modalities of an individual human being, although this Reality remains,

---

25. Nārada Maha Thera, *The Buddha and His Teachings* (Bangkok: Buddhadhamma Foundation, 1980), 162.
26. Xing, *The Concept of the Buddha*, 101.
27. Xing, *The Concept of the Buddha*,142.
28. Xing, *The Concept of the Buddha*, 72.

as we have seen, totally independent from the latter. From another point of view, the *Nirmānakāya* can also be considered as a "skillful" and compassionate "manifestation" of the *Dharmakāya*, the latter being one and the former many. Thus, the avatāric nature of the Buddha, explicitly claimed by some Hindu *purānas* as the ninth "descent" of Vishnu, remains clearly conceivable, *mutatis mutandis*, in Buddhist language both because of the co-presence of the two dimensions of the Ultimate, *paramārtha-satya*, and the conventional, *samvriti-satya*, and because of the archetypical reality of the historical Buddha as founder of a spiritual tradition, which implies a "divine" and cosmic function on his part. In this context it is highly significant that, following the Enlightenment of the Buddha, it is actually the god Brahma who convinces him to "turn the wheel of the Dharma."[29]

With respect to the ultimate aspect of the Buddha, the relationship between the two "natures" or, rather, "dimensions" of Siddharta, reveals an inflection that is, however, significantly different from its equivalent in Christianity. Thus, while the co-reality of the human and divine natures in Christ remains theologically irreducible, the human "locus of realization" of *Bodhi* is as if dissolved by the realization of the latter, at least in the sense that reaching *Nirvāna* amounts to recognizing the emptiness and impermanence of that which is held as real from a conventional point of view. This is the reason why we encounter such typically startling expressions as Nāgārjuna's "No Dharma was taught by the Buddha at any time, in any place, to any person."[30] This paradoxical statement corresponds to the ultimate truth of non-duality and non-objectification, as it obviously cannot make sense on the level of conventional reality. From the vantage point of conventional truth, and therefore on the level of the *Nirmānakāya*, it is as if the individual were reabsorbed into the universal, with a primary stress on the spiritually "upward" motion of *Nirvāna*. From the point of view of "no view," which is that of the *Dharmakāya*, there is either "manifestation" in the sense that form "manifests" emptiness or,

---

29. "*After the Buddha attained enlightenment he remained* silent for seven weeks. Then the god Brahma came and offered a golden mandala requesting that the Buddha teach sentient beings. Because of this request the Buddha began to turn the wheel of the Dharma." Gheze Lhundub Sopa, *Steps on the Path to Enlightenment: A Commentary on Tsongkhapa's Lamrim Chenmo—Volume 3: The Way of the Bodhisattva*, edited by Beth Newman (Boston: Wisdom Publications, 2008), 152.

30. Rje Tsong Khapa, *Ocean of Reasoning: A Great Commentary on Nāgārjuna's Mūlamadhyamakakārikā*, translated by Geshe Ngawang Samten and Jay L. Garfield (Oxford: Oxford University Press, 2006), 532.

better, pure ontological coincidence whereby form *is* emptiness. In both cases, which obviously do not imply any ontological duality, there is no emphasis on the human site of enlightenment *as such*. In fact, Suchness is universal and has, ultimately, no privileged dwelling. By contrast, the Christic incarnation entails a downward direction, a Divine intent, and, in a way, a soteriological emphasis on the specifically human nature of Christ, without which the redemptive drama of the Passion and Resurrection would be neither possible nor, if one may say so, crucial. Here humanity is marked by a cardinal significance that makes the "Man-God" all the more powerfully striking and necessary. In the Buddhist outlook, on the other hand, the spiritual "reabsorption" of the human that we have highlighted, or even ultimately its non-dual identity with the *Dharma*, runs parallel to a greater contingency of the human channel of Enlightenment, when compared to the soteriological "necessity" of the *Redemptor hominis*. The historical Buddha, like all other Enlightened beings, is no more than an occurrence of Awakening. The Mahāyāna teachings of the *trikāya*, or three natures, brings this point home in a most powerful and eloquent way.

The fundamental reality of the *avatāra* lies, for Schuon, not only in what constitutes its metaphysical principle, that is his divinity or his identity with the Ultimate, but also, and consequently, in his spiritual and eschatological function, his saving grace. In a chapter entitled "Christianity and Buddhism,"[31] Schuon highlights this saving function of the *avatāra* as being one of the fundamental common characteristics shared by the two traditions initiated by the Buddha and the Christ. More specifically, Schuon attributes this salvific function to the spiritual corporeity, if one may say so, of the two founding figures of Buddhism and Christianity. Taking as a starting point the fact that the two traditions are distinguished by the soteriological centrality of their respective human founders, Schuon highlights, in this regard, the essential function of the "sacramental body" of the avatāric figure. By emphasizing "the very Body of the Man-God, thus offering a so to speak 'consubstantial' participation in the Word,"[32] Schuon is evidently taking stock of the Christian paradigm of the redemptive virtue of the very substance of the body of Christ. The term "consubstantial," directly borrowed from the vocabulary of the Christian credo, in which it refers to the substance of the Son in relation to the Father, was also used—in the cognate form of consubstantiation—in

---

31. Schuon, *Treasures of Buddhism*, 95–106.
32. Schuon, *Treasures of Buddhism*, 104.

some schools of Christian theology as a way of preserving the idea of two substances, one natural and one supernatural, in the Eucharist. It is, therefore, quite appropriate to apply this term to the body of the Man-God, in whom the Divine substance does not obliterate the human nature, as the Divine Presence does not cancel the physical substance of the Eucharistic species. The fact that Schuon capitalizes the word *Body* implies, in this case, that there is more at work than a mere physical reality. The body itself is transfigured into a reality that partakes of the supernatural, in a numinous and transformational way. To wit, the main point made by Schuon in this regard is less metaphysical than spiritual and soteriological. The key point is the reality of one's participation in the Word as principle of salvation and transformation. Schuon is much less interested in specifying the ontological status of the avatāric body—a point that is confirmed *a fortiori* by his reticence to over-theologize the mystery of the Divine Presence in the Eucharist[33]—than he is to underline the role of the physical and tangible dimension of spiritual presence in the process of contemplative transformation.

It goes without saying, moreover, that the Christian associations of the concepts at play do not allow for a literal application of the aforementioned principles to Buddhism or, *a fortiori*, to other faiths. However, Schuon extends the principle of participating in the grace of the Word to the physical representation of the Buddha. The insight that the Buddhas save by their supernatural beauty is one that Schuon frequently reiterates throughout his work in order to stress the significance of the spiritual and transformative vibrations that emanate from sacred and aesthetic forms. The significance of this dimension of beauty, in the Schuonian definition of the spiritual impact of the *avatāra*, finds one of its main traditional sources in Pure Land Buddhism. Schuon quotes a passage from one of the early Patriarchs of Chinese Pure Land tradition, Tao-ch'o (Jp. Doshaku) who, in his *Collection of Passages on the Land of Peace and Bliss (An-lo chi)*, enumerates four ways in which the Buddhas save; namely through their oral teachings, their supernatural beauty, their spiritual powers of transformation, and their Names. D. T. Suzuki quotes a *sūtra* mentioned

---

33. "What actualizes the ontological relation between the Mass and Calvary is the Real Presence, independently of the question of transubstantiation; that one may conceive transubstantiation as a change of substance—an elliptical idea if ever there was one—is an entirely different question." Schuon, *In the Face of the Absolute* (Bloomington, IN: World Wisdom, 2014), 53.

by Tao-ch'o according to which "All the Buddhas save beings in four ways: 1. In oral teachings such as recorded in the twelve divisions of Buddhist literature; 2. By their physical features of supernatural beauty; 3. By their wonderful powers and virtues and transformations; and 4. By their names, which, when uttered by beings, will remove obstacles and assure their rebirth in the presence of the Buddha."[34] Among these four aspects of the Buddha, only the first pertains to what Schuon would call the dimension of Truth, akin to the discernment of Reality through the metaphysical doctrine, whereas the three others belong to the dimension of Presence, which regards the spiritual and transformative aspects of religion through their "sacramental" and theurgic channels of grace. This is not surprising inasmuch as the avatāric figure is, by virtue of his very function, a "conveyor of Presence." Moreover, one of the most interesting points with regard to the four aforementioned aspects is that they are universalized by Schuon in order to be applied to Christianity and also, *mutatis mutandis*, to all religions. Thus, Schuon mentions the doctrine of Redemption by, and through, Love, the Eucharist, the Paraclete, and the Name of Jesus, as the four functional equivalents of the Buddhist soteriological quaternity. What is visual in Buddhism, that is, the physical beauty of the Buddha and his artistic representations, becomes more directly bodily in the case of Christ, with the actual species of the Eucharist, in keeping with the Christian emphasis on the Word made *flesh*. Although Schuon does not develop this fourfold criteriology beyond the cases of Buddhism and Christianity, he affirms that it is "to be found in appropriate forms in every divine Messenger."[35] In the case of Islam, for instance, the third of the world religions to claim a universal vocation, it is obvious that the doctrine of *tawhīd*, or Divine Unity, the transformative power of the Qur'ān and the Names of God as invoked in remembrance or *dhikr*, correspond to the first, third, and fourth characters. With respect to the second, which involves a physical mode of presence, it can be deemed that the Tradition of the Prophet, the *sunnah*, especially in its most outward aspects, constitutes a quasi-bodily modality of participation in the Prophet's blessings. In the non-avatāric context of Islam, the physical appearance of the Messenger cannot possibly take a central place, nor is there any channel through which a physical "sacramental" contact with the Prophet

---

34. Daisetz Teitaro Suzuki, *The Zen Koan as a Means of Attaining Enlightenment* (Boston: Charles E. Tuttle Co., 1994), 98.
35. Schuon, *Treasures of Buddhism*, 106.

could be part of a religion centered on the dangers of idolatry and the consequent relentless emphasis on Transcendence. Visual and tangible dimensions of the Prophetic presence can only manifest sporadically in the context of esoteric or popular perspectives, and the canonical *hadīth* itself provides a few instances of such possibilities.[36]

In whatever form and degree one may consider the phenomenon of the *avatāra* under its general aspect of saving manifestation or conveyance of the Absolute, we have seen that it presupposes a relativization of the latter *in divinis*, without which the very relationship between the Absolute and the relative would not be possible and, hence, no theophanic human could be thinkable. This amounts to saying that the manifestation of the Absolute in the relative is a sort of inverted reflection of the presence of the relative in the Absolute, or, to use Schuon's phrase, the prefiguration of the relative in the Absolute. Thus, the principle at stake is encapsulated in one of the most synthetic expressions of the metaphysical underpinnings of the *avatāra*: "That man, who is relative, could be identified with God, who is the Absolute, presupposes that relativity has an aspect of absoluteness and that therefore relativity be prefigured in *divinis*."[37] The matter is couched here in terms of an identification of the human with the Divine, being understood, as indicated earlier, that such identification can only be subjective—in the sense of referring to an inner reality of union—in that it does not concern the Essence, which lies beyond such identifications since it is pure Identity in and of itself. This being specified, Schuon makes it clear in this passage that the human, in its avatāric paradigm, cannot but be "present" in God as a prefiguring possibility, therefore as Ultimate Relativity, if one may say so. Such is one of the highest meanings of the biblical notion that "mankind was created in the image and resemblance of God," since this Ultimate Relativity is none other than Being, God as the Principle and Creator of the universe. Thus, the first, and therefore the

---

36. There is, for instance, a *hadīth* in which Abu Bakr, after having stared at 'Alī's face for a while declares that "to look at the face of 'Alī is to worship" (*An-nadhar ilā wajhu 'Alī 'ibādah*). Muhammad Mahmood Ali Qutbi, *Fragrance of Sufism* (Karachi: Royal Book Co., 1993), 22. Another interesting example is the transmission of *barakah* or blessing through bodily fluids: "Narrated Mahmud ibn al-Rabī': 'When I was a boy of five, I remember the Prophet took water from a bucket with his mouth and threw it on my face.'" Tayeb Chouiref, *Spiritual Teachings of the Prophet: Hadith with Commentaries by Saints and Sages of Islam* (Louisville: Fons Vitae, 2011), 90.

37. Schuon, *Form and Substance in the Religions* (Bloomington, IN: World Wisdom, 2005), 212.

most fundamental, Self-determination or Self-delimitation of the Divine Essence is Being as the "Word of Beyond-Being" and, therefore, as the source of all further determinations and manifestations. It is important to understand that this prefiguring determination is the seed of transcendence in God, so to speak, the Divine Essence *qua* Essence being neither intrinsically transcendent nor immanent—in the sense that it accounts, among other metaphysical gaps, for mankind not being God: "The hiatus between Creator and creature is necessarily prefigured *in divinis* by the differentiation between the Absolute as such and the Absolute that is relativized with respect to a dimension of Its infinitude; but this difference, precisely, is real only from the standpoint of Relativity."[38] This means that any distinction within the Principle itself, and in fact any distinction whatsoever, is entailed by relativity, and has no reality and no meaning from the point of view of the Absolute itself. In order to understand the *avatāra*, therefore, one must understand that his dual nature of "Man-God," with the radical distinction that this expression both involves and negates, is in a sense the relative reflection of the prefiguration of relativity within absoluteness. The *avatāra* is both human and divine, but the very distinction between the two natures can have meaning only from a relative, and therefore human, point of view. Absolutely speaking, the distinction has no reality, which allows one to fathom why the terrestrial "manifestation of God" as *avatāra* constitutes both a kind of miracle and a kind of enigma.

However, besides the level of Being, the prefiguration that is the principle of the avatāric possibility can and must be envisaged on other, quite different, levels. On a lower level, Being as the first determination of Beyond-Being gives rise to Existence, that is the Principle *as manifested*. For God is also Existence, not in the sense of accidental existence, of course, but in the sense in which the Islamic tradition refers to Him as *az-Zāhir*, the Manifest, or the Outward. Since, according to the non-dualistic perspective of Sufi gnosis, there is none other than Him, Existence cannot but be a dimension of His Reality. Now, at the metaphysical center of Existence lies the Word or the Logos "through which everything was made." This is the Logos as Principle, whose manifestations are like cosmic reflections of its Light. Envisaged as the lowest degree of Divine manifestation, that is to say, reaching below the metacosmic level, the Logos must be considered,

---

38. Schuon, *Form and Substance in the Religions*, 208.

for Schuon, as both divine and created, a point that lies at the foundation of Schuon's avatāric doctrine. Schuon characterizes the Logos as the "end-point of theogenesis."[39] The concept of "theogenesis," which, Schuon concedes, is somewhat "ill-sounding," inasmuch as it appears to imply a sort of becoming in God—*quod absit*—pertains to the various levels of determination and manifestation of the Principle, which involve degrees and aspects without altering the essential unity of the Divine Reality. This is what the Islamic tradition would refer to as a *barzakh*, a reality that operates the junction between two domains of reality while, at the same time, presupposing them, and therefore affirming them in their difference. Schuon specifies that the Logos, or the Divine Spirit, is the transcendent prefiguration of both humankind as terrestrial reflection of God on earth and the "supernatural representative of God amongst men," that is, the *avatāra*. This remark is not without important implications, since it allows one to fathom both the way the human participates in the Divine and the way the Divine participates in the human. The first participation is theomorphic. The term "representative" is specifically borrowed from the vocabulary of Islam, since it refers to the human being as *khalifatu-Llāh*, or vice-regent of God on earth. Beyond the specific connotations of the term in an Islamic context, "representative" points to the fact that mankind is a "representation" of God, which is expressed by the biblical concept of mankind being created "in the image and in the resemblance of God," while being also, as such, endowed with particular faculties and capacities that situate it at the "epistemological center," as it were, of creation. It is within this epistemological context, so to speak, that the *avatāra* is able to appear. While mankind may be deemed to be "divinely human" in the sense of bearing the imprint of the Ultimate within its nature, as a reflection of the Logos, this makes for the possibility of a being who is "humanly divine," that is the *avatāra*. As such, the *avatāra* actualizes the highest potential of the human nature by referring back the latter's roots to the Divine.

Unity and distinction are therefore to be found, both in the Divine Order, where they originate, and in the human and terrestrial order, where

---

39. "The end-point of theogenesis is the most relative or the most outward *Hypostasis*, namely the 'Spirit of God,' which is still divine even though, having already been created, it occupies the luminous center of creation; this is the *Logos*, which prefigures both the human species as the natural representative of God on earth and the *Avatāra* as the supernatural representative of God among men." Schuon, *Esoterism as Principle and as Way* (London: Perennial Books, 1981), 50.

they are reflected. In both cases, although in different, and in a sense reverse, ways, unity and distinction coincide without ceasing to imply difference. *In divinis*, as we have seen, difference is only real extrinsically, that is, in relation to the relative field. It could be said, therefore, that difference is included, or integrated, into Unity. Within the human world, by contrast, difference is the rule and unity the exception, an exception that cannot but be, however, since pure difference would run contrary to metaphysical Unity. This exception is precisely none other than the *avatāra*. From another point of view, it is because there is distinction above that there can be union below. It is because the Divine Reality determines itself and opens the way, therefore, to the very possibility of otherness, that the end-point of this otherness, or relativity, may be re-absorbed into Unity.

While, as we have seen, the Hindu tradition clearly refers to the avatāric being as a divine "descent," Schuon's texts are indeed quite nuanced in their characterization of the ontological status of the *avatāra* since the perennialist metaphysician holds on to the human nature of the phenomenon without however reducing it to the human, hence a recognition of the "supernatural" dimension of the *avatāra*. In his essay "The Mystery of the Veil," Schuon develops in fact a very penetrating and detailed meditation on the relationship between the human and the divine in the *avatāra*. He distinguishes three levels: namely, the Divine Reality itself, or the Divine Self; the Divine Spirit or Universal Intellect as a reflection of the latter in and for a given cosmic sector; and human reality itself. These three ontological degrees must be carefully distinguished lest one run the risk of abusive interpretations of what is conveyed by the term *avatāra*. There is, evidently, a separation between the Divine Selfhood as such and the human "accident" as such, this gap being prefigured, as we have seen earlier, in the distinction between the *purum absolutum* and the "relatively Absolute" or Being. On the other hand, Schuon refers to a "mixing" (*mélange*) between the latter and the reflection of a cosmic aspect of the Divine for a particular sector.[40] The Divine Selfhood, which is none other than the Essence, remains obviously

---

40. "In the *Avatāra* there is quite obviously a separation between the human and the divine—or between accident and Substance—then there is a mixing, not of human accident and divine Substance, but of the human and the direct reflection of Substance in the cosmic accident; relatively to the human this reflection may be called divine, on condition that the Cause is not in any way reduced to the effect." Schuon, *Esoterism as Principle and as Way*, 63.

transcendent vis-à-vis the human "accident," while being also immanent to it but without involving any sort of inherence. Another way to express this is to conceive of it as involving continuity from the point of view of the Substance-Essence but not from that of the accident. The Divine Self does not incarnate, while being the Essence of everything that is. This is in keeping with Sufi expressions, including—among the most daring ones—Hallāj's, that reject any possibility of combination or admixture of God as such and the creature as such, thereby protecting the Divine Essence from any humanizing *shirk,* or polytheistic association. Thus, we read in Hallāj these beautifully suggestive and perplexing words: "Oh you who are uncertain, do not identify 'I am' with the Divine 'I'—not now, nor in the future, nor in the past. Even if the 'I am' was a consummated gnostic, and if this was my state, it was not the perfection. Even though I am His I am not He."[41] For Schuon, this paradox of unity in difference and difference in unity can only be intimated, on a theoretical level—for its spiritual reality remains what it is for whomever it *is*—by preserving a clear sense that the "union" of the divine and human realities can only involve, as far as the former are concerned, that which in the Divine is already cosmic while still being divine, a reality that Schuon refers to as the *Buddhi* of Hinduism, or the Universal Intellect or Logos at the center of Existence. Moreover, we must keep in mind that it is only an "aspect" of the Logos-Intellect that "incarnates," and not its totality. For instance, a given *avatāra* of Vishnu is a "mixing" of the cosmic light projected by the god, so to speak, with a particular human being. Schuon asserts, moreover, that the divinity of this cosmic reflection can only be recognized "relatively to the human," therefore in its dimension of relativity, and not in any way as referring to the Essence as such. When the Qur'ān states unequivocally that "He is the One, God, the Independent, and He does not beget and is not begotten," it refers to this "unmixable" Essence of the Divine Reality that does not "descend" and does not "incarnate." And these considerations allow us, moreover, to understand how the Hindu tradition can be characterized by the harmonious coexistence of the most metaphysically exclusive concept of the Absolute and the most pervasive incarnationist religious mythology. This point of view raises, obviously, a number of issues and questions from the vantage point of Christian theology. It is impossible to address these questions and the manner in

---

41. Al-Husayn ibn Mansūr Hallāj, *Kitāb al-Tawāsīn* (Berkeley: Diwan Press, 1974), 25.

which Schuon modulates the notion of the *avatāra* in a Christian context, without broaching his interpretation of the Trinity, which is moreover the focus, per se, of another chapter of this book in which we will return to this topic in further depth. At any rate, considering the various ways in which Schuon envisages the Christian Trinity places one in a better position to understand how the Incarnation can be approached from his esoteric point of view.

In the context of its theological meaning, Schuon considers the Trinity in three, or four, different ways.[42] The first of these perspectives on the Trinity is termed by him "supreme" and "horizontal." It is supreme because it concerns the Essence as such, and horizontal inasmuch as it considers dimensions of the Essence that do not entail Relativity, therefore "situated" on the same level of Absolute Reality. This level of consideration refers to the Essence, or Beyond-Being, as containing the three Persons *qua* its three fundamental dimensions. It is analogous to the way Hindu metaphysics points to the nature of the Supreme Reality of *Nirguna Brahman* as *Sat*, *Cit* and *Ānanda*; that is, Being, Consciousness, and Bliss. In a different context, Schuon also refers to the Absolute, the Infinite, and the Perfect as being the three dimensions of the Ultimate. A correlation can be established, therefore, between the Father as Absolute Being, the Son as Perfect Consciousness, and the Holy Spirit as Infinite Bliss. Such correspondences can be buttressed by bringing in other passages from Schuon's works in which he provides his readers with a geometric symbolism of the Trinity of the Father, the Son and the Holy Spirit as represented, respectively, by the central point, the perfect circle, and the limitless ray. From the perspective of this Trinitarian interpretation, it is quite clear, first of all, that as a "hidden dimension" of the Ultimate, the "Son" *qua* Essence is not susceptible to any incarnation, being, from this vantage point, none other than the Unconditioned itself. The first point to emphasize, therefore, is that Schuon does not consider the Incarnation, or any incarnation, as referring to the Essence or Divine Selfhood itself. It is clear that the Essence cannot possibly "incarnate" since it lies beyond all determinations and, therefore, all relations. In other words, any incarnation presupposes a distinction—between the incarnating and incarnated realities—that has no meaning whatsoever on the level

---

42. On Schuon's "vertical" and "horizontal" view of the Trinity, see, among other passages, "Man in the Face of the Sovereign Good," in *Roots of the Human Condition* (Bloomington, IN: World Wisdom, 2002), 71.

of the Divine Essence, hence the Judaic and Islamic anathema against the very idea of Divine incarnation. What is religiously an Abrahamic protestation against idolatry amounts, metaphysically, to a most rigorous understanding of the ultimate reality of the Absolute. However, inasmuch as the "Son" corresponds to the dimension of Perfection, and insofar as He is identifiable with Consciousness, it is possible to understand how the cosmic manifestation of the Word would be, at the same time, the locus of realization of the Essence. The latter is indeed pure Consciousness and its recognition is, *ipso facto*, the actualization of human perfection and therefore, in a way, of human nature as such. In other words, the Word as Son *is* within the Essence, that is, that dimension of Consciousness which is the privilege of mankind and which is fully actualized by the avatāric being. From another point of view, however, the Incarnation can be thought to be potentially "contained" within the dimension of Infinitude proper to the Essence, insofar as the latter is the source of all manifestation, of which the Incarnation can be considered a central and, as it were, a prototypical instance. The association of the Infinite with the third Person of the Trinity, the Holy Spirit, does not invalidate this point since it is through the Holy Spirit that the Incarnation becomes a reality at the time of the Annunciation.

The second way to consider the Trinity is also "horizontal," since it envisages the three aspects of God as Being, Wisdom, and Will on the same ontological level of Reality. However, being non-supreme, it refers only to Being as the first determination of the Principle and not to the Essence as Beyond-Being. Would this contemplation of the non-supreme Trinity indicate the possibility that the Incarnation may, in fact, pertain to Being? It would not, precisely by reason of the ontological status of Being as first Relativity *in divinis*. This amounts to saying that Being is intrinsically relational to the extent that it presupposes a relative otherness without which it would have no meaning. Therefore, Being as such cannot incarnate presupposing, as it does, the irreducible distinction between the Lord and the servant, and the transcendence of the former in relation to the latter, to put it in Schuon's own language. In a sense, it could be argued that this principle is implied in Christian theology, at least in its subordinationist aspects, by the fact that the Father does not incarnate.[43]

---

43. "The tradition teaches us first that it was the Son or Logos, the second Person of the Holy Trinity, who was incarnate in Jesus, not the first Person of the Father. On the contrary, the Father is the *aitia* or cause of both the Son and the Spirit, whether by

Here again, while it is quite clear that Being as such cannot be the "subject" of the Incarnation, the aspect of Wisdom associated with the Son epitomizes the specificity of the Word as principle of illumination through the Intellect. This opens the way to a theology of the Son as "Wisdom of the Father" which, as we will develop further on, crystallizes in the gnostic concept of the "Christ-Intellect."

Finally, the third understanding of the Trinity is "vertical," as it considers the three hypostases as different degrees of the Real; namely, Beyond-Being, Being and Existence, each of which corresponds, respectively, to the three Persons of the Trinity. This interpretation, while equating the Son with Being, may open the way to a principial understanding of the Incarnation, as Schuon has suggested, where the latter would be understood as the determination of a higher hypostasis into a lower one. This way of apprehending the Incarnation highlights the first ontological determination of Being—*qua* the Word of Beyond-Being—and therefore as the metaphysical archetype, if one may say so, of the historical Incarnation. By highlighting an aspect of discontinuous continuity among the hypostases, this interpretation provides one with a model for apprehending the paradox of the Incarnation, a paradox that is provoked by the manifestation of the higher in, and through, the lower.

To these three interpretations of the Trinity must be added a fourth that, again, considers it "horizontally" but on the level of Existence; that is, as the Divine Reality as manifested through, and within, creation. This is also the perspective that would correspond, in a sense, to what Christian theology refers to as the "economical Trinity"; in other words, that which unfolds as, and in, the history of Redemption. Thus, Schuon writes: "One could also envisage a third plane, which is already cosmic, but still Divine however from the human point of view which, as for it, determines theology, and this is the Luminous Centre of the cosmos, the 'Triple Manifestation' (*Trimūrti*) of the Hindu doctrine, or the Spirit (*Rūh*) of the Islamic doctrine."[44] This is the plane of the Incarnation in the strict sense of the term, since it pertains to the cosmos, its axial center,

---

filiation or spiration; He is the Unity, according to St Gregory the Theologian, 'from whom and to whom the order of the Persons runs its course,' and He remains forever, therefore—despite the Incarnation—a transcendent and inaccessible mystery." James Cutsinger, "The Mystery of the Two Natures," *Every Branch in Me: Essays on the Meaning of Man*, edited by Barry McDonald (Bloomington, IN: World Wisdom, 2002), 94.

44. Schuon, *Logic and Transcendence* (Bloomington, IN: World Wisdom, 2009), 85.

and the reflection of this center in the existential unity of the Man-God. By designating Jesus as *Rūh Allāh*, the Islamic tradition alludes to this understanding of the relationship between the Divine and the human without, however, drawing from it incarnationist conclusions that would be incompatible with its exoteric and theological system. We note, from this perspective, that all human beings, in the image of Adam, have been breathed in the *Rūh* upon their creation and that, moreover, the specific identification of Jesus with this *Rūh* may be understood as suggesting his being the prototype and perfection of mankind, at least from the point of view of the latter's Divine origination.

In order to summarize the implications of Schuon's various interpretations of the Trinity with regard to the Incarnation, one can begin by recognizing that, within the perspective of supreme and horizontal readings of the Trinity, the Incarnation can only be conceived as a reality potentially included within the Infinite dimension of the Ultimate as source of all determinations and manifestations. With respect to the non-supreme horizontal reading on the level of Being, it is the aspect of Wisdom that prefigures the Incarnation. As for the vertical understanding of the Trinity, it allows one to understand how each lower degree of the Chain of Being may be read as a principial foundation for the Incarnation. Finally, on the level of Existence, the Incarnation becomes "effective" as an existentiation of the Logos.

The metaphysical picture of the Trinitarian underpinnings of the doctrine of the Incarnation in Schuon's esoteric perspective would not be complete without considering the respective correlations between the Father and the metacosm, the Son and the macrocosm, and the Holy Ghost and the microcosm. In this respect, the Incarnation takes on a universal meaning that equates the Logos with the entire manifested universe. Thus, in this view of things, the Incarnation assumes the mode of manifestation, as a whole, by the Divine Reality, the Man-God being thus identified with the prototype of creation and its perfection. This way of considering the *avatāra* appears in Schuon's commentary on the second testimony of faith of Islam in his *Understanding Islam*. In this context, Schuon characterizes the metaphysical meaning of the sentence *Muhammadun Rasūl Allāh* as follows: "The name of the Prophet (Muhammad), in the second *shahādah*, designates the world in so far as it is real because nothing can be outside of God; in some respects, everything is Him."[45] It is quite clear, however,

---

45. Schuon, *Understanding Islam* (Bloomington, IN: World Wisdom, 2011), 5.

that we are not speaking here of incarnation in the theological sense but, rather, of Divine immanence in the most universal way. It must be added, though, that the *avatāra* concentrates and crystallizes, as it were, this immanence in a particularly central mode.

It is only on the level of Existence, therefore, that the Incarnation can have a plausible meaning. It refers, more specifically, to the Logos, the ontological and epistemological center of Existence, as well as to its "combination" with the human nature in the person of Jesus Christ. On the one hand, the Divine nature of Christ is relative, in the Schuonian sense of the "relatively absolute"; on the other hand, his human nature is universal, inasmuch as he manifests the *raison d'être* of its existence. In other words, Christ is not the Absolute as such, nor is he just an individual person. His Divinity necessarily participates in relativity, and his humanity is necessarily raised above individual accidentality. The latter does not adulterate the Divine in the least, nor does the former affect his human nature as such. There is, in a sense, no humanization of the Divine which would amount to a sort of Jesuanism, an idolatrous reduction of Divinity, and no divinization of the human as such, which would result in a kind of docetism; that is, in a de facto negation of the human side of the Incarnation. The latter is therefore a "mixture," not in the sense of a confusion, but in the manner of an inalterable unity of personhood and will that does not cancel out the separation of the two natures, or alter the reality of each of them. In other words, the inherence of the Divine Intellect in mankind, or the inherence of the Word in the Incarnation, do not abolish the incommensurability between the Divine and the human. The inherence of the Divine, in whichever mode one may conceive of it, does not nullify transcendence but rather (and paradoxically), makes its Presence irresistible.[46] From another point of view, inasmuch as the Intellect-Logos, as a "direct reflection of Substance," is the center of Existence, its irruption in human flesh cannot but epitomize the perfection of mankind and, beyond, that of creation itself. The universal dimension of the Word as perfection of existence accounts, in the Christian perspective, for the seemingly exclusive claim of salvation that has been most often read into it. However, one must contend, following Schuon's argument, that if the Christian Incarnation is unique, it is because the Logos is one, as the Center of the cosmos, whereas by contrast, if the Hindu *avatāras* are

---

46. "The decisive argument is that the two orders, created and uncreated, have no common measure and that nothing simply natural—whatever its ultimate cause—can oppose the Presence of God." Schuon, *Form and Substance in the Religions*, 143.

many, it is because the cosmic reflections of the Logos are diverse, since the Light of the latter is refracted in different ways. Therefore, Schuon can write that "by naming himself 'the Way, the Truth and the Life,' in an absolute and therefore principial sense, Christ did not thereby intend in the least to limit the universal manifestation of the Word, but affirmed on the contrary his essential identity with the latter, the cosmic manifestation of which he lived himself in subjective mode."[47]

Here we find, once again, the distinction between the Logos and its cosmic reflection or manifestation, a distinction that highlights both continuity and discontinuity, suggesting thereby how the Man-God is, and is not, Divine. We also come across the suggestion that there is a distinction to be drawn between the objective and the subjective modes of the manifestations of the Logos. The latter allows for the possibility of a pure identification with the Logos. In other words, subjectively speaking, the Logos is lived by the Man-God as his true identity or selfhood, independently from the objective multiplicity of the reflections of the Logos, which do not enter into his spiritual and eschatological equation, as it were. We can thus understand how what appears to be on the surface a claim of exclusiveness—that is, one excluding the possibility of other "truths," "ways" and "lives"—is in fact none other than an inner and, therefore, subjective recognition and consequent self-proclamation. This two-fold aspect is also significant in that the objective manifestation of the Logos in the *avatāra* is transcendent in relation to human beings, whereas its subjective dimension is immanent, and gives access—through its door—to the Divine Self.[48] While the objective mode, being necessarily tied up with the formal realm, gives rise to exclusive worship and claims of absoluteness, the subjective mode opens the path to a universal recognition of the Logos beyond forms and, therefore, to a greater degree of inclusiveness. The fact that mystics, when placed in contexts conducive

---

47. Schuon, *The Transcendent Unity of Religions* (Wheaton, IL: Quest Books, 1984), 27–28.

48. "There is no difficulty in conceiving the transcendence and immanence of Beyond-Being and Being, but it may be asked what these two aspects mean on the plane of theophanic projection; the answer is that the Logos—the *Avatāra*—presents himself either objectively as 'Divine Image,' in which case he is transcendent in relation to the ordinary man, or subjectively as the Intellect, in which case he is immanent; he is then like the door towards the Divine Self, the immanent Divine Subject within our immortal substance." Schuon, *Roots of the Human Condition* (Bloomington, IN: World Wisdom, 2002), 72.

to such recognition, have been most susceptible to universalist forays, provides an evidence for this observation.

While the objective and subjective modes of manifestation of the Logos tend to take us in the direction of either formal exclusiveness or supra-formal inclusiveness, these tendencies cannot be taken as universal and necessary. To wit, the subjective dimension of the Logos can also give rise to formal and exclusivist bents, particularly in the climate of a personalist *bhakti*. This is to be observed, for example, in devotional forms of Christian mysticism as well as the path of bodhisattvic grace found in *Jōdo-Shinshū*. The focus of those spiritual ways is so intensely brought to bear on the saving manifestation of the Logos, as Jesus or Amida, that even the inward dimension of practice cannot but remain largely suffused with a sense of personal exclusivism, given the uniqueness of the Saviour or Redemptor.

As for the inclusive and supra-formal aspect of the Logos, which is always available—in principle—in the inner layers of the *avatāra*'s teachings and spiritual presence, it also manifests itself objectively, according to Schuon, in the feminine aspect of the avatāric Logos, in the form of the Virgin. This is one of the most important dimensions of Schuon's avatāric doctrine, and one that deserves, therefore, some further consideration. Schuon considers the Blessed Virgin as the Prophetess, the female *avatāra*, of the informal, or supra-formal, dimension of the Logos.[49] From a religious point of view, this consideration flows from the cross-confessional function of Mary at the intersection of the three Abrahamic traditions. As a "descendant of David," her ancestry makes her an "heiress" and "queen" in the Jewish tradition,[50] while her eminent position in Christianity and Islam gives her the status of "Prophetess of the whole Abrahamic lineage."[51] On a more inward plane, moreover, this privilege is akin to the aspects of contemplative inwardness and Divine Femininity, which she embodies. Spiritual inwardness frees one from

---

49. "In Hindu terminology, we would say that Mary is a feminine *Avatāra* of supreme degree, which is proven by her qualities of 'Bride of the Holy Spirit' and 'Co-Redemptress,' not to mention the epithet, all things considered problematic, 'Mother of God'; and as is also indicated by the practice of the *Ave Maria*, which pertains to the worship of the Logos, and consequently to the cosmic prolongation of the Divine Order." Schuon, *To Have a Center* (Bloomington, IN: World Wisdom, 2015), 95–96.

50. Schuon, *In the Face of the Absolute*, 69.

51. Schuon, *Form and Substance in the Religions*, 111.

the limitative aspects of outwardness, as already indicated in the context of our discussion on the subjective dimension of the avatāric Logos. Its relationship with Mary flows from the fact that both the Bible and the Qur'ān[52] emphasize her contemplative receptivity to the Word, and her identification with inner prayer. Femininity, for its part, also denotes essentiality, both metaphysically and in regard to the aforementioned emphasis on inwardness, as is developed more fully in a chapter of the present book. The latter refers to an ability to perceive the "divine intention" of religious practices beyond their formal literalness, while the former relates to the Divine Essence as the unfathomable Mystery of the Infinite. It is also connoted by the observation that "woman is 'mother,' therefore 'creative,' and moreover—or rather a priori—she manifests the Informal, the Infinite, the Mystery."[53] Moreover, this dimension of the Feminine, embodied by the female *avatāra*, is associated with the Divine dimension of Mercy that reconciles and unites. All these considerations lead Schuon to conclude that "femininity appears in this instance, given the spiritual and cosmic supereminence of the personage, as the inverted reflection of pure essentiality, which amounts to saying that, in her 'transcendent body' (*dharmakāya*), the Virgin is the virginal Mother of all the Prophets; she is identified with Divine Femininity or the Wisdom that 'was in the beginning.'"[54] The traditional centrality of Mary at the intersection of the various streams of Abrahamic inspiration, her *Nirmānakāya*, as it were, is a reflection of the transcendent Essence that lies beyond polarities, her *Dharmakāya*. This reflection is inverted, however, inasmuch as the traditional role of Mary appears outwardly subordinate to that of Jesus in Christianity and, in a different way, to that of Muhammad in Islam. The relationship between the avatāric function of the prophetess and her earthly destiny is, as is also the case *mutatis mutandis* with Fātima, discontinuous, providing thereby an allusion to the incommensurate, and in a way sacrificial, privilege of inner contemplation over outer action. If women are rarely, if ever, explicitly recognized as *avatāras*, it is precisely

---

52. "And Mary said, 'Behold the handmaid of the Lord; be it unto me according to thy word.'" Luke 1:38 (King James Version). "Whenever Zachariah went into the sanctuary where she was, he found that she had food. He said: O Mary! Whence cometh unto thee this (food). She answered: It is from Allah. Allah giveth without stint to whom He will" (*Qur'ān* 3:37, translated by Marmaduke Pickthall).

53. Schuon, *To Have a Center*, 95.

54. Schuon, *Logic and Transcendence*, 101.

on account of this paradoxical but profoundly meaningful privilege of spiritual inwardness. This is particularly so in the Abrahamic world, where the legal framework of religious traditions weighs in favor of the formal and therefore in a way masculine dimension of religion. This observation sheds light, *a contrario*, on the identification of the female *avatāra* with universal and inner Wisdom, both in a Christian and Buddhist context, by virtue of the association of *Sophia* and *Prajñāpāramitā* with the innermost layers of the human heart.[55] Ultimately, like the *guru*, the *avatāra* cannot but be identified with the core substance of the human being and consciousness, since he highlights and embodies the very entelechy of the human being as a potential or virtual "knower of God."

The identification of the *avatāra* with human inwardness can be envisaged, moreover, from two different vantage points that crystallize the onto-epistemological status of the Man-God. On the one hand, the *avatāra* amounts to an objectification of the Divine Intellect that flows through the vessels of the entire creation. One of the best illustrations of this principle lies in Christ's statement "I am the Way, the Truth and the Life."[56] While the inner reality of the Intellect may be out of reach—a priori—for most human beings, the *avatāra* provides an outer access to the latter, in a symbolic or actual manner. On the other hand, the *avatāra* can also be contemplated as a "subjectification" of creation. In other words, outer manifestation is both interiorized and synthetized by the Man-God. "The *Avatāra* is subjective in relation to creation in that he personifies it in a human subject";[57] as perfection of manifested Being, the Man-God provides the archetype of all creation. This is all the more so that

---

55. "Being the Throne of Wisdom—the 'Throne quickened by the Almighty,' according to a Byzantine hymn—Mary is *ipso facto* identified with the Divine Sophia, as is attested by the Marian interpretation of a given eulogy of Wisdom in the Bible. Mary could not have been the locus of the Incarnation did she not bear in her very nature the Wisdom to be incarnated." Schuon, *In the Face of the Absolute*, 68. "From the point of view of the human support or of the 'glorious body' one can recognize Prajñāpāramitā or Tārā in queen Māyā, mother of the historical Buddha: in the same way as the Buddha can be said to be a manifestation of the Absolute Buddha—the Ādi-Buddha or Vajradhara, or Mahāvairochana depending on the various terminologies—so does his august Mother manifest the complementary power of the universal Buddha, or the saving grace inherent in Nirvāna and emanating from It." Schuon, "Note on the Feminine Element in Mahāyāna," *Form and Substance in the Religions*, 135–36.
56. John 14:6.
57. *Stations of Wisdom*, 82.

the tradition emphasizes the centrality of the *avatāra* in the economy of salvation which, in turn, tends to leave little room for the "metaphysical transparency" of creation, to use one of Schuon's favorite expressions. It has been asserted, for instance, that the prototypical centrality of Christ has not uncommonly led, in a Christian context, to an impoverishment of the sense of the sacredness of nature. The aspect of synthesis of the Man-God in relation to nature cannot be severed, however, from his interiorizing function with regard to the latter. By "subjectivising" creation, the *avatāra* restores it back, so to speak, to its primordial state of "metaphysical transparency." The objectification of the Intellect, and the subjectification of creation that the *avatāra* crystallizes, "unites . . . in his person both the totality of the 'objective' macrocosm and the center of the 'subjective' microcosm."[58]

The subjective significance of the Man-God as reflection of the Logos and "sacramental Symbol" of one's deepest substance is brought to the fore with Schuon's gnostic interpretation of Christ as the "illuminating reality of the Christ-Intellect." Here, the Intellect must be understood as the principle of Divine intelligence and order that flows from above and innervates the entire creation. This reality can be envisaged on the metacosmic, macrocosmic, and microcosmic degrees of reality. By making use of the expression "illuminating reality," Schuon implies that the spiritual symbolism of the Light is best fitted to account for both the dimensions of continuity and discontinuity between the Divine source and human selfhood. It evokes the connection of the latter to its source through universal intelligence while highlighting its dependence upon the former. According to Schuon, "In the perspective of gnosis, Christ, 'Light of the world,' is the universal Intellect, as the Word is the 'Wisdom of the Father.' Christ is the Intellect of microcosms as well as that of the macrocosm; he is thus the Intellect in us as well as the Intellect in the Universe and *a fortiori* in God."[59] It is clear, in this perspective, that the Divine Intellect remains transcendent as source of all knowledge, being indistinguishable from God as Divine reality, while being prolonged or reflected in the world of creation as well as in the human soul. It is all too obvious that the very notion of "Christ-Intellect in us" amounts to a consideration of Christ as—essentially, necessarily, and inseparably—identified with the Intellect by contrast with a fallible

---

58. Schuon, *Stations of Wisdom*, 113.
59. Schuon, *Gnosis Divine Wisdom*, 103.

human reception of the Intellect. This distinction is analogous, in a sense, to the one drawn between human nature as such, which is intrinsically "intellectual," and its fallen manifestations that may not actualize this intellectual virtuality.

The interplay of transcendence and immanence that lies at the core of the concept of the *avatāra* can be further illuminated by considering a complex chapter of Schuon's *The Eye of the Heart*, entitled "*An-Nūr*," in which he analyzes the definitions and correlations of some of the principles of Islamic cosmology, namely, *al-'Arsh*, "the Throne," *ar-Rūh*, "the Spirit" and *an-Nūr*, "the Light." Schuon highlights the two-fold function of those principles, which are different aspects or modes of the Logos-Intellect, as "separating walls" and "transmitting openings."[60] This dual function is best illustrated by the Qur'ānic notion of *barzakh*, or isthmus, which plays an important role, in Sufi theosophy, as a principle of "continuous discontinuity" between higher and lower ontological realms. In other words, the *barzakh* is a zone of ontological separation that is, at the same time, a nexus of communication. Such a characterization can be applied to the Man-God, or the *avatāra*, inasmuch as it highlights the fundamentally paradoxical status of the latter. The *avatāra*, and Christ inasmuch as he mediates incommensurable realities in an avatāric way, may therefore be understood as a kind of human crystallization of transcendence within immanence. When Christ declares "only the Father is perfect," he affirms the aspect of separation, whereas, in Schuon's terms, the Spirit—not in the Christian sense of the Holy Ghost but more in the general sense of the mediating Logos-Intellect—"hides the incommensurability of *Allāh*" but it also "expresses and transmits it." It hides it by expressing it. Or, in other words, its veiling of transcendence is at the same time an unveiling. The *avatāra* proclaims that the Divine is radically transcendent by conveying it within immanence.

More specifically, the three Islamic concepts of *al-'Arsh*, *ar-Rūh*, and *an-Nūr* provide ways of understanding further the Divine roots of the mystery of the Man-God. *Ar-Rūh* corresponds, according to Schuon, to the creator of Hinduism, the god Brahma (and first figure of the *Trimūrti*), which is itself ontologically and functionally equivalent to the archangelic realm in the Abrahamic traditions. However, *ar-Rūh*, like other onto-cosmological realities, can be considered either as referring

---

60. This chapter is included in the English volume titled *Dimensions of Islam* (Lahore: Suheyl Academy, 1999), 102–120.

to a particular degree of existence or as a principle that flows through a diversity of ontological levels of reality. This means that it is, in Schuon's words, "an essential or 'vertical' reality which, as such, can be considered independently from the degrees of reality in which it affirms itself."[61] From this point of view, *ar-Rūh* can be defined, as Schuon puts it, as "the affirmation of Unity at all degrees of universal Existence."[62] This remark also applies to *an-Nūr*, which Schuon characterizes as the "Substance" or the "matter" of the Divine reality of which *ar-Rūh* is the center. This point is highlighted in the Qur'ān's assertion that God is "*nūr as-samawāti wa al-ard*" ("Light of Heaven and Earth"), which indicates how *an-Nūr* is the thread of Unity, as it were, that runs through all worlds. While the angels, who participate in this thread, are immediately subordinate to *ar-Rūh*, which is their archangelic summit, they are deprived of the Spirit's totality that informs the ontological center, and thus reflect only partial aspects of the Real. By contrast, mankind, in spite of its lower ontological position in relation to the angels, lies in the very continuity of the Spirit and, therefore, constitutes "the final reach of the vertical axis that is the locus of the Prophetic revelation."[63] This amounts to saying that mankind is potentially, or virtually, avatāric to the extent that it is directly situated under this vertical axis of Light that is *ar-Rūh*. The analogy, drawn by Schuon, between the number 1 and the Divine Spirit on the one hand, and the number 3 and the human being on the other hand,[64] allows one to further understand why and how the *avatāra* is both fully human and truly Divine, in the sense of being both the first odd number that reflects oneness, and oneness itself as the essential qualitative content of being an odd number. If it is possible, when considering the number 3, to comprehend both its being a number (therefore entailing multiplicity) and its being odd (therefore implying unity), it is also possible, analogously, to consider the *avatāra* as both human and Divine. What makes the Christian perspective on the *avatāra* unique is that it highlights oneness over multiplicity, therefore overwhelming the human with divinity, so to speak,

---

61. Schuon, *Dimensions of Islam* (Lahore: Suhayl Academy, 1999), 119.

62. Schuon, *Dimensions of Islam*.

63. Schuon, *Dimensions of Islam*, 120.

64. "One could symbolize *ar-Rūh* by the number 1, the Angels by the number 2, and Adam by the number 3; now, the number 2 is closer to Unity than the number 3, but the latter reflects unity in a integral and adequate, or not 'fragmentary,' way, as does the number 2." Schuon, *Dimensions of Islam*, 120.

while considering the Divine Center of Existence in its totality, and not in one or another of its archangelic aspects; hence, also, its incarnationist unicity and exclusiveness. Celestial multiplicity, in its angelic modes, is kept radically distinct from the Incarnation of the Word. While the gods of Hinduism, who are the ontological equivalent of the angels, do incarnate inasmuch as they express different facets of the One Spirit crystallized as the *Trimūrti*—the emphasis then being on the unity of the light of *Buddhi* in which they participate—angels do not and cannot incarnate in Christianity because it is their aspect of refraction, and therefore fragmentariness, in relation to Unity that defines them intrinsically.

As we have seen, for Schuon, the Incarnation can only involve the cosmic refraction of the Word and not the Word itself in its metacosmic divinity. What this means is that the Word is, and is not, identifiable with its incarnation. The ideational symbol of the refraction indicates both a continuity, since the same reality is propagated, and a discontinuity, since it implies a change of direction as it passes through different mediums or strata of being. Schuon's point, in essence, is that the metacosmic cannot incarnate in the cosmic, that it cannot be mixed with it. This is in keeping with the teachings, among others, of representatives of the Sufi tradition that espouse the "Unicity of existence" (*wahdat al-wujūd*), such as the Emir 'Abd al-Qādir al-Jazāirī, who conceived of the intermediary of the human theophany as the instrument for illuminating the various degrees of heavenly and creaturely realms without this entailing "union, mixture, or conjunction."[65]

This understanding of the Incarnation preserves the transcendence of the Divine while making it possible to grasp how the Divine and the human can become united within the realm of cosmic manifestation. This is a vision that allows one to make sense of both the Christian and Islamic points of view on the matter. From an Islamic perspective, the reason why the idea of incarnation is anathema is that it appears to jeopardize the transcendence and, therefore, the metaphysical integrity

---

65. The illumination of the various orders of reality is explained by the Emir 'Abd al-Qādir in a commentary on the *Verse of Light*, through an analogy with the niche, the glass, and the lamp, which are as many elements of the propagation of the Light without any contact or admixture: "By recourse to the symbol of the niche, the glass and the lamp, He lets us know that this illumination operates without union, mixture or conjunction through the intermediary of the Muhammadan Reality." *Spiritual Writings of Amir 'Abd al-Kader* (Albany: State University of New York Press, 1995), 116.

of the Divine Essence, of God as He is. Schuon's understanding of the incarnation does not blur the transcendence of the Essence inasmuch as it sees the Incarnation as concerning exclusively the lowest degree of Divine Reality, which is still Divine—from a human point of view—but already cosmic in its mode of manifestation. This is also compatible with the Christian view of the Trinity, at least inasmuch as this is understood either in terms of degrees of Reality, that is "vertically," or as relating to an already relative realm of Divine Reality, and not to the Essence as such. What this conception cannot accommodate, however, is the idea that the relationships between the Persons or Hypostases are the Essence in the sense in which normative Christian theology understands it. For Schuon, this metaphysically unsound absolutization of Divine Relativity results from an inability to recognize the degrees of Divine Reality and a failure to acknowledge the necessary relativity of the Trinity Itself.

With respect to Islam, Schuon's understanding might also be considered problematic from the point of view of exoteric religion and rational theology. This is so inasmuch as the latter tend to be exclusively focused on avoiding any kind of divinization of the relative, so to speak.[66] Thus, even though the common notion of the uncreatedness of the Qur'ān and the existence of traditional supports for a metacosmic view of the Prophet could, in principle, lend ways to notions of an encounter between the lowest range of the Divine and the highest degree of the cosmic, this possibility is only actualized within the exclusive confines of some schools of Sufi theosophy.[67]

---

66. An interesting point made by Guénon is that the *avatāra*'s place of birth is in the cave of the heart. Symbolically, the latter refers to the deepest part of the human being or manifestation, which is both void and fullness, or a void and an obscurity from which fullness and light radiates. The *avatāra* is born out of pure nothingness, or out of pure "ontological humility." The divine glory coincides with a type of human extinction which is also, in itself, a glorification of the human vessel.

67. "Reference was made above to the avatāric nature of Muhammad, to which it might be objected that for Islam or, what comes to the same thing, by his own conviction Muhammad was not and could not be an *Avatāra*. But this is not really the question because it is perfectly obvious that Islam is not Hinduism and notably excludes any idea of incarnation (*hulūl*); quite simply, and using Hindu terminology, which is the most direct or the least inadequate, we would reply that a certain Divine Aspect took on, under particular cyclic circumstances, a particular terrestrial form, something in full conformity with what the Envoy of *Allāh* testified as to his own nature, for he said: 'He who has seen me has seen God' (*Al-Haqq*, 'The Truth'); 'I am He and He is I, save that I am he who I am and He is He who He is'; 'I was a Prophet when Adam

At any rate, it is clear that Schuon's understanding of the Incarnation precludes conceiving it as a reality pertaining to either the Divine Essence or Divine Being. The avatāric incarnation only engages the direct cosmic reflection of the Center of Divine Existence that, being in the prolongation of the Divine Ray of Light that runs through all degrees of reality, cannot but be considered as Divine from a certain point of view. This is a metaphysical vision of the Incarnation that can be accounted for both from a Christian and an Islamic point of view, although once again not within the strictures of exoteric theology, and with obviously different emphases in each case. As we have seen, the Islamic "transcendentism" is fully compatible with Schuon's vision of the matter, since any incarnation of the Essence *qua* Essence is most fundamentally precluded. From a Christian aspect, the reality of the "Word made flesh" must allow for the union of the two natures, the Divine and the human, in a coexistence that implies neither a confusion of the two nor the exclusion of one or the other. Schuon's nuanced interpretation of the Trinity makes it possible to fathom how it can be real and operative on different metaphysical planes of Reality. It also allows for a consideration of the Incarnation that is both metaphysically grounded in the highest degrees of Reality, that is, incarnation as determination, as well as engaged with the cosmic stuff of existence, including the human physical envelope.

In conclusion, it is important to reassert that the metaphysically non-dualistic perspective of Schuonian gnosis means that differences cannot but be existentially mediated, and essentially annulled, through points of junction between the Absolute and the relative. In God, the root of these necessary mediations is none other than the relatively Absolute, the God of Relativity. The Divine Essence, by virtue of its infinitude, makes relativity ontologically and existentially possible, as it were. In the cosmos, this mediating function is that of the *avatāra*, who is like an emergence of the Absolute in the relative, thereby linking the two within the field of relativity. The necessity of the communication between the two realms calls for points of intersection, while their utter incommensurability makes the latter seemingly impossible. Even though traditions vastly differ in the ways they crystallize their respective theological understandings of those avatāric metaphysical points of junction and contact, they cannot avoid

---

was still between water and clay' (before the creation); 'I have been charged to fulfill my mission since the best of the ages of Adam (the origin of the world), from age to age down to the age in which I now am.'" *Understanding Islam*, 87–88.

involving—within the fold of their religious mythologies—the awe, mystery, and paradoxes of those luminous instances of "impossible necessity" and "unveiling veils."[68]

---

[68]. "Therefore the incommensurability between the two terms [God and humans] must in a certain way veil itself and does so precisely by way of those 'points of intersection' which we can call 'divine manifestations.'" Schuon, *Stations of Wisdom*, 69.

3

Upāya: Religion as Relatively Absolute

The debate about religious pluralism largely revolves around the nature of the Real (to use John Hick's term)[1] and the sacred means of spiritual realization that religious traditions consider essential in providing access to it. In order to simplify matters, one may consider the following two aspects. The first refers to religious movements and sensibilities that tend to conflate, at least practically speaking, the Divine—or the beatific state that is believed to flow from its grace—with the formal requirements of a religion deemed necessary to approach them. The term fundamentalism, for all its flaws and derogatory undertones, suggests an emphasis on literal, exclusive, and dogmatist representations and formal practices. By contrast, many contemporary religious paths are characterized by a dissociation—not to say schism—between the realm of the Ultimate and religious forms (whether theological or ritual) traditionally regarded as imperative conditions for the spiritual life. Thus, contemporary neo-spirituality is, by and large, informal and little concerned with, and indeed even often hostile to, traditional mediations. The advent of New Age spirituality is chiefly

---

1. "Such terms as the Real, the Ultimate, Ultimate Reality are commonly used to refer to this supposed *ne plus ultra*. None of them will suit everybody's linguistic taste. Accepting this I propose, arbitrarily, to speak of the Real, corresponding as it does in some degree to the Sanskrit *sat*, the Arabic *Al Haqq*, and the Chinese *zhen*. And I shall be distinguishing between, on the one hand, the Real *an sich*—to use an expression which avoids the neuter as well as the masculine and the feminine—and on the other hand the Real as variously thought and experienced within the different religious traditions." John Hick, *Disputed Questions in Theology and the Philosophy of Religion* (London: Palgrave Macmillan, 1997), 165.

characterized by a breaking away from traditional forms involved in the expression of religious belief and the practice of religion. In fact, current popular discourse tends to distinguish, and sometimes even oppose, religion and spirituality, conceiving the former as limiting or distorting the latter.

In a sense, the tension between religious forms or institutions and the spiritual realm of the inner life is not new. A consideration of religious traditions the world over reveals that they are inclined to absolutize the formal and institutional dimension of their worldviews. However, the highest reaches of spirituality have been prone to relativize religious concepts and practices in the name of love or spiritual knowledge. It must be stressed, though, that this freedom from forms did not proceed from any a priori rejection of traditional mediations, which is what we find in contemporary forms of new spirituality. Rūmī, to choose one of the most celebrated examples, extols the power of Love to transcend all dualities and all forms, while clearly situating himself within an Islamic universe of meaning.[2] In fact, the number of great mystics having dispensed with the formal aspects of their religion is negligible. In the very rare cases where this occurred, it was not a rejection of tradition as such but a spiritual "pull" to transcend its human limitations. It is only in our times, through the erosion of sacred forms and an increasingly individualistic view of religion, that spiritual aspirations find themselves often largely disconnected from traditional mediations.

Beyond the historical and contextual conditions within which it arises, this polarity points to a tension between a vision of religion as absolutely binding and a sense, especially among its esoteric adherents, of the rela-

---

2. ". . . . I am neither Christian nor Jew, neither Magian nor Muslim,
I am not from east or west, not from land or sea,
not from the shafts of nature nor from the spheres of the firmament,
not of the earth, not of water, not of air, not of fire.
I am not from the highest heaven, not from this world,
not from existence, not from being . . .
My place is placeless, my trace is traceless,
no body, no soul, I am from the soul of souls.
I have chased out duality, lived the two worlds as one.
One I seek, one I know, one I see, one I call.
He is the first, he is the last, he is the outer, he is the inner.
Beyond *He* and *He is* I know no other."

Jalāl-ad-Dīn Rūmī, *Music of a Distant Drum: Classical Arabic, Persian, Turkish, and Hebrew Poems*, edited and translated by Bernard Lewis (Princeton, NJ: Princeton University Press, 2001), 122.

tivity of its forms. It is this dual character of religion and its phenomena that we will explore further in this chapter, in light of its implications for religious pluralism. A theoretical framework conducive to this exploration is the notion of the *perennial religion*, as reformulated in our times by the current of thought referred to as the "perennialist" or traditionalist school. As the most prominent representative of the perennialist perspective, Schuon provides a clear definition and defense of tradition, understood as a comprehensive set of principles, practices, and phenomena rooted in Divine revelation and inspiration. However, the most significant aspect of his thought lies in a much less emphasized dimension of his perspective, that is, its penetrating discussion of the limitations, overemphases, and biases of the various religious traditions conceived as semi-divine and semi-human approximations of Reality. Schuon demonstrates the absolute dimension of religion while also highlighting—and this is no doubt one of his unique contributions—its relative aspects. This is directly connected to his emphasis on what he refers to as "quintessential esoterism," which he conceives as the gnostic core of all religious traditions. Only this essential core is absolute in the sense that it implies a disinterested objectivity with regard to "the nature of things." Notwithstanding this focus on the esoteric quintessence that underlies traditional messages, Schuon is also keen to highlight the need for strict adherence to traditional means of spiritual realization. It is this dual characteristic of Schuon's perspective that is relevant to the confrontation of contemporary religious pluralism with traditional religious identities. Our concern in this chapter will be to show how Schuon makes use of the Buddhist concept of *upāya* to articulate the absolute and relative dimensions of religions. This approach provides vital keys to a supra-confessional esoterism that averts the pitfalls of radical fundamentalist exclusivism and superficially pluralistic inclusivism, while being necessarily lived within—but not intellectually or spiritually limited by—the objective framework of a single spiritual tradition.

Upāya is, among Buddhist concepts, the one that is most frequently used in Schuon's lexicon. This is true to the extent that that there is no Sanskrit word, with the possible exceptions of *Ātman* and *Māyā*, which is more commonly found in Schuon's opus. This is significant in two ways. First, it suggests the affinity of Schuon's esoteric perspective with a prominent dimension of Buddhist thought—indeed with what may be regarded as a defining feature of its teachings—in contrast to other spiritual traditions. This dimension could be thought of as the "relativity of means" or the relativization of forms. This specifically Buddhist emphasis lies, for Schuon, in the fact that the Buddha's perspective was both subjective and methodical. This means that Buddhism begins with a subjective experience, namely that of suffering, and not with an objective metaphysical account of Reality. It also signifies that its focus is on the spiritual, methodical, and practical ways of overcoming suffering, rather than articulating a merely doctrinal response to the problem of *dukkha*. Interestingly, Schuon's perspective is not in itself aligned with these two chief characteristics of Buddhism but is firmly rooted in the principle of objectivity and sapiential metaphysics. As we will see, the Schuonian affinity with the Buddhist notion of *upāya* pertains to other imperatives.

In addition to the relatively absolute, which characterizes much of his work, Schuon's frequent use of *upāya* suggests how central its implications are in reaching a deeper understanding of what he refers to as esoterism or, rather, quintessential esoterism. For him, esoterism is a certain way of apprehending Reality and phenomena such as religion and the sacred, in that it focuses on the "nature of things," independently of any confessional partiality. The latter is inherent in a sentimental need for exclusiveness: "The average man is not disposed to grasp this character of Absoluteness [inherent to any religious tradition] if it is not suggested to him by the uniqueness of its expression."[3] This need is all the stronger in that the motivating sources of religious engagement are more emotional than intellectual, although Schuon is also quite clear that emotions can represent modes of objectivity and intellectual positions can be disguised passions or unconsciously determined by sentimental prejudices. To the extent that mankind as a whole—as a result of the metaphysical and epistemological rift or fall that religions depict in various mythological idioms—is largely determined by sub-intellectual factors, it is quite clear that religious forms are necessarily expedient and symbolic, which is to say partial but adequate, rather than exhaustive. The term adequate indicates a relationship with Reality that is founded less on the recognition of the Real as such, and the diversity of its aspects, than it is on mediating representations that function as mobilizing motivations of subjective engagement. In contrast to the subjective expediency that is part and parcel of what Schuon calls the "believing mentality," the esoteric perspective—to the extent that it is consistent with its own tendencies—can best be characterized by an unflinching adherence to the principle of objectivity. This is undoubtedly a key notion in Schuon's work that deserves further consideration.

---

3. Schuon, *From the Divine to the Human* (Bloomington, IN: World Wisdom, 2013), 114.

While the term objectivity tends to connote, in contemporary parlance, an attitude of cool and fair impartiality, this is far from being sufficient to account for its integral scope in Schuon's vocabulary. Objectivity could be best characterized as the predominance of the objective pole over a subjective one.[4] It therefore runs counter to ways of thinking that promote either the exclusive primacy of subjectivity—which essentially amounts to relativism—or the enlisting of subjective experiences, feelings, and passions to such an extent as to blur one's capacity to contemplate reality with utter disinterestedness. What this means, in fact, is that esoterism is an intellective perspective and not a religious outlook, at least to the extent that religion necessarily involves a predominance of sentimental factors that are, unavoidably, sources of bias and a lack of imagination. As Schuon observes: "A climate of religious belief calls for emotivity, and emotivity is evidently opposed to perfect objectivity, at least when it exceeds its rights."[5] The issue is not the presence of emotions and sentiments. All human beings are made of sentiments on the psychic level. The issue is the role they play in the identification with the truth. The esoteric outlook begins with intellectual evidence whereas the exoteric point of view is intrinsically sentimental and experiential, or volitive. This is to say that the exoteric path, parallel in that to bhaktic ways, is often triggered by an emotional, aesthetic, existential, response to a human manifestation of the Absolute. The *bhakta* is convinced by Christ or by the Buddha, rather than by metaphysical principles themselves. This being said, it must be admitted that there can exist instances of identification with esoteric and metaphysical truths on the basis of sentiments, and even some sort of sentimentalism. However, in such cases the sentimentalist priority tends to manifest itself through abusive biases, like a disdaining belittling of formal religions, for instance, or a rejection of other expressions of esoterism. Thus, any doctrine, including esoteric teachings, can give rise to some kind of sentimental identification. In fact, any intellectual perception may be accompanied by an emotional concomitance. The realization of a mathematical truth, for

---

4. For Schuon, this predominance of the objective, both in terms of content and style, is the chief characteristic of traditional and ancient mankind, by contrast with modern subjectivism: "The ancient and medieval man was 'objective' in the sense that his mind was still strongly determined by the element 'object,' on the plane of ideas as well as on that of sensory things." Schuon, *Light on the Ancient Worlds* (Bloomington, IN: World Wisdom, 2006), 19.

5. Schuon, *In the Face of the Absolute* (Bloonmington, IN: World Wisdom, 2014), 17.

instance, can produce a feeling of joyful satisfaction, and it may even be accompanied by a form of emotional attachment to the truth; but this does not alter in any way the objectivity of the intellectual perception, nor does it imply that any a priori sentimental bias has determined, or entered into, the inner phenomenon of the recognition of the truth. That an esoteric knowledge may entail emotional concomitances does not mean that it proceeds from sentiments. A religious faith, by contrast, cannot but involve a sentimental and exclusivist identification with its formal object, be it in a subtle and subconscious way, without which it could not be fully effective. This sentimental bias manifests, among other traits, by a lack of imagination that makes it impossible, or very difficult, for a believer to recognize truth, beauty, and virtues in other religious climates, or at least to draw from them some acknowledgment of the validity of the other religion. Obviously, sentimental partiality can even intrude into the esoteric domain, humans being human, but this possibility is only adventitious, not inherent in esoterism, or constitutive of it. Schuon has even asserted, in this connection, that one may adhere to esoteric teachings for wrong reasons, and that there is an esoterism de jure, and another one de facto.

Notwithstanding, the adjective intellectual refers to the *Intellect*, which is taken to be the organ that enables us to know truth in the Scholastic sense of an *adaequatio rei et intellectus*. For Schuon, as with Platonic and Scholastic traditions, the Intellect in the human being knows—*in potentia*—everything that is to be known. It is the divine principle of all knowledge because it is indeed adequate to all knowable objects. It is this epistemic proportionality of the Intellect to all objects of knowledge—from metaphysical principles to relative beings—that makes it the very principle of objectivity; in other words, it can know all things in principle because it is, in and of itself, unhampered by subjectivist and contextual limitations that would undermine an adequate cognition of realities. Thus, the Intellect, when fully actualized, has been compared to a mirror that reflects the reality of all things placed before it.[6] It must be kept in mind, however, that the actualization of the Intellect is, in religious contexts, largely dependent upon limitations of aspects and points of view. An actualization of the Intellect allowing for a full recognition of the "transcendent unity of religions" is a rare occurrence indeed, one

---

6. Cf., for instance, Titus Burckhardt, *Mirror of the Intellect* (Albany: State University of New York Press, 1987).

that requires subjective and objective conditions that are hardly met in most religious ambiences.

For Schuon, a religion primarily comprises a certain sensibility nourished by a particular outlook on the Real; that is to say, a more or less exclusive concentration on some of its aspects at the expense of others. The partiality and sentimentality that are inherent in the religious perspective do converge with some important insights into *upāya* that Schuon develops beyond their strictly Buddhist implications. This universalizing treatment of *upāya* appears in the way the term is translated by Schuon—in particular, the manner in which he applies it to religious phenomena.

Schuon renders the concept of *upāya* in a variety of ways. In most scholarly translations, the term is understood as "provisional" or "expedient" means, which approximates another frequently used rendition, "skillful means" or "skill-in-means." Schuon himself offers the image of a "saving mirage" and the term "saving stratagem."[7] There are a few points to note in relation to this terminology. First of all, Schuon sometimes stresses the non-ultimacy, therefore relative incompleteness, of the *upāya* while emphasizing, at other times, its dimension of spiritual efficacy. However, even the adjective expedient, which suggests the aspect of effectiveness, also connotes imperfection, since expediency is ordinarily involved at the expense of some element of truth, whether intellectual or moral. As for provisional, it echoes the classical Buddhist view of the conventional nature of the *upāya* in contrast to the ultimate truth; that is, the fundamental distinction between *paramārtha-satya* and *samvriti-satya*. In other words, the *upāya* remains true, as does the conventional perspective, only as long as the ultimate reality has not been recognized. Hence its provisional aspect, like the raft that is no longer needed once the other shore has been reached. As for Schuon's more characteristic references to "saving mirages" and "saving stratagems," these highlight both the epistemological limits and the divine intentionality of the *upāya*. The first expression allows Schuon to point out that mankind is inherently part of

---

7. "To offer images to souls at their own level and to transmute these souls without their being aware of it is the very definition of *upāya*, the 'provisional means' or 'saving mirage' of Buddhism." Schuon, *Sufism: Veil and Quintessence* (Bloomington, IN: World Wisdom, 2006), 10. "Let us not lose sight of the fact that on the religious plane, hyperbole veils an intention that in the end is merciful; it is then a question of *upāya*, of a 'saving stratagem.'" *The Eye of the Heart* (Bloomington, IN: World Wisdom, 1997), 138.

the relative order—or *Māyā*—and, therefore, can only respond a priori to realities that also partake in *Māyā*. By contrast, the term stratagem appears to echo the notion of a scheme or ruse of the Absolute, which is to be found—in varying degrees—in philosophical and religious traditions as radically diverse as Hegel's philosophy of history and the Qur'ān.[8] At any rate, the use of this term by Schuon points to the eschatological and soteriological finality of the *upāya*, while its ambiguous connotations, not unlike those of ruse and scheme in other contexts, clearly signal that the formal strategy of salvation that it entails lies beyond a strict consideration of truth and morality per se. It is amoral, although certainly not immoral, since its goal is none other than the essence of morality. The domain of "expedient truths" may appear, in that sense, as reflecting the moral ambiguities inherent in the inexhaustible potential of All-Possibility.

Beyond matters of terminology and translation, the originality—in the sense of an inspiration flowing from the original intent of the concept—of Schuon's use of *upāya* lies in its application to historical religions. In fact, his use of *upāya* to refer to religious forms, as in the expressions "Christian *upāya*"[9] or "Islamic *upāya*," constitutes an important key to his understanding of religions. Indeed, a firm grasp of this point reveals, at least on a theoretical level, the distinction between the "quintessentially esoteric" dimension of Schuon's perspective and the traditionalist recognition of Schuon's contribution. In other words, while Schuon is indeed a traditionalist in the sense of being a philosopher who highlights the metaphysical validity, transmuting beauty and spiritual necessity of religious traditions, he is also—first and foremost—an esoterist who is keenly aware of the limitations of religions as providential salvific systems. For him, it is quite clear that the latter necessarily fall short, from the outset and not simply out of decay or corruption, of providing a total and disinterested conception of Reality, to the extent that this is possible given the unbridgeable gap between the Real and its doctrinal expressions. Moreover,

---

8. "And they (the disbelievers) schemed, and *Allāh* schemed (against them): and *Allāh* is the best of schemers" (3:54). Translated by Marmaduke Pickthall.

9. "To say that the Christian *upāya* requires the intervention of an *Avatāra*, of a 'man-God,' amounts to saying that it is founded, doctrinally and emotionally, not on the Divine Nature as such—as is Islam, for example—but on the Divine Manifestation in the world." Schuon, *Christianity-Islam: Perspectives on Esoteric Ecumenism* (Bloomington, IN: World Wisdom, 2008), 67. "Through the average man, necessarily 'horizontal' in certain respects, the Islamic *upāya* seeks to reach every man as such." Schuon, *Sufism: Veil and Quintessence*, 77.

this highlights a delineation between an esoterism that is predicated upon religious forms and one—clearly favored by Schuon—whose foundations are exclusively metaphysical and, therefore, supra-confessional. While Schuon's intention, *a contrario*, in treating the concept of *upāya* esoterically is unambiguous, it is also true that he uses this Buddhist term with various shades of meaning which helps to delineate more clearly his assessment of religious phenomena.

In one way, Schuon's view of *upāya* is linked to the distinction between doctrine and method. This is clear in the following passage, where he alludes to the classical Buddhist distinction between *upāya* and *prajñā*, or wisdom, in the context of a general phenomenology of religion: "The fundamental intention of every religion or wisdom is the following: first, discernment between the real and the unreal, and then concentration upon the real. One could also render this intention otherwise: truth and the way, *prajñā* and *upāya*, doctrine and its corresponding method."[10] Here, *upāya* refers to the spiritual way as embodied in various traditional paths; that is, the diversity of spiritual approaches, contemplative methods, rites, moral codes and religious practices that make it possible to realize the Ultimate. In fact, this distinction is in the spirit of the Buddhist tradition, which considers *upāya* as eminently *practical*.[11] In this sense, *upāya* refers

---

10. Cf. "No Activity without Truth" in *The Sword of Gnosis*, edited by Jacob Needleman (New York: Penguin, 1974).

11. The story of Kisa Gotami and the mustard seed is considered by the tradition to be a paradigm of the *upāya*: "Kisa Gotami had an only son, and he died. In her grief she carried the dead child to all her neighbors, asking them for medicine. . . . At length Kisa Gotami met a man who replied to her request: 'I cannot give thee medicine for thy child, but I know a physician who can. . . .' Go to Sakyamuni, the Buddha. Kisa Gotami repaired to the Buddha and cried: 'Lord and Master, give me the medicine that will cure my boy. The Buddha answered: 'I want a handful of mustard-seed. . . . The mustard-seed must be taken from a house where no one has lost a child, husband, parent, or friend. Poor Kisa Gotami now went from house to house . . . and there was no house but some beloved one had died in it. Kisa Gotami became weary and hopeless, and sat down at the wayside, watching the lights of the city, as they flickered up and were extinguished again. At last the darkness of the night reigned everywhere. And she considered the fate of men, that their lives flicker up and are extinguished. And she thought to herself: 'How selfish am I in my grief! Death is common to all; yet in this valley of desolation there is a path that leads him to immortality who has surrendered all selfishness. . . . Returning to the Buddha, she took refuge in him and found comfort in the Dharma, which is a balm that will soothe all the pains of our troubled hearts." Paul Carus, *The Gospel of Buddha According to Old Records* (Chicago: Open Court, 2004), 210.

to the methodical dimension of religion; in other words, to everything that pertains to the means of liberation, in contrast to the theoretical aspects of doctrine. This Buddhist emphasis on the operative dimension of religion leads to a certain wariness, even suspicion, with respect to rigid doctrinal formulations. The so-called "unanswered questions" (*avyākata*), about which the Buddha intentionally chose to remain silent, epitomize the Buddhist relativization of metaphysical and cosmological doctrines on the basis of giving primacy to existential realization and direct metaphysical cognition. These questions pertain to the temporal and spatial status of the world and, most importantly, to the status of a person who has attained Buddhahood after death. The reason for the Buddha's reticence is that these questions have no real object in the state of *Nirvāna*; any meaning they may have in our relative world of forms becomes consumed in the state of realization.[12] In other words, the Buddha was inclined to shun metaphysical and cosmological speculation in his teachings precisely to the extent that their arising presupposed a distorted perspective lying outside the orbit of *Nirvāna*. This helps us to understand his preferred focus on the *means* for attaining Buddhahood rather than on the doctrinal content associated with such an experience.

Accordingly, it is clearly apparent that, in Buddhism, the doctrine itself may also function as a methodical means of spiritual realization. There are, indeed, individuals for whom doctrinal concepts have an instrumental value in the quest for enlightenment. The very fact that Buddhism, not unlike other traditions, has spawned a number of highly sophisticated metaphysical teachings does indicate that the latter may well have a central role to play in the Buddha's way. This way of understanding the function of metaphysics is akin to the Neo-Platonic philosophical path, which Pierre Hadot characterized as a set of spiritual exercises[13] leading to self-transformation as it is to the Advaitin practice of doctrinal

---

12. "The Buddha introduces the well-known simile of fire, which contributes to the title of the discourse. Just like fire, which cannot be said to travel to any direction after the material that feeds it is exhausted, the Buddha has quit feeding the human fire of the aggregates and thus, after he passes away, there is no way by which he can be said to be reborn (*upapajjati*) / not-reborn / both / neither. For him the aggregates are 'forsaken, their root severed, made like an uprooted palm-tree, eradicated with no future arising.'" Eviatar Shulman, *Rethinking the Buddha: Early Buddhist Philosophy as Meditative Perception* (Cambridge: Cambridge University Press, 2014), 68.

13. Cf. Pierre Hadot, *Philosophy as a Way of Life: Spiritual Exercises from Socrates to Foucault* (New York: Wiley, 1995).

meditation.[14] Taking into account this broader conception of metaphysics, one sees how it can be viewed as a variety of *upāya*.

The wider comprehension of the notion of *upāya* to which we have just referred is not unconnected to Schuon's increasing use of the term *upāya*—as his opus unfolded, and particularly in his later works—to refer to religion as a whole, that is both *qua* doctrine and *qua* method. In such cases, Schuon's intention is to stress the expedient character of religious forms, in contrast to the objective apprehension of metaphysical realities that he sees as the prerogative of esoterism. The use of the term "objective" may need some further consideration, as it is commonly considered, in a modern context, that such objectivity is impossible. Objectivity does not mean here the absence of any subjective element, which would be impossible and absurd; it means that the determining pole of the subject is the object. In other words, schematically speaking, the esoterist is not a priori seeking an answer to the question "What saves me?" but is rather in search of a response to the interrogation "What is real?" or "What is Reality?" There are obviously degrees in this distinction, which cannot be absolute for, in the relative field, there is no object without a subject and no subject without an object. Moreover, it is true that esoteric teachings are themselves, in a way, *upāyas*, since any doctrine or method can be considered as a "saving means." However, what differentiates them from exoteric teachings is that they entail a measure of awareness of their own nature of *upāyas*. Furthermore, their "conventional" character stems from the provisional nature of language in general, rather than as a result of the limitations of a particular symbolic appropriation of Reality. This amounts to saying that they are, as it were, transparent *upāyas*, therefore undoing themselves, so to speak, for the sake of *prajña*.

Now, to go back to the specifically religious *upāya*, it must be noted that its expedient character is not necessarily confined to the methodical dimension, since it also entails the limitations of the respective doctrinal outlooks regarding Reality. Nevertheless, the inclusion of theological teachings, within the fold of "*upāyic* means," is intimately connected to the salvific efficacy of the former. Thus, confessional theology may be

---

14. "Verily, my dear Maitreyi, it is the Self that should be realized—should be heard of, reflected on, and meditated upon. By the realization of the Self, my dear—through hearing, reflection, and meditation—all this is known." Bṛhad-Āraṇyaka-Upaniṣad, 2, iv, 5. Swami Satchidanandendra Saraswati, *The Method of the Vedanta: A Critical Account of the Advaita Tradition* (Delhi: Motilal Banarsidass, 1997), 251.

understood as expedient metaphysics that aims at garnering spiritual and moral resources to stimulate religious sincerity and fervor.

In light of the above, one may contrast two ways of envisaging religions or, more exactly, religious doctrines. One is akin to *upāya* while the other pertains to *prajñā*. From the point of view of *prajña*—what Schuon would call the *Sophia Perennis*—it is the intrinsic conformity of the teachings to Reality, or the "nature of things," that is the principal concern and emphasis. In fact, this is what Schuon considers to be the "absolute" content of religions. For him, each and every tradition provides its followers with a kernel through, and by, which the essential truth is conveyed and with which it may be identified. This can be illustrated with one of Schuon's recurrent symbols. When a given religion is symbolized by the geometric figure of a square, then its differences from, say, a triangle or a rectangle are accidental by comparison with the fact that all three figures are, fundamentally, modalities of space. The essential content of a square is space, while the latter obviously escapes any geometric confinement. From this point of view, which is that of esoterism, the fact that the square is not the circle is effectively much less important than its being a configuration within space. Moreover, it is quite obvious that space itself, in essence, is undefinable as such in geometric terms. By contrast, *upāya*—in its aspect of limitation—corresponds to a particular geometric form (a square for instance), and it is precisely in this respect that the constraints of a square make it incapable of being identified with space as such. Thus, the instrumental and expedient dimension of religion is the very source, as well as the symptom, of its limitations. This is so to the extent that the primary aspect of any given religious perspective is not an accurate representation of the Ultimate—to the extent that it is possible for limitations to convey this—but a means to effectively ensure acceptance and assimilation on the part of the human collectivity for which it is intended.

This being the case, an important question that arises is whether the concept of *upāya* must be restricted to religions in their dogmatic aspect or be further extended to their sacramental and theurgic, or spiritually transformative, means. This distinction is predicated on the observation that all dogmas crystallize a particular outlook on Reality, or a number of key principles that define a religious perspective, whereas the *sacramental* refers, in this context, to the ritual practices and religious injunctions that facilitate an inner transformation conducive to salvation or emancipation. In his essay "Alternations in Semitic Monotheism," Schuon contends that both "dogmatic premises and sacramental means" have a relative, and not absolute, scope. However, it is important to note that this is so "insofar as the characteristics of the particular form or *upāya* are emphasized."[15] In other words, what makes a religion relative is not so much its defining characteristics as its exclusive emphasis, or overemphasis, on those characteristics. This implies, quite evidently, the possibility of two different accentuations: one stressing the universal and another emphasizing the particular. Although there is obviously no absolute line of demarcation between these two approaches, it is quite clear that the restrictive character of *upāya* is all the more relevant when considered from the point of view of the particular. Conversely, a consideration of the "dogmas and sacramental means" in which the characteristics of the particular forms as such are not emphasized, but rather contemplated as symbolic supports of spiritual awakening, is more likely to focus on the universal—and therefore "absolute"—content of the religion. This is, needless to say, a point that most religious believers would deny or challenge, precisely because their beliefs are essentially defined and motivated, or let us say energized, by that which in their religion is *significantly* and *decisively* different to other faiths. In other words, for the immense majority of the faithful, it is precisely the particular that is clothed with absoluteness, de facto if not de jure. Moreover, the distinction between particularizing and universalizing tendencies parallels that between a literal meaning that is exclusive, and a symbolic one that is virtually or actually inclusive, by virtue of the polysemic and quasi-inexhaustible nature of a religious symbol.

While it is probably not too difficult to see how a particular dogma could be envisaged in a way that would not be primarily exclusive— inasmuch as its intellectual scope could be expanded beyond the literal meaning of a creed and therefore in a way that opens onto its universal metaphysical horizon—it is perhaps more challenging to envisage how

---

15. "First, each religion has a specific character that is destined to lay claim to a given set of mental tendencies and develop what is best in them; second, the dogmatic premises and sacramental means of each religion—insofar as the characteristics of the particular form or *upāya* are emphasized—have a relative and not an absolute significance at the level of their literal interpretation, even though they reflect in their own way absolute, and not relative, realities. Dogmas and sacraments are keys to the divine Reality, but they do not represent it in an exclusive and irreplaceable fashion." Schuon, *Christianity/Islam: Visions of Esoteric Ecumenism* (Bloomington, IN: World Wisdom, 2008), 65.

it could be so for sacramental means since the latter are, by definition, practically exclusive of other ways. Aside from marginal, and most often problematic, attempts at combining various spiritual elements in some contemporary spiritual trends (e.g., "Christian Zen" or "Islamic Yoga"), one practice normally excludes another. For instance, can we consider the Eucharist, the person of Christ, the Qur'ān, or even practices such as invoking a Divine Name, as *upāyas*? In the aforementioned essay, Schuon seems to place in the category of *upāya* both dogmas and sacraments seeing them as "keys to the Divine Reality." However, he is also careful to note that these "do not represent it [the Divine Reality] in an exclusive and irreplaceable fashion"; rather, their aspect of *upāya* is considered "relative" to the extent that it is "emphasized," at least inordinately so.

When considering dogmas and sacramental means, it is important to observe that the first are conceptual while the second are essentially ritual in nature. This distinction largely corresponds to Schuon's soteriological categories of Truth and Presence.[16] This amounts to saying that dogmas relate to Reality indirectly, or as its theological reflections, so to speak. By contrast, sacraments relate to Reality directly or, more specifically, by participation in the Platonic sense of partaking (*methexis*) in the supreme ontological reality. The sacramental dimension amounts, in that sense, to a prolongation of the *nirvānic*. Thus, the concept of *upāya* assumes a different meaning depending on whether it is applied to dogmatic or sacramental realities. Schuon uses the expressions "saving mirage" and "saving stratagem" to suggest both the spiritual efficacy of the *upāya* as well as its provisional nature in face of the Absolute as such; therefore, its comparative lack of reality in an ultimate sense. Considered in this light, it is clear that the saving dimension is stronger with respect to the sacramental order than it is to dogma; and it is no less clear that the aspect of "mirage" or "stratagem" is more relevant to the dogmatic realm. This is so because a dogma is like a doctrinal mapping out of Reality, whereas a sacrament is a transformative manifestation of that same Reality. In Schuon's parlance, this could be expressed by stating that doctrinal dogma lies symbolically on the circumference of a concentric circle that revolves around the Real, as it were, whereas the sacramental is situated on a ray that emanates from, and returns to, the Real. If there

---

16. "The saving manifestation of the Absolute is either Truth or Presence, but it is not one or the other in an exclusive fashion, for as Truth It comprises Presence, and as Presence It comprises Truth." Schuon, *Form and Substance in the Religions*, 1.

is also an aspect of mirage or even stratagem in the sacrament, it is only to the extent that it does not exhaust the nature of Reality and cannot therefore be considered as the Real itself. While a dogma ceases being an *upāya* when it is fully grasped in its universal and metaphysical roots, a sacrament is lived as an *upāya* when its dependence on the Real—which manifests in its being effectively theurgic in the economy of a given tradition—becomes a constricting force as its limitations are identified with the Real. In other words, a dogmatic *upāya* is no longer an *upāya* by virtue of a subjective and intellective assimilation of its essence, while sacramental means function as *upāya* to the extent that they impose their exclusiveness on apprehensions of the Absolute.

We now have sufficient context for understanding why and how Schuon presents the notion of *upāya* from two different perspectives. On the one hand, an *upāya* proceeds from the Divine, and is therefore a mercy, that is a saving dispensation that flows from the fundamentally inclusive nature of the Infinite. On the other hand, Schuon also sees *upāyas* as being "tolerated" by God as a concession to human limitations. In a sense, these perspectives correspond to two sides of the same reality, since the matter here is one of an interplay between the finite and the Infinite. Nevertheless, the aspect of Divine toleration is more relevant to what Schuon refers to as theological traditions in contrast to metaphysical perspectives. The first category refers to religions that envisage, primarily or exclusively, the Divine as Supreme Being and, therefore, give particular attention to the relationship between the human self and God. Such is the case, typically, in the Abrahamic religions. The second category encompasses metaphysics and mystical knowledge that are largely centered on what Schuon refers to as Beyond-Being, that is, the Divine Essence in its unconditioned and non-dual Selfhood. Given their exclusive focus on the relationship between Divine Being and the individual, the former have a more functional, rather than ultimate, apprehension of *upāyas*, while claiming, quite understandably, ultimacy for their own traditional perspective as a matter of principle and soteriological efficacy. By contrast, the latter are dedicated to the metaphysical "nature of things" or Reality in its essence. This means, first of all, that Reality is considered in this case independently of any relationship with mankind or with relativity in general. There is little doubt, though, that to the extent metaphysics manifests itself within the context of a religious message—therefore in a formal garb inherently limited—it must reflect, objectively, a measure of *upāya*. At any rate, that which is actively a manifestation of Divine Compassion is also passively an adaptation to human limitations. The *upāya* comes from above but is soteriologically determined by human factors below. To sum up, religion is absolute because, or to the extent that, it comes from God; but it assumes an aspect of relativity insofar as it must respond to human needs, that are, of necessity, limited and particular. In that sense, every religion is both divine and human, not only in terms of its historical foundations, but also in its revelatory or paradigmatic substance. A purely divine formless religion would be, indeed, a contradiction in terms.

According to this perspective, what is the status of "relatively absolute" realities such as Christ or the Qur'ān? Let us note, first of all, that Schuon never makes use of the term *upāya* to refer to such central manifestations, which he explicitly identifies with the Divine Logos. This is in keeping with the fact that the Buddha himself—or Buddhas in general—are not traditionally considered as being *upāyas*. This is because Buddhas, who embody *prajña*, are seen as sources of *upāya*, not examples thereof. A Buddha dispenses these "saving stratagems" commensurate with the aptitude and temperament of his audience. This a Buddha can do precisely by virtue of his identification with *prajña* as the goal and source of all *upāyas*. Analogously, Christ and the Qur'ān are, in their respective traditions, central and necessary vehicles of the Real, as it were, which makes it impossible, from within religious traditions that are essentially dualistic, to relativize the status of their theophany as skillful means.

On the other hand, it is readily apparent that numerous Buddhist texts teach the ultimate emptiness of all Buddhas, thus opening the way to a reduction of the latter to the status of conventional means; something that would be unthinkable in any specifically religious perspective as it would undermine the very foundations of its sacred dispensation. Typically iconoclastic Buddhist expressions, to this effect, are to be found, for instance, in some of Nāgārjuna's classic treatises as well as in the teachings of many Zen masters.[17] These are a natural outflow from the distinction between ultimate and conventional truths, since reliance on the latter rests on a mistaken perception regarding the true nature of phenomena. In a

---

17. "Followers of the Way, there is no Buddha to be gained, and the Three Vehicles, the five natures, the teachings of the perfect and immediate enlightenment are all simply medicines to cure diseases of the moment. None have any true reality. Even if they had, they would still all be mere shams, placards proclaiming superficial matters, so many words lined up, pronouncements of such kind." Burton Watson, *The Zen Teachings of Master Lin-chi* (Boston: Shambhala Publications, 1993), 76.

sense, these negations amount to rejecting the reification of the Buddha as a conventional phenomenon, although this is not, of course, to deny its reality as a perfect manifestation of the Buddha-nature. It is quite remarkable that a spiritual tradition can be so consistent in its premises as to call into question the ontological status of its very founder. There is, it would appear, no equivalent position in other traditions (other than a very few exceptions restricted to esoteric schools). One could mention, in this regard, the Advaitin statement according to which the domain of *Māyā*, or the principle of relativity and nescience, ranges from "the god Brahma to a blade of grass." It is beyond doubt, however, that most religious perspectives would be reluctant, to say the least, to implicate the God they consider as Creator of all things within the domain of appearance or illusion.

That being said, it seems difficult to deny that Buddhism is, by and large, the tradition most intent on stressing the relativity of its salvific means. The Zen maxim "If you meet the Buddha, kill him!" suggests that, at least from a certain methodical stance, the Buddha himself could be considered as an *upāya*. This conclusion flows from the fact that the Buddha's teachings focus on the realization of a state of consciousness, and not on an ontological principle as such, hence an emphasis on the pedagogical means of attaining this state of consciousness, which renders everything else instrumental. Thus, Buddhism as a whole, comprising the Four Noble Truths and the Eightfold Path, is nothing else—from its own point of view—than an *upāya*. This is not only because of its practical emphasis—as suggested by the allegory of the raft that takes one to the Other Shore before being abandoned, but also because of its being centered, metaphysically speaking, on a non-objectified, non-anthropomorphic, non-personal, and non-relatable reality that cannot be usurped by any religious form. Nāgārjuna's statement that there "has never been ever any Dharma taught"[18] reinforces this attitude while highlighting the non-formal and non-substantial character of Nirvānic reality, making it thus void in the sense of being untainted by all relative phenomenal defilements that appear on it as dust on a mirror.

This uncompromising approach to *upāya* has led some non-Buddhist commentators to conclude that it confirms the delusory character of

---

18. "No Dharma was taught by the Buddha at any time, in any place, to any person." *Mūlamadhyamakakārikā*, 25.24, in *Ocean of Reasoning: A Great Commentary on Nāgārjuna's Mūlamadhyamakakārikā*, translated by Geshe Ngawang Samten and Jay L. Garfield (Oxford: Oxford University Press, 2006), 532.

Buddhist wisdom. In his essay "Originality of Buddhism,"[19] Schuon challenges Father De Lubac's polemics against Pure Land Buddhism by showing that it fails to take into account the degrees of reality implied by the notion of *upāya*. To say that the paradise of Amida Buddha is illusory, compared to *Nirvāna*, does not in the least invalidate the reality of this paradise at a conventional level which is, precisely, that on which the very reality of its enjoyment is situated. Schuon argues that the view of *upāya* as mere illusion is a misapprehension typical of many Western critics who forget that it is, in fact, a subtle and multilayered concept not easily dispensed with through unbalanced theological simplifications. When De Lubac argues, for example, that the Buddhist view of paradises as *upāya* betrays the fundamentally deluded character of Pure Land faith, he fails to take into account that any degree of existence, including our terrestrial one, can be taken as less real from a higher point of view and is, therefore, illusory in a fundamental sense, that is, from the vantage point of Enlightened Consciousness. This distinction is directly connected to Schuon's frequent discernment between the Self, or Spirit—the transpersonal and universal Subject—and the empirical self immersed in the current of forms.[20] Only a perspective grounded in the former is capable of true spiritual perception and of piercing the veil of existential illusion. These reflections indicate the need for greater attention, subtlety, and discrimination when dealing with Eastern concepts that qualify the reality of conditioned phenomena. Schuon sees much of Western theology as being unable—given its largely rational, discursive, and reductionist disposition—to fully fathom the metaphysical implications inherent in the degrees of reality.

As we find in the Advaitin doctrine of *Māyā*, but in a more methodical than doctrinal manner, *upāyas* can be said to possess a provisional nature. This amounts to saying that they represent conventional truth (*saṃvṛti-satya*) or that which is ontologically metaphorical. The distinction between conventional and ultimate can be considered either from the point of view of expression only, as we find in the Pāli Canon, or as pertaining to Reality and its realization. In the Pāli canon, conventional refers to an indirect way of expressing the truth, as in the use of metaphors, as

---

19. Schuon, *Treasures of Buddhism* (Bloomington, IN: World Wisdom, 1993), 25.

20. "This brings us back to the question—which we have discussed in other writings—of the two spiritual subjectivities, one being that of the empirical individual, who cannot sincerely desire a 'union' beyond Paradise, and the other, that of the spirit, which tends towards its own source and remains independent of every consideration of individual interest." Schuon, *Sufism: Veil and Quintessence*, 56.

opposed to an ultimate approach that is more direct. This resonates with Schuon's distinction between theological expressions and metaphysical teachings. Later in Buddhist history, this distinction extended to conceptions of absolute reality, beyond the reach of discursive expression. Thus Nāgārjuna states that "the Buddha's teaching of the Dharma is based on two truths: a truth of worldly convention and an ultimate truth. Those who do not understand the distinction drawn between these two truths do not understand the Buddha's profound truth. Without a foundation in the conventional truth the significance of the ultimate cannot be taught. Without understanding the significance of the ultimate, liberation is not achieved."[21] In other words, there is a truth that governs conventional teaching and one that pertains to realization, with only the latter being ultimate. The affinity of *upāya* with the first type of truth is reflected in its indirect and pedagogical nature, while ultimate truth pertains to *prajña* as supreme transcendental wisdom. This more radical distinction is not commonly encountered in the writings of Schuon for whom *upāya* is intrinsically connected to religious and formal crystallization.

Mention was made earlier of such Schuonian notions as "Christian *upāya*" and "Islamic *upāya*." This may lead his readers to question the extent to which, in his perspective, all religions can be deemed *upāyas*, or whether the upāyic aspect is more prominent in some rather than others. As we saw earlier, the concept is used by Schuon in a very general sense and could therefore be applied, in principle, to any and all sets of religious forms *qua* forms, to the extent that form is distinct from essence. It is certainly true, though, that Schuon tends to make use of the notion of *upāya* in the context of religions as understood conventionally; that is, with regard to religious traditions comprised of well-defined dogmas, universal ritual practices, and ethical injunctions. Generally speaking, although religion can be reduced to these three components, it is safe to say that they are particularly applicable to the Abrahamic religions. It is hardly a simple task, for instance, to define the dogmas of Hinduism, or the general ritual practices of Buddhism. This suggests that non-Abrahamic faiths and traditions pertain to the realm of *upāya* in a way that differs markedly from the latter.

The fact that Buddhism embraces *upāya* within its very fold cannot but make it a very distinctive form of religious expression. On the one

---

21. Nagarjuna, *Mūlamadhyamakakārika* 24:8–10, translated by Jay L. Garfield, *Fundamental Wisdom of the Middle Way* (Oxford: Oxford University Press, 1995), 296–298.

hand, Buddhism—or rather each of its various schools—can undoubtedly be reduced to a formal doctrinal system with all the expedient means that characterize it as *upāya*; on the other hand, however, its unique sensitivity to the reality of *upāyas* makes it particularly prone to relativize its own claims. Accordingly, even though Buddhism includes many metaphysical statements about the Nirvānic Reality, it is very difficult to speak of Buddhism in inflexible dogmatic terms since its overall emphasis is not, predominantly, on metaphysical pronouncements about reality, but on the means for becoming awakened. Ultimately, Schuon's association of *upāya* with a dogmatic and confessional outlook makes it less attributable to Buddhism than to other religions, since it tends to favor, on the whole, methodical means over doctrinal exactitude. For these reasons, Buddhism is most likely—among all spiritual traditions—to acknowledge the provisional nature of its own "skillful means." This suggests that *upāya*, in the Schuonian sense, is less likely to be applicable to Buddhism, given that this tradition is less prone to emphasizing the function of dogmatic pronouncements as a means of salvation.

If we turn our attention to Hinduism, or to the manifold traditions, schools and ways that come under the *Sanātana Dharma*, we can also—for somewhat different reasons—both affirm and qualify its specific character of *upāya*. This is because this tradition cannot be defined as a set of dogmatic statements about Reality, a fact of which Schuon was keenly aware when he referred to the "contemplative plasticity" of the Hindu spirit.[22] In keeping with the original implications of the term *upāya*, the various Hindu *yogas* and *margas* may be understood in terms of their spiritual effectiveness, rather than in regard to their metaphysical adequacy. This is so to the extent that Hindu schools of spirituality and mysticism are considered to be a priori vocational. Their diversity relates to the wide spectrum of human predispositions and temperaments, including with regard to objects of worship, as indicated by the pervasive concept of *ishta devatā*, the divinity of affinity or choice. This remains true even though, in contrast to Buddhism, metaphysical principles are often foundational in their own right. The hearing of, and reflection on, the doctrine in

---

22. "One must take into account the spiritual temperament of the Hindus, their contemplative plasticity, the particular character of their emotivity, which is more 'cosmic' and less individualistic than that of Europeans, as well as more 'aesthetic' and less prone to moralizing." Schuon, *Language of the Self* (Bloomington, IN: World Wisdom, 1999), 47.

Shankara's *Advaita*, for example, are necessary preliminary stages on the way to spiritual realization. However, here again, the diversity of the *darshanas*, or so-called orthodox points of view, bears witness to the fact that metaphysical approaches in Hinduism are largely correlative to the multiplicity of human vantage points and the diversity of motivating principles or emphases.

It is, therefore, with regard to each Abrahamic religion—taken as a whole—that, in the specifically Schuonian sense, the notion of *upāya* can be applied with most relevance. In point of fact, to the best of our knowledge, Schuon never made use of the terms "Buddhist *upāya*" or "Hindu *upāya*" (or else "Taoist *upāya*"). Indeed, Schuon makes reference to the first verse of the *Tao Te Ching*, not to apply the concept of *upāya* to the Taoist tradition but to illustrate its meaning in light of Lao-tzu's awareness of the limitations it implies: "The Name that can be named is not the true Name."[23] It is quite clear that this paradigmatic statement of the gap between expression and reality on the one hand, and ultimate and provisional truths on the other, cannot be compatible with the kind of one-sided religious interest or bias that lies at the core of the *upāya* as understood by Schuon. In the Abrahamic traditions, on the other hand, the universal call to adhere to a creed is the most evident manifestation of the "religious nationalism" inherent in confessional identification. As we have indicated earlier, Schuon sees the formal absolutism and exclusivism of such faiths as a necessary way to enlist both individual and collective spiritual enthusiasm. What is outwardly absolute in religious identity results, in fact, from the expedient need to align dogmatic representation with an exclusively particular aspect of the Real. Schuon refers to "aspects" and "points of view" as being the two sources and dimensions of religious diversity. The first of these concepts refers to the infinitely diverse facets of Ultimate Reality, while the second relates to the indefinite number of human vantage points regarding that Reality. As a matter of fact, the inability to take into account (theologically and vocationally) these two kinds of diversity can be deemed as the hallmark of the Jewish, Christian, and Islamic *upāyas*.

---

23. "Let us note here that the idea of *upāya* essentially implies the ideas of 'aspect' and 'standpoint'; it means that every formulation derives objectively from 'aspect' and subjectively from 'standpoint'; this is also stated by the introductory sentence of the *Tao-Te-King*: 'The Name that can be named is not the true Name.'" Schuon, *Islam and the Perennial Philosophy* (London: World of Islam Publishing Co., 1976), 137.

Schuon argues that the character of *upāya* mainly appears, in Islam, in the tendency to reduce the whole metaphysical doctrine of Unity to a one-sided theology emphasizing Divine Omnipotence and human obedience.[24] This means that the Divine Essence is limited to the dimension of Will in ways that may all too often contradict the very definition of this Essence, as if God had the power not to be what He is, i.e., the power to be arbitrary or unjust. It also entails a theology that tends to deny the integrally theomorphic nature of mankind by reducing it to a single dimension of obedience, as if human beings could be exclusively characterized as slaves of God. We can see, therefore, how the *upāya* responds to the priority of particular human predicaments as appears, in the case of Islam, in the need to strike down any potential idol by overemphasizing the compelling power of God. In parallel, the Islamic *upāya* also needs to define mankind in terms of this emphasis on power by stressing human limitations, thus translating this emphasis into a de facto negation of God-given human intelligence and initiative. It would be a grave mistake, however, to reduce the whole tradition to those two fundamental characters of the *upāya*, for behind the limitative schema of this formal emphasis lies the infinite reality of the Essence. This appears, in Islam, as the Divine Essence—being envisaged in its ultimate absoluteness—cannot but encompass everything into its merciful Unity, thus effectively transcending the limited aspect of compelling power. Similarly, human servitude before God, which lies at the forefront of the exoteric system, cannot always veil the fundamentally intellective dimension of human nature in Islam. This is demonstrated by the paramount principle of *tawhīd*, which calls for an intellectual recognition on the part of mankind, on account of its primordial nature or *fitra*.

In Christianity, on the other hand, the limitations of the *upāya* are apparent in a de facto Trinitarian relativization of the Absolute and, concomitantly, in an exclusive focus on the power of Redemptive Presence that becomes embedded in a one-sided emphasis on mankind's corrupted will. In other words, God is reduced to that which, in the Divine Nature, is implied by the Incarnation, and mankind thereby limited to what makes Redemption necessary. The absoluteness of the Divine Essence is relativ-

---

24. "In totalitarian obedientialism there are two flagrant nonsenses: one concerning God, whom one would have sublime by means of a blind hyperbolism of freedom, and the other concerning man, of whom one would make a nothingness by means of a no less blind abdication of commonsense." Schuon, *Islam and the Perennial Philosophy*, 119.

ized by its identification with the internal life of the Trinity, while the theomorphic intelligence of humankind is kept in abeyance by dint of a relentless insistence on the fragmentation of the human will in the wake of the Fall. Here again, however, the limits of the *upāya* cannot always prevent a metaphysical understanding of the Trinity that provides access to a recognition of the Divine immanence and its power of grace—as an essential dimension commensurate with a proper conception of the Absolute—as well as to the potential "divinity" of mankind.

While the limitative dimensions of Islam and Christian as *upāyas* constitute both the provisional strength and ultimate weakness of those two traditions, it is also obvious that the fundamental dimensions of the Divine Nature and the human vocation remain fully accessible at the core of their respective messages, which is the objective foundation of their spiritual efficacy. Furthermore, an esoteric and universal grasp of each tradition's core truths ensures access to an effective recognition of the fullness of Reality, or what Schuon likes to call "the nature of things," beyond confessional biases. By contrast, a primary focus on the exclusive dimensions of the *upāya* cannot but give rise to limitations that fail to respond to the integrity of the intellectual, spiritual, and moral needs of the human intellect, will, and soul.

To conclude these considerations, it may be deemed paradoxical that religions like the Abrahamic monotheisms—given their universal imperatives—are arguably the least adjusted to individual and vocational modes of diversity, i.e., those which most deservedly warrant being thought of as an *upāya*, since the latter is normally thought of as an adaptation to the needs of particular human needs. Such an assessment would be justified were it not the case that—for Schuon—the concept of *upāya* does not so much comprise the individual needs of a given person as the common denominators shared by a collectivity of people who are historically, geographically, ethnically, and culturally bound. It is to the needs of this collective self and, by extension, to the attributes of those who constitute it that the religious *upāya* responds. There are also, no doubt—both in Christianity and Islam—historical and eschatological reasons for such expedient emphases and shortcuts, given the need to parry individualistic tendencies, and to provide elementary saving keys accessible to all. Schuon is particularly explicit, in this respect, in recognizing the necessary connection between religion as an inevitable adaptation and an unavoidable limitation. He does not hesitate to stress, moreover, that the aspect of limitation inherent to any religious tradition, particularly those which are more religious than metaphysical, carries in its wake the very seeds of its own corruption and self-destruction.[25] This happens through a growing hypertrophy and opacity of the limitative aspects of that tradition, which are either unconsciously substituted for the fundamental core that lies beyond them or corrupted and abused through being subverted by dark forces that ape their formal contours while standing diametrically opposed to their essence. Be that as it may, the truth is that, in an apparent paradox, the religions that are least conducive to recognizing their *upāyic* tendencies are those that are, indeed, the most aptly characterized—within Schuon's esoteric perspective—as *upāya*. This is so precisely because their dogmatic emphases and exclusivism, which are immune to relativization, are a providential response in the absence of a contemplative disposition that enables an objective metaphysical recognition of a multiplicity of spiritual points of view.

In his correspondence,[26] Schuon defines *upāya* as referring to "all the dogmas inasmuch as they are subjectively effective—although not necessarily as objectively true—in the sense that they determine attitudes of faith, love, or fear depending on the case; and these attitudes, precisely, are supposed to contribute to salvation. This is the meaning of the Buddhist term *upāya*, 'technical device' or 'spiritual stratagem' (in German *Kūnstgriff*), and it is by virtue of this effective intention and this virtually saving 'truth' that all dogmas have their justification and are, in the last analysis, mutually compatible." This passage reveals the way in which the notion of *upāya* is essential in fostering a recognition of both the differ-

---

25. "Every religion is necessarily an adaptation, and adaptation implies limitation. If that is true of the purely metaphysical religions, it is still more true of the exoteric religions, which represent adaptations for the sake of more limited mentalities. These limitations must needs be found in one manner or another in the origins of the religious forms and it is inevitable that they should be manifested in the course of the development of these forms becoming most marked at the end of their cycle to which they themselves necessarily contribute. If these limitations are necessary for the vitality of a religion, they remain nonetheless limitations with the consequences that that implies. The heterodox doctrines themselves are indirect consequences of this need for curtailing the amplitude of the religious form and for limiting it in proportion with the advance of the Dark Age. It could not indeed be otherwise, even in the case of the sacred symbols, because only the infinite, eternal and formless Essence is absolutely pure and inviolable, and because Its transcendence must be made manifest by the dissolution of forms as well as by Its radiation through them." Schuon, *The Transcendent Unity of Religions* (Chennai: Theosophical Publishing House, 1984), 104–5.

26. Private correspondence, May 2, 1982.

ences and the convergence among religious traditions, or what Schuon calls "the transcendent unity of religions." The important difference between the "subjectively effective" and the "objectively true" is parallel, *mutatis mutandis*, to the Mahāyāna differentiation between conventional truth (*samvriti*) and the ultimate truth (*paramārtha*). A classical expression of this distinction can be found in verse 24:8 of Nāgārjuna's *Mūlamadhyamakakārikā*, which David Kalupahana translates as follows: "The teaching of the doctrine by the Buddhas is based upon two truths: truth relating to worldly convention and truths in terms of ultimate fruit."[27] This translation clearly accentuates the subjective and spiritual thrust of the Buddha's teachings in contrast to the tendency to understand *paramārtha* in a metaphysically objective way, hence the choice of the word "fruit" instead of "reality." Verse 10, moreover, clarifies the distinction between the two in terms of a contrast between teaching and realization: "Without relying upon convention, the ultimate fruit is not taught. Without understanding the ultimate fruit, freedom is not attained."[28] Here, freedom is taken to be *Nirvāna*. Some identify *Nirvāna* with the ultimate truth, while other translators would keep them separate. According to the first view, there is an intimate association between intellectual penetration and spiritual emancipation. However, the second perspective envisages ultimate truth as implicated in the limits of representation, since mental understanding unavoidably remains involved, whereas only *Nirvāna* comprises the spiritual realization to which *paramārtha* refers. This *distinguo* could be expressed by making use of the terms "recognition" and "realization," respectively.

At any rate, in Schuon's conceptual vocabulary, *upāya* pertains to *samvriti* whereas the objectively true corresponds to *paramārtha*, with its realization through wisdom or sanctity being *Nirvāna*. The obvious difference is that, in Buddhist terms, *paramārtha* is not always understood as objective, given the highly realizational and therefore subjective bent of the tradition. Be that as it may, it is quite clear that in both cases *upāya* pertains to teaching; that is, with subordinating—to a certain degree—the objectively true to the pedagogically effective. This is illustrated, more generally, by the fact that, according to Schuon, religious truth cannot simply be equated with metaphysical truth. The latter is a matter of ontological adequateness, whereas the former pertains to soteriological adaptation.

---

27. Nāgārjuna's *Mūlamadhyamakakārikā: The Philosophy of the Middle Way*, 331.
28. *Mūlamadhyamakakārikā*, 333.

This is a very important point to grasp if one is to reach a consistent understanding of Schuon's spiritual anthropology. In this view, it is not the Intellect that primarily determines collective mankind in its fallen state but the will, feelings, and imagination. Schuon asserts the normative primacy of the Intellect that, when unhampered by sentimental biases and properly informed, recognizes the universality of the Truth; however, he also acknowledges that the Intellect in itself, or metaphysical doctrines inasmuch as they directly express its content, do not suffice to move most individuals, and certainly not collective mankind, to a recognition of the Truth. Hence, precisely, the need for religions as *upāyas*.

As a conclusion, it must be acknowledged that Schuon's esoteric and universalist point of view will not be acceptable in a purely confessional environment, even though it flows from a consistent and integral metaphysical point of view. This means that, within a religious tradition, it is only by envisaging reality from a metaphysical point of view—one rooted in ultimate non-duality underlying all phenomena—that one can fully recognize a transcendent unity of religions. This is only possible to the extent that one comprehends the relevance of the notion of *upāya* to all religions and traditional perspectives, including one's own; something that one cannot expect, precisely, from the religious point of view as such which is, by definition, identified with a particular *upāya*. Nevertheless, even when the metaphysical and spiritual implications of *upāya* are not strictly drawn, it remains true that this notion can provide the intellectual and spiritual keys to determine a sense of the essential and the secondary in religions.[29] Such insight may also contribute to a more just assessment regarding the value of other traditions and the points of convergence between religions. It must be added, however, that a reverse evidence of the human need for *upāyas* lies in that the highest truths themselves may very well end up being turned into errors within the subjective purview of those who are not adequate to them. While the "error" of the *upāya* is a way to convey the truth, the truth itself—which is objectively what it is—can be a source of error when not properly discerned and situated.

---

29. "The Buddhist solution to the problem of fundamentalism, from which other traditions may gain a useful perspective, is to see dogma as supple and diaphanous; something that still captures the profoundest insights of a spiritual tradition but which, nonetheless, does not fix them into a rigid or inflexible posture." John Paraskevopoulos, *The Unhindered Path: Ruminations on Shin Buddhism* (Kettering, OH: Sophia Perennis, 2016), 135.

According to Schuon this may be the case when a human consciousness is ill prepared or lacks contemplative disinteredness. "Herein is the meaning of the Buddhist *upāya*, the 'saving means' which is itself illusory: a spiritually effective 'absurdity' is a mercy, and it is its very efficacy that here takes the place of truth; in fact, a notion which for any reason leads to the truth is virtually true, which amounts to saying that truths that are too elevated may, on the contrary, actually become errors in the consciousness of a man who is too earthly or too passionate."[30] Since the very notion of *upāya* does rank among such elevated truths, it may in its turn be a source of error for those who do not adequately understand its epistemological status. This means that the objective reality and effectiveness of the notion of *upāya* ought to be distinguished from misinterpretations arising from a hasty dispensation, or facile contempt for religious forms. One of the most effective ways of keeping oneself immune from such subjective error lies, no doubt, in cultivating a sense of the sacred. When understood as the "emergence of the 'metaphysical' Center within the periphery," the sense of the sacred bestows on humans—beyond any confessional formalism and the careless disregard of traditional forms—a receptivity toward the transformative intimations of the Real.

---

30. Schuon, *Islam and the Perennial Philosophy*, 137.

4

The Nature of Things
and the Human Margin

The title of this chapter may *prima facie* be enigmatic since it relates two concepts that may not be immediately recognized as being connected in any way. While these are used repeatedly in Schuon's work, he does not explicitly relate them to each other. Our juxtaposition of these key expressions is intended to stress that the esoteric perspective articulated by Schuon comprises two dimensions. Esoterism is both central and total. These are the hallmarks of the esoteric outlook as defined by Schuon: core essentiality and a virtually unlimited inclusion of manifold perspectives, together with a consideration of the whole of human experience. By this is meant that esoterism, as the word plainly indicates, aims at reaching the innermost truth of religious phenomena. The esoteric outlook also claims, perhaps less obviously, to embrace the whole spectrum of manifestation, including religious phenomena, through a discernment of its various degrees and modes.[1] It would be a misconception, therefore, to think of esoterism in the way it is most often understood; that is, as an arcane and highly specialized field of knowledge. While Schuon's definition of esoterism does encompass some dimensions of reality that are its specific purview (e.g., the notions of Beyond-Being and Intellect), it also refers to a way of contemplating matters in general and, therefore, the whole spectrum of phenomena in principle.

---

1. This is expressed by Schuon's paraphrase of the Duke of Orléans's motto that "all that is national is ours" in the form of "all that is human is ours."

As for the notion of a "nature of things," it pertains to the dimension of essentiality typical of the esoteric outlook inasmuch as it points to the ultimate reality of things, to their "true nature." Esoterism also aims at unveiling a universal standard for assessing the value of all other realities. This essential aspect of beings and phenomena is in itself independent of our human perceptions and evaluations. However, it is also true that, in this universe at least, mankind occupies a privileged position with regard to the capacity for being fully adequate to the "nature of things," both in depth and breadth. As the "supernaturally natural" criterion of reality and truth, the "nature of things" has an aspect of simplicity, in the sense that it reduces everything to the meaningful architecture of the universe. Thus, it reduces forms to essences, and accidents to the Substance. It also entails an aspect of complexity, however, inasmuch as it considers what Schuon refers to as aspects and points of view. These two terms are connected in pointing to the objective and subjective sides of multiplicity. When considering a single phenomenon, it must be recognized that it includes a multiplicity of aspects, presenting as it does diverse attributes. Moreover, the same phenomenon may be contemplated from a variety of vantage points. This complexity can be a source of ambivalence in the field of religion as in other domains.

The "human margin," by contrast, is never a simple matter. It pertains to limitations, adaptations, approximations, and ambiguities. Schuon distinguishes, in this respect, between that which in religion "must be, and which consequently cannot not be," or the Divine intent, and "that which may or may not be, and which therefore does not necessarily have to be," or the "human margin."[2] The "human margin" can only be understood, to the extent that it can, when situated within a range of cosmic possibilities, of which it is but one manifestation. Given the encompassing essentiality of its outlook, esoterism is, in principle, in a position to account for these various intricacies and ramifications. Even though they are clearly not its focus, it has a capacity for evaluating the extent of their legitimate significance as well as their limitations. It must be added that this margin is confined to the human domain by reason of the intermediary status of mankind between the Divine and the terrestrial, whereas the "nature of things" is evidently universal in scope, as it refers to the way things are, or as Shunryu Suzuki put it suggestively, "the way things *is*." This signifies

---

2. Schuon, *From the Divine to the Human* (Bloomington, IN: World Wisdom, 2013), 101.

that while the esoteric focus lies in the dimension of depth, the esoteric awareness of human reality—and the discernment of the extrinsic necessity and limitations of the human margin—belongs to a wisdom of breadth. This aspect of esoterism addresses relativity and, as such, is symbolically akin to a broad unfolding that embraces areas of complexity, ambivalence, and approximations.[3] Such is the province of human and religious forms that both manifest and conceal the ontological core of Reality.

To the extent that exoteric mentalities are generally satisfied with being fixated on the formal aspects of religion—what Ghazālī would call the "mould of truth"[4]—they tend to absolutize, subjectively speaking, the entire spectrum of religious realities; including those that are all too human but which they see as a monolithic whole. The esoteric outlook, by contrast, is drawn to the essence of phenomena, the latter being sensed as symbols of transcendent realities. Further, this deeper perspective cannot but reveal the unevenness of the layers in religious and traditional dispensations which it therefore situates within a graduated range of spiritual relevance. In other words, the "nature of things" signifies the ultimate standard of reality—the meaning of phenomena *sub specie aeternitatis*—while the human margin, which is confined to the realm of religious phenomena, includes a maximum of plausible and expedient means of asserting Reality. This margin is ambiguous and even largely problematic, by contrast with the nature of things the complexity of which should not be confused with obscurity. Through its discernment of the degrees of religious reality, the esoteric perspective—to the extent that it is free from religious *a priori* identifications—can, in principle, dispel the enigmas of the human margin, thus exposing both its spiritual intentions and human pitfalls. It aims at situating things at their proper level; esoterically, idealism and realism coincide in the sense that a consideration of the archetypes and ultimate finalities of religious phenomena accounts for the ambivalence in human adaptations of transcendent realities.

---

3. "It is always a question of the notions of absoluteness and relativity, which are so important or so fateful in the context of the 'human margin.'" Schuon, *Form and Substance in the Religions* (Bloomington, IN: World Wisdom, 2002), 210.

4. "That belief which the commonalty of mankind learns is the mould of truth, not truth itself. Complete gnosis is that the truths be uncovered from that mould, as a kernel is taken out of the husk." Al-Ghazālī, *On Knowing Yourself and God*, translated by Muhammad Nur Abdus Salam (Chicago: Great Books of the Islamic World, 2002), 31.

The expression "the nature of things" gained philosophical credence with Lucretius's *De natura rerum*. This is the celebrated philosophical poem in which the first-century Roman philosopher propounded a theory of the universe based on atomism that, for Lucretius, was the necessary principle of natural production. Needless to say, this atomistic and incidentalist view of the universe—which excludes Divine intervention—has no affinity whatsoever with Schuon's metaphysics. The latter is not only theocentric but also non-dualistic and immanentist in the sense that it sees manifestation as "none other" than the Principle. Thus, the term "nature of things" refers simply, in Schuon's idiom, to the metaphysical order of the universe and to the laws of verticality and equilibrium that preside over it. "The way things are" encompasses where they come from, where they lead to, and the patterns that govern their functioning. What is remarkable about Schuon's use of the term is not so much that he borrows it from Lucretius's usage but rather that its philosophical and neutral wording perfectly fits the sense of objectivity that he wishes to convey. The nature of things, in Schuon's terminology, suggests the elementarity, primordiality, and simplicity of Reality. It does so, moreover, not only in marked contrast to atheism and agnosticism but also to religious biases, devotional hyperboles, and theological convolutions. This amounts to saying that the use of the expression "nature of things" implies a reduction of religious symbols to metaphysical and spiritual realities. For the esoterist, as Schuon understands the term, what matters most is not how a particular Revelation communicates a sense of Reality but rather apprehending Reality itself in its naked objectivity. There is, in a way, nothing religious about such a claim, at least if religion means what is understood by theologians and most of the faithful.[5] This objectivity distanced from extrinsic religious identifications is also evidenced, characteristically, by Schuon's positive evaluation of the term philosophy, which he understands in the etymological sense as love of wisdom. There is no doubt that, for him, philosophical traditions such as Neo-Platonism hardly lack anything in terms of their capacity to lead to the summits of realized gnosis. As we will see, the only indisputable superiority of religions over philosophies, understood as schools of intellective and contemplative wisdom, lies in

---

5. "'What about religion?' 'For these last [those who seek spiritual realization] religion is only a starting point.' 'Then is there anything above religion?' 'Above the religion there is the doctrine.'" Martin Lings, *A Sufi Saint of the Twentieth Century* (Cambridge: Islamic Texts Society, 1993), 26.

their ability to address the lowest common denominators of mankind, both from an intellectual and an ethico-spiritual point of view.

Independently of any specific connection to Lucretius's work, the term *natura* refers to what we have been bestowed with at birth (from the verb *nascor*, to be born). In Schuon's perspective, this is obviously not only a matter of physical and psychological constitution but, primarily, of ontological and epistemological endowment. Human nature is, in his gnostic perspective, fundamentally theomorphic, which means that there is an intrinsic relationship between what God is and what mankind was made, by Him, to be. To be made "in the form of God" can be understood, in this respect, both symbolically and literally. Since the Divine Reality transcends all forms, whether bodily or animic, it is clear that the adjective theomorphic must be understood, first of all, in a way that only symbolically refers to form. This symbolic meaning is thus an allusion to the faculties with which mankind is endowed, all of which draw their reality from their Divine prototypes. Most importantly for Schuon's anthropology, these include the intelligence, the will, and the capacity for sentiment or love. For mankind to be theomorphic means to enjoy and fructify its capacity for objectivity, freedom, and disinterested compassion. These faculties, which Schuon sees as integral to human nature, reflect—in diverse ways—the Divine Qualities of Wisdom, Power, and Mercy. The objectivity of intelligence, which is akin to a Zen-like reflection of the way things are—a "speculative" receptivity to being—is the key to the objectivity of the will. This is so inasmuch as the latter amounts to a freedom from the internal constraints that flow from a subjectivist misreading of reality: "They will know the truth, and the truth will set them free." It is, moreover, through inner freedom from self-delusion and the tyranny of egoic impulses that true love and compassion may flourish. Accordingly, the nature of things, as expressed in the realm of human existence, ought to serve as a framework for discerning all religious phenomena.

Schuon has woven rich meditations on the spiritual significance of various aspects of the human bodily form. These insights confirm the privilege of the vertical state as uniquely represented by the human body. To be human is to be shaped for transcendence, as it were, and the privilege of a vertical physical posture is the clearest indication that our true vocation is to ascend to the Ultimate. It is, at any rate, what essentially distinguishes mankind from animals. Other aspects of the human body express different aspects of being and consciousness, and therefore of their Divine prototypes. This is illustrated, first of all, by the distinction between the face, which expresses a mode of consciousness, and the rest of the body that conveys a state of being. What this means is that nature is an image of the supernatural. The natural is supernatural as the supernatural is natural: any natural phenomenon is grounded in its transcendent archetype, while what we call the supernatural is just that dimension of the nature of things that ordinarily escapes our terrestrial perception.

Schuon's understanding of the nature of things often appears as a contrast to religious or traditional norms and practices. In fact, Schuon states quite unambiguously that the quintessentially esoteric perspective that he propounds is characterized by its primary consideration of the nature of things. In the same way, as esoterism has an inherent precedence over exoterism—both doctrinally and spiritually—so "sacred facts are true because they retrace on their own plane the nature of things, and not conversely: the nature of things is not real or normative because it evokes certain sacred facts."[6] This is a crucial distinction to bear in mind: what lies at the very core of the distinction between the exoteric and the esoteric could not be expressed more directly and unambiguously. While specifically religious perspectives are founded on "sacred facts," without which they would have no bearing on reality, quintessential esoterism is based on a recognition of the nature of things that, in principle, is independent of any sacred myths. At any rate, the distinction between "sacred facts" and "nature of things" does not, as such, entail opposition or conflict, although it does involve significant differences of outlook in the way religion is conceived and experienced. Sacred facts represent symbolic modes of apprehending the nature of things, it being understood that the symbolic implies much more than merely figurative representation, involving as it does sacramental and theurgic means of spiritual transformation. Moreover, "symbolic reality" also means a key idea or a narrative that expresses fundamental aspects of the Essence of Reality. For Schuon, any sacred narrative—to the extent that it is "intrinsically orthodox"—is like a limited and "congealed" fragment of the nature of things, which it expresses intrinsically but limits extrinsically. Taking the Christian tradition as an example, one can appreciate how it is founded, a priori, on the sacred facts of the Incarnation and Redemption. This presents us with just one possible account of the relationship between God and mankind, the Absolute and the relative. Its truth and effectiveness stem from the

---

6. Schuon, *Light on the Ancient Worlds* (Bloomington, IN: World Wisdom, 2006), 56.

fact that the relative is none other than the Absolute, and that the latter can therefore manifest in and through the former in order to reintegrate it within the Essence. Schuon likes to quote, in this respect, the Patristic formula: "God has become man so that man may become God." When considering the Christian point of view, the question at stake is therefore not whether the nature of things conforms to it, but whether it corresponds to an essential aspect of the nature of things. While the latter is undeniably true, since it articulates a dimension of Absolute Reality, the former is only relatively true, for the incarnationist perspective does not exhaust the nature of the Absolute, nor the full range of its relationships to the relative. In other words, religions are true when they embody salvific aspects of the Absolute, but they cease being absolutely true to the extent that they deny other manifestations of the Real.

Claims that esoterism represents an intrinsic objectivity cannot but prompt the question of how the nature of things may be known. This sounds like an extraordinary claim in the context of modernity where the very notion of nature is held in deep suspicion, and in which the classical concept of truth as *adaequatio* has been discarded. Schuon's view, by contrast, is akin to premodern types of ontology and epistemology. It sees the universe as structured and infused with transcendent intelligence. Being an integral part of this universe, mankind is also endowed with a sense of adequateness in relation to it. The key to this matter is that epistemology and ontology ultimately coincide. It could be said that intelligence is consciousness of being, and being is crystallized intelligence or consciousness. The very concept of Intellect encompasses the two poles of being and intelligence since the Intellect manifests in various ways of being: the growth of a plant toward the light is an example of this kind of intellective being. It goes without saying, therefore, that Schuon's view of the Intellect is profoundly different from the ordinary equation of the intellectual domain with the realm of the mind. For him, to know is to be; each mode of knowing is a mode of being, and vice versa. If we consider perspectives such as Advaita Vedānta and Zuangzi's Taoism, for instance, we can see how both traditions conceive of being as consciousness and consciousness as being. The Tao is intelligence as much as being, and this holds true as well for the Supreme *Brahman*, which is being and consciousness. This coincidence of the ontological and the epistemological lies, in a sense, at the root of Schuon's view of the relationship of the Intellect to the nature of things, since it entails an identity of the knower and the known. It must be observed, moreover, that while ontology may be reduced to epistemology with regard to the Supreme Principle, the reverse is true when we consider the lowest ranges of manifestation. In other words, the "being" of the Supreme may be reduced to its Selfhood as objects are reintegrated into the sole Subject, God being Subject or "I am" "before" being Object. Conversely, the lowest ranges of manifestation, such as minerals—but also to a lesser extent vegetables and animals—are characterized by a reduction of the epistemological to the ontological. This means that the intelligence of the mineral lies in its being. Mankind lies in between the Supreme and lower realms of reality, since its intelligence and its being do not immediately correspond, as it were. In mankind, the distance between knowing and being may result in cerebral intellectualism or in brutish materialism. The integrated human being harmonizes being with intelligence. His knowledge is not only a recognition of the nature of things but also a participation in it.

We have earlier alluded to the possibility that a particular religious outlook may be superseded, as it were, by a consideration of the nature of things. This is particularly the case when considering the distinction, already discussed in our chapter on *upāya*, between theological traditions and metaphysical wisdom. The former are specifically religious in character, which means that they give precedence to sacred facts that crystallize a certain vision of Reality. In that sense, they are more collectively subjective, if one may say so, than impersonally objective. Metaphysical traditions, on the other hand, are primarily—if not exclusively—focused on the nature of things. Needless to say, sacred facts and collective subjectivism are also at work in those traditions since mankind, as a whole, requires symbolic orientations and principles of exclusive identification. However, the quintessence of metaphysics is completely free of symbolic reductions and religious biases. An Advaitin may share, to an extent at least, in the collective prejudices of the Hindu mindset but the core truths of Advaita, as found in the doctrine of *Ātman* and *avidyā*, are totally independent of religious reductionism and confessional identity. In the Abrahamic religions, by contrast, the core truths are virtually indistinguishable from symbolic events and theurgic manifestations which are, for all practical purposes, identified with "the way things are." The Incarnation of the Word and Christ's crucifixion are the Truth, which overshadows, without denying it, the doctrine of Divine Unity that he preaches. Schuon makes the point that, in such contexts, there is little room for a disinterested account of the truth, since everything is envisaged a priori through the prism of a particular soteriological perspective. Therefore, to expect objectivity from the religious faithful would be in vain. Objectivity means to fully recognize the spiritual and ethical values of foreign religions and, even more so, acknowledging the limitations of one's own. The religious universe is defined by a subjective effectiveness that hardly makes room for any unbiased consideration of religious phenomena. This amounts to saying that the main motivating factors of religious traditions are not intellectual but emotional and volitional. The depth and intensity of faith do not necessarily require intelligence, since faith itself provides a functional equivalent of the latter within the realm of religious life. Faith is a mode of intelligence in the sense that it involves a degree of epistemic *adaequatio* to the Real, but the modes of this intelligence are mostly colored by sentimental and experiential conditionings.

Religious mentalities represent a departure from a strict concern with the nature of things, and this is what accounts for the growing development of the human margin. This is so inasmuch as human partiality precipitates ways of thinking, feeling, and acting that become increasingly disconnected from the essence of religion, that is the discernment between the Absolute and the relative and the concentration on the Absolute.

What does the term "margin" mean and what are its implications? On the one hand, it may refer to a spectrum of acceptable possibilities. This is the edge or the further limit of a given religious manifestation. In this respect, margin refers to something that does not belong to the center—*stricto sensu*—but which still falls within the scope of legitimate, acceptable, or approximate realities. In other words, it is a possible but ambiguous accretion on the substance that, nevertheless, manifests itself in a very relative and borderline manner. Thinking of this margin as a type of commentary on the Divine Message may be a helpful way of envisaging the concept. In that sense, the human margin is like an "error" that is grafted onto the truth or is, perhaps, even the truth itself, in the sense of Zuangzi's "only error is transmitted."[7]

From another point of view, Schuon characterizes the human margin in religion as a Divine condescension to human limitations and weaknesses, but one that cannot, nevertheless, be fully approved. This is why Schuon questions the religious claim that each and every theological crystallization

---

7. "If a Taoist master could say that 'only error is transmitted,' it is because there is an inverse relationship between 'idea' and 'reality,' the 'thought' and the 'lived,' the 'conceived' and the 'realized.'" Schuon, *Stations of Wisdom* (Bloomington, IN: World Wisdom, 1995), 20.

is, in the religious domain, directly inspired by the Holy Spirit. In other words, there is a complex and ambiguous amalgamation of the Divine and the human in religion, one that defies hasty and zealous absolutizations as well as facile and individualistic rejections of traditional phenomena. The following passage makes the meaning of this margin quite explicit: "There is a sector which, while being orthodox and traditional, is nonetheless human in a certain sense; this means that the Divine influence is total only for the Scriptures and for the essential consequences of the Revelation, and that it always leaves a 'human margin' where it exerts no more than an indirect action, letting ethnic or cultural factors speak. It is to this sector or margin that many of the speculations of exoterism belong."[8] On a most fundamental level, this amounts to saying that the Absolute cannot absolutely determine the relative and human fields without denying the latter's freedom and, in a sense, their very existence. There cannot but be a marginal grey zone of relative leeway that mediates, with unavoidable ambiguities, the encounter of the Absolute and the relative on the level of religious phenomena. The second point that this passage makes is that, in the absence of a direct and all-encompassing Divine determination, the impetus of the development of the tradition must necessarily be left to the collective genius of the sections of mankind that have become the providential receptacles of the religion. In other terms, the form of the Divine inspiration combines with the matter of the human receptacle in a way that particularizes the former in different ways. Thus, a most significant aspect of the human margin lies in its connection with the cultural predispositions of the specific peoples among which religious realities crystallize and spread. Schuon mentions the major impact of "ethnic and cultural factors," to which the diversity of expressions of the same faith in different geo-cultural contexts bears witness. In fact, the Divine message also accommodates itself to the specific character of given communities. It is not for nothing that celestial appearances, when they involve spoken words, generally do so in the vernacular language of the recipients and, sometimes, even with reference to particular cultural traits or phenomena. However, it is with the human margin, properly so-called, that ambiguous elements tied to a particular cultural ambience come to the fore, thus coloring the religious message through commentaries, interpretations, and formalizations that do not necessarily reflect—in the most

---

8. Schuon, *Form and Substance in the Religions*, 201.

direct way—the core metaphysical and spiritual teachings of a religion. It is interesting to note, in this respect, that the all-too-human aspect of these external trappings of the tradition tend to be wedded to the message itself to the point of precluding any differentiation between the two. This is all the more so as the tradition loses its spiritual sap—something of which it may not be aware since a consciousness of what is being lost would presuppose an adequate idea of what spirituality entails. In any event, such a loss tends to become transformed, by way of a compensatory process, into an intensification of the formal concretions resulting from the human margin. Hence the more or less unavoidable phenomenon, on a collective level, of an ethnicization or "nationalization" of religion, either through identification of a particular people with a specific faith or through a more or less explicit turning of the religion into a "nation."

Another facet of the ethnic dimension of the human margin lies in the complex question of the relationship between ethnic groups, cultures, and religions. The historical experiences of the last centuries and their impact on contemporary sensibilities, inasmuch as the latter have been characterized by a heightened sense of identity and a focus on relations of power, make all the more difficult and delicate any approach to these matters. There is no question, however, that the human margin also pervades the ambience of given human collectivities and not just metaphysical or theological concepts.

With regard to Schuon's consideration of racial factors in religion, it is most important to begin with his premise that "race is a form while caste is a spirit."[9] This means, quite evidently, that racial factors can in no way determine the level of spirituality of any individual nor the metaphysical content of any given teachings, although they may inform their modalities of expression. "Racial determination can only be relative"[10] being subordinate, as it is, to the human as such. While caste, for Schuon, is not a priori a sociological category but a certain way of apprehending the world and Reality—hence a "spirit"—the race is a "form" that affects extrinsically, and in a partial manner, the ways in which this "spirit" is lived. "Formal" racial characteristics must therefore be differentiated from ethnic identity, which involves extra-racial determinations. For instance, Schuon explicitly rejects the notion of an Aryan or Semitic race, considering these

---

9. Schuon, *Language of the Self* (Bloomington, IN: World Wisdom, 1999),147.
10. Schuon, *Language of the Self*, 147.

as merely linguistic and psychological realities.[11] Furthermore, Schuon's writings provide explicit refutations of racist theories, and his anthropology emphasizes the universality of spiritual capacity and potential regarding our human relationship with the Ultimate.[12] It is this differentiated universality that Western sociopolitical domination and expansion has undermined through a cult of European "culturism (that) is practically synonymous with civilizationism, and thus with implicit racism."[13] There is, moreover, an important analogy to be drawn between Schuon's displacement of the notion of caste from the social to a spiritual level, and his understanding of ethnic identity as referring to characteristics that do not necessarily, or primarily, pertain to race and which can even be abstracted from the group to which they refer outwardly and in an approximate fashion. When Schuon writes, for instance, that there is in Christ an Aryan dimension,[14] he plainly refers to a generic way of apprehending Reality that is independent of ethnic identity even though, from another point of view, its spiritual qualities are by and large more representative of a given civilizational sector. Elsewhere, and in an altogether different context, Schuon would mention the fact that Jesus was a Semite, without it being possible to understand this term in strictly ethnic terms. In other words, the terms "Aryan" and "Semite" refer here to complex combinations of religious, historical, and cultural factors that are associated with given peoples, and in which can be recognized, to some extent, a collective homogeneity largely reflecting their perceptions and expressions of the Divine. If one is ready to admit that the religious and spiritual climate of the Bible, the Talmud, and the Islamic *sharī'ah* can be distinguished from that of the Upanishads, the idea of *Moksha* and the institution of the *varnas*, then one may consider the

---

11. "What is important to recall here is that there is no Aryan, Semitic, Hamitic, or Uralo-Altaic race, nor a Germanic, Celtic, Latin, Slavic or Greek race; even though there may be racial predominances in these linguistic groups, and even though each language corresponds to a greater or lesser extent to what may be called a 'psychological race.'" Schuon, *To Have a Center* (Bloomington, IN: World Wisdom, 2015), 35.

12. Schuon notes that racist theories are "unaware of the fact that in each race repetition of certain types is due, not to mixtures, but to the homogeneity of mankind and to the ubiquity of the same typological possibilities, not to mention the role of astrological types, the universality of the temperaments, and other factors both diversifying and repetitive." *To Have a Center*, 37.

13. Schuon, *Esoterism as Principle and as Way* (Pates Manor, Bedfont: Perennial Books, 1990), 189.

14. Schuon, *Form and Substance in the Religions*, nn. 19, 24.

possibility that the terms Semite and Aryan may refer to distinct realities.

Schuon was born in 1907, and his language was shaped by the linguistic conventions of the times and his intellectual formation during the first half of the twentieth century. His use of the term "Aryan," for instance, may suggest to a number of readers associations of ideas that a thorough and careful consideration of his work as a whole—particularly its anthropological and spiritual thrust—would dispel.[15] While the use of the term Aryan is likely to evoke, in some minds, the racist ideologies of the first half of the twentieth century, it is used by Schuon in a manner that pertains not only to the general cultural traits of peoples belonging to the Indo-European linguistic groups but, more significantly, to an intellectual and spiritual typology that transcends mere ethnic determinations. On the other hand, Schuon does not shun from adopting certain simplifying distinctions that he readily acknowledges. For instance, he writes: "*Grosso modo*, Aryans . . . are above all metaphysicians and therefore logicians whereas Semites . . . are *a priori* mystics and moralists, each of the two mentalities or capacities repeating itself within the framework of the other in keeping with the Taoist symbol of the *yin-yang*."[16] He also refers to "Aryans" as "objectivists" and to "Semites" as "subjectivists" while emphasizing the "good or ill" of each tendency.[17] When Schuon contrasts the metaphysical and the mystical, he hardly presupposes an intrinsic eminence of one over the other. For him, metaphysics is discernment and mysticism is union. The typological and largely "symbolic" association of the Indo-European, or Aryan, religious sensibilities with metaphysics and of Abrahamic, hence Semitic, traditions with mysticism points to a difference of emphasis that, although recognizable through their respective religious productions, is neither exclusive nor one-sided. Indeed, Schuon criticizes the inspirational pitfalls of mystical subjectivism as well as the intellectualist and abstruse bent of certain metaphysical tendencies when abused. He points to the excesses of inspirationism that are the negative tradeoffs arising from particular prophetic and mystical

---

15. See for example Gregory A. Lipton, "De-Semitizing Ibn 'Arabī: Aryanism and the Schuonian Discourse of Religious Authenticity," *Numen* 64, no. 2-3 (2017), 258-93.

16. *Sufism Veil and Quintessence* (Bloomington, IN: World Wisdom, 2006), 21.

17. "Or again, Aryans are objectivists, for good or ill, while the Semites are subjectivists; deviated objectivism gives rise to rationalism and scientism whereas excessive subjectivism engenders all the illogicalities and pious absurdities of which a sentimental, zealous, and conventional fideism is capable." Schuon, *Sufism: Veil and Quintessence*, 21.

emphases in religious traditions of Semitic origin, while also highlighting the grave distortions of mental ratiocination that can be attributed to Indo-European, and particularly European, intellectual developments.[18] Moreover, the objective is not intrinsically superior to the subjective and vice versa. *In divinis*, the subjective aspect precedes the objective one, since God is Self before being Other or Object. It is actually by virtue of Divine "subjective" Selfhood that the Divine Reality can "become" an Object through the objectifying dimension of its Self-Determination and Self-Manifestation, but this Divine Subjectivity transcends, in another sense, the very notion of a polarity between subject and object. The notions of subjective and objective are therefore fundamentally relative. While mankind must strive toward objectivity inasmuch as the Divine Subject is, a priori, an object—indeed its Supreme Object—for human beings it must also realize this objectivity subjectively, that is mystically or inwardly. In his essay "Stations of Wisdom," Schuon describes six spiritual perfections. The fifth corresponds to discernment between the Real and the unreal, while the sixth is union with the Real. From the highest point of view, they are but two sides of the same perfection, whereby the Real is seen as the only Real, either exclusively in the first case or inclusively in the second.

The association of a tradition with a culture or an ethnic group can also result in an overevaluation of the latter, through a de facto identification of the two. Furthermore, this can lead, by extension, to excessive generalizations concerning particular civilizations or specific peoples. In fact, this tendency to over-essentialize the historical identity of given peoples on the basis of their close association with a particular religious tradition lies at the foundation—*a contrario*—of Schuon's critique of overly systematic and dichotomic understandings of the distinction between East and West. René Guénon's keen—but sometimes one-sided—critique of the West (and apologia for the East) is particularly susceptible to this kind of thinking. In his *East and West*, first published in 1924, and three years later in *The Crisis of the Modern World*, Guénon opposed the materialism of the West to the spirituality of the East, primarily understood as being inclusive of India, China, and Islam, which he considered to be the remaining bastions of tradition and metaphysics. He did so in ways

---

18. And similarly: "As for the 'independence' of the Aryan spirit, it must be specified that this can be a quality or a defect, depending on the case, exactly as Semitic formalism can be; all told, the whole question is relative, and each thing must be put in its proper place." Schuon, *Form and Substance in the Religions*, nn.19, 24.

that were pedagogically meaningful in terms of bringing out the spiritual crisis prevalent in the West, hence the profound influence he had in some circles, although this was done in too unqualified a manner in the sense that he sometimes overestimated the East and underestimated the West. At any rate, Schuon, while certainly appreciating Guénon's seminal contribution to the "intellectual restoration" of the West, was also critical of his insufficient awareness of the fragilities and pitfalls of the East, coupled with an appearance of ignorance regarding some of the major metaphysical and spiritual streams of Europe, such as Neo-Platonism and Christian Orthodox mystical theology. More importantly in the present context, Schuon attributes Guénon's inability to provide a more nuanced and accurate evaluation of the East to a lack of consideration of the human dimensions of tradition, which touches very directly on the problem of the human margin.[19] This tendency also relates to an underestimation of the universal human traits and tendencies that must necessarily relativize civilizational differences. What can be deemed to have amounted to an idealization of the East on the part of Guénon flows mostly from a tendency to conflate the metaphysical and spiritual core of the tradition with the human substance of the peoples who participate in it. On the one hand, tradition and religion shape the character of a given people, ethnic group, and culture, but on the other hand, human nature remains what it is irrespective of the civilization in question, and its negative tendencies cannot but corrode, with time, the integrity of the tradition as such. In other words, there is a sense in which metaphysical and spiritual principles inform and elevate the segment of mankind that they address, but there is another way in which the latter tends to lower and thicken the former, although the manner in which this is actualized varies from one religious civilization to the next. The significance and power of this human component cannot be underestimated, but it must also be understood to play a role in the law of entropy that determines the gradual decline and degeneracy of a given tradition.

Metaphysically speaking, the spiritual history of religions cannot but obey a law of gradual decline, given that the Divine and the terrestrial are incommensurate. There is, therefore, no way the latter could sustain the former without a gradual weakening and breaking down of its ability to function as an immanent conduit for the transcendent. This is why the

---

19. Cf. Schuon, *René Guénon: Some Observations* (Hillsdale, NY: Sophia Perennis, 2004).

human margin tends to increasingly expand past the "apostolic age" that was still characterized, in contrast, by a sort of immersion of the human within the celestial and the Divine. Schuon describes this phenomenon in a very striking manner in *The Transcendent Unity of Religions*:

> Every Tradition is necessarily an adaptation, and adaptation implies limitation.... These limitations must needs be found in some manner or other in the origins of the traditional forms and it is inevitable that they should be manifested in the course of the development of these forms, becoming most marked at the end of this development, to which they themselves contribute. If these limitations are necessary for the vitality of a Tradition, they remain none the less limitations with the consequences which that implies.... It could not indeed be otherwise, even in the case of the sacred symbols, because only the infinite, eternal, and formless Essence is absolutely pure and unassailable, and because its transcendence must be made manifest by the dissolution of forms as well as by its radiation through them.[20]

Implicit in this passage is the idea that the Real, or the Truth, transcends any particular formulations of it, the latter flowing from the specific needs of a given people or a given time. The Essence is and always remains the Essence, and it is in this transcendent and supra-formal dimension that we find the ultimate meaning of religion as such. If the Essence remains unassailable by contingencies and limitations, it is precisely because it is not relational as such. By contrast, the necessity of formulating religious doctrines—*qua* adaptation—is intrinsically tied to human limitations. Now this is a crucial point in terms of understanding the meaning and the extent of the human margin. While the latter is by definition exclusively human, it must also be admitted that this is prefigured in the Divine message itself; not inasmuch as it is Divine but insofar as it is a message intended for human beings. The Divine must limit itself in order to be known by limited humanity, although believers further limit this Self-limitation through their own inherent shortcomings. They do so by focusing—mostly and increasingly so as the tradition ages—on the

---

20. Schuon, *The Transcendent Unity of Religions*, 104–5.

aspect of relativity inherent in the Divine rather than striving to fathom that which participates in the Divine Illimitation. Thus, what is perhaps most significant in Schuon's passage is a recognition that religious limitations, stemming from both the Divine and the human, play a role that is indispensable yet hazardous. These limitations are necessary because, in their absence, there would be no possibility for religious principles to be widely received and for traditions to develop. Accordingly, one must acknowledge these inherent defects or imperfections in mankind and accept, thereby, that these restrictions must give rise to the host of perils inherent in the human margin.

As long as the spiritual energy of the Revelation remains strong, the limitations of religious phenomena can be neutralized and, to an extent, integrated in the powerful stream of a healthy and robust tradition. It is only when its spiritual sap dries up that these impediments begin to bring about corruption and demise. It must be noted that this process is passive and "may be compared to the decay of a physical organism worn out with age."[21] Schuon refers to this as a "decadence," whether it be of civilizations, religions, or initiatory orders. Concretely, it means that traditional ideas and institutions are gradually "taken for granted" and eventually become largely ossified. The contemporary theologian Wilfred Cantwell Smith has accounted for this process in a way that is analogous to Schuon's view, in terms of a "reification" that leads from the prevalent inner faith of an apostolic era to the objectified "religion" or rigid theological systematization of later times.[22] It is not clear, though, whether Cantwell Smith considers this process as "natural" and unavoidable, whereas it is quite apparent that Schuon sees it as inscribed in the very nature of things. Another more clearly perceptible difference in their respective evaluation of this phenomenon is that Schuon—contrary to Cantwell Smith's by and large negative assessment of intellectual crystallizations—sees the process of theological objectification as a necessity and even a "perfection" in its own right. In other words, the theological formalization of the tradition is not only the symptom—and measure—of a spiritual decline, it is also, from another perspective, a kind of flourishing. Actually, any such exteriorization,

---

21. Schuon, *The Transcendent Unity of Religions*, 82.

22. "Here, then, is a process of institutionalization, of conceptual reification. Concepts, terminology, and attention shift from personal orientation to an ideal, then to an abstraction, finally to an institution." Wilfred Cantwell Smith, *The Meaning and End of Religion* (Minneapolis: Fortress Press, 1991), 76.

including in the artistic domain, can be perceived both as a sign of atrophy as well as one of renewal. Such theological crystallizations bear witness to a lack of the spiritual intuition that was ubiquitous during apostolic times. In other words, conceptual enrichment is, in a way, a compensatory response to a tradition's increasing degeneration.

What Cantwell Smith tends to see as a fateful intellectualization of faith—while recognizing some of its positive contributions within the context of what he refers to as the "cumulative tradition"—Schuon perceives as a necessary unfolding of a tradition's incipient spiritual seed. The theological, but also artistic, maturation of the tradition constitutes a culmination of sorts, at least from the point of view of forms and the stability of a religion over time. This productive spectrum constitutes the most positive aspect of the human margin inasmuch as it contributes to an intellectual framework for sustaining a tradition. However, it does not go without negative concomitances in terms of excluding potentialities that could have been beneficial to the development of the religion itself. Schuon is particularly sensitive to what he considers an unfortunate tendency to scrupulous pedantry among theologians: "When the divine Light descends onto the human plane—embodying itself, as it were—it undergoes an initial limitation, resulting from human language and from the requirements of a given collective mentality, or cycle of humanity; then it undergoes a second limitation, owing to the fact that this mentality pushes the specific limitation of the *upāya* as far as possible by needlessly dotting i's and hence provoking divergences and heresies."[23] This is, in a sense, what theology is all about: an inflexible and apologetic systematization of the core principles in a particular faith. This limitation is reflected in a bifurcation of the tradition, whereby what remained implicit—and therefore perfectly compatible with unity—becomes exclusive and explicit, leading to opposition, schisms, and differences in interpretation. The human margin is, needless to say, relevant to the polemical implications of this scission, which it tends to foster and intensify. It manifests in religions that are intrinsically orthodox; that is, traditions that conform essentially to the nature of things within a particular perspective and through a specific sacred symbolism. What Schuon refers to as "intrinsic orthodoxy" is demonstrated by a sufficiently explicit concept of the Absolute, a way that leads to it, providing a means for attaining sanctity and, secondarily,

---

23. Schuon, *Christianity/Islam: Perpectives in Esoteric Ecumenism* (Bloomington, IN: World Wisdom, 2008), 107.

the creation of sacred art as a tangible manifestation of this way.[24] While a discussion of these points is developed in another chapter of this book, what interests us more here is how the human margin functions as a principle of scission within orthodox traditions, a phenomenon that is universal in the history of religion, particularly in post-axial traditions. These scissions within religions such as Islam and Christianity are quite different in nature from the diversity that is inherent in traditions such as Hinduism and Buddhism. In the latter, there is either no dogmatic orthodoxy—aside from the recognition of scriptures and the tradition as a whole—or a very flexible attitude with regard to the latter, on account of human diversity and the consequent need for a plethora of *upāyas*. In such contexts, exclusivism rarely goes so far as to excommunicate schools and perspectives other than one's own, even though there is, quite often and understandably, a confident belief in the superiority of one's own path. While the diversity of Hinduism and Buddhism is extensive, the human margin does not influence them to the same extent that one finds in the monotheistic faiths. It tends to manifest itself in Eastern traditions more in terms of orthopraxy rather than in orthodoxy. In other words, its influence is largely restricted to the development of socioreligious practices and institutions.[25] The case of dogmatic monotheism is different, and it is in this context only that it is possible to speak of scissions properly so called. In most cases, the vehemence—even violence—of competing views can assume an intensity that is more acute than the one that opposes a given religion to another. It must be conceded, however, that the development of divergences leading to sectarian divisions can also be a principle of renewal and revitalization. Schuon shows, for instance, how Lutheranism made it possible for a particular Christian possibility to flourish, while at the same time—via a corresponding reaction—reenergizing the spirituality of the Catholic Church through the Counter-Reformation. Notwithstanding

---

24. "For a religion to be considered as intrinsically orthodox it must be founded upon a fully adequate doctrine of the Absolute (extrinsic orthodoxy depending upon particular formal elements which cannot be applied literally outside the perspective to which they refer); it must also advocate and realize a spirituality that is adequate to this doctrine, which means that it must comprise both the notion and the fact of sanctity." Schuon, *Form and Substance in the Religions*, 13.

25. Thus, on several occasions, Schuon notes the pedantic formalism found in Hindu brahmanism, where a type of "professional priest . . . has become narrow and pedantic, even pharisaic, through 'specialization.'" Schuon, *Sufism: Veil and Quintessence*, 85.

the extrinsic benefits that may result from it, the "dotting of the i's" that Schuon criticizes invites a greater theological rigidity that risks disorder, while also strengthening—over time—an increasingly passive reliance on dogmatic forms and external practices with which religions have often become almost entirely identified. What a certain degree of "conceptual indeterminacy" may have contributed in fostering intellectual and spiritual fluidity, theological systematization has tended to obstruct. This is particularly exemplified by the sedimentation of a certain type of institutionalized scholasticism that may not reflect the intellectual vitality prominent at a tradition's inception and during the peak phases of its flourishing. This passivity is not restricted to the realm of dogma, as it may manifest in other domains, such as ceremonialism and religious law.

In contrast to this largely passive process of sedimentation and decay—the traces of which Schuon mostly perceives in the Asian traditions and the increasingly negative impact of theological hardening that is representative of Abrahamic religions—there also exists an active deviation that is consciously opposed to tradition and seeks to sever itself from it.[26] This trend first appeared in Europe as early as the Renaissance and has spread to wherever European thought has been influential. Thus, the equation between the East and tradition, on the one hand, and the West and modernity, on the other, has often been proposed as a distinguishing feature of the traditionalist or perennialist outlook. This is an oversimplification, however, since even from the point of view of Guénon, the real opposition is that between tradition and modernity, with the opposition of East and West simply serving as its most evident illustration. It is also worth noting that Guénon himself was careful to stress that by Western he meant that which was essentially modern and by Eastern that which

---

26. "We will take this opportunity of pointing out that the East was already in a state of great decadence at the time when Western expansion began, though this decadence can by no means be compared with the decadence of the modern West, the nature of which is, in certain secondary respects at least, the very reverse of that of Eastern decadence. Whereas the latter is 'passive' and may be compared to the decay of a physical organism worn out with age, the specifically modern decadence is, on the contrary, 'active' and 'voluntary,' 'cerebral' so to speak, and it is this that gives to the Westerner the illusion of a 'superiority' which, even if it really exists on a certain psychological plane by reason of the difference we have just mentioned, is none the less very relative and disappears altogether when contrasted with the spiritual superiority of the East." Schuon, *The Transcendent Unity of Religions*, 82.

is traditional.[27] While the dominant presence of a spiritual tradition in any civilization normally affords protection against the materialism that Guénon attributes to the modern West, it must also be recognized that the same causes, of human provenance, produce the same effects. This is why, according to Schuon, there should be no surprise at the rapidity with which Asian and African societies, while still remaining semi-traditional in many ways, have adopted most—if not all—of modernity's ideas and ways of living, even to the extent of sometimes going beyond what one finds in the West. The unity of mankind, and the fundamental tendencies and vocations of the human spirit (which Schuon discusses in the context of the underpinnings of the caste system), is a much deeper and determining reality than the differences found between cultures, ethnic groups, or civilizations. The excessive—and rather alarming—zeal with which Easterners have pursued modernization and—*a contrario*—the growing interest, albeit uneven and ambivalent, of many Westerners in Asian spirituality are sufficient proof of this universal human tendency.[28] Therefore, all manner of pitfalls can be found in schematizing oppositions between East and West, today more than ever, even though these may have had a fruitful heuristic and symbolic value a century or so ago.

Even those features that were seen by Guénon as characteristic of modern Western deviations, such as rationalism and activism, must also be considered—according to Schuon—from the point of view of their positive content and contribution. While rationalism and activism constitute, respectively, a reduction of the scope of intelligence and an obstacle to contemplation, there is also a sense in which reason and action constitute intrinsically positive values. Although it may sound like a truism, Schuon believes that to rely on reason—where it is legitimate and necessary to do so—is evidently a virtue. The critical sense that it entails, far from being destructive in itself, amounts to "considering the nature of things rather

---

27. "There was no reason for opposition between East and West as long as there were traditional civilizations in the West as well as in the East; the opposition has meaning only as far as the modern West is concerned, for it is far more an opposition between two mentalities than between two more or less clearly defined geographical entities." René Guénon, *The Crisis of the Modern World* (Hillsdale, NY: Sophia Perennis, 2001), 22–23.

28. Responding to Guénon's idea of a reform of the West by means of Eastern values and tools, Schuon prefers to assert that "the problem—or the solution—is not a reform of the West by the East, it is a reform of the entire world by the Truth as such." Schuon, *The Eye of the Heart* (Bloomington, IN: World Wisdom, 1997), 68.

than obeying conventional reflexes."[29] For Schuon, traditional worlds, as a result of the human margin, are prone to capitulate to the abuses of conventionalism. It is at this point that the modern Western mentality can provide a positive counterpart to what remains of traditional Eastern structures and values. The former may compensate for the ill effects of conventionalism through a fresh, critical look at the excessive accretions of the human margin. Reason, critical reflection, and "free thinking"—in the sense of a thorough exercise of one's God-given ability to think—are aspects of the nature of things, meaning that they are gifts with which humankind is endowed. What is noteworthy is that religious traditions, because of their human margin, can sometimes move further away from the nature of things than a neutral, or even de facto, secular rationality is apt to do. This is a claim that most traditional faithful would utterly reject, precisely because their standard is not the nature of things but the Divine Will as expressed through a religious law, the human components of which they tend to ignore or downplay.

As we have alluded to, the human margin is also present in the literality of scriptures and its prototypical historical events. There is a contingency inherent in the terrestrial dimension of Revelation which means that, on that level, "it could be other than it is."[30] The best evidence of this appears in the fact that some revealed injunctions have been abrogated, either under the imperative of a new revelation or—even within the same religion—at different stages of its development. The first case pertains to Christianity, in relation to the prescriptions of the Judaic law, while the second is apparent in the different levels of Divine Will as they apply, for instance, to the prohibition of wine in the Qur'ān.[31] It goes without saying that the exoteric mentality is given to absolutizing scriptural contingencies and is little disposed to draw any conditional conclusions from them.

---

29. Schuon, *The Eye of the Heart*, 63.

30. Schuon, *Form and Substance in the Religions*, 233.

31. The Qur'ān first condemns prayer in a state of inebriation: "O ye who believe! Draw not near unto prayer when ye are drunken, till ye know that which ye utter" (4:43). It then rejects intoxicants as exercising an evil influence on human behaviour: "O ye who believe! Strong drink and games of chance and idols and divining arrows are only an infamy of Satan's handiwork. Leave it aside in order that ye may succeed" (5:90). Exoterism is not going to consider the rationale behind the interdiction (i.e., the need for lucidity in exercising one's religious and daily duties) as it can only focus on the rejection itself, since it expresses God's Will.

When it does so, it is generally a sure sign of the influence of a modern or secular influence, which means a distancing from the tradition rather than an interiorization of its message. As for the exoteric resistance to any spiritual exegesis, it is attuned to a subjective "divinization" of contingent factors, seen as coming from God, and shows little intuition of the nature of things underlying the *raison d'être* of these factors. By contrast, the esoteric outlook tends to focus on the divine intentions that are immanent to religious phenomena rather than concentrating on the latter themselves. The recognition of a human capacity to understand these intentions, which the exoterist strongly questions or perceives as a dangerous self-divinization, is predicated on the presupposition of a nature of things, precisely, which human intelligence can recognize by virtue of the Divine imprint sealed upon it. This distinction appears, for instance, in Islam[32] in connection with the veiling of women. Within a typically exoteric outlook, the latter is a subjectively absolute symbolic marker of religious adherence. Esoterically, it is symbolically meaningful—and socially plausible within a traditional context—but also given to an excessive formalization, not to mention fanatical abuses.

It is in relation to these kinds of ambiguous phenomena that Schuon refers to the human margin as unfolding "in the shadow of Divine inspiration."[33] This is a particularly striking image that suggests both a dependence of the human margin on a tradition's source of light but also the corresponding obscuration that it entails. Comparing this margin to a shadow projected by the human contours of the Divine Light suggests a symbolic way of characterizing the shortcomings "revealed" by Divine inspiration. In a sense, these limitations bear witness to the presence of the Light while, in another, they serve to obstruct it. The challenging question, in this respect, lies in discerning what pertains to the Divine Will—*stricto sensu*—and what participates in the human margin. As we

---

32. "An example of excessive formalism—and of a conventionalism which is definitely superstitious—is provided by certain garments of Moslem women: in Islamic India there are certain ways of veiling women that have something truly sinister about them—they are like walking prisons or phantoms—which to say the least is contrary to nature, and which demonstrates to what extent the exoteric spirit can be pedantic, blind and desiccated; by contrast, the veil of Moroccan women is morally and aesthetically acceptable, being so to speak 'one point of view among others.'" Schuon, "Ambiguity of Exoterism," in *The Face of the Absolute*, 22.

33. Schuon, *Form and Substance in the Religions*, 219.

have intimated above, there are no absolute boundaries in this domain, which means that objective and subjective circumstances cannot but play a determining role in the religious evaluations of what is essential and what is marginal.

Many in the modern world subscribe to the idea that religion has all too often been subjected to human interferences and abuses. Some critics of traditional religion share a fundamentalist point of view: they reject human accretions, interpretations, or adaptations that they see as adulterating the scriptural integrity of religion. In other cases, we find anti-traditional objections stemming from a modernist point of view that highlight the rigidities and abuses of dogmatic traditions and hierarchical institutions. In a sense, these concerns echo some of Schuon's reflections on the human margin, both in terms of theological hyperbole along with institutional or sociocultural excesses. However, what distinguishes Schuon's position from most contemporary critiques of religion is his view that this human margin is inevitable. The latter is seen as a kind of extrinsic necessity that has an ambiguous, but also integrating, function. The latter is most apparent in the earlier phases of a tradition's development, whereas the former—together with its negative potential—tends to manifest "with a vengeance" in its later stages. Furthermore, Schuon's consideration of the sacred roots of this phenomenon—in the sense of a Divine condescension that permits a "humanizing" of religion—implies that the gap between the Absolute and the human domain is not as unbridgeable as it may initially appear from a "puritanical" point of view. As for the excessive institutionalization of religion, Schuon often deplores its detrimental effects, although he also acknowledges the reality of the human factors that give rise to it. For instance, in considering the institutional formalism of the Roman Catholic Church,[34] he attributes its proliferation to certain traits and needs that are ingrained in the mentality of Latin cultures.[35] At any rate, for Schuon, it

---

34. "On the Catholic side, there is a certain bureaucratization of the sacred, which goes hand in hand with a kind of militarization of sanctity, if one may be allowed to express oneself thus; in particular, there is the cult of the monastic 'Rules' and that of the liturgical 'rubrics.'" Schuon, *In the Face of the Absolute*, 58.

35. "One example, among others, of 'Tradition' as a 'precept of men,' is the cardinalate: whereas bishops and patriarchs derive from the apostles, there is nothing in the New Testament that prefigures the cardinals. At the beginning of this papal institution, even the laity could obtain this dignity; after the 11th century, it was attributed only to the bishops, priests and deacons who surrounded the Pope; in the 13th century, every cardinal received the rank of bishop and the red hat; finally, in the 17th century, the

is clear that any response to this challenge is not to be found on the level of collective dogmatic or ritual reforms—these may be necessary, in some cases, but they also yield consequences that are often worse than what they seek to remedy—but rather in an interiorization of traditional forms in a spirit of contemplative focus on the essential metaphysical and sacramental dimensions of religion. This essentialization may vary in form and extent, as the history of mysticism demonstrates, but it allows one to situate and relativize phenomena pertaining to the human margin without losing sight of the integrating and transformative powers of a tradition.

In a sense, we could draw a meaningful analogy between a discrimination of the human margin and the discernment that contemplatives bring to their relationship with the world. How can contemplatives know what they can give to the world without taking something away from God, since there is a sense in which the spiritual path is an alternative between the two? The criterion here is what Schuon calls the predominance of "the inner pole of attraction."[36] This pole comprises a concentration on the Heart or the Intellect through contemplative practices. In other words, that which does not run contrary to the predominance of this pole can be conceded to the outer world, which may then become a support for spiritual interiorization. Accordingly, it could be said that the criterion of discernment between the necessity of the essential and the contingency of the marginal may lie in giving priority to the inner kingdom. This reality is grounded in the Essence, which allows a discrimination of what is essential, as well as a capacity to situate more contingent elements within a spectrum of relativity.

---

cardinals received the title of 'Eminence.' All this has a more imperial than sacerdotal character and scarcely accords with the principle 'everywhere, always, by everyone' (*quod ubique, quod semper, quod ab omnibus creditum est*); having said this, we do not contest that such an institution may be required by the Roman or Latin mentality any more than we contest the requirements of the play of Providence." Schuon, *In the Face of the Absolute*, nn. 13, 59.

36. "The criterion of the balance between the outward and the inward is the predominance of the internal pole of attraction. The 'man of prayer' is capable of measuring what he is able to offer to his ambience, and what he is able to accept from it, without dispersing himself and without being unfaithful to his vocation of inwardness; nothing should be to the detriment of our relationship with immanent Heaven. Only those who give themselves to God can know what they have a right, or duty, to give to the world and to receive from it." Schuon, *The Play of Masks* (Bloomington, IN: World Wisdom, 2003), 33.

Aside from the confessional divisions and entanglements that it provokes, the human margin also lends support to a fideist antagonism toward non-religious expressions or intimations of the nature of things. Thus, Schuon also attributes to this margin the attacks of theologians against philosophy; we are referring here, primarily, to the Christian rejection of Platonism based on Saint Paul's opposition between the "wisdom according to the Spirit" (that of the Gospel) and the "wisdom according to the flesh" (that of Greek philosophy), but also to Ghazālī's scathing critique of Muslim philosophers. The matter at stake in such polemics is not so much the lack of conformity of philosophy to principles that are foundational for theology as it is the independence of the former from the Holy Spirit and, therefore, the alleged human pretensions of a "wisdom according to the flesh." Most Platonic theses, for instance, do not necessarily contradict the Christian worldview—quite the contrary, as the assimilation of Neo-Platonism into mystical theology clearly demonstrates. The real issue lies in such theses being claimed by philosophers as proceeding from the Intellect, independently of Revelation, hence the vehemence of early Christian polemics against philosophy by virtue of an instinct of preservation, which Schuon does not hesitate in attributing to the sentimental partialities of the human margin. The attacks of some Sufis and theologians, like al-Ghazālī, against Muslim philosophers is of the same type. What is targeted by Christian and Muslim apologists is the allegedly natural character of human intelligence. There is no question for them of meditating upon the implications of the Divine roots of the Intellect, since the latter is de facto primarily, if not only, considered in its human accidentality, and for the sake of extolling the exclusive privileges of Revelation. From a certain point of view, the theological bias is a clear limitation of the scope of human intelligence in the Name of Divine Power while, from another point of view, the expediency of the means can be deemed legitimate in light of imperatives dictated by soteriological ends. Here, the human margin plays the role—*mutatis mutandis*—of conventional truth in Buddhism, or perhaps even that of an *upāya*, but one which is not directly backed by the Transcendent, so to speak. In this respect, it makes it possible for the truth to be formalized in conformity with the human needs and limitations of a particular community, and it further mobilizes the emotions and energies of those it enlists at the service of this restricted expression of the truth.

The aforementioned considerations, along with Schuon's assertion that the Platonic argument—in contrast to the historicity of salvation in Christianity—is in the nature of things,[37] must lead us to raise the question of the relative merits of religion and philosophy. Could it be said that philosophy—in the highest sense of exercizing the actualization of the Intellect—is superior to religion? Yes and no, depending on the context and vantage point. There is an eminence in philosophy in that it can awaken wisdom and the Intellect independently of the limitations inherent to the religious point of view. Yet there is, in ordinary circumstances, an imperative for religion as a transformative reality grounded in the Will of the Transcendent, what Schuon refers to as the "means of grace." The following contrast highlights both the strengths and limits of the two perspectives: "For the Greeks, truth is that which is in conformity with the nature of things; for the Christians, truth is that which leads to God."[38] On the Platonic side, a recognition of the nature of things is, in principle, sufficient to realize the truth, but the fact is that such a direct correlation presupposes human and civilizational conditions that are most rarely fulfilled. The gnostic outlook implies that, in principle, everything lies within the heart of man, that is, in primordial intelligence,[39] although, in fact, mankind in its fallen state of spiritual hardening—and certainly collective mankind as the most direct manifestation of the latter—cannot be saved by intelligence alone. Schuon opines, in this respect, that "the Greeks can be reproached for having only at their disposal a way that is inaccessible in fact to the majority."[40] This allows one to understand why he also goes so far as to say that "Hellenist (philosophers) were predominantly right in principle and the Christians in fact";[41] since principles are more real than facts, one cannot but draw the conclusion that the highest sapiential philosophy is closer to Reality than religion understood as a system of sacred symbols. This relative superiority of philosophy can even be reflected—when contrasted with the ever-widening of the

---

37. Schuon, *Light on the Ancient Worlds*, 55.
38. Schuon, *Light on the Ancient Worlds*, 47.
39. "In esoterism there are two principles which may be actualized sporadically and at different levels, but always in a partial and contained manner: the first is that fundamentally, there is only one religion with various forms, for humanity is one and the spirit is one; the second principle is that man bears everything within himself, potentially at least, by reason of the immanence of the one Truth." Schuon, *In the Face of the Absolute*, 19.
40. Schuon, *Light on the Ancient Worlds*, 49.
41. Schuon, *Light on the Ancient Worlds*, 47.

human margin in religion—in the relative wisdom of political authority. The latter can, in some cases, represent a realism that is closer to the nature of things than "idealist" or fanatical religious institutions and figures largely disconnected from the spiritual sources of the tradition.[42] In both cases, the philosophical and the political—although obviously to markedly different degrees—may function as an intellectual and cultural corrective to the negative consequences flowing from the abusive spread of the human margin in the religious domain.

The question most keenly raised by the notions of the nature of things and the human margin is evidently that of the very nature of religious truth. Considering the sharp contrast between the two, truth can be conceived either as a matter of intellective *adaequatio* to the nature of things, which it rarely is, or as a largely sentimental and experiential adherence to symbolic facts that convey a sense of compelling reality. It is obviously in the context of the latter conception that the human margin manifests its most powerful influence. The humanization of religion is an unavoidable reality because religion is about human totality—totality of faith and integral engagement of the whole person—and because intelligence by itself cannot provide, in most cases, a sufficient foundation for such a totality. On a more circumstantial level, the notion of a human margin could be particularly useful in our day and age. At a time when the limitations and abuses of religious traditions have become increasingly apparent due to the erosive effect of time and the manifold corruptions and excesses of religious mankind, a capacity to discern the implications of the human margin may keep one from discarding what is essential out of a misguided focus on the contingent. However, this discrimination is a difficult exercise; first on account of the margin of indeterminacy found in traditional religious phenomena, and second because it presupposes a deep spiritual anchoring in the essential teachings of a tradition, along with a genuine receptivity to the emanations of the sacred.

It should, by now, be evident that one of the major questions concerning the human margin lies in assessing the boundaries of its scope and the degree of its acceptability or toleration. Indeed, the very notion

---

42. "The Muslims in Spain were not persecuted until the clergy had become too powerful in comparison with the temporal power; the temporal power, which appertains to the emperor, represents in this case universality or 'realism,' and therefore 'tolerance,' and therefore also in the nature of things a certain element of wisdom." Schuon, *Light on the Ancient Worlds*, 3.

of margin entails an element of relativity and imprecision that cannot be reduced to clear and distinct boundaries. Contemplating the human margin means, therefore, dealing with a measure of unintelligibility inherent to relative reality, including religion as a humanly contingent matter. Ultimately, the confrontation of the nature of things and the human margin must be linked to the principle of the two subjectivities: "In one sense it is evidently the fallen and sinful individuality that is 'ourselves'; in another sense it is the transcendent and unalterable Self: the planes are different; there is no common measure between them."[43] In the religious order, the first "self" necessarily involves the human margin to some degree, whereas the second entails the nature of things since it is its very principle. The paradoxes and perplexing ambiguities of religion, not to say its blemishes and "pious absurdities," flow from the confrontation of two realities that have "no common measure."

---

43. Schuon, *Light on the Ancient Worlds*, 54.

5

Trinitarian Metaphysics

Schuon's metaphysics can be characterized as unconditionally focused on the strictest concept of the Absolute. Indeed, he considers this emphasis the hallmark, and starting point, of any truly esoteric perspective. In *Understanding Islam*, Schuon notes, in the context of a contrast between Christianity and Islam, that "exoterism must always start from the relative while esoterism starts from the Absolute to which it gives a more strict, and even the strictest possible meaning."[1] This is so inasmuch as exoterism and esoterism have both different subjects and different objects. The subject of exoterism, or the subject of ordinary religion, cannot be other than the individual self, which is primarily interested in its terrestrial happiness and postmortem condition. Religions, in their exoteric dimension, address the needs of the individual, both in the here-below and in the hereafter. "Starting from the relative" means starting from relative consciousness, therefore, from the individual, empirical, self that the Hindu tradition denotes as *jīvātman*. This holds true intellectually, volitionally, sentimentally, and eschatologically. Intellectually, this means that the exoteric doctrine must satisfy an individual mode of understanding, thereby remaining within the strictures of the limitations that are inherent to the individual order. Concretely speaking, such needs cannot but translate to a merely rational formulation of theological principles that is, perforce, analytical and exclusionary, given the nature of rational thought and its inability to make sense of a plurality of aspects and points of view. Volitionally, the individual scope of exoterism is expressed in a strong emphasis on the actions and merits of the individual. For all practical purposes, religious

---

1. Schuon, *Understanding Islam* (Bloomington, IN: World Wisdom, 2011), 13.

life is understood as what Hindus would refer to as a *karma-yoga*, a way of action primarily—but not exclusively—characterized by one's adherence to prescriptions and proscriptions. Emotionally, the exoteric system provides a powerful means of sentimental identification, the effectiveness of which is largely dependent on an exclusivist conviction of being "the true religion" and a subsequent lack of imagination with regard to the spiritual degrees and modes of realization of religious perspectives that lie outside the perimeter of the familiar. Eschatologically, the aspiration of the "exoteric self" is primarily concentrated on obtaining a state of bliss in the hereafter, even though the intensity of devotional love that enters, at its peak, into its spiritual economy may overwhelm this merely individual aspiration under the universality of Love. Thus, the individual scope of exoterism cannot always exclude glimmers of universal and even at times supra-confessional realities and insights. In this regard, for instance, the rational modalities of the theological creed cannot prevent it from opening the way to a sense of the unfathomable Mystery that is also a manner of recognizing, albeit indirectly and as if symbolically, the supra-rational—hence intellective—horizon of religious faith. Similarly, the exoteric perspective of action and merits cannot completely veil the supra-individual dimensions of faith and grace, which are bound to function—in lieu of the objectivity of the Intellect—as a kind of modality of the latter in relation to the individual. As for the perspective of individual salvation, it is not immune from faint intimations of the unconditioned Deliverance, even more so when it reaches the mystical heights of loving extinction in the Beloved.

Besides the aforementioned characters of the exoteric path, it must also be stressed that the nature of the exoteric subject is intrinsically connected to the definition of the exoteric object or, rather, Object. In other words, the individual perspective that is integral to exoterism is necessarily dependent on an understanding of the Divine as a Personal Being. This is Being in the Schuonian sense, not as an impersonal principle but as a Divine Interlocutor, if one may put it this way. To wit, a human being *qua* individual cannot relate to the Non-dual Essence as such, insofar as the latter not only transcends the former but also annihilates it, as it were, and encompasses it. This amounts to saying that the exoteric point of view as such cannot reach a fully adequate concept of the Absolute as the one supra-ontological and supra-personal Principle.

The unity of the supra-ontological Principle, to which Schuon refers as Beyond-Being, is inherent in the very understanding of its absoluteness and infinitude. The Absolute is One because any duality or multiplicity is ontologically, and logically, incompatible with metaphysical absoluteness. A plurality within the Absolute would amount to relativity—and therefore non-absoluteness—inasmuch as it would necessarily postulate a relationality between the constituents of this plurality. It would signify the reality of several Absolutes since the Absolute *qua* Absolute cannot admit of any reality *beside* it. Plurality, including any ternary, is also incompatible with the Infinite since it involves the limitations that are inherent to the exclusive reality of the plural constituents. The Ultimate is, therefore, emphatically One, both in the exclusive sense of absolute unity and in the inclusive sense of infinite unity.

The foregoing suggests that there is, in the exoteric point of view—paradoxically considering the religious emphasis on the uniqueness of the Object of worship—a quasi-irreducible duality,[2] that is in keeping with the conventional etymology of the word religion as a link or bond between the human and the Divine (but which also presupposes separation). When religion is exclusively defined in terms of relationship and worship, it cannot but amount to a sort of absolutization of both the worshipper and the worshipped. By contrast with this intrinsic religious tendency toward dualism, it is no coincidence that an emphasis on the Trinity, or triads, in religious metaphysics can also often be evidence of an esoteric perspective. This is so inasmuch as a metaphysical ternary points to a reintegration within Unity, through a retrospective addition of one to two. It is also true to the extent that a ternary may symbolize non-duality, rather than Unity as such, whether within a gnostic perspective or through an alchemy of Love and Union. This appears in the fact that the third element is a synthesis—and therefore in a way a negation—of two, rather than being a mere equivalent of one. Finally, the esoteric meaning of three-ness suggests a consideration of Unity from the dimension of its internal plurality, so to speak, and therefore an ability to move from one perspective to the other by virtue of a receptivity to the various angles and vantage points of Relativity.[3] Such is obviously the case in the context of Christianity,

---

2. We use the restriction "quasi" because the mysticism of love tend toward an "asymptotic" Union that comes close to Unity but never quite reaches it.

3. "The Trinity, inasmuch as it corresponds to a more differentiated point of view and represents a particular development of the Doctrine of Unity among others that are equally possible, is not strictly speaking capable of exoteric formulation, for the simple reason that a 'differentiated' or 'derived' metaphysical conception is not accessible to everyone." Schuon, *The Transcendent Unity of Religions* (Wheaton, IL: Theosophical Publishing House, 1984), 133.

since the ideas of the "Word made flesh" and the procession of the Holy Spirit is characteristically esoteric (albeit within the language of Love) in its highest, supra-rational, reaches and transmutational implications. As we will see, though, the Trinitarian theology that ensues constitutes a sort of exotericization of this esoteric Trinity. Nevertheless, there is, within the Trinity, an intimation of the One that cuts short any danger of dualistic reduction. This is already symbolized, mathematically speaking, by the fact that three is considered to be the first odd number; therefore, the first retrospective number, inasmuch as it adds unity to the even number, and thus refers it back toward its numerical source.[4] While four often symbolizes the Earth, or manifestation as such, three tends to refer to manifestation as a point, or way, of return to the One.

This chapter will explore the ways in which Schuon articulates a metaphysics of the Trinity that he sees as consistent with the Christian *idée-force* and applicable to it, even though it clearly remains at odds with mainstream theological views on the Tri-une God. As we have seen, traditional metaphysics is particularly connected to the number Three insofar as it accounts for non-duality within multiplicity. It adds One to Two in a way that produces plurality but also integrates the latter under the rule of Unity, by expressing the plural in terms of the One. Buddhists would argue, in the same order of ideas, that one must recognize and express the Ultimate truth according to its conventional manifestations. Accordingly, the conventional realm of relativity is intrinsically dualistic and, therefore, plural. In the religious order, inasmuch as it is bound to relative existence, the confrontation of the Divine and the human has something absolute about it, even though the deepest principles of the religious outlook cannot but open onto non-duality as exemplified, in a most striking way, by the following Qur'ānic verse: "Everything perishes but the face of God" (28:88). Thus, the number Three symbolizes, among other interpretations, the remembrance of the One within the world of multiplicity that it produces.[5] In this sense, while the dialectics of duality

---

4. "The odd numbers are 'retrospective' in the sense that they express an infolding towards Unity, or the Divine Origin, whereas the even numbers are 'prospective' in the sense that they express on the contrary a movement in the direction of Manifestation, the world or the Universe." Schuon, *In the Face of the Absolute* (Bloomington, IN: World Wisdom, 2014), 124.

5. This appears most clearly, in Schuon's works, in the Sufi ternary of the human rememberer, the Divine Remembered and spiritual remembrance: "The three words

comprises opposition and complementarity, that of the number Three connotes production and reintegration.

It could be added, that the number Three saves Two and, by extension plurality in general, from its negative potentialities. Three prevents Two from becoming a principle of opposition and, by bringing in unity within plurality, actualizes within the dyad its potential of harmonious complementarity. Schuon writes that this is exemplified, in human existence, by the implications of the relationship between a man and a woman, and the need for this confrontation to be, in some way, opened up by a third element.[6] In this connection, Schuon goes as far as to suggest that "the number Three, for its part, has about it something messianic."[7] This amounts to saying that Three can symbolize and actualize a redemption from the vicissitudes and evils that are the concomitants of duality as a principle of division and opposition. It is not, therefore, a matter of coincidence that the number Three plays such a central role in many metaphysical and theological teachings of salvation and emancipation.

In order to understand his overall interpretation of the metaphysical Trinity, it is important to note that Schuon makes it explicit that there exist two types of ternaries. The first essentially amounts to a synthesis of the One and the Two through a third element that is, either essential and inward, or productive and outward, in relation to it. The triangle provides a fitting geometric representation of this type of triad, whether in a productive mode, from the apex to the base, or a reintegrative mode, from the base to the apex. In this schema, Three evokes the inner life or the "inner breathing" of Unity, an aspect that is fundamental, for instance,

---

dhākir, dhikr, madhkūr—a classical ternary in Sufism—correspond exactly to the ternary Muhammad, *Rasūl*, Allāh: Muhammad is the invoker, *Rasūl* the invocation, Allāh the invoked. In the invocation, the invoker and the invoked meet, just as Muhammad and Allāh meet in the *Rasūl*, or in the *Risālah*, the Message." Schuon, *Sufism: Veil and Quintessence* (Bloomington, IN: World Wisdom, 2006), 106.

6. "In a permanent confrontation of two beings, there must be two equilibrium-producing openings, one towards Heaven and the other on earth itself: there must be an opening towards God, who is the third element above the two spouses, without which the duality would become opposition; and there must be an opening or a void—a ventilation, so to speak—on the immediate human plane, and this is abstinence, which is both a sacrifice before God and a homage of respect and gratitude towards the spouse." Schuon, *Esoterism as Principle and as Way* (Pates Manor, Bedfont, Middlesex: Perennial Books, 1981), 134.

7. Schuon, *The Eye of the Heart* (Bloomington, IN: World Wisdom, 1997), 25.

to Christian theology. As we will see, this type of ternary corresponds to the highest metaphysical meaning of the number Three such as is illustrated, for example, by the Hindu triplicity of *Sat*, *Cit*, and *Ānanda*. The second type of ternary does not involve any direct unfolding of or reduction to Unity, but it establishes a kind of spatial hierarchy from the point of view of "a consciousness which is situated within it."[8] This sort of ternary is, therefore, relative in the sense that it involves degrees that are envisaged from a particular vantage point. A reference to a subjective consciousness situated within the space of the hierarchy of the ternary presupposes a relative outlook and, therefore, Relativity itself. Moreover, this pattern is exclusive of any union or synthesis of two of the terms. It also precludes that one be a mediating element between the two others, even though one can obviously be situated in between two others in the scale of the ternary. Schuon mentions the Hindu cosmological triad of *sattva*, *rajas*, and *tamas* and the traditional tripartition of body, soul, and spirit[9] as representative of this type of ternary. The first type of ternary is "synthetically horizontal" in the sense that it does not involve a hierarchy of the three terms and is underpinned by Unity, whereas the second type is necessarily "gradationally vertical" inasmuch it entails an ontological or epistemological hierarchy. The first ternary is therefore objective in that it refers to different dimensions of the same object in and of itself, whereas the second presupposes a subjective and relative position. As we shall see, this distinction is important in paving the ground for a differentiation between a "vertical Trinity," which corresponds to the second type of ternary and presupposes a relative point of view, and several instances of a "horizontal Trinity" that do not involve any relativity in regard to the distinction between the three terms themselves. A consideration of these distinctions lies at the foundation of Schuon's interpretation of the Trinity.

Schuon's treatment of this subject cannot be approached without first recognizing that it is based on the premise that any major historical religious event, such as the birth, teaching, and death of Christ, must be situated in relation to its foundations *in divinis*. In other words, Schuon's perspective is decidedly supra-historical, not only in that it asserts the

---

8. Schuon, *Esoterism as Principle and as Way*, 67.

9. "But there is still another type of ternary, the most immediate example of which is the hierarchy of the constituent elements of the microcosm, *corpus*, *anima*, *spiritus*, or *soma*, *psyche*, *pneuma*; the Vedantic ternary of the cosmic qualities, *tamas*, *rajas*, *sattwa*, is of the same order." Schuon, *Esoterism as Principle and as Way*, 67.

metaphysical primacy of principles over events but also, and above all, in that it understands the latter as being the manifestations of realities that are already present in the Divine *eminently*. The traditional theological distinction between the immanent Trinity and the economical Trinity parallels, to a certain extent, this way of apprehending the relationship between metaphysical principles or archetypes and historical manifestations. The first notion refers to the intrinsic interplay of the relationships between the Persons within the Divine Reality itself, whereas the second pertains to the respective functions and relations of the Persons in the economy of salvation.

This perspective allows one to understand why Schuon may provide several readings of the meaning of the Trinity. In other words, the historical drama that involves the Father, the Son, and the Holy Spirit is rooted in realities that span the range of metaphysical dimensions and onto-cosmological degrees that are relevant here. It is precisely at this juncture that we find the main difference between Schuon's meditations on the Trinity and normative Christian Trinitarian theology. His perspective emphasizes the plurality of the Trinity's manifestations, on different planes of Reality, while also being careful not to confuse them. What this means, in effect, is that Schuon's understanding of the Trinity cannot be reduced to the theological level as it is, primarily, metaphysical. This distinction is crucial in Schuon's vocabulary: while theology is a discourse on God as Personal Being, metaphysics is the science of the Unconditioned, or Beyond-Being, together with its Self-determinations and Self-manifestations. This distinction may sound like an abstraction and a puzzle to many, but it actually refers to a most fundamental principle that entails many consequences with respect to one's understanding of Reality and its spiritual correlates. Theology, in a Christian and more generally monotheistic context, pertains to God conceived as the Ultimate Being and the Principle, through creation, of all beings. The use of the term "being" to refer both to the Creator and to creation is evidence of the "commensurate measure" that makes it possible to think of their reciprocal relationship. Hence, when Schuon makes use of the adjective ontological, he wishes to designate the Divinity as first and supreme Being, as well as to its engagement in multiple relationships with mankind and creation. Therefore, when used in contrast to theological, the term metaphysical means meta-ontological. This expression does not, in any way, refer to an absence of being but to a radically transcendent order of Reality that the term Being cannot satisfactorily denote since it is already redolent with a sense of relativity.

By contrast, Schuon has coined the term Beyond-Being to suggest that the Ultimate Reality lies beyond any polarity, relationality, or hypostatic determination.

It is on this supra-ontological level that the highest triad in Schuon's metaphysics can be contemplated. It corresponds to the Hindu *Sat-Cit-Ānanda*, most often translated as Being-Consciousness-Bliss. These are, particularly in *Advaita Vedānta*, the three characterizations of the absolute and ultimate *Brahman*. *Sat*, *Cit*, and *Ānanda* are not qualities as such since they pertain to *Nirguna Brahman*, that is, the *Brahman* without qualities, in contrast to *Saguna Brahman*, the *Brahman* possessed of qualities. In other words, as Eliot Deutsch has suggested, it would be a mistake to understand *Sat*, *Cit*, and *Ānanda* as "qualifying attributes" since they pertain to the intrinsic reality, or essence, of *Brahman*. However, this does not mean that these terms are definitions of *Brahman*, which—strictly speaking—is indefinable. Rather, they should be considered as modes of apprehending its Reality within the context of relative human understanding.[10] It must be added that *Sat-Cit-Ānanda* cannot be reduced to either the status of mere concepts or to subjective modes of contemplation of Reality, for the attributes of *Nirguna Brahman* are objectively one with Reality as its internal and substantial contents.

In a similar way, Schuon uses the term "dimensions" to refer to that which is intrinsic to the Ultimate but cannot be differentiated objectively. This term clearly pertains to the element of space, which is the most accurate approach to the Supreme Ternary, since "the natural symbol of the trinity is provided by the three dimensions of space."[11] The ternary of dimensions is that of height, width, and depth, the definitions of which may vary depending on the perspective on a given object but which, in all cases, provide approaches to "measuring" the "immeasurable." However, any Trinity involves a necessary division between One and Two, while the modes of this division vary depending on the point of view. This means that the triangular symbolism that illustrates the Trinity may show the

---

10. "With the designation of Brahman as *saccidānanda*, we have an essential identification of *sat, cit, ānanda* with Brahman rather than an adjectival qualifying of Brahman. . . . These terms are really being used properly not so much in a logical as in a phenomenological manner, for the problem is not so much one of defining Brahman as it is one of describing the fundamental features of man's experience of Oneness." Deutsch, *Advaita Vedānta*, 9–10, n.2.

11. Deutsch, *Advaita Vedānta*, 69.

apex at the top and the base at the bottom, or the reverse. Schuon makes use of both forms of symbolism, sometimes initiating his metaphysical account with the unicity of the Sovereign Good and, at other times, with the complementary polarity of the Absolute and the Infinite. Thus, according to the first pattern, the Ultimate is the Sovereign Good: it is first Absolute and, as such, Infinite, and then Perfect. The connection between absoluteness and infinitude is intrinsic and, as such, represented by the two extremities of the base, "the one being inconceivable without the other."[12] The Absolute is that which is totally itself without any qualification and is, at the same time, necessary and independent from anything else. There is, in the concept of the Absolute, a reality of self-sufficiency that entails a necessary lack of constraints or boundaries and is, therefore, a synonym of infinitude. An Absolute that is not Infinite would leave something out of itself, as it were, by which it would be—*ipso facto*—limited and, in a sense, determined. The Absolute is exclusive of everything, while the Infinite is inclusive of everything. It could also be said that the Absolute is No-Thing—which is to be understood here as unconditioned—while the Infinite is Everything, that is, equivalent to All-Possibility. The second point of view, the reversed triangle, begins with the aforementioned two dimensions as a dyad, to which is added a third that pertains to a "less synthetic point of view," that is, "closer to *Māyā*."[13] It is referred to by Schuon as Perfection. One may wonder why this Perfection is deemed to be closer to relativity than it is to the Absolute and the Infinite. If Perfection is defined as the absence of defects, it follows that it excludes imperfection and thus cannot accommodate it in any way. In other words, there is in the Absolute an exclusive and an inclusive aspect: by affirming its exclusive Reality, the Absolute also includes everything within it. Similarly, the Infinite would not be the Infinite without having the capacity to "become" finite. These two dimensions of absoluteness and infinitude, the two "sides" of Beyond-Being, derive, so to speak, from the core reality of the One as such, the Ultimate beyond all relativities, which is why its exclusiveness cannot exclude inclusiveness and why its inclusiveness includes, as it were, exclusiveness. Perfection, the third dimension, for its part, does exclude imperfections and flaws, without it being possible to say that it also includes them intrinsically, or by virtue of its very perfection, in a

---

12. Schuon, *Survey of Metaphysics and Esoterism* (Bloomington, IN: World Wisdom, 2000), 15.
13. Schuon, *Survey of Metaphysics and Esoterism*, 25.

manner that would be analogous to the way the Absolute and the Infinite do with respect to the relative and the finite. This greater exclusiveness is, in a sense, a mark of a closer proximity to *Māyā*, since essential and all-embracing inclusiveness characterizes the highest consideration of Reality, while more relative degrees, including with respect to the Divine Order, entail increasingly greater measures of exclusiveness. This is evident, first and foremost, in the way Beyond-Being envelops everything while the Divine Being or Personality excludes creaturely relativity through its transcendence. As we have indicated, when the three dimensions of the Absolute, the Infinite, and the Perfect are represented by a triangle, the base would be at the top, consisting of the horizontal axis of the Absolute and the Infinite while the apex would be at the bottom, representing Perfection. This triangular structure illustrates the way Perfection may appear as a product of the "combination" of the Absolute and the Infinite. It has the exclusiveness of the former, in terms of its incompatibility with relative flaws, and the inclusiveness of the latter in the way it includes every quality without lacking anything. It must be added that Perfection is the projection of the Absolute through the radiation of the Infinite. Thus, it may be conceived as the Divine archetype of *Māyā* and, thereby, the super-essential Root of Existence.[14]

Now, a confusion may arise with respect to Perfection from the fact that, at times, Schuon also, as we have seen, makes use of the concept of Sovereign Good to refer to the highest dimension of the Ultimate Principle. Given their common qualitative super-eminence, these two concepts may be equated, as they sometimes are by Schuon himself,[15] but they may also be distinguished to highlight a difference in perspective. For instance, in his chapter "The Onto-Cosmological Chain," Schuon symbolically refers to the Supreme as a triangle, the apex of which is the Sovereign Good while the basis is the polarity of the Absolute and the Infinite. The expression "Sovereign Good" is derived from the Platonic Good, *to agathón*, which Plato in his *Republic* characterizes as being *epékeina tēs ousías*, that is,

---

14. "Relativity cannot be personified in the Trinity because it is itself, in a way, the framework for the personifications." Schuon, *Form and Substance in the Religions*, 37.

15. "If we were to be asked what Perfection or the Sovereign Good is . . . we would say it is that which, in the world, is manifested as qualities." Schuon, *From the Divine to the Human* (Bloomington, IN: World Wisdom, 2013), 31–32.

beyond Being.[16] The term Sovereign Good indicates both the ultimate character of the Principle and the reality of its substance. Schuon does not ignore, however, that the concept of Good presents a potential problem for some readers in that it is morally and linguistically related to its opposite, namely evil. This reality is inherent in the nature of conditioned experience that is characterized by the possibility of negation and privation and to the nature of language that cannot but bear witness to this intrinsic limitation of the relative order. This is the reason why, like other gnostics, Schuon specifies that it "is necessary to distinguish between the Good in itself and the manifestations of the Good."[17] The first is absolute while the latter are relative. The absoluteness of the Supreme Good—the fact that it has no opposite—explains, but does not totally justify, the assertion that the Absolute is beyond good and evil. In this case, the Supreme Good is Perfection as the apex of the supra-ontological triangle whose base is the dyad Absolute-Infinite but, when used as a synonym of Perfection, is the lowest tip of the reversed triangle that points toward *Māyā* from above it, so to speak. At any rate, Schuon sometimes refers to these three dimensions as "hypostases," not to indicate that they are "below" the Essence as mere Qualities would be, but in order to highlight their intrinsic substantiality or the fact that they constitute the very foundations of Reality as such.

As we have indicated, Schuon's most elevated interpretation of the Trinity is metaphysical. This is the "supreme horizontal" interpretation, which is equated by Schuon to the ternary *Sat*, *Cit*, and *Ānanda* but that remains, albeit less explicitly, connected to the three dimensions of absoluteness, infinitude, and perfection. In a sense, the two ternaries (and the order in which they unfold), present us with two different ways of understanding the relationships between the Persons, ways that echo the respective Roman Catholic and Eastern Orthodox interpretations of the procession of the Spirit. When referring to the Hindu ternary, it is quite clear that the Father corresponds to *Sat*, the Son to *Cit*, and the Holy Spirit to *Ānanda*. The Father is the ontological and un-originated Cause. The Son actualizes the dimension of Consciousness of Reality—*Cit*—as refraction, that is, "begotten" by Being in the sense of its intrinsic and

---

16. ". . . *ouk ousías ontos toū agathoū, all' eti epékeina tēs ousías presbeía kai dynámei hyperéchontos.*" Plato, *Republic*, Book 6, 509b, 8–10.
17. Schuon, *Survey of Metaphysics*, 27.

internal reverberation, as it were. As for the Holy Spirit, it refers to *Ānanda* in that the latter is the principle of Bliss that communicates the internal life of Being and Consciousness. It is important to insist on the principle that Being, Consciousness, and Bliss are not differentiated objectively and that they refer to a single Unity of Essence, as indicated by the reference to the Ultimate by the single word *Saccitānanda*. With respect to the three dimensions of absoluteness, infinitude, and perfection, they can also be correlated respectively to the three Persons of the Trinity. In this case, the Father refers to the Absolute, the Son to Perfection, and the Holy Spirit to Infinitude. The Father is the Absolute as "unbegotten," without an originating cause. The Holy Spirit evokes the Infinite as principle of projection, radiation, and diffusion, while the Son is the crystallized perfection of the Real. In the Hindu ternary, the Holy Spirit comes in third as Bliss, while it comes in second in the Schuonian ternary as the Infinite. The latter sequence emphasizes the principle that the Spirit proceeds from the Father through the Son, whereas the former may be interpreted as meaning that the Spirit proceeds from the Father and the Son, which corresponds to the Latin theological view of the *filioque*.[18] As Infinite, the Holy Spirit is pure radiation from the center, that is the Absolute; as Bliss, the Holy Spirit is communication of the Good from Being through Consciousness.

Besides this interpretation of the Trinity as a supreme and horizontal ternary, Schuon introduces three other ways in which the Trinity may be understood. One is vertical, in the sense that involves degrees of Reality, while the two others are horizontal, like the supra-ontological Trinity, but situated on the level of Being and Existence. Schuon distinguishes between dimensions, degrees, and modes of the Divine Principle. As we have seen, the word dimensions pertain to ways of "measuring" the intrinsic reality of Beyond-Being. It also refers to an internal plurality that is inherent to undifferentiated Unity. Degrees, by contrast, imply an onto-cosmological

---

18. "The principle of radiation or projection—inherent in the Absolute, in the 'Father'—corresponds to the 'Holy Spirit,' and the principle of polarization or refraction, to the 'Son.' The 'Son' is to the 'Father' what the circle is to the center; and the 'Holy Spirit' is to the 'Father' what the radius is to the center. And as the radius, which 'emanates' from the center, does not stop at the circle but traverses it, it could be said that starting from the circle, the radius is 'delegated' by the circle, just as the 'Spirit' emanates from the 'Father' and is delegated by the 'Son'; the nature of the *filioque*, at once justifiable and problematical, becomes clear with the aid of this image." Schuon, *From the Divine to the Human*, 34–35.

unfolding, whereby the transcendent Unity of the Principle is first determined and then made manifest. This refers to a version of the classical notion of the Great Chain of Being, which consists in Beyond Being, Being, and Existence. The latter does not refer to the manifested universe as such but to its Center, which is the direct reflection of the Ultimate within Manifestation, or to Manifestation inasmuch as it is none other than the Principle. Finally, the concept of modes refers to aspects of the Divine Nature, inasmuch as they are differentiated, that is, below the level of the pure Absolute or Beyond-Being.

The vertical interpretation of the Trinity is fundamentally subordinationist and it is, as such, at odds with the main theological streams of Christianity that insist on not giving any Person, including the Father, any metaphysical preeminence. For Schuon, on the contrary, there is no way to exclude such a vertical reading of the Trinity, since it flows from the respective concepts of the Father and the Son and since some of Christ's words, in the Gospel, clearly establish the superiority of the Father in relation to the Son. Now in the vertical Trinity, the Father corresponds to Beyond-Being, the pure undifferentiated Essence, while the Son refers to the Self-Determination of the Essence as Being, and the Holy Spirit to Divine Self-Manifestation as Existence. The correspondence between the Son and Being appears in the fact that "Being is the Word of Beyond-Being" as First Determination; thus, it could be said that it is metaphysically begotten by Beyond-Being. As for the Holy Spirit, it refers to Existence inasmuch as the latter is the very manifestation of Divine Reality through the expansive radiation of its infinitude and, insofar as it constitutes the spiritual center of the cosmos, or the point of junction between the transcendent Order and the immanent realm. Existence flows from Beyond-Being as infinite and it does so through the Self-Determination of the latter as Being. It could be said, therefore, that what theology envisions as generation is akin to the determination of Self in and by the Other, while procession is tantamount to the manifestation of Self both through and from the Other. This metaphysical Trinity is based, first of all, on the primary recognition that Beyond-Being is the ultimate metaphysical foundation of everything, and that this originating status makes it symbolically analogous to the Father. It is based, second, on the idea of "metaphysical generation" as "productive determination." To say that Beyond-Being and Being are con-substantial could mean, from this point of view, that they share in the transcendence of the Divine Reality. Third, the "delegation" of Existence can be interpreted as the manifestation of the infinite wealth of Reality of Beyond-Being by, and through, the creative Being.

As mentioned earlier, the horizontal undifferentiated Trinity is not the only one to be considered as referring to a similar metaphysical degree of Reality. Schuon actually mentions two other such considerations of the Trinity: one on the level of Being and another on the level of Existence. As we go down the levels of Reality, the same fundamental triplicity can be contemplated but only according to very different modalities. At the degree of the supreme horizontal Trinity, the Trinity is undifferentiated which means that the three dimensions refer to the eminent "substance" of the Highest Reality within the pure Unity of Beyond Being. One could, therefore, make use, *mutatis mutandis*, of Thomistic categories to state that the Trinity is entitatively in the Essence but not intentionally, so to speak. Or else that the three dimensions are undifferentiated metaphysically but distinct cognitively. Now, as a consequence of the infinitude of the Trinity's supra-ontological reality, there must be also a determinative projection of its undifferentiated eminence on the level of Being. In other words, that which is supra-ontologically latent must be ontologically patent: "(The supreme horizontal perspective) envisages the Trinity inasmuch as It is hidden in Unity; the non-supreme horizontal perspective on the contrary situates Unity as an essence hidden within the Trinity, which is then ontological and represents the three fundamental aspects or modes of Pure Being, whence the triad: Being, Wisdom, Will (Father, Son, Spirit)."[19] On the ontological level, the Divine Unity underlies the Trinity that modalizes Being, as it were. The Father is Being as foundation of all the other modes of reality and the Son, which Saint Paul calls "the Wisdom of the Father" (2 Corinthians 13:13) crystallizes, so to speak, the Intelligence that is inherent to Divine Being; hence the identification of Christ with the Intellect in Christian gnosis. Finally, the ontological mode of the Holy Spirit is Will, inasmuch as the latter is the principle of production and diffusion of Being.[20]

Schuon also makes mention, at times, of a third horizontal Trinity situated on the level of Existence.[21] This is, one will recall, the degree

---

19. Schuon, *Understanding Islam*, 45.

20. This is not without relevance to Saint Augustine's Trinity of "Memory, Understanding and Will," the first being conceived as the repository of all that is, hence its relationship with Being.

21. "One could envisage a third plane, already cosmic but nevertheless still divine from the human point of view, which is the point of view that determines theology,

TRINITARIAN METAPHYSICS | 167

that corresponds to the Holy Spirit in the vertical Trinity, that is to say, the degree of the projection of the Divine into Manifestation. Interestingly, Schuon refers to two non-Christian equivalent of this theo-cosmic Reality: the Hindu *Trimūrti* and the Islamic *Rūh*. With respect to the ternary Brahmā-Vishnu-Śiva, it must be observed that it presents some correlations with the functions of the Persons of the Trinity. Brahmā is the god of Creation, the Originator. Vishnu is the Conservator and he is, as such, associated with avatāric descents for the sake of the salvation of the world. As for Śiva, he "incarnates" the principle of dissolution and revivification thus echoing some of the characteristics of the Holy Spirit, particularly with respect to its freedom from forms: "The Spirit bloweth where it listeth" (John 3:8). As for *ar-Rūh*, Schuon associates it with Brahmā, "the Spirit of God hovereth over the waters," which he compares to the center of which *al-'Arsh* ("the Throne") is the circumference and *an-Nūr* the "substance" or the "matter."[22] Here again, it is possible to highlight: (i) "resonances" between *Ar-Rūh* and the principle of creation, *Al-'Arsh*; (ii) the Divine "circumference" or "crystallizing projection" of the Divine and the authority of the Kingdom of Heaven—"my Kingdom is not of this world"; and (iii) *An-Nūr* and the principle of diffusion of the Divine Light that illuminates the totality of the universe, which is associated with the Holy Spirit.

As a synthesis, the combination of the vertical Trinity and the three horizontal ones illustrates both the relational inequality of the Persons—as a descending ternary—and their "substantial" equality on each of the three metaphysical planes of consideration. Among these four interpretations, the meta-cosmic and differentiated view of the Persons reflects the concept of the theological Trinity. Furthermore, it can be argued that Schuon's distinction between the ontological and the theo-cosmic Trinity parallels, in some ways, the traditional theological distinction between the immanent and the economical Trinity. Thus, Handley Moule suggests that "the Immanent Trinity is a phrase pointing to the internal inner relation of the Persons . . . [while] the Economical Trinity is a phrase pointing to what may be called with reverence the redeeming activities

---

and this is the luminous Center of the cosmos, the 'Triple Manifestation' (*Trimūrti*) of Hindu doctrine and the 'Spirit' (*Rūh*) of Islamic doctrine the Trinity is also present here, radiating and acting." Schuon, *Logic and Transcendence*, 85.

22. "*Al-'Arsh* is the 'circumference' of which *Ar-Rūh* will be the 'center' and *An-Nūr* the 'matter.'" Schuon, *Dimensions of Islam*, 120.

of the Persons."[23] There is, in this distinction, something that echoes the Schuonian distinction between Being and Existence. Notwithstanding, a number of contemporary theologians, including Karl Rahner, claim that the immanent Trinity is none other than the economical Trinity.[24] This is, of course, a consequence, of the historicizing tendencies of contemporary theology in a Christian context; it points to a desire not to let go of any relational and soteriological differentiations while keeping them equated with transcendence. As we will see, this integration of both relational inequality and subsisting equality is the primary difficulty raised by Christian trinitarianism.

For Schuon, it is clear that one must distinguish between the Trinity and trinitarian theology. The former is in the nature of things and also inherent to the vision of the Divine as Manifestation: "Trinitarianism is a concept of God determined by the mystery of Divine Manifestation; if we seek the prefiguration of this mystery in God, we discern the Trinity."[25] In other words, the "mystery of Divine Manifestation" presupposes the Non-Manifested, the Manifested and Manifestation; or else, the Father, the Son, and the Holy Spirit. Trinitarianism is also, quite obviously, a theological elaboration on the basis of scriptural data that provide various standpoints on the relationship between the Father, the Son, and the Holy Spirit. Schuon's main critique of Christian trinitarianism, in its ordinary formulation, is that it proceeds from "a summation of different points of view that are related to different dimensions of the Real."[26] In other words, Christian trinitarianism reveals its weaknesses by confusing ontological levels of consideration. Schuon considers that theological trinitarianism abusively identifies the Trinity—or rather the differentiated ontological Trinity—with the Essence. As we have seen, Schuon argues that the Trinity can be applied horizontally to the degrees of Beyond-Being, Being, and Existence although the status of the Trinity is very different in each case. Beyond-Being is the Divine Essence as such, which means that is contains eminently all perfections to be found in the universe. Therefore, the

---

23. Handley C.G. Moule, *Outlines of Christian Doctrine* (Eugene, OR: Wipf & Stock, 2007), 25.

24. "When God reveals himself in creation and in Jesus, he is truly revealing himself as he is." Wilfrid Stinissen, *The Holy Spirit, Fire of Divine Love* (San Francisco: Ignatius Press, 1989), 153.

25. Schuon, *Form and Substance in the Religions*, 206–7.

26. Schuon, *Logic and Transcendence*, 82.

Trinity cannot but be "real" in the Essence. On the other hand, however, the Essence is pure Unity, and thus cannot admit any differentiation. The ternary *Sat, Cit, Ānanda* does not involve objective differentiations within *Ātman-Brahman*, since the three "aspects" merely refer to various ways in which the Ultimate can be apprehended and experienced within the world of difference as seen from a human point of view. One may be at a loss, of course, to conceive of what an undifferentiated inclusion of the three Persons actually means objectively, since the human mind is by definition working on differences that exclude unity and that cannot, therefore, fathom what an undifferentiated co-presence could amount to. There are, however, symbolic ways in which analogous perplexing realities have been conveyed by non-dual metaphysical doctrines. One of them, in the Hindu tradition, consists in considering the presence of diluted salt (as discerned through taste) within water. In salted water, there is no visually perceptible differentiation between water and salt, even though both substances are undoubtedly present. So the Persons of the Trinity can be envisaged, in this perspective, as undifferentiated dimensions of the Essence.

Returning to the analogy with *Sat, Cit,* and *Ānanda*, it could be said that the Father corresponds to Being, the Son to Consciousness, and the Holy Spirit to Bliss. Schuon himself, without explicitly relating the respective Hindu and Christian terms, writes that "the supreme horizontal perspective corresponds to the Vedantic triad *Sat* (supra-ontological Reality), *Cit* (Absolute Consciousness) and *Ānanda* (Infinite Beatitude), which means that it envisages the Trinity inasmuch as it is hidden in Unity."[27] The identification of the Father with *Sat* refers to His metaphysical status as ultimate foundation of the Trinity, while the connection between the Son and Consciousness echoes the relationship of the Word with Knowledge. Schuon writes that "the Father is being as such and the Son the 'Consciousness' of Being."[28] As for the Holy Spirit, it evokes the diffusion and communication of infinite freedom and bliss. The latter are associated with manifestation as such, which is a way of saying that creation emerges "out of Love" and Schuon actually refers to the Holy Spirit as "at once the 'inner life' and the 'creative projection' of Divinity."[29] Thus we see that the

---

27. Schuon, *Understanding Islam*, 44–45.
28. Schuon, *Gnosis: Divine Wisdom* (Bloomington, IN: World Wisdom, 2006), 104.
29. Schuon, *Gnosis: Divine Wisdom*, 104.

supra-ontological "conjunction" of Being, Consciousness, and Bliss does not involve any differentiation, in the way the *Ātman-Brahman*, as *Saccitananda*, is not conceived by *Advaita Vedānta* as being differentiated. As we see from the previous passage from Schuon, this absence of differentiation, which is a transcendent and eminent integration of the differentiated aspects (and not a negation of their reality), is not incompatible with what constitutes the primary claim of much of Christian theology; namely, the insistence on Life, Love, and Relation: "For extreme trinitarianism, God is of course One, but He is only so while being Three, and there is no One God except in and by the Trinity; the God who is One without Trinity, or independently of all hypostatic unfolding, is not the true God for, without this unfolding, Unity is meaningless."[30] It is important to stress, in this regard, that Schuon highlights the living and creative dimensions of the Holy Spirit in reference to both the supra-ontological and ontological unfolding degrees of the Divinity; in other words, both in terms of the undifferentiation and differentiation of the Hypostases.

It is with regard to the ontological degree of this unfolding that there occurs a differentiation between the Persons. Being is to be conceived, here, as the first determination of Beyond-Being; so it could also be said that Being is the highest differentiation that is possible and the principle of all further differentiations. The problem with Christian trinitarianism, from Schuon's "absolutist" point of view, is that it introduces the differentiations inherent to the ontological Trinity into the supra-ontological Essence which is, by definition, incompatible with any notion of multiplicity: "That God is triune is true in a relative sense—or in a 'relatively absolute' sense if one prefers—unity alone being unconditionally absolute; inversely, that God is one does not prevent Him from having an aspect of trinity on the already relative level of hypostatic differentiation; but the two theses become irreconcilable when both are placed on the level of absoluteness, through 'piety' and by confusing the absolute with the sublime."[31] What this means, concretely, is that most Christian theology is disposed to abandon a strict notion of the Absolute to accommodate the needs of a religious sensibility centered on the God-man. Christ is the only direct "manifestation" of God through the one and only Incarnation; therefore, he is God in a way that cannot be relativized without lessen-

---

30. Schuon, *Form and Substance in the Religions*, 206.
31. Schuon, *Christianity/Islam: Perspectives on Esoteric Ecumenism* (Bloomington, IN: World Wisdom, 2008), 82.

ing—subjectively—his status of *Redemptor*, which means that the relation that binds Him to the Father must also be absolutized in an unqualified way. This is what Schuon sometimes refers to as a "sublimicization" of metaphysics, whereby the subjective spiritual bias of a particular religious mentality is taken as "the Truth." It is worth mentioning, as a historical corroboration of Schuon's claim, that the theological need to elaborate a theology of the Trinity originally arose from devotional demands, that is, a need to clarify the economy of Christian piety. This spiritual intentionality may invite one to consider trinitarianism less as a rigorous metaphysical account and more as a mystical ellipsis, not so say antimony: "The idea of the Trinity is perhaps less a metaphysical definition of the Absolute than an instrument of mystical interiorization."[32] This is, by and large, the point of view of the Eastern Orthodox tradition, where the tendency to resist any intellectual reduction of the antinomies and apophatic implications of the Trinity is very strong. Incidentally, Schuon acknowledges that the information on which he relied with respect to the Trinitarian definition of the Essence—as being strictly identical with the hypostatic Trinity—was primarily drawn from a Christian Orthodox source.[33] The distinction between Orthodox and Catholic sources is not without relevance in that there exists, in the Orthodox mystical impulse, a tendency to oppose any philosophical rationalization, as it were, of the Trinity. This results in a strong emphasis on the antinomic and apophatic dimensions of the Trinitarian doctrine, hence the extreme resistance to any kind of reduction of the Trinity to Unity as such. Whereas Western Thomist theology tends to draw the Trinity from an integral concept of the Unity of God that is inclusive of all perfections, including that of relationality, Orthodox mystical theology resists any such reduction as being rationalist in bent, while insisting on the irreducible, perplexing, humbling, and mystically illuminating coincidence of the Unity and the Trinity, hence the accusation of "tritheism" that is sometimes leveled against Orthodox trinitarianism. Schuon himself appears, sometimes, to consider that Thomistic trinitarianism comes closer to providing keys for

---

32. Schuon, *Christianity/Islam: Perspectives on Esoteric Ecumenism*, 82.

33. Schuon does not specify the nature or identity of this source: "The opinion that the trinitarian relationships—or the three hypostatic Persons—'constitute' the Absolute is not inherent in Christianity; it has come down to us from an Orthodox source, not a Catholic one; but it has possibly rather more the meaning of a 'sublimation' than a strict definition." Schuon, *Form and Substance in the Religions*, nn. 3, 32.

a genuinely metaphysical recognition of the meaning of the Trinity.[34] He observes that Aquinas recognizes that the Divine Reality includes both absoluteness and relativity *eminenter formaliter*. However, he deems that Scholastics do not draw, from these two adverbs, the conclusions that ought to be reached with respect to the metaphysical status of the Relations with regard to the Essence. At any rate, from Schuon's "absolutist" point of view, any attempt at including the differentiated Persons into the Essence is a confessional confusion of planes—between the supra-ontological and ontological degrees of Reality—that does not consistently recognize that eminence excludes differentiated relations.

Although Christian trinitarianism, as a whole, is undoubtedly characterized by this conflation of the super-ontological and the ontological, some mystical insights from within the tradition intimate that the ontological Trinity is indeed transcended in the undifferentiated Reality of the Essence. Dionysius and Meister Eckhart are two of the most eminent mystical authors to have suggested, at least in some of their writings, this type of radically "absolutist" views. Thus one finds, in Dionysius's *Divine Names* and *Mystical Theology*, an apophatic emphasis on the relationship between Unity and Trinity, and all other determinations, that is clearly difficult to reconcile with an identification of the Divine Essence with a differentiated Trinity: "No unity or trinity, no number or oneness, no fruitfulness, indeed, nothing that is or is known can proclaim that hiddenness beyond every mind and reason of the transcendent Godhead which transcends every being."[35] Moreover, in the opening lines of his *Mystical*

---

34. "According to the Scholastics, Divine Reality is neither purely absolute nor purely relative, but contains *formaliter eminenter* both absoluteness and relativity; this has not prevented the theologians from being apparently disinclined to grasp the implication of these two terms, since they do not draw the obvious conclusions from them. We shall take this opportunity to make the following observation: that the hypostases should have a Personal character—or should be 'Persons'—because the Substance imparts its own Personality to them, does not in any way prevent them from being in another respect, or from another point of view, Modes of the One Substance, as Sabellius maintained." Schuon, *Form and Substance in the Religions*, nn. 3, 32.

35. "And the fact that the transcendent Godhead is one and triune must not be understood in any of our own typical senses. No. There is the transcendent unity of God and the fruitfulness of God, and as we prepare to sing this truth we use the names Trinity and Unity for that which is in fact beyond every name, calling it the transcendent being above every being. But no unity or trinity, no number or oneness, no fruitfulness, indeed, nothing that is or is known can proclaim that hiddenness beyond every mind and reason of the transcendent Godhead which transcends every

Theology, when marveling at the Trinity contemplated as "higher than any being, any divinity, any goodness," Dionysius adds that it is "not sonship or fatherhood and it is nothing known to us or to any other being." It is clear, here, that the eminent reality of the Trinity, as that of the Divine Unity, resists any human attempts at understanding it in terms of relative differences and conceptual distinctions. The "hiddenness" of the Essence is pure super-essential undifferentiation, to the extent, precisely, that its wealth of Reality defies any definitions, distinctions, and relations. If the Essence consisted in ontological relations of the kind that is referred to in most instances of theological trinitarianism, such apophatic maximalism would be out of place indeed. While it is true that Dionysius's point of view is more epistemological and spiritual than metaphysical as such—since his objective is, evidently, to humble the rational pretenses of the human mind—it is clear that this apophatic approach toward the Ultimate is based on an explicit recognition of its "pre-eminently simple and absolute nature."[36]

Similarly, Meister Eckhart observes that it is the "indistinction" of the Essence that makes it, paradoxically, distinct from everything else: "God is distinguished by his indistinction from any other distinct thing, and this is why in the Godhead the essence or existence (*essentia sive esse*) is unbegotten and does not beget."[37] If the Essence does not beget, it is hardly possible to identify it with the Father and, therefore, with any other Person of the Trinity. Furthermore, there are a number of texts by Eckhart in which the Essence is explicitly recognized as lying beyond the Persons of the Trinity. Thus, in a famous passage, he refers to the "simple ground," the "quiet desert, into which distinction never gazed, not the Father, nor the Son, nor the Holy Spirit."[38] One could not express more clearly that the differentiated Trinity cannot be the Essence, since it cannot even "gaze into" its naked Reality. The simplicity of the Essence, whether it be conceived as pure being or pure unity, cannot admit of any internal distinctions, even though it has to be inclusive of the latter in

---

being. There is no name for it nor expression." Pseudo-Dionysius, *The Complete Works*, translated by Colm Luibhead (New York: Paulist Press, 1987), 129.

36. Louis Dupré and James A. Wiseman, eds., *Light from Light: An Anthology of Christian Mysticism* (New York: Paulist Press, 2001), 92.

37. Edmund Colledge and Bernard McGinn, eds., *Meister Eckhart: The Essential Sermons, Commentaries, Treatises, and Defense* (Mahwah, NJ: Paulist Press, 1981), 35.

38. Colledge and McGinn, *Meister Eckhart*, 36.

an undifferentiated way. This is because, as Eckhart writes in Sermon 66, "the distinction in the Trinity comes from the unity . . . the unity is the distinction, and the distinction *is* the unity" and "the greater the distinction, the greater the unity, for that is the distinction without distinction."[39] This paradoxical statement implies that Unity cannot exclude the "content" or "substance" of the qualitative differentiation within the Trinity, but it does so without thereby embracing its exclusiveness. As Bernard McGinn has perspicaciously suggested, this perplexing paradox is analogous to the metaphysical principle of the Essence being both transcendent and immanent to the universe of plurality.[40] It must be stressed that this "distinction without distinction" implies both the reality of the Trinity in the Essence and its not being differentiated. This is in keeping with Schuon's view of the Trinity as three undifferentiated dimensions of the Essence. The triad, like other Pythagorean numbers, is eminently contained within Unity but in a way that is "distinctly indistinct," to paraphrase Eckhart. In other words, while triplicity—and multiplicity in general—implies increasingly marked distinctions as one descends on the chain of Being, its distinctions become more and more indistinct as one ascends to the higher reaches of Reality. Thus, there is no "room" in the Essence itself for the very distinction of transcendence and immanence.

While, for Eckhart, the Essence "contains" the Trinity in an "indistinct distinction," it is also true that it is transcendent in another respect, to the extent that it can be distinguished from it, or insofar as the Trinity is differentiated and, therefore, situated "below" the Essence. This is parallel to Schuon's distinction between the metaphysical and the ontological perspectives. Eckhart has two ways of distinguishing the Essence from the Trinity: either the Essence is conceived as pure Unity (*unum*), while the Persons are respectively contemplated as *ens, verum*, and *bonum*; or the Essence is pure Being, *esse*, and the Persons seen as the hypostases of *unum, verum,* and *bonum*.[41] The first perspective emphasizes, in conformity with the view of the undifferentiated Trinity, that the Essence is

---

39. Colledge and McGinn, *Meister Eckhart*, 37.

40. "If we paraphrase the language of indistinction and distinction into the image of immanence and transcendence, we see better what the Meister was after—a way of speaking about God as simultaneously totally immanent to creatures as their real existence and by that very fact absolutely transcendent to them as *esse simpliciter* or *esse absolutum*." Colledge and McGinn, *Meister Eckhart*, 34.

41. Colledge and McGinn, *Meister Eckhart*, 35.

one, therefore negating the plurality as "negation," whereas the second emphasizes that it is pure being, in a sense that transcends the analogical meaning of "beings" and therefore the purely ontological meaning of the term, referring thereby to what Schuon would call Beyond-Being. In the first case, the Trinity as Being, Truth, and Goodness presents striking analogies with *Sat*, *Cit*, and *Ānanda*, even though it appears to be situated on a different level than the Hindu triad. In the second case, the Unity of the Father is stressed, no doubt as an allusion to its status as the origin of both generation and procession. In order to symbolize this origination, Meister Eckhart makes use of the Latin term *bullitio*, a productive "boiling" that evokes the internal Life of the Essence; an infinite "gestation" that Schuon conceptualizes as a dimension of infinitude that is inherent to the Absolute. What is apparent, at any rate, is that this *bullitio* is not understood by Eckhart as productive of a Person in the likeness of the Father but, rather, of "what is one and the same as itself."[42] Therefore, generation may correspond, following Schuonian categories, either to the infinite "origin" of the supra-ontological and undifferentiated Essence considered in its own "horizontal" integrity, or to a "vertical" begetting in which, without affecting their unity of Essence, the Father is identified with the Essence as such and the Son to its Word as Being. These two possible ways of understanding *bullitio* would be equivalent, therefore, to the super-ontological All-Possibility, inasmuch as it "gestates" multiplicity, or to the Divine Self-Determination. In addition and by contrast, Eckhart makes use of the term *ebullitio* to refer to the Self-diffusive outpour that Schuon would call Existence. In *bullitio*, "the three Persons are simply and absolutely one,"[43] whereas *ebullitio* distinguishes the Persons inasmuch as they relate to creation and refers to the latter itself. In both cases, but in different degrees, the Holy Spirit is "at once the 'inner life' and the 'creative projection' of Divinity."[44]

All these considerations are connected to the difficult question of the meaning of the Persons and their relations, with respect to their identification or distinction. On the basis of his absolutist and non-dualistic outlook, Schuon argues that the Persons must be considered both as "three

---

42. Meister Eckhart, *Commentary on the Gospel of John*, n. 342, *Meister Eckhart. Die deutschen und lateinischen Werke III* (Stuttgart and Berlin: W. Kohlhammer, 1936), 291.
43. Colledge and McGinn, *Meister Eckhart*, 37.
44. Schuon, *Gnosis: Divine Wisdom*, 104.

modes of one Divine Person and three relatively distinct Persons."[45] This implies, as we have seen, a distinction between a super-ontological degree of Unity and an ontological one that envisages the Trinity as "relatively absolute." Such positions have been rejected in traditional Christian trinitarian theology. The view that the three Hypostases are "modes" of a single Divine Person has been associated to Sabellius, a third-century theologian who was excommunicated from the Church for teaching that God is one single Person who "manifested" himself in three different "modes" as Father, Son, and Holy Spirit. Sabellius's modalism is sometimes associated with a form of sequentialism that sees the Trinity as comprising consecutive modal manifestations of the One God, and is often associated with monarchianism, the theological position of a single supreme God or of a Divine Essence that transcends the Persons of the Trinity. Accordingly, the traditional reaction to Sabellianism is that it represents a heterodox theological reading of the Trinity, in that it appears to negate the personal reality of the Father, Son, and Holy Spirit, thus reducing them to various manifested modes of the one and only Divine Person. It goes without saying that the term mode can be conceived in different ways, which leads Schuon to argue that the two conceptions of person and mode are in no way incompatible: "In fact modes can perfectly well have a personal nature, and this tri-personalism in no way prevents God from being a unique Person, to the extent that, or on the plane on which, this definition can properly be applied to Him."[46] While the last restriction implies that the highest consideration of the Essence pertains to a Supra-Personal Reality, the main thrust of Schuon's argument lies with a vision of modes that includes the possibility of personal ones. In other words, modalities can be personal inasmuch as they entail identity and relationality. This is what Hindu metaphysics readily admits, since it recognizes the plurality of Divine hypostatic modes, whether incarnated or not, in the form of its many gods, who are both distinct in their onto-cosmic *līlā* and identified with the supreme *Brahman*, who is also the one and only Self of all selves.

It is worth noting, in this regard, that some contemporary theologians (first and foremost the Protestant theologian Karl Barth) have indicated that the term mode—understood as a "manner of being"—does indeed correspond to some early teachings of the Church: "God is One in *three ways of being*, Father, Son and Holy Ghost . . . 'Mode (or way) of being'

---

45. Schuon, *Logic and Transcendence*, nn. 7, 82.
46. Schuon, *Logic and Transcendence*, nn. 9, 87.

(*Seinsweise*) is the literal translation of the concept τρόπος ὑπάρξεως or *modus entitativus* as, e.g., Quenstedt . . . put it in Latin."[47] At the core of this understanding lies God's Self-characterization as *I am*, as found in the book of Genesis, as well as a consistent care to preserve the Unicity of this Divine "I-ness," lest one be led to misrepresent the Trinity as a kind of tri-theism comprising three autonomous Divine subjectivities. Barth specifies his concern by stating that "we are speaking not of three divine I's, but thrice of the one divine I."[48] In other words, for him, there is only one Divine "I" in three different modes of being. Moreover, it is important to note that Barth not only proposes the concept of "mode of being" in order to parry the pitfalls of tri-theism but also on account of the misleading connotations of the term person in a contemporary context. To speak of three persons—today in particular—amounts to speaking of three different "personalities," three centers of consciousness that are independent from each other. It bears remembering that *persona*, by contrast, means "mask"; that is, something in, and by, which the identity of he who wears it "appears," even though his intrinsic selfhood cannot be equated with the *persona* as such. This modal understanding of the Persons is not acceptable to most theologians because it implies that the Essence lies behind the three modes, which is exactly the position defended by Schuon. However, Schuon does not reduce the Trinity to this ontological modalism since he also refers to the undifferentiated Trinity that is the Essence, the Unity within which the Trinity is hidden, as he puts it. In the ontological Trinity, conversely, it is Unity that is hidden in the Trinity, alhough the term hidden would be unacceptable to most Christian theologians precisely because it appears to distance this Unity from the Trinity. It is worth adding that, despite its theological antecedents and qualifications, Barth's position itself has become a target in theological controversies. Thus, Jürgen Moltmann, for instance, has claimed that Barth's views are "a late triumph for the Sabellian modalism which the early church condemned. The result would be to transfer the subjectivity of action to a deity concealed 'behind' the three Persons."[49]

---

47. Karl Barth, *Church Dogmatics—The Doctrine of the Word of God, Volume II* (London: T & T Clark, 2010), 359–60.

48. Karl Barth, *Church Dogmatics—The Doctrine of the Word of God, Volume I* (London: T & T Clark, 2010), 56.

49. Jürgen Moltmann, *The Trinity and the Kingdom: The Doctrine of God* (Minneapolis: Fortress, 1993), 139.

As is evident from Moltmann's remarks, the fear among many Christian theologians lies in witnessing an "objectification" of the One God "behind" the Trinity, an objectification that would therefore dissolve the intrinsically relational nature of the Divine. In response, it could be said that the One is not a priori an Object but, first and foremost, *the* one and only true Subject. Therefore, the reproach of objectification could be turned back on their theological contradictors by the proponents of a personalist modalism. When considering Schuon's perspective, in particular, it is imperative not to forget that the Absolute "I" is not exclusive of supra-ontological modes, *mutatis mutandis*, by virtue of the diversity of its dimensions. When they oppose any form of modalism, Christian theologians want to save the relational nature of the Trinity from what they conceive as a static monism. They situate themselves within a *bhaktic* perspective that precludes an adequate articulation of non-duality and duality. This is so because they posit duality as spiritually and, therefore, de facto ontologically ultimate, while conceiving of non-dual Reality as inert, "neutral," and objectified. By contrast, Advaita Vedānta and Śaivism, for instance, are keenly aware that the ultimate *Brahman* or *ParamaŚiva* is Consciousness, Bliss, Infinite creativity and, therefore, also encompasses what could be called "intrinsic relationality." The mere mention of the Śaivite view of the Ultimate illustrates the way in which a polarity of Principles, such as *Śiva* and *Śakti*, can be differentiated at a conditional degree of Reality but undifferentiated on a higher one.

The debate over the objectification of the Divine is evidently related to the question of the definition of the Divine Persons, since the latter notion is central to the trinitarian view of the Essence. In this regard, the theological understanding of this notion has been intrinsically connected, in the West, to an attempt at preserving both the unity and diversity of the Persons. This means that all three must "subsist" in the Essence while being "relations" inasmuch as they necessarily differ from the point of view of their "origin." This is because the Father is unbegotten, the Son begotten by the Father, and the Holy Spirit spirated by both; hence the Thomistic concept of the Persons in the way of "relations as subsistent." Aquinas elaborated this idea by clarifying that it means "relation by way of substance, which is a hypostasis subsisting in the divine nature," while emphasizing that "it remains that which subsists in the divine nature is the divine nature itself."[50] Such a notion of the Persons as relations asserts

---

50. Anton C. Pegis, ed., *Basic Writings of Saint Thomas Aquinas, Volume 1* (Indianapolis: Hackett Publishing, 1997), 298 (Q.29 Art. 4).

the trinitarian thrust of the Christian outlook against monarchianism, conceived as an incomplete Judaic understanding of God, while the assertion that these relations are "subsisting"—and therefore one with the Essence—is a way of avoiding the pitfalls of pagan tri-theism, that is, the position that there are three Divine substances. The definition of the Persons as relations is evidently not unrelated to an emphasis on Divine Love as the principle of their Unity through generation and spiration. Moreover, it is important to note that, in this view of things, there is no Person without relation. As a contemporary theologian has put it: "The Persons are not prior to the relations. The Persons are constituted by the relations."[51] There is, in this way of thinking, an implicit rejection of the Absolute as unrelatable and unconditioned Reality.

Schuon considers the Thomistic definition of the Person as a "relation as subsistent" in a critical way.[52] He recognizes that the concept of relation is an implicit reference to the principle of inequality between the Hypostases, and sees the quality of subsisting as a reference to their equality. However, one excludes the other from a theological point of view, so that there is a need to define "relation" in a way that makes it a synonym of "Essence," thereby not entailing any subordination. Such a definition derives from the fact that there are no real distinctions in God since the three Persons are One, except from the point of view of their respective origin, such as generation for the Son and spiration for the Holy Spirit. Thus, the only difference between the Father and the Son is that the Father is self-originated while the Son is engendered by the Father, but it remains that these relations are none other than the Essence and, since the Essence subsists, then so too must the relations. This is the crux of the identification of the Persons with the Essence *qua* Essence, but it is also the very point of metaphysical contention. In response to this view, which he considers to be metaphysically self-contradictory, Schuon observes that the notion of relation can be understood either in reference to the Persons or in regard to the Essence. If the Person, as distinguishable from

---

51. "There is not a pre-existing substrate for gift and relation. They are in so far as they are reciprocally relative. Relation unites and distinguishes at the same time. The unity of God is not that of a solitary, but that of a perfect communion. The being of God is identified with relation, and is an eternal exchange of love: relation, in so far as it is a divine reality, is the essence itself." Ángel Cordovilla Pérez, "The Trinitarian Concept of Person," in *Rethinking Trinitarian Theology*, edited by Giulio Maspero and Robert J. Wozniak (New York: T & T Clark International, 2012).
52. Schuon, *From the Divine to the Human*, 35.

the other Persons, is exclusively a relation, then it must mean that it is also in some way a substance, as is indirectly conceded by the Thomistic expression "by way of substance." In other words, there is no relation that does not entail substance, unless the relation be taken as a pure abstraction. If we contemplate, for instance, the relation of Paternity, we can see that it obviously entails the two substances of a begetter and a begotten. This does not mean that the substances are produced by the relation but simply that the position of relations does entail that of substances, without which the relation is a pure *nihil*. Furthermore, if the relation is taken in reference to the Essence, then it must mean that it is inherent to the Essence. Given that the Essence is one and cannot admit of plurality, it must logically imply that the "essential" relations remain undifferentiated, while eminently and formally present in the Essence.

One of the paradoxes of trinitarianism, specifically among the Eastern Church Fathers, is that the Trinity is to be contemplated, on the one hand, as the one and simple Godhead and, on the other, as being caused or "unified" by the Father. Thus, the twentieth-century Orthodox scholar John Meyendorff writes that "the Father is the cause (*aitia*) and the 'principle' (*archē*) of the divine nature." He quotes Gregory of Nazianzus as teaching that "God is the common nature of the three, but the Father is their union (*henōsis*)."[53] The biblical monotheistic heritage of Christianity had to be articulated with the notion of the Triune God in a way that would preserve both respective theological intents, although, in doing so, it could not but skirt antinomies. To say that the Father is the source of the Godhead is a manner of saying that the Godhead is not the source of the Trinity and, therefore, to equate the former with the latter, thereby absolutizing the relative.[54] It must be added, however, that there are a number of doctrinal statements—as already illustrated in the teachings of Dionysius and Meister Eckhart—which explicitly assert the transcendence of the Godhead with respect to the three Persons. Such mystical insights

---

53. John Meyendorff, *Byzantine Theology: Historical Trends and Doctrinal Themes* (New York: Fordham University Press, 1979), 183.

54. Timothy Mahoney writes that if the Trinity were subordinated to the Essence, "then we should see statements to the effect that the Godhead generates the Trinity. By contrast, what we see are statements such as this by Dionysius: 'The Father is the originating source (*pēgaia theotēs*) of the Godhead'" (*Divine Names* II.7.645B). "Christian Metaphysics: Trinity, Incarnation and Creation," http://www.theveil.net/meta/mah/xmet_3.html.

must lead one to understand the meaning of the Father as cause, source, and principle in a way that transcends its mere unbegottenness. In point of fact, if the Father is the source of the Godhead, and if the Godhead is the Trinity, it follows that the Father is also the source of Himself as a distinct Person, in addition to being the cause of the Son and the Holy Spirit. Thus, He would logically need to be, *qua* source of the Trinity, "the Father" of the Father *qua* begetting the Son and spirating the Spirit. This could be intelligible if, as Schuon suggests in one of his readings of the Trinity, we identify the Father with Beyond-Being, that is, with the Self-originated Essence and Principle of all, while contemplating the Son and the Holy Spirit as the descending hypostatic degrees of Being and Existence. Understood in this way, the Father is indeed the source and principle of the whole vertical ontological Trinity but only on the basis of His exclusive identification with the Essence and, therefore, while acknowledging that the Son and the Spirit are only "relatively absolute." It could also be understood that the definition of the Father as source of the Godhead refers to the super-ontological dimension of Absoluteness inasmuch as it contains Infinitude and Perfection. However, such an identification is hardly coherent when one understands Fatherhood in a merely ontological—hence differentiated—sense, for then we are confronted with a self-contradictory assertion of monarchianism and tri-unity.

The difficulties raised by the conflation of absoluteness and relativity in Christian trinitarianism appear in full light when considering the quasi-unqualified identification of each of the Persons with the "entirety" of the Essence. When we read, in the words of the Fourth Lateran Council of 1215, that "each of the persons is that supreme reality, viz., the divine substance, essence or nature,"[55] it is obvious that this is a question of vantage point; for it is one thing for a person to be "entirely" the Essence, in the sense in which the Essence is obviously indivisible, and another thing to say, for instance, that the Father is entirely the Essence and therefore entirely the Son. Such unqualified identifications are intended to absolutize the reality of the Trinity, although they cannot but negate the distinction of Persons and therefore the very reality of their relations, unless "entirely the Son" is meant as "entirely the Son *qua* Essence." However, this would imply that both the Father and the Son together do not comprise the entirety of the Essence in an absolute and unconditioned

---

55. Thus, commenting on this teaching, Timothy Mahoney writes that "each person is the entirety of God." "Christian Metaphysics: Trinity, Incarnation and Creation."

sense. In other words, the Trinitarian postulation is that each Hypostasis makes up the entirety of the *Ousia* but that, nevertheless, the Hypostases are still distinguished from each other. This, in fact, signifies that they are both absolute and relative.

Taking stock of these two postulations of trinitarianism, Schuon notes that, in scholasticism, God includes both absoluteness and relativity but that He does so *formaliter eminenter*.[56] However, as we have indicated earlier, he also remarks that Trinitarian Thomism does not appear to draw all the consequences from these two terms. The adverb *formaliter* means that absoluteness and relativity are inscribed in the very nature of the Divinity, while *eminenter* signifies that they are *in divinis* in a way that is "incomparably analogous"—if one may use this seemingly self-contradictory expression—to the manner in which they exist "outside" of God. Let us note that absoluteness, as predicated of something other-than-God, can only mean, as Schuon would say, that anything that exists is "absolutely" other than nothingness. Divine absoluteness, for its part, adds to this absolute gap the total absence of contingency, whereby absoluteness acquires its proper implication of full necessity. This is another way of saying that while existence has something "absolute" about it, it is only in God that essence and existence coincide and that absoluteness reaches its eminent meaning. Accordingly, there is, among the two degrees of absoluteness, a transcendent jump that is none other than the very hallmark that distinguishes the *eminentia* of the Divine Essence.

With respect to relativity, the question of the eminent and formal mode of its inherence in the Divine appears in a way more complex, simply because the ordinary concept of Divinity includes absoluteness but excludes relativity. That relativity can be formally contained in the Essence only means that it is so in a way that coincides, so to speak, with its intrinsic absoluteness, and this is what Schuon would refer to as the

---

56. "Absolute perfections are found both in God and in creatures, not univocally, and not equivocally, but analogically. This is the precise meaning of the term *formaliter eminenter*, where *eminenter* is equivalent to 'not univocally, but analogically.' Let us listen to St. Thomas: [347]. 'Any effect which does not show the full power of its cause receives indeed a perfection like that of its cause, but not in the same essential fullness [that is, in context, not univocally]: but in a deficient measure. Hence the perfection found divided and multiplied in effects pre-exists in unified simplicity in their cause.' Hence all perfections found divided among numerous creatures pre-exist as one, absolute, and simple unity in God." Reginald Garrigou-Lagrange, *Reality: A Synthesis of Thomistic Thought* (London: Aeterna Press, 2016).

Infinite: the Infinite is what the Absolute would be if it could be relative. The undifferentiation of the Absolute and the relative in the Essence is none other than the unity of the two dimensions of absoluteness and infinitude; that is, the Absolute *qua* Infinite. Moreover, to say that relativity is contained in the Essence *eminenter* means that it is so in a way that is eminently different from what relativity is in the contingent realm; it means, therefore, that it is relative in a way that is absolute. This is the crucial, albeit paradoxical, notion of the "relatively absolute." In other words, the "relative" that is formally "inherent" in the Absolute is none other than the Infinite, and the relative that is eminently in the Absolute is the "relatively absolute" reality of Being.

Such an understanding of the "relationship" between the Divine Essence and the Hypostases is deemed by Schuon to be not incompatible with Islam, inasmuch as it entails an acknowledgment of the highest consideration of the Divine Essence: "The concept of a Trinity seen as a deployment (*tajallī*) of Unity or of the Absolute is in no way opposed to the unitary doctrine of Islam; what is opposed to it is solely the attribution of absoluteness to the Trinity alone, or even to the ontological Trinity alone, as it is envisaged exoterically."[57] As a refutation of this abusive attribution, the Schuonian distinction between the Absolute per se and the "relatively Absolute" is analogous to the differentiation, within Sufism, between the Divine Essence and the Divine Qualities or Names. The former is the Divine Aseity whereas the latter are, for Sufi metaphysicians like Ibn ʿArabī, relationships. Referring to the Divine Names, or Attributes, Ibn ʿArabī specifies that "they are one in God's eyes, but many in our eyes."[58] Thus, each Divine Name has two sides, so to speak; one in regard to which it is, *qua* Essence, all the other Names, and one with respect to which it is different from other Names. Schuon's notion of the "relatively absolute" corresponds, therefore, quite adequately to "the Names."

The fact that a Divine Name, as a Quality, can be invoked by the faithful, demonstrates that *al-Rahmān*, the Compassionate, or *al-Karīm*, the Generous, are personal realities, in a way that is not fundamentally different, from this perspective at least, from a Barthian "mode of being." Doubtlessly, Islam and Sufism do not ponder the question of the relationships between the various "personal" qualities of the One God, and certainly

---

57. Schuon, *Understanding Islam*, 45.
58. *Futūhāt al-Makkiyāt* IV 419.7, in William Chittick, *The Sufi Path of Knowledge* (Albany: State University of New York Press, 1989), 36.

not in the way of a relationship of Love or by reference to relations of generation and procession. In fact, Islam, given its strictly unitarian or tawhīdic perspective, tends to envisage Divine plurality as a principle of "discord," rather than one of reciprocal Love. This is, for instance, quite apparent—and indeed most forcefully so—in the Qur'ānic critique of the idea of Divine sonship: "*Allāh* hath not chosen any son, nor is there any god along with Him; else would each god have assuredly championed that which he created, and some of them would assuredly have overcome others. Glorified be Allah above all that they allege" (23:91). In the Islamic imagination, Divine plurality is divisive and destructive. This vision is mostly couched, however, in regard to creation, or extrinsically, rather than with respect to the Divine Aspects *in divinis*. In other words, the rejection of any fragmentation of the Divine is connected to a rejection of any "chasm" within creation itself, although this does not preclude a diversity of creaturely qualities. On the contrary, the latter are nothing but cosmic illustrations of the Divine Omnipotence and the diversity of God's Attributes. However, inasmuch as a given Divine Quality is none other than an aspect of the Essence, it could be said that it is "united" with the other Qualities through, in, and by the Essence itself. Moreover, Sufi metaphysics recognizes that the various Names cannot but relate to each other to the extent that they are cosmic manifestations of the Divine Aspects. In this sense, these relationships can be understood as existentiations flowing from All-Possibility, the Infinite, and inexhaustible Divine "Will" of the Essence.

These analogies with the Persons of the Trinity having been established, it must be stressed that the personal aspects of the Divinity obviously do not involve, in Islam, generation and procession, or any other such relational mode; nor do they manifest reciprocal relationships of Love. Nevertheless, Islam acknowledges, and indeed emphasizes, that the most intrinsic dimension of the Divine Essence is Mercy which encompasses everything. As Mercy, the Essence is the Ultimate Reality in which the Names and Attributes reflect, and are thus reconciled to, each other. Commenting on verse 19:85 of the Qur'ān, Ibn 'Arabī argues that the Divine Name "The Overbearing" is, as it were, superseded by the Name "The All-Merciful" with which it coincides as Essence, and this is because "each name has two denotations: a denotation of the Named and a denotation of its own reality through which it is distinguished from every other name."[59] Thus, when Timothy Mahoney writes that "simplicity

---

59. Chittick, *The Sufi Path of Knowledge*, 37.

and multiplicity are necessary for the Absolute,"[60] he in a sense expresses the foundation of Mercy, which is both unitive in terms of its drawing back everything to the Absolute, and self-diffusive or productive with regard to the world of multiplicity that it already "contains" within itself by virtue of its blissful infinitude. The One could not be Self-diffusive *ad extra*, as principle of creative emanation, if it were not Self-diffusive *ab intra*, in terms of its dimension of Infinitude and *Ānanda*. This is, no doubt, the most universal lesson to be drawn from a metaphysical meditation on the highest implications of the Christian Trinity. Such is also the foundation of Schuon's aforementioned characterization of the Trinity as a "prefiguration" of the "mystery of Divine Manifestation": "As we have pointed out before on more than one occasion, trinitarianism is a concept of God determined by the mystery of Divine Manifestation; if we seek the prefiguration of this mystery in God, we discern the Trinity. Applied to any religion, monotheistic or not, the same idea calls for the following formulation: the Essence has become form in order that form may become Essence; all Revelation is a humanization of the Divine for the sake of deification of the human."[61]

In a more exclusive and critical mode, Schuon's challenging and no doubt controversial meditations on Christian theological trinitarianism reveal a keen and rigorous defense of an uncompromisingly consistent metaphysics of the Absolute. The notion of the Absolute is not simply a philosophical abstraction, as too many Christian theologians believe. For Schuon, it is the ontological foundation of all intellectual and spiritual values: "The worth of man lies in his consciousness of the Absolute."[62] Without a clear foundation in the Absolute, intellectual and spiritual ways are bound to be compromised with sensualism and rationalism, or else determined by a subjective sublimism that "absolutizes" theophanic realities, or their prototypes, *in divinis*. For Schuon, it is quite clear that the prime content of human intelligence is the sense of the Absolute—which amounts to a form of the ontological proof of God—and that this core intellectual reality is the foundation for any real and consistent objectivity on any level of Reality. Without a recognition of the strictest conception of the Absolute, and a recognition of its inscription within the human Intellect, intelligence betrays its highest vocation and, as a consequence,

---

60. "Christian Metaphysics: Trinity, Incarnation and Creation."
61. Schuon, *Form and Substance in the Religions*, 206–7.
62. Schuon, *From the Divine to the Human*, 127.

cannot but seek foundations for its convictions and endeavors on lower levels of reality, such as a sensory epistemology or materialistic empiricism.

Schuon's focus on a purely non-dualistic and absolutist understanding of the Divine is particularly consonant with the Trinity as a symbol of the inner, pluri-dimensional depth of Ultimate Reality. This metaphysical conception of the Trinity evokes meditations that strike an essentially esoteric chord, by contrast with rationalistic and one-dimensional monistic theological doctrines of the Divine. It is clear from his writings that Schuon is quite sensitive to these subtle considerations when he emphasizes that "Reality has to remain one, notwithstanding the undeniable complexity of the Divine Mystery."[63] It is this transcendent complexity that enables the Trinity to be understood in the context of an onto-cosmological unfolding of the One. As such, it is a fundamental key for grasping the full implications of the idea of the relatively absolute, in all its perplexing necessity.

---

63. Schuon, *From the Divine to the Human*, 18.

6

Necessary Sufism and the Archetype of Islam

The last half-century has been characterized by the growing impact of Sufism in the West, along with burgeoning scholarship on Sufism in North America and Europe.[1] This has been a result of several factors, not least of which being a sense that Sufism has for too long been dismissed or misread as an extra-Islamic phenomenon. This negative assessment was—and still is—a result of the objective convergence between the Orientalist claim that there is no intrinsically Islamic spirituality and Muslim reformist discourses that are critical of Sufism, from both modernist and puritanical perspectives. With regard to the latter, Sufi spirituality was not uncommonly denounced as a source of intellectual and cultural sterility, and even called into question with respect to the very validity and legitimacy of its manifestations from an Islamic point of view. Since the mid-twentieth century—and occasionally even earlier—a growing number of European and American scholars have challenged these early interpretations and worked on correcting them by taking a fresh look at the Qur'ānic and Islamic sources of Sufi phenomena. Louis Massignon's contribution has remained, in that sense, seminal, irrespective of the reservations one may have concerning some of the French Islamicist's methodology and conclusions. His *Essay on the Origins of the Technical Language of Islamic Mysticism* provided concrete lexical evidence

---

1. This includes the growing field of study of the transformation of Sufism in western contexts. William Rory Dickson's *Living Sufism in North America: Between Tradition and Transformation* (Albany: State University of New York Press, 2005) is an interesting study that shows, through a series of interviews with contemporary Sufi Shaykhs, the ways in which Sufism has adapted its traditional principles to contemporary realities.

for the Qur'ānic grounding of Sufi practices and principles.[2] A plethora of more recent studies has approached Sufi ideas, movements, and practices as intrinsically representative of some of the most influential forms of Islamic thought and culture. Moreover, in the last decades, the academic and popular interest in Sufism has grown stronger in a climate of perplexity, apprehension, or hostility toward the most visible and audible realities of the Islamic world. In this regard, Sufism has been often highlighted as an antidote to militant and violent discourses and actions emanating from Islamic ideological movements in a way that, quite paradoxically, may be deemed to have all too often politicized it against the grain of its own spiritual leanings.

Among the intellectual currents that can be credited with having contributed to a growth of information and interest in Sufism, perennialism is no doubt one of the most significant. Perennialism is the name given, in English-speaking countries, to the school of thought that developed in the first half of the twentieth century around the works of the French metaphysician René Guénon (1886–1951) and the Anglo-Singhalese art historian and religious studies scholar Ananda K. Coomaraswamy (1877–1947). The tenets of the perennialist vision lie in the notion of Tradition as a divinely inspired and instituted reality whose core principle, the transcendent wisdom of the ages, is manifested through a diversity of revelations and symbols in response to the various conditions of time and place. As James Cutsinger has rightly observed, perennialism, especially in its Schuonian articulation, is esoteric, traditional, and universalist.[3] These three adjectives can be applied equally—*mutatis mutandis*—to Sufism (including its most important streams) as it is understood by perennialists. Sufi intellectual and spiritual trends reveal an affinity with the inner dimensions of Islam, whether it be in terms of the purification of the soul or the focus on inner *bāṭinī* interpretations of the Qur'ān. Sufi Masters have also given emphasis to tradition and lineage, both in the sense of a focus on the Qur'ān and the Prophetic tradition, as well as to matters of

---

2. Louis Massignon, *Essay on the Origins of the Technical Language of Islamic Mysticism* (Notre Dame, IN: University of Notre Dame Press, 2003).

3. "The teaching of Frithjof Schuon is at once metaphysical, esoteric, traditional, and perennial. . . . This 'universalist' or perennialist dimension is summed up in the assertion that there is a 'transcendent unity of religions.'" James Cutsinger, *Advice to the Serious Seeker: Meditations on the Teaching of Frithjof Schuon* (Albany: State University of New York Press, 1997), 193.

spiritual heritage and the transmission of spiritual influence. As for the universalist dimension, it has been highlighted by some luminaries such as Rūmī, Hallāj, and Ibn Arabī. Inasmuch as the perennialist introduction to Sufism tends to emphasize these three dimensions, Sufism has often been understood, as a consequence and rightly or not, within a universalist outlook. This has its parallel, albeit with less conceptual and spiritual rigor, with the immense popularity of Jalāl-ad-Dīn Rūmī's poetry throughout the world, especially in North America.

It is in this context that Schuon's contribution needs to be considered. Schuon's thought is complex and circumstantiated, and although doctrinal shortcuts may be tempting when addressing his opus, one must pay heed to this complexity in order to avoid the pitfalls of hasty categorization. This is particularly true when it comes to his assessment of Sufism. Our contention is that Schuon redefines Sufism, as it were, in a way that manifests continuity with the historical and scholarly concepts of *tasawwuf* but that nevertheless is also significantly different from them in its esoteric inflection. Schuon's Sufism prolongs classical and popular streams of Sufism inasmuch as it emphasizes general spiritual bents such as essentialization, interiorization, and universalization in ways that are largely parallel to traditional *tasawwuf*. However, it is quite distinct from them in several important respects. One of the theses presented below is that, although Schuon has sometimes been presented as an intellectual representative of Sufism, there is much evidence to argue that his work is paradoxically more consonant with Islam than with Sufism—to the extent that the two can be distinguished; and being understood that the meaning of these two words needs to be refined to do justice to Schuon's understanding of them. This *prima facie* astonishing claim becomes more plausible when one considers that Schuon's "quintessential esoterism" is significantly more aligned with the foundational principles and practices of Islam than with the speculative developments and spiritual bents of major trends in Sufism. Furthermore, this Islamic character derives, in fact, no doubt quite paradoxically and unexpectedly for many, from Schuon's esoteric and universalist outlook. Thus, in his articulation of Sufism as esoterism, Schuon builds on Guénon's schematic definition of Sufism as "Islamic esoterism." Schuon generally accepts this characterization but also feels the need to further qualify the notion of esoterism by adding the adjective quintessential, which he sees as necessary to distinguish the paradigm of gnostic *tasawwuf* from the spiritually uneven manifestations of Sufism as a historical reality.

When approaching Schuon's writings on Sufism one cannot but notice that only two of his works are primarily devoted to Islam and to the metaphysics and spirituality of *tasawwuf*. The first is *Understanding Islam*, one of his earliest books, first published in French in 1961. Schuon did not consider this work as a description of Islam but as a wide-ranging intellectual and spiritual foray into "why Muslims believe in it."[4] The second book, *Sufism: Veil and Quintessence*, appeared almost two decades later (in 1980) and arguably contains the most explicit and complete crystallization of Schuon's understanding of Sufism. While Schuon's bibliography includes two other volumes (in English) primarily centered on Islam, *Dimensions of Islam* and *Islam and the Perennial Philosophy*, the publication of these works was circumstantial and not intended by Schuon himself. These are collections of essays that had already been published in French in other volumes under different titles, and their publication was conceived in the context of the World of Islam Festival that took place in London in 1976. Nevertheless, as several scholars have noted, Schuon's writings include numerous passages in which readers familiar with Sufism can recognize themes and ways of thinking that are deeply consonant with some aspects of this spiritual tradition. On the other hand, however, it cannot escape a careful reader that Schuon developed a point of view that can in no way be limited to, or even assimilated with, that of Sufism.

While some scholars have emphasized the Sufi, and even Islamic, character of Schuon's work and life, others have underplayed—or even denied—its intellectual and spiritual centrality, notwithstanding Schuon's own repeated and unambiguous assertions. The first interpretations of Schuon relied on everything connected, in his writings, to Islamic concepts and practices. Without ignoring the prominent non-Islamic themes and ideas that inform his perspective, some analysts have deliberately chosen not to highlight them, or have striven to connect them to Sufi themes to such an extent that, in the last analysis, they could be conceptually reduced to the latter. Thus, Islamic interpretations of Schuon's work have been argued by way of enumerating a number of recurrent aspects of Schuon's works considered to bear the hallmarks of Sufism, with a view to building a case for the strictly Islamic credentials of Schuon.[5] This

---

4. Schuon, *Understanding Islam* (Bloomington, IN: World Wisdom, 2011), xvii.

5. Foremost among these readings of Schuon, one must mention Seyyed Hossein Nasr's comprehensive study "Frithjof Schuon and the Islamic Tradition," *Sophia—The Journal of Traditional Studies* 5, no. 1 (Summer 1999): 27–48.

inevitably amounts to giving preeminence to all those components of Schuon's work that participate in the conceptual world of Islam, thereby resulting in an inflection of his work that Islamicizes his universal gnosis in a misleading way. Correlatively, such readings of Schuon also tend to translate the universal and non-Islamic concepts that are central to his perspective into Islamic terms, or to reduce them to Sufi ideas. This type of translation is indeed often possible, given the gnostic and universal thrust of important streams of historical Sufism. However, such an appropriation occurs de facto at the exclusion of other possible doctrinal languages, which have no less—and often more—legitimacy than Sufism with regard to the expression of gnostic principles and, more importantly, which do greater justice to the intrinsically supra-confessional inspiration of the Schuonian corpus. To borrow an image from Schuon's work, it is as if one were claiming that the light is green because green conveys light. Thus, while this kind of *pro domo* interpretation of Schuon is not in itself synonymous with a negation of the universalist scope of his work, there is no question—for the objective, disinterested, and attentive reader—that it lends to Schuon's work a specifically Islamic bent that is not conducive to acknowledging, and benefitting from, its unarguably supra-confessional vantage point. In other words, such reductively Islamic readings of Schuon, however expediently beneficial they may be in some respects, do not give their due to the doctrinal principles and modes of expression that are the main hallmarks of his work.[6] The fact that Schuon himself lived most of his adult life within the ritual forms of a particular tradition does not in the least invalidate, or even relativize, the aforementioned points. Such biographical evidence only pertains to the practical dimension of spiritual

---

6. Let us note that Schuon's view of the place and modalities of Sufism in the West was, in this respect, quite divergent from René Guénon's. In a letter written to Michel Valsân in 1960, Schuon distinguishes most clearly between Sufism as understood by Guénon—an understanding which would be echoed later on, *mutatis mutandis*, by Seyyed Hossein Nasr, and his own concept and practice of synthetic and quintessential Sufism: "For Guénon . . . [Sufism] could only be an extension of Shadhilism implanted in the West; for . . . [me] on the contrary . . . [it] must realize both a synthesis and a quintessence determined on the one hand by the awareness of the metaphysical significance of forms and on the other hand by the contingencies of the modern world, with the simplifications and compensations this implies." Pully, Switzerland, October 9, 1960, letter to Michel Vâlsan, in *Letters of Frithjof Schuon: Reflections on the Perennial Philosophy*, edited by Michael Oren Fitzgerald (Bloomington, IN: World Wisdom, 2019).

life in which, given that it belongs to the formal order, one form is in principle necessarily exclusive of another. By specifying "in principle," we mean that this is not always necessarily so in fact, even though the exceptions in this regard—one thinks of Ramakrishna's Christian and Islamic devotional occurrences—are indeed quite marginal and, most often, temporary. When he remarked that "explicitly to practice one religion is implicitly to practice them all,"[7] Schuon was clearly suggesting that the ritual and methodical exclusiveness of a religious path is both inevitable and, in no way, incompatible with a fully fledged and unbiased universalist outlook. Needless to say, it is difficult—perhaps sometimes impossible—for most scholars and religious faithful to conceive that one can live within the forms of a religious universe without espousing its confessional limitations and biases, even more so while being critical of them. There is in religion, including most of its esoteric currents, a principle of sentimental identification that functions, for most believers, as a necessary devotional lever but also as a protective blinker. Be that as it may, even on the immanent level of religious phenomena, Schuon's deep affinities with some non-Islamic artistic, cultural, and ceremonial forms—be they Native American, Mahāyānic, or other—bear witness to the fact that his spiritual universe was utterly immune from any "religious nationalism" or "confessional bias," to use but two expressions directly taken from his own works.[8] At any rate, the crux of the matter lies in Schuon's frequent

---

7. Schuon, *Gnosis: Divine Wisdom* (Blomington, IN: World Wisdom, 2006), 20.

8. "Religious loyalty is nothing else than the sincerity of our human relations with God, on the basis of the means which He has put at our disposal; these means, being of the formal order, ipso facto exclude other forms without for all that lacking anything whatsoever from the point of view of our relationship with Heaven; in this intrinsic sense, form is really unique and irreplaceable, precisely because our relationship with God is so. Nevertheless, this uniqueness of the intrinsic support and the sincerity of our worship within the framework of this support do not authorize for us what we might call 'religious nationalism'; if we condemn this attitude—inevitable for the average man, but this is not the question—it is because it implies opinions contrary to the truth, which are all the more contradictory when the believer lays claim to an esoteric wisdom and claims that he possesses knowledge that permits him to take note of the limits of the religious formalism with which he sentimentally and abusively identifies himself." Schuon, *Esoterism as Principle and as Way* (Pates Manor, Bedfont, Middlesex: Perennial Books, 1981), 31–32. "Not all historical esoterism is esoterism pure and simple, far from it; an exegesis colored by confessional bias, or overly involved in mystical subjectivism is hardly true gnosis." Schuon, *To Have a Center* (Bloomington, IN: World Wisdom, 2015), nn. 2, 45.

emphasis on the independence of esoterism vis-à-vis any and all traditional forms. In this, he followed in the tracks of Guénon, with whom his name is often associated, and who also considered esoterism as being utterly free from religion, indeed as belonging to a radically different order of reality.[9]

Schuon's rigorously esoteric perspective is affirmed in his explicit and repeated critique of the intrinsic limitations of the perspectival and theological forms of Abrahamic religions including, of course, Islam. This critical dimension of Schuon's work comes to the fore in the way he associated the general theological perspective of the Abrahamic religions with the monistic *bhakti* of Rāmānuja, in contrast to the Advaitin non-dualism of Shankara, which he favored as reflecting a more directly integral metaphysics.[10] For him, it is clear that the former represents a methodically legitimate but metaphysically limited point of view, whereas the latter corresponds to one of the most direct expressions of Reality. More importantly, Schuon has repeatedly remarked that the religions originating in the biblical world are characterized—in their mainstream but also mystical currents—by individualist, sentimentalist, and voluntaristic accents[11] that he deems incompatible with the disinterested objectivity of gnosis. Religions address large collectivities at historical junctures when the Message must be all-inclusively effective and therefore, in a way, reduced

---

9. "The presence of an esoteric nucleus in a civilization that possesses a specifically religious character guarantees to it a normal development and a maximum of stability; this nucleus, however, is not in any sense a part, even an inner part, of the exotericism, but represents, on the contrary, a quasi-independent 'dimension' in relation to the latter." Schuon, *The Transcendent Unity of Religions* (Wheaton, IL: Theosophical Publishing House, 1984), 9–10.

10. "Apart from secondary elements that are not in point, the three Semitic religions share their general perspective with the monism of Ramanuja and not with the non-dualism of Shankara, although this non-dualism shows itself sporadically within these religions, that is, in their sapential esoterism." Schuon, *Esoterism as Principle and as Way*, 23. By monism Schuon means here the qualified non-dualism (*viśiṣṭādvaita*) that includes, as it were, the duality of the servant and the Lord within the Unicity of the latter.

11. "Like every religion, Islam includes both a Message, and a Language. We have given an account of the Message; as for the Language, being Semitic it is distinctively voluntaristic, moralistic and inspirationist, and to the extent that exoterism is the equilibrium and salvation of the greatest number, this Language is specifically addressed to the 'average man.'" Schuon, *Christianity/Islam: Perspectives on Esoteric Ecumenism* (Bloomington, IN: World Wisdom, 2008), 113.

to the smallest common religious denominator.[12] This does not, in itself, contradict the presence of esoteric dimensions within these religions, but it cannot but affect their modalities of manifestation, as well as their normative dialectics.

While it is clear that Schuon's perspective cannot be exclusively couched in Islamic terms or characterized as giving any sort of religious or metaphysical eminence to Islam, one should note that his supra-confessional perspective must necessarily be lived within the formal framework of a particular religion, be it Islam or another faith. A specific concern or emphasis on this necessity could be referred to as provisional, to use a Buddhist expression, on account of the climate of informal neo-spirituality and, more generally, rejection or distrust of religious forms that are prevalent among contemporary Western cultural elites. In other words, it is important to be aware that Schuon's supra-confessional perspective—the intellective objectivity of which does not allow for any religious nationalism—is founded on radically different grounds to that of New Age or globalized postmodern spirituality. Indeed, the traditional emphasis on revelation, ritual, traditional lineages, and sacramental integrity—so central to Schuon's understanding of religion—could not be more antithetical to contemporary calls for individually tailored or "post-religious" forms of spirituality. Schuon, like other perennialists, emphasizes the transcendent source of tradition that—without being able to neutralize the limitations, ambiguities, and human imperfections of religious universes—is the principal guarantor of doctrinal efficacy, as well as the irreplaceable means of transforming grace. From another point of view, insisting on the primacy of elements in Schuon's work that are, directly or indirectly, Islamic in form and content may correspond to an aspect of expedient or conventional truth, in the sense that this emphasis can contribute to inviting Muslim intellectuals to consider the tenets of perennialism, or even to accept them, by offering a universalizing and essentializing version of their creed. While this has clearly contributed to the dissemination of perennialism in Muslim areas such as the Persian world, the Indian subcontinent, and

---

12. "Semitic religions of Abrahamic lineage present themselves as gifts descended from Heaven at a moment of history; now in order to impose themselves to entire collectivities, that is to say in order to be able to convert and integrate them, they must call on volitional and emotional factors, which is obviously without relation with pure intellection and a qualified dialectics." Schuon, *Form and Substance in the Religions* (Bloomington, IN: World Wisdom, 2002), 181.

Southeast Asia, not to mention among Western Muslims, it falls short of presenting an objective and integral picture of Schuon's perspective.

With these controversial issues now being laid to rest, it is important to note that the two chapters that, in the final sections of the aforementioned books, consist most directly of a presentation of Sufism do not include the word "Sufism" itself. *Understanding Islam* treats Sufism in the chapter titled "The Way," while another lengthy chapter in *Sufism Veil and Quintessence* is titled "The Quintessential Esoterism of Islam." This surprising absence of the very term Sufism is also noticeable in the two final chapters of *Esoterism as Principle and as Way* included in the section "Sufism," namely, "The Religion of the Heart" and "The Way of Oneness." Such a deliberate omission is highly significant. Indeed, what could be considered, at first sight, as a purely formal and incidental matter reveals, on further analysis, a significant connection to the very vision of Sufism that emerges from Schuon's writings. Thus we read in the first sentence of the chapter "The Path": "Our aim in this section is not so much to treat of Sufism exhaustively or in detail—other writers have had the merit of doing so with varying degrees of success—but rather to envisage the 'path' (*tarīqah*) in its general aspects or in its universal reality; therefore the terms used will not always be those proper to Islam alone."[13] Considering that this chapter concludes a book that is counted as a classic study of Islam, one is struck by the decidedly universal outlook that it propounds, which differentiates it, markedly, from other perennialist books devoted to Islam and Sufism. While the latter are representative of a universalist outlook on Islam, they do not as explicitly undertake their survey with a direct reference to the *sophia perennis* as their guiding perspective, nor do they make systematic use of terminology borrowed from other traditions. This characteristic is likely to be at least partially a matter of intended audience and specific objectives or contexts, but there is undoubtedly more to this. Furthermore, the following sentences of the aforementioned chapter synthesize the whole reality of Sufism according to Schuon's fundamental doctrinal dyad, entailing discernment between the Absolute and the relative, along with the corresponding method of exclusive concentration on the Absolute. This, in a nutshell, is the most accurate and succinct definition of Schuon's Sufism. In light of the perennialist perspective, based on the axiom of the unity of the various forms of wisdom throughout the ages,

---

13. Schuon, *Understanding Islam*, 105.

Schuon's understanding of Sufism is undeniably informed by a universal outlook. However, universality is but an extrinsic aspect of the matter, one that follows from an intrinsic reality that Schuon held to be more significant than the former. Esoteric gnosis is the intrinsic reality to which he refers as either *religio perennis* or *sophia perennis*, the latter emphasizing its intellectual dimension and the former its operative aspect. This inner sapience is, for Schuon, not only the very essence of Sufism but of all forms of traditional spirituality.

Indeed, Schuon's distance from any specifically Sufi understanding of Reality[14] is to be found in numerous passages of his works. It is most clearly highlighted in his assertion that the main prerogative of esoterism lies in its objectivity, that is, its intellectual and spiritual conformity to reality as it is, independent of any confessional limitations or biases. This claim stems from a consideration of the Intellect as being the very principle of adequateness and objectivity; one that is symbolically and mythologically reflected in revelations and religions, while also being independent of them in principle. It must be noted, however, that such an actualization of the Intellect can operate on different degrees. This explains why it may be limited to particular aspects of Reality, those that are taken into primary consideration within a given tradition. In other words, the Intellect is not likely to be actualized in a traditional Muslim gnostic in a way that would account for extra-Islamic aspects of the Truth. The Intellect is in principle free from religious conditionings, but its full supra-confessional actualization is conditioned by specific contextual concurrences, which are unlikely to be present in normative traditional circumstances.[15] The supra-confessional objectivity of an actualization of

---

14. It has been stated by some of his close associates that Schuon did not wish to be publicly identified with Sufism, and even less so with Islam; not only for reasons of opportuneness having to do with the current crisis of the Islamic world and the negative perceptions of that religion in the West but also, more importantly, for reasons of principle in the sense that he was keenly aware that his esoteric perspective could not be considered as orthodox from a strictly Islamic point of view. Contrary opinions can only appear as wishful thinking and *pro domo* apologetic exercises to an attentive and objective reader of his works. Schuon distinguishes intrinsic orthodoxy, in relation to Reality as such, and extrinsic orthodoxy, in relation to a particular dogmatic system; it is clearly the latter that we have in view here.

15. This is analogous to what happens with celestial appearances, which are de facto conditioned by a particular religious psycho-spiritual climate. Bodhisatvas do not normally appear to traditional Kabbalists.

the Intellect cannot be validated externally by authorities belonging to a given tradition. It could be said that the Intellect is self-validated, and that its recognition is itself a measure of actualization of its epistemological potential. Academically speaking, the concept of the Intellect raises, of course, important questions as to the epistemological premises of Schuon's claim of objectivity. Without being able to get into all the implications and underpinnings of this claim, one may simply note that Schuon's epistemology is basically akin to the Platonic view of archetypal realism and noetic *adaequatio* that also characterizes the main metaphysical streams of Sufism (as well as significant streams of Judaeo-Christian philosophy and theosophy). Schuon considered himself a Platonist, but he took Platonic epistemological realism one step further, as it were, by applying it to the domain of religions. For him, religions are first and foremost realities "in the mind of God," if one may say so, which enables him to refer to the reality of a Christian or Islamic "archetype." These archetypes are not necessarily manifested in a single religion only, since their transcendent character make them independent—in principle—of any particular realm of cosmic manifestation.[16] The metaphysical objectivity of the archetypes is one of the main foundations of the human capacity—quite rare and precarious in fact—to recognize the spiritual legitimacy and effectiveness of all religious forms and thus be free from confessional bias.

The preceding remarks are most significant when considering the way Schuon approaches Sufism in the only book of his explicitly devoted to Islamic mysticism, *Sufism: Veil and Quintessence*. This is so inasmuch as his delineation of Sufism stems from a comprehensive consideration of what he conceives as the "Islamic archetype." In a sense, the whole book is based on a distinction between Sufism as a religious phenomenon or a set of religious phenomena and Sufism as an archetype or, rather, as the most direct manifestation of the Islamic archetype. The work largely addresses the former, in a way that is intended to clear the ground, as it were, for a strict definition of the latter. A number of chapters are devoted to the main pitfalls of historical Sufism, that is, the ways in which the latter may veil the esoteric core, *haqīqah*, of Islam. These include matters

---

16. "To understand our point of view, one has to know that religions are determined by archetypes which are so many spiritual possibilities: on the one hand every religion a priori manifests an archetype, but on the other hand, any archetype can manifest itself a posteriori within every religion." Schuon, *Christianity/Islam: Perspectives on Esoteric Ecumenism*, 23.

of dialectics, religious anthropology, theology, pietism, and mystical exegesis. In all these areas, Schuon traces what he refers to as the individualist, voluntarist, and sentimental characters of historical Sufism, highlighting the ways in which they obscure or hamper one's access to the spiritual core. By "individualist" is not meant a focus on the individual as such, but a spiritual perspective too tied up with the reality of the individual in his way to God. This translates into a path that is overly concerned with the motivations, deeds, worth, and standing of the individual—in contrast to the gnostic outlook, where one begins and ends with the Divine Reality and the universal, while integrating the individual only "by way of consequence," as it were. Such spiritual "individualism," if such an oxymoronic expression may be used, cannot be immune from excesses, pitfalls, and deviations; at any rate, it veils the objectivity of the *haqīqah* under layers of subjective distractions and detours, while giving rise to formalistic excesses. A typical case, examined critically by Schuon, appears in the kind of pious scruples that betray the lack of a sense of metaphysical proportion, sometimes bordering on absurdity. What is at stake here is an effort at cultivating inner sincerity beyond the minimal formal demands of the Law. As Schuon puts it: "Excess . . . [is] a way of sublimating legalism through sincerity, hence by the absence of hypocrisy—whereas from the vantage point of gnosis, excessive scruple appears on the contrary as an element of exoterism, given that no formalistic zeal can lead to knowledge."[17] Not only is "formalistic zeal" unable to lead to knowledge—since knowledge transcends the realm of forms and actions—it also opens the way to an individualistic sedimentation of the path, via its emphasis on spiritual self-refinement through personal effort and practice. Schuon's criticism of such an individualization of Sufism is founded on a clear distinction between voluntaristic mysticism, on the one hand, and gnosis, on the other. In fact, Schuon repeatedly highlights the incompatibility between voluntarism, or a voluntaristic emphasis, and gnosis. This incompatibility finds its source in the principle that the exercise of the will pertains a priori—from an operative point of view—to the individual initiative, while intellective discernment is a priori an affirmation of the universal: "Truth . . . makes us conscious of an absolute and transcendent Reality—at once personal and suprapersonal—and the will . . . attaches itself to it and recognizes in it its own supernatural essence and its ultimate

---

17. Schuon, *In the Face of the Absolute* (Bloomington, IN: World Wisdom, 2014), 105.

end."[18] Thus, the universal Truth is a priori the initiating subject or agent of discernment within the human consciousness, while the individual attaches himself to the Truth through his efforts of assimilation and concentration. In contemplative disciplines, the striving of the will results ultimately in the recognition of its own essential identity with the Self, therefore with the Truth.[19] Thus, in Schuon's gnosis, the will is the *Śakti*, or actualizing power, of intelligence, with which it is identified in the Heart, whereas, by contrast, voluntaristic mysticism places its main emphasis on the individual dimension of the will, its perspective giving thereby preeminence to actions and the acquisition of merit through action, or even to a misguided subjective subordination of gnosis to one's ascetic efforts.[20] For Schuon, a focus on the saving power of intelligence highlights the central function of metaphysics and the transformative virtue of the Divine Name, hence a conjunction of discernment and concentration—the latter necessarily entailing individual efforts of assimilation. The efficacy of those efforts flows from the sacramental reality of the Name, and not from the human striving per se. From a gnostic point of view, the objective of knowledge, which is non-dual and non-formal, cannot possibly result from any form that takes root in the field of subject-object consciousness. Knowledge can only be an outcome of actions indirectly, as it were, inasmuch as the latter constitute a symbolic allusion to it, or insofar as they facilitate removing the veils that prevent it from being actualized. As Schuon observes, in

---

18. Schuon, *Light on the Ancient World*, 18. This is independent of the fact that the essential root of the will is the Self—all human volitional initiatives being ultimately an illusion—and that the will may—or must—recognize a posteriori its deepest identity with the transpersonal *Ātman*. Conversely, the mental reflection of the Truth and the exercise of the rational faculty pertain to the individual realm, while its intellective principle is universal.

19. "The application of the will to the spiritual way culminates in contemplative concentration, or in the practice that supports this, namely prayer in all its forms or meditation, in short the 'remembrance of God'; this is why we may give the name of 'union' to this supreme function of the will, although it is not a question of a union of grace, such as ecstasy or the station of unity. The summit that is contemplative concentration is identified with the intrinsic will in the sense that the will, in this application, is united to its immanent source." Schuon, *Esoterism as Principle and as Way*, 97–98.

20. "One must take care not to transfer the voluntaristic and sentimental individualism of religious zeal onto the plane of transpersonal awareness; one cannot wish for gnosis with a will which is contrary to the nature of gnosis. It is not we who know God, it is God who knows Himself in us." Schuon, *Esoterism as Principle and as Way*, 32–33.

another context, one "falls upward" into knowledge, so to speak, rather than acquiring it; and the manifold practices and efforts that facilitate its actualization have the metaphysical weight of a "single gesture," symbolically speaking.[21] By contrast with this gnostic focus on intelligence as the prime mover of the spiritual path—which far from excluding the will confers upon it an objective style—the voluntaristic character of much mainstream Sufi piety results, in parallel to its individualistic thrust, in an overemphasis on the power of the human will as the principal catalyst of the way. The will, which is intrinsically connected to the realm of action, appears, in this context, as the cause of spiritual wayfaring. Even though no Sufi perspective can be unaware of the primacy of Divine Grace, it functions methodically in such a way as to give precedence subjectively—if not objectively—to some forms of asceticism, in the most general sense of the term, pertaining to the domain of action. In this sense, voluntaristic Sufism is akin to the exoteric point of view in its de facto absolutization of the individual and the will.

Furthermore, the strong sentimental component of Islamic mysticism functions as a means of sincere identification with the religion, its standard bearers and the various forms in which it has become crystallized. The beauties and the pitfalls of the sentimental dimension of Sufism are particularly evident in the climate of "personalist *bhakti*" that surrounds the Messenger as embodiment of the religion. For example, such sentimental piety precludes objective recognition of the spiritual eminence of other figures, such as Jesus. Moreover, the climate of extreme emotionalism that characterizes early Sufism—including weeping, fainting, and other powerful manifestations of pious sentiments—bears witness to the intensity of devotion and spiritual life even while leading to excesses that blur the sober functioning of the intelligence that Schuon sees as one of the hallmarks of Islam as such.[22] These manifestations are, a fortiori, hardly compatible with the perspective of gnosis inasmuch as the latter finds

---

21. "After efforts worth no more than a gesture, man is breathed in by the Heavens and falls upwards, as it were, into his own Deliverance; our merits have no positive value: they do but eliminate—more symbolically than effectively—the obstacles that cut us off from the celestial attraction." Schuon, *Form and Substance in the Religions*, 127.

22. "Excessive emotivity damages the power of reflection or even—with all due reservations—intelligence itself, while plainly favoring a fundamental sentimentalism, extending from an initial biased attitude to harmless prejudices." Schuon, *In the Face of the Absolute*, 17.

its source in a "disinterested contemplation."[23] Thus, while there is no question, for Schuon, that sentiments have an important role to play in the spiritual alchemy of mysticism and gnosis alike, their function is one of prolonging intelligence rather than being a substitute for it. Whether they are colored with individualistic, voluntaristic, or sentimental shades, Schuon contrasts these various veils with the quintessence of Sufism as he conceives it.

The term quintessence evokes cosmology and alchemy, since it refers etymologically to the "fifth essence"—*quinta essentia*—a term denoting the fifth element, ether, that lies beyond the four basic elements of earth, water, fire, and air. Ether refers to that which burns and shines, as a terrestrial reflection of the luminous sky, a symbol of transcendence and the highest degrees of reality. This symbolism is all the more suggestive when one considers that Schuon has also described esoterism as belonging to the spiritual "stratosphere,"[24] by contrast with the "atmosphere" of religion. Moreover, as the *quinta essentia*, ether is one of the five elements that is "quasi-transcendent" in relation to the other four.[25] This is akin to the status of "quintessential Sufism," which, as we shall discover, is one of the key spiritual elements of Islam that transcends all the other aspects of the religion.

Looking more closely at Schuon's categorization of Sufism's various manifestations, one can recognize that his evaluation rests upon four

---

23. "The question that arises here concerns the basic nature of the soul: whether it is made of a partial and interested zeal, or of disinterested contemplation; in other words, whether the soul finds its happiness and its development in a passion directed towards God, in a fervent desire for heavenly reward—which is certainly honourable, though it does not exhaust the whole spiritual possibility of man—or whether the soul finds its happiness and unfolding in a profound comprehension of the nature of things, and consequently in a return to the Substance of which it is an accident." Schuon, *Esoterism as Principle and as Way*, 33.

24. "It results from all these considerations that God is the same for all the religions only in the Divine 'stratosphere,' and not in the human 'atmosphere'; in the latter, each religion has practically its own God, and there are as many Gods as there are religions." Schuon, *Sufism: Veil and Quintessence* (Bloomington, IN: World Wisdom, 2006), 41.

25. "The four sensible elements and all chemical aggregates and substances emerge from ether which, being simple—and inherent in every sensible substance—is the center of this unfolding. Here too, the central element cannot be merely a so to speak quantitative beginning; quite to the contrary, it is quasi-transcendent in relation to its modalities or projections." Schuon, *Sufism: Veil and Quintessence*, 127.

key notions that are introduced in contrast to each other. Firstly, there is quintessential Sufism in opposition to, or rather in tension with, average Sufism that Schuon sometimes characterizes as an "exo-esoteric" symbiosis. Furthermore, there is also a "possible Sufism" as opposed to a "necessary Sufism." While the former largely overlaps with "average Sufism" and "exo-esoterism," it also extends to hermeneutic and mystical phenomena that cannot be equated with the latter. For instance, Schuon considers some of the hermeneutic speculations of Ibn ʿArabī as only "possible forms" of Sufism, given that they derive from inspirations that do not necessarily flow from the essentials of the tradition. Thus, the distinction between the necessary and possible runs parallel to the difference between, on the one hand, direct manifestations of the tenets of Islam within the realm of spirituality—that which cannot but bloom by virtue of the intersection of those tenets with the need for a spiritual interiorization of the religion—and, on the other, manifestations of piety, imaginal inspiration, and speculative theosophy that pertain to interpretations and needs that are, arguably, not intrinsic to the Islamic archetype. The latter respond, to a large extent, to vocational requirements or mystical forays that tend not to bear the hallmarks of normative Islamic principles and values.

The difference between "average" and "quintessential" Sufism echoes the very distinction between exoterism and esoterism. In other words, quintessential esoterism can be contrasted with what Schuon refers to as "exo-esoterism." The latter refers to manifestations of Sufism that largely reflect exoteric phenomena such as the intensification of pious acts, emotional exteriorization, obediential zeal, and an inordinate emphasis on formal scruples and the perspective of fear. In Hindu parlance, such Sufi phenomena pertain to *karma-yoga* and *bhakti*—the way of action and the path of love—but not to gnosis, which primarily involves intellective discernment in addition to a propaedeutic methodical ascesis. Schuon observes that what is historically referred to as Sufism, at least in the early centuries of the Hegira, can actually be characterized as asceticism[26] or what would be referred to in Arabic as *zuhd*. Early specialists of Sufism have readily noted this fact, and it was taken by Orientalists as strong evidence of Sufism's heterogeneity to Islam, given that the latter is characterized, normatively, by moderation and a sense of equilibrium.

---

26. "The undisputed authorities of Sufism—those of the first centuries—refer only to the ascetical and mystical method, and not to a sapiential doctrine properly so-called." Schuon, *Sufism: Veil and Quintessence*, 70.

Be that as it may, the notion of exo-esoterism bears witness to the fact that there cannot be any absolute boundaries between the outer and the inner, without which the former could not even exist. Such is the meaning of the notion of *barzakh* as applied to the intermediary range of esoterism.[27] The *barzakh* separates and unites at the same time, in the sense that it shows the exo-esoteric domain as esoteric from the exoteric point of view, and the same as exoteric from an esoteric point of view.[28] It amounts to esoterism being, as it were, translated into exoteric terms. This allows one to understand how esoterism can penetrate the exoteric domain within the terms of the latter, making it thereby possible to connect the two domains. By and large, Sufi exo-esoterism, as Schuon understands it, has been responsible—particularly since the integration of its explicit presence within the fold of the tradition during the classical period—for the spiritualization of Muslim society. It has contributed to the injection of a spiritual sap, so to speak, into the formal structure of the tradition. This is all the more important given that Islam is outwardly a legal religion defined by prescriptions and proscriptions, not by spiritual principles as such.

Accordingly, exo-esoterism—whether considered as "average" or "possible"—can be understood as an esoterization of exoterism, that is, an intensification of pious practices and a deepening of one's concern with the ethico-spiritual refinement of the soul. There is no question that Sufism, in this respect, can be best defined as an interiorization of the Qur'ān and the Prophetic exemplar. On the other hand, exo-esoterism is also seen by Schuon as an exoterization of esoterism, as epitomized by

---

27. "The Arabic word *barzakh* means 'isthmus': it is a dividing line between two domains, and this line appears, from the standpoint of each side, to belong to the other side." Schuon, *In the Face of the Absolute*, 105.

28. The following excerpt from one of Schuon's letters develops this point: "Concerning the question of the 'formal' and the 'informal,' or the 'letter' (which occasionally kills) and the 'spirit' (which vivifies), I would like to note that there is always or almost always between exoterism and esoterism an intermediary region, a *barzakh*, which appears both like an esoterised exoterism and an exoterized esoterism; Christianity is nothing else, hence its paradoxical character, and as for Islam, we find this *barzakh* in the ritualism of a Ghazālī and in popular Sufism, but also spread everywhere in the collective forms of *Tasawwuf*. Between exoterism and esoterism, there always lies a ritualistic and moral *karma-yoga*; now the latter, by its invidualistic nature itself—for action and merit necessarily belong to the individual—is opposed to the metaphysical perspective as well as to the way of the saving Name."

abuses encountered in some trends of Sufi theosophy with inherent theological limitations: "Esoterism prolongs and deepens religion or, inversely, religion adapts esoterism to a certain level of consciousness and activity."[29] Religion cannot do the latter without limiting the scope of esoterism. In Islam, the exoteric limitations of esoterism include a voluntarist view of the Divine, whereby the Divine Essence is erroneously conflated with a dimension of the Divine Will that is "relative" to the created order, and where an obedientialist understanding of humanity reduces the latter—as a human reflection of the voluntarist view of the Divine—to its dimension of relative will in submission to the Divine Order. These two tendencies overlook what constitutes the Essence of God and of the human being, precisely inasmuch as "God and man are defined as will."[30] Thus, the anthropomorphic way in which the Divine Will is envisaged in Ash'arite *kalām* infiltrated some important streams of Sufism thereby leading to serious misconceptions. Rejecting the "rationalism" of the Mu'tazilite school, al-Ash'arī defended a purely Qur'ānic interpretation of the relationship of the Divine and the human that suspends both the laws of nature and the morality of actions to an All Powerful but unintelligible Divine Will. The result is that the distinction between good and evil is severed from any ontological grounding and bereft of an intellective or "Platonic" transparency, leading to what Schuon refers to as an opaque and tyrannical appearance of arbitrariness. What such Ash'arite reductions ignore is that the Divine Will must be first identified with the Divine Essence itself or, rather, with its dimension of infinitude that, as Schuon has repeatedly asserted, is the very principle of Manifestation. In other words, many Sufis tend to confuse the impersonal Principle of Manifestation, which is the ultimate cause of relativity—hence separation, fragmentation and thus evil—with the Will of the Personal God who creates, legislates, and saves. What is bypassed by such anthropomorphic conflation is the principle that the Will of God is in no way independent of His Nature, so that He cannot possibly will and act in ways that would contradict Himself, as it were. Short of recognizing this fundamental distinction, the typical bent of Islamic mysticism is to see God as a sort of tyrant whose omnipotence is abstracted, as it were, from His Nature, in ways that render the doctrine absurd. As indicated earlier, this metaphysical voluntarism is linked to an anthropological one that reduces mankind to its will, failing thereby

---

29. Schuon, *Esoterism as Principle and as Way*, 233.
30. Schuon, *Sufism: Veil and Quintessence*, 31.

to take into account its fully theomorphic nature. The theomorphism of humanity does not annul the unbridgeable distance between mankind and God, although it does prevent the absolutizing of this separation by asserting that which is most central to the human state in terms of its relationship with God, namely intelligence, which flows from the Divine Spirit. Schuon concurs with the Platonic tradition when he highlights intelligence as the principle that determines our connection and unity with the Supreme Good. Even though the chasm between the human and the Divine needs to be emphasized exoterically in order to affirm the transcendence of God that Islam must unambiguously profess to prevent any idolatrous tendencies, esoterism should be in a position—according to Schuon—to reestablish an equilibrium by stressing the primary function of the Intellect.

The voluntaristic concept of God that one finds in many Sufi accounts betrays a reduction or lowering of the Divine Essence that cannot be "measured" in any way and, therefore, not identified with the extrinsic Will that is its determination on the level of relativity. What this means, quite paradoxically, is that too many Sufi teachings and mystical statements do not fully conform to the deepest metaphysical implications inherent in the Islamic message. First, they fail to do so by not recognizing that the Divine Essence cannot be anthropomorphized or subject to the theological systematizations that are bound up with this reductionism. In doing so, they project the unfathomable absolutenesss and infinitude of the Ultimate onto the plane of relative "measurability," thereby denying God's inaccessible depth of being. To paraphrase the Qur'ān, voluntarist theology does not measure God "with His true measure" (6:91). This kind of theological debasement—which Schuon sees reflected in the ascetic feats of many early Sufis that appear to compromise the intelligibility of both the Divine and the human[31]—may be deemed to not do justice to

---

31. Schuon quotes a number of stories or traditions that illustrate a legalistic sense of fear that borders on the absurd, like the following: "In this connection we shall quote the following utterances, attributed to the caliph Ali: 'If even a single drop of wine were to fall into a well, which afterwards one were to fill in order to build a minaret there, I would not climb that minaret to make the call to prayer. If one drop of wine were to fall into a river, which were then to dry up and grasses grow on its bed, I would not pasture an animal there.' Taken literally, these utterances are properly absurd because contrary to the nature of things, both with respect to wine and to its prohibition." Schuon, *Survey of Metaphysics and Esoterism*, 179. While Schuon qualifies his assessment of these statements by highlighting that one has to take into account, beyond their literalism, the implicit spiritual message that they convey, that

"extra-theological" Islam itself. This is so to the extent that the latter defines God's Essence as Mercy and human nature as having received both the light of the spirit, *ar-rūh*, and the imprint of primordial nature, *al-fitra*.

The pitfalls that we have mentioned stem from the fact that, in Schuon's view, Sufism all too often treats metaphysics "according to the categories of an anthropomorphist theology and an individualist piety the main character of which is obediential."[32] For him, while metaphysics is not theology, even the latter must remain free from any reduction resulting from anthropomorphism and voluntarism. To say that metaphysics is not theology means that it encompasses the whole of Reality beyond the duality of the Creator and His Creation. According to Schuon, what decisively distinguishes metaphysics—as universal science of the Real—from theology—as a revelation-based rational discourse on the Divine Being and its manifestations—is the former's focus on Beyond-Being, or the Non-Dual Essence that transcends the domain of relativity, including that of Creator and creature, or *Māyā*. The perspective of Ash'arite theology, inherited by many a Sufi theosophist, remains trapped within a limited conception of Divinity that reduces the latter to the level of principle of creation. This can lead only to an abusive anthropomorphism and a reductionist voluntarism. What Schuon refers to as "moralizing metaphysics" results from a confusion between two dimensions of the Divine that William Chittick, translating from classical theological terminology, has referred to as "creative command" (*al-amr al-kawnī*) and "religious command" (*al-amr al-dīnī*).[33] The view that Satan or Iblis has obeyed God by disobeying Him is representative of such confusions. Hallāj manifests such a paradoxical understanding when he asserts that Iblis was the best of believers when he disobeyed God's command to prostrate before Adam, thereby confusing the "creative" and "religious" dimensions of the Divine command.

There is no question that, in doing away with what he deems to be impediments to the unveiling of the quintessence of spiritual Islam, Schuon paves the ground for an approach of Sufism that is less based on the wealth of elliptical, hyperbolic, and paradoxical utterances of traditional

---

is, the spiritual pitfalls of psychic inebriation as symbolized or induced by wine, it remains nevertheless true that the mystical hyperbole may hinder the intelligibility of the Divine and the human condition.

32. Schuon, *Sufism: Veil and Quintessence*, 102.

33. William Chittick, "The Ambiguity of the Qur'anic Command," in Muhammad Hassan Khalil, *Between Heaven and Hell—Islam, Salvation, and the Fate of Others* (New York: Oxford University Press, 2013), 70.

Sufism, or the ascetic and devotional prowess and charisma of early Muslim mystics, and more focused on the basic principles and practices of what he sometimes refers to as "pre-theological Islam." In this regard, it can be argued that the extent of the spiritualization of Islam by Sufism has been proportionate to its reflecting, albeit partially and not always consistently, the principles and practices of what Schuon refers to as necessary Sufism. This intrinsic dimension of Schuon's view of Sufism is specifically addressed in three chapters entitled "The Quintessential Esoterism of Islam,"[34] "The Religion of the Heart,"[35] and "The Way of Oneness."[36] It would be accurate to state that these works, which refer both to the doctrine and method of Sufism, constitute the most direct expressions of what Schuon has in mind when referring to necessary Sufism. The opening sentence of "The Way of Oneness"—"the oneness [or unity] of the object demands the totality of the subject" that is significantly repeated in "The Religion of the Heart" and several other passages from Schuon's works—provides the most direct and succinct characterization of quintessential Sufism. This assertion is based on a structure that articulates metaphysics and spirituality, along with doctrine and method, in a manner suggesting the interconnection of all dimensions of Reality and the essential Unity that underpins them.

In fact, the four terms "religion," "heart," "way," and "oneness" capture Schuon's integral understanding in this regard. The word Oneness refers to the Unity and Unicity of God, which is here taken to mean that the Divine is both exclusively and inclusively One. This amounts to saying that there is an exclusive way to the One and an inclusive one. The first understanding is specifically Islamic in that it relates transcendence to human contingency, unity and totality; unity referring to God and totality to the Law. A Muslim is one who, recognizing the Unicity of God, concludes from this awareness that he must surrender to the Law that expresses the Will of the One God. As for the inclusive meaning, it is obviously more esoteric in nature, since it refers to the idea of the Unicity of Essence, "there is none in existence save God" (*laysa fī'l wujūd ill'Allāh*), to use Ghazālī's powerful expression.[37] Accordingly, the demands of Unicity do not

---

34. Schuon, *Sufism: Veil and Quintessence*, 101–24.
35. Schuon, *Esoterism as Principle and as Way*, 229–34.
36. Schuon, *Esoterism as Principle and as Way*, 235–40.
37. Al-Ghazālī, *The Niche of Lights*, a parallel English-Arabic text translated, introduced, and annotated by David Buchman (Provo, UT: Brigham Young University Press, 1998), 16–17.

pertain to the will and its surrender to God through the Law but—more radically—to the existential totality of the human being, which is perfected in extinction (*fanā'*) and permanence in God (*baqā'*). This is the way of Oneness and the only true way, both in the sense of a return to the One and of the "way things are." As for the "Religion of the Heart," it implies totality—both objectively and subjectively: objectively, because religion is that which binds us to the One in a manner that cannot be partial or selective, and subjectively, because the Heart means "all that we are."[38]

It is significant that, in order to delineate the characteristics of the "Religion of the Heart," Schuon begins with a consideration of Ghazālī's introduction to his *Revivification of the Religious Sciences* in which the diagnosis of the spiritual sickness in Muslim society leads the theologian to highlight the orthodoxy—indeed necessity—of Islamic spirituality, which he equates with Sufism as *ihsān* or "perfect practice." Thus, Ghazālī demonstrates that Islam cannot survive as a spiritual reality if it is not vivified by the essentializing and interiorizing stream of Sufism. This demonstration is, for Schuon, evidence of the fact that Islam contains within its fold what he calls two "religions"; that is, the "outward religion" of the Law and the "inward religion" of the Heart. For Schuon, this distinction amounts to a recognition that the relationship between the inner and outer dimensions of the tradition implies both continuity and discontinuity between them. This is a reflection of the relationship between essence and form; in Schuon's terms, "Form proceeds from essence, but the latter remains eminently free in regard to form."[39] While acknowledging that Ghazālī does not necessarily—or fully—recognize the "irreversibility of relationships" between the two, Schuon sees, in his affirmation of the need to revivify the essence of faith and practice, evidence of Ghazālī's intuition of the latter. The fact that Ghazālī may not acknowledge the irreversible supereminence of the essence in relation to forms, or that he could not draw all the consequences from his clear intimation of the former's deeper reality, may be taken as a clear demonstration of what distinguishes mainstream classical Sufism from the quintessential variety that Schuon has in view. This is evidence that Sufism has necessarily been pulled back and forth, in its historical development, between two poles:

---

38. "The saving power of Islam stems from the principle that the oneness of the truth demands the totality of faith; this totality engages all that we are, and thus the heart which sums up what we are." Schuon, *Esoterism as Principle and as Way*, 231.

39. Schuon, *Esoterism as Principle and as Way*, 230.

on the one hand, its conventional religious framework and sensibilities and, on the other, its esoteric—and therefore universalist—dimension. While Schuon is keenly aware of both the benefits and limitations of this polarity—spiritual benefits for society and the formal hampering of gnosis—he sees the Heart as being the point of convergence of all that, in Islam as in other religions, tends toward essentialization, totality, and inwardness. This is so to the extent that he considers the point of encounter between Islam and Christianity to be situated in the recognition of Divine Unicity as the principle of human totality, therefore Heart-knowledge. If "the uniqueness of Christ means that only the Logos can save us," this is "basically . . . a more relative way of saying that 'there is no god other than the sole God."[40] Far from diluting the Unicity of the Divine Object, the focus on the Word appears as a manifestation of the same principle of Unity on a relative level, independently of the problematic intricacies of Trinitarian theology. While this question is not directly at stake in our current discussion of Sufism, what we need to retain from his understanding of the quintessence of Sufism is that it is founded on the fundamental relationship between "unity of the object" and "totality of the subject," and that this relationship is deemed by Schuon to be paradigmatic for every religion. Thus, Schuon's Sufism as a "Way of Oneness" and "Religion of the Heart" articulates both essential Islam and religion in general; indeed, it provides a synthesis, or "schema," of religion as such: "This perspective is specifically Islamic, but in its fashion it summarizes all integral—or, in other words, transforming and uniting—spirituality."[41]

Leaving aside for now the paradigmatic and universalist aspects of the matter, it is important to ponder the implications of Schuon's articulation of Sufism as quintessential esoterism in direct relation to Islam itself and, therefore, independently of the historical developments and complexities of *tasawwuf*. This is, no doubt, the most unexpected and puzzling aspect of Schuon's view of Sufism: on the one hand, his understanding is uncompromisingly esoteric and universalist to the point that he has been sometimes criticized for "de-islamicizing" Sufism; on the other, it can be fairly argued that his reflections on Sufism are more rooted in Islam itself than in the intellectual and spiritual traditions of Sufism per se, to the extent that the two can actually be distinguished. Indeed, this seeming

---

40. Schuon, *Esoterism as Principle and as Way*, 231.
41. Schuon, *Esoterism as Principle and as Way*, 235.

paradox is compounded by Schuon's critical appreciation of certain Sufi phenomena in light of the normative standards of pre-theological Islam. In order to understand the nature of this ostensible paradox, it is necessary to consider a few important aspects of Schuon's thinking on the matter.

First, and as we have already seen, the fundamental distinction between the exoteric and the esoteric draws a line, in Schuon's view, between the outer and inner dimensions of traditional religions. It is actually in Islam—and no doubt also in Judaism—that this distinction is most clearly attested. Thus, the delineation of Sufism within Islam corresponds to the theoretical differentiation between exoterism and esoterism, as formulated in the works of the French metaphysician René Guénon. However, Schuon is well aware—as evinced by notions such as "average Sufism" and "possible Sufism"—that the realities of historical and sociological Islam are far from corresponding to such a neat configuration. Moreover, numerous passages from Schuon's works bear witness to his acknowledgment that the theoretical differentiation between esoterism and exoterism does not show the same degree of distinctiveness across all religious traditions. This is already an indication that Schuon's understanding of esoterism, by contrast with René Guénon's work, is less technical and systematic than metaphysical and spiritual. In other words, esoterism is not a category but an intellectual and spiritual orientation. Suffice it to say that notions such as a rigorous conception of the Absolute and an emphasis on transpersonal inwardness are revealed in varied ways through the structures, proportions, modes, and articulations of different religious traditions.

Second, Schuon's definition of Islam is decidedly less theological and legal than metaphysical and spiritual. By contrast with Ghazālī and other Sufis, whose perspectives are more complex and in many ways more indirect, Schuon contemplates Islam from the point of view of the metaphysics of Unity, and the spiritual and moral implications of the very term *islām*. In other words, he defines Islam—as we have seen—as the "Way of Oneness" and the "Religion of the Heart." This is what he refers to, at times, as "absolute Islam" in contrast to "contingent Islam."[42] This is also what allows him to characterize Islam as a "synthesis"—even a "schema"—of all religions. As a matter of fact, Schuon accounts for the rapid expansion of Islam, and its stability throughout time, in terms of its having "given a religious form to that which constitutes the essence of

---

42. Schuon, *Sufism: Veil and Quintessence*, xiv.

all religion."[43] In doing so, Schuon rejoins those Sufis, such as Rūmī and Hallāj, who have seen in the primordiality and terminality of Islam an evidence of its constituting an archetype of all religions. Needless to say, individual religions can be considered as so many archetypes of religion itself, since there is always a sense in which a given religion coincides with religion as such. However, what makes Islam particularly suited to being an archetypical religion is, first, its emphasis on Unity and, second, the simplicity and totality of its means of salvation. These hallmarks of Islam are what makes it, on the one hand, particularly inclusive while being, on the other, also conducive to contemplation and gnosis. In considering Islam, there is, however, the danger of confusing its surface with its fundamentals; a danger that is all the more apparent in the forms associated with its specifically Arab cultural traits and its rapid transformation into a contemporary ideology.[44] This, no doubt, is why Schuon was inclined to regard the pillars of Islam as the keys to Islamic spirituality, both inasmuch as they constitute the fundamentals of the religion—as confirmed by the Prophet himself[45]—and to the extent that they provide access to the gnostic quintessence of necessary Sufism.

That Schuon considers the quintessence of Sufism in the context of these pillars reflects a perspective implying that form derives from, and gives access to, the Essence, but only to the extent that a keen sense of the latter informs the way in which one envisages the former. In other words, in order to understand Sufism, one has first to understand Islam, because Sufism is nothing else—in its quintessence—than the interiorization and (as circumstances permit) the essentialization and universalization of Islam. In that sense, Schuon reclaims the essential principles of Sufism in order to disassociate it from its external and "mythological" representations; in

---

43. Schuon, *Roots of the Human Condition* (Bloomington, IN: World Wisdom, 1991), 81.

44. "On the surface of Islam we meet with the features of the Bedouin mentality, which obviously have nothing universal about them; in the fundamental elements, however, we encounter as it were religion as such, which by its essentiality opens quite naturally onto metaphysics and gnosis." Schuon, *Roots of the Human Condition*, 81.

45. "The angel Gabriel, appearing as a man dressed in a pure white gown, approached Muhammad while he was among his friends and interrogated him about his religion. When Gabriel asked Muhammad about Islam, he replied, 'Islam is that you witness that there is no god but God and that Muhammad is God's messenger; that you perform prayer; give alms; fast [the month of] Ramadan; and perform the *hajj* to the house [of God in Mecca] if you are able to do so.'" Juan E. Campo, ed., *Encyclopedia of Islam* (New York: Facts on File, 2009), xxiii.

other words, to rehabilitate its roots in Islamic spirituality based on the pillars. One can think, for instance, of the striking traditional dictum from the twelfth century: "Sufism is the five prayers and waiting for death."[46] Aside from its typically elliptical and hyperbolic character, this precept corresponds to Schuon's spiritual distillation of Sufism into the two principles of *dhikr* and *faqr*. The first refers to the remembrance of God, which Schuon sees as the essence of all religious practices, while the second suggests the ethical and spiritual precondition for such methodical recollection, that is, humility as the absence of all egocentricity and an emptiness for God. In other words, canonical prayers are the most direct exoteric "symbol" of *dhikr* as the esoteric practice of contemplative concentration, whereas "waiting for death" points to spiritual renunciation, detachment, and, ultimately, extinction in God—*fanā' fī-Llāh*—the esoteric consummation of the Islamic virtue of "poverty" or *faqr*.

When looking for the foundations of Sufism, Schuon considers the five pillars, or *arkān*, as gateways to the esoteric meaning of Sufi doctrine and method. This does not mean that he equates the *sharī'ah* with the *haqīqah*. While Schuon considers the former as a "symbolic" representation of the latter, he still rejects Ibn 'Arabī's idea of their conjunction.[47] For him, this equation results from a legalistic emphasis that he sees as incompatible with gnosis. It remains true, however, that each of the pillars gives access to one of the major metaphysical and spiritual dimensions of Islamic spirituality. This is true, first and foremost, with respect to the *shahādah* that encapsulates the whole metaphysics of Unity—the central doctrine of the *wahdat al-wujūd* school associated with the disciples of Ibn 'Arabī.[48] For Schuon, Islam can be identified with the *shahādah*. Considering that Islam is a variant of what Hindus would call *karma-yoga*—a way of action through an adherence to prescriptions—one may be sur-

---

46. Quoted in Eric Geoffroy, *Introduction to Sufism* (Bloomington, IN: World Wisdom, 2010), 68.

47. "[For Ibn 'Arabī] There is no illumination without obedience. The *sharī'ah* (Law) and the *haqīqa* (the highest and most secret of truths) are inextricably conjoined." Michel Chodkiewicz, *An Ocean without Shore—Ibn 'Arabī, The Book, and the Law* (Albany: State University of New York Press, 1993), 101.

48. "Ibn 'Arabī . . . had the great merit of enunciating the mystery of radiating and inclusive Unity in a fully Ash'arite environment, and thus of putting the emphasis on the implicitly divine character of cosmic Manifestation, which brings us back to pure and integral metaphysics." Schuon, *Sufism: Veil and Quintessence*, 33.

prised by Schuon's stress on the intimate relationship between Islam and intelligence, and his frequent affirmation that Islam provides a religious avenue particularly conducive to gnosis. It must be stressed, however, that the network of legal injunctions that constitutes the pillars of Islam and the *sharī'ah* flow from a recognition of Divine Unity, as expressed by the *shahādah*, and has no meaning outside it. In a sense, the formal witnessing of *tawhīd*—which affirms the existence of one God—is symbolic of this metaphysical attestation, which alone realizes the fullness of its meaning. By symbolic is meant a relatively external dimension that does not plumb the full depths of the Reality at stake. In other words, the religious attestation of Unity is like a reflection of metaphysical *tawhīd* on the plane of mental and volitional duality. Only a recognition of the metaphysical meaning of the *shahādah* does justice to both the unicity and totality of the Divine Principle, and reabsorbs the human reality into its archetype in God. The negative, or exclusive, aspect of the *shahādah* extinguishes all realities before God. In this respect, Schuon notes that "in Arabic script the word *lā* resembles a pair of scissors."[49] This principle is realized subjectively as *fanā'* or extinction. As for the aspect of totality, which is associated with the infinitude of the Principle, it means the inclusion of everything within the Essence of the One without a second. This is the aspect of immanence regarding the truth of Islam that is realized inwardly as *baqā*, or permanence, in God. This is also a dimension that is the specific province of Sufism.

The second *arkān* of Islam is *salāt*, or the canonical prayer, which is key to the spiritual recognition of one's utter dependence on God and the main content of Sufi consciousness. The very reality of God entails a relationship between Him and mankind, which is the evident foundation of prayer. In more strictly metaphysical terms, *salāt* means, esoterically, "the submission of Manifestation to the Principle."[50] There is, therefore, in prayer a reality that exceeds the mere relationship of mankind with God, since the human submission that it achieves reflects the metaphysical status of the entire universe. In this sense, the prostration in which the canonical prayer culminates expresses the summit of the universal worship of creation, as the Qur'ān teaches when declaring that "the stars and the trees prostrate" (55:6). However, the full metaphysical recognition

---

49. Schuon, *Sufism: Veil and Quintessence*, nn. 5, 46.
50. Schuon, *Sufism: Veil and Quintessence*, 116.

of this relationship is achieved only through internal prayer, which is—at its summit—the "prayer of God within us." In other words, invocation or *dhikr* is the essence of *salāt* but it is also the realization of our utter dependence on God's order, meaning that we are intrinsically "attached" to God within the *barzakh* of the heart, the seat of Divine immanence.

Concerning the central function of *dhikr*, or remembrance of God through His Name, a number of points need be grasped in order to reach a deeper understanding of Schuon's view of Sufism. First, with respect to the core God-consciousness mentioned above, *dhikr* can embody, in and of itself, the very reality of the Sufi path in its entirety. This is so to the extent that it epitomizes the whole metaphysical reality of mankind and its concomitant spiritual vocation. To remember God is to remember the Real, and to remember the Real is to remember, and recover, one's true nature in, and by, God. Therefore, Schuon, in agreement with the whole Sufi tradition, considers *dhikr* to be the central practice of *tasawwuf*. The way in which he articulates this centrality is remarkable in that it directly identifies the Name with the Named. Few Sufis have been so explicit in highlighting the spiritual significance of this ontological equation. Although numerous Sufis have affirmed that God's grace works through His Name or Names, the idea that God is none other than His Name is more familiar in Hindu spirituality than in Islam. Schuon likes to mention Ramakrishna's assertion that "God and His Name are one," a declaration of immanence that most Muslims would find difficult to fathom and, indeed, might even reject as a form of *shirk*—or association—whereby something relative is idolized as God Himself. Schuon's point of view, by contrast, is akin to the *Advaita* perspective on the Name, in the sense that the latter is conceived, and experienced, as the most direct manifestation of the Unity of Essence that is intrinsic to the whole creation. Second, and by way of consequence, *dhikr* is clearly identified by Schuon as the highest form of prayer, one in which the ordinary notion of prayer as petition is ultimately transcended, since it presupposes a duality that—at its summit—the invocation of the Name dispels. In an essay entitled "Modes of Prayer,"[51] Schuon contrasts invocatory orison, of which *dhikr* is the manifestation in Islam, with two other kinds of prayer, one being personal prayer—in which the individual articulates petitions, difficulties, or expressions of gratitude before God—and the other being the canonical prayers that are divinely instituted in

---

51. Schuon, *Stations of Wisdom* (Bloomington, IN: World Wisdom, 1961), 121–45.

all traditions. Schuon makes the point that while personal prayer (*du'ā*) is the prayer of "such and such human being" and the canonical prayers (*salāt*) are those of "humanity as such," invocation (*dhikr*) is the prayer of God in a human being. This shows that *dhikr*, at its highest level of realization, is the consummation of all religious practices and leads to union with the Divine Self. In this regard, Schuon likes to quote Shaykh Ahmad al-'Alawī, according to whom "the law was not enjoined . . . , neither were the rites of worship ordained but for the sake of establishing the remembrance of God."[52]

Compared to the *shahādah* and its operative complement, prayer, the third and fourth pillars of Islam—fasting during Ramadan and giving alms—appear as informing the requisite predisposition of the soul. Esoterically, Schuon characterizes *siyām*, or fasting, as "detachment . . . with regard to the ego" and *zakāt*, or almsgiving, as "detachment . . . with regard to the world."[53] The spiritual meaning of fasting is the need for a reduction in desires, therefore a diminution of the *nafs* or the concupiscent passions of the soul.[54] As for almsgiving, it fosters an awareness regarding the emptiness of mundane existence, thus predisposing one to recognize the exclusive nature of Divine reality. In both cases, a given practice gives potential access to a mode of consciousness, or rather stimulates its awakening, without ever being the actual cause of it, since Schuon remains fully cognizant of the Advaitan principle that "only knowledge delivers."

An esoteric interpretation of these two pillars raises the question of the relationship between ascetic practice, or abstention, and knowledge; and, indeed, Schuon's view of asceticism is critical to understanding his assessment of early and classical Sufism. As we have seen, Schuon stresses the limitations of a voluntaristic perspective that appears to subordinate knowledge to action, or make the latter the cause of the former. This does not mean that any form of asceticism should be, or could be, excluded

---

52. Martin Lings, *A Sufi Saint of the Twentieth Century: Shaikh Ahmad al-'Alawī—His Spiritual Heritage and Legacy* (Berkeley: University of California Press, 1971), 96.

53. Schuon, *Sufism: Veil and Quintessence*, 116.

54. In his treatise *The Four Pillars of Spiritual Transformation*, Ibn 'Arabī makes a similar point when he states that the hunger resulting from fasting "is characterized by humility, submission, servility, lack of self-importance, indigence, discretion, tranquil emotions and an absence of base thoughts." *The Four Pillars of Spiritual Transformation: The Adornment of the Spiritually Transformed (Hilyat al-abdāl)*, translated by Stephen Hirtenstein (Oxford: Anqa Publications, 2008), 36.

from the perspective of gnosis. In fact, Schuon distinguishes between two kinds of asceticism, both of which may play a role in the path of knowledge. The first is physical and indirect in relation to knowledge, as it consists in mastering or curbing the passional element of the soul, with a view to making this energy available to serve spiritual ends, as we find *mutatis mutandis* in the tantric traditions of India. In a sense, fasting and almsgiving address this need to keep the appetites under control, and to channel desires toward their ultimate object. It is in the domain of this type of asceticism, however, that one finds numerous examples of hyperbole and excess pertaining to an overemphasis on the fear of God that is so characteristic of original Sufism. As we have seen, Schuon deplores the fact that such exaggerations often contribute to veiling the intelligibility of Sufism, both from the point of view of gnosis and from that of Islamic sensibilities in general. It must be added, though, that not all such purgative asceticism is necessarily given to dramatic and passional excesses. In and of itself—and independent of any penitentialist tendencies—asceticism can be equated with mere sobriety and detachment from worldly proclivities, whether normatively—as a necessary and general context for spiritual life—or more particularly in response, and in proportion to, the passional tendencies of a given individual or a collectivity.[55]

The second type of asceticism brings us closer to gnosis since it relates to the cultivation of virtues understood as ethical modalities of knowledge. Thus Schuon may write, quite suggestively, that "every virtue is an eye that sees God."[56] In contrast to the first type of asceticism that is purgative—the inner purification envisaged as the main aspect of early Sufism—the second kind is "receptive" and "participatory," which amounts to saying that it corresponds to a strictly Platonic view of the virtues. This means that virtue is a reflection of a higher reality that is archetypical and grounded in God, or ultimately identified with a given attribute of

---

55. "There is an ascesis that consists simply in sobriety, and which is sufficient for the naturally spiritual man; and there is another which consists in fighting against passions, the degree of this ascesis depending upon the demands of the individual nature; finally, there is the ascesis of those who mistakenly believe themselves to be charged with all sins, or who identify themselves with sin through mystical subjectivism, without forgetting to mention those who practice an extreme asceticism in order to expiate the faults of others, or even simply in order to give a good example in a world that has need of it." Schuon, *Christianity/Islam: Perspectives on Esoteric Ecumenism*, 40.

56. Schuon, *Esoterism as Principle and as Way*, 104.

the Divine. From a slightly different point of view, virtue is a mode of participation in the archetype or the Divine itself. To be virtuous, therefore, amounts to partaking of a Divine Quality in the Platonic sense of *methexis*, the participation of a phenomenon in the Idea or the archetype. This Platonic dimension of Schuon's view of spiritual asceticism allows us to better understand its deep connections with knowledge, since it refers to the coincidence of knowing and being.[57] In early Sufism, this aspect of *methexis* found a religious correspondence in the mystical idea of an "exchange of qualities," *tabaddul as-sifāt*. Ghazālī refers to this as one of the most distinctive aspects of Sufi asceticism. In extolling the virtues of *mutasawwifūn* and the excellence of Sufism, he states: "It became clear to me that their [the Sufis] most distinctive characteristic is something that can be attained, not by study, but rather by fruitional experience (*dhawq*), the state of ecstasy (*hāl*) and the exchange of qualities."[58] The notion of an exchange of qualities is both comparable to, and distinct from, the Platonic *methexis* that allows one to further elucidate the differences between various streams of Sufism. In classical Sufism, to speak of *tabaddul as-sifāt* is to suggest an extinction of the human will in the Divine—an "extinction" and "permanence" in God, as Sufis would put it—whereby the Divine is substituted, as it were, for the human. There is a reciprocity here in the sense that God is "the Rich" (*al-Ghanī*) while mankind is poor (*faqīr*), the latter term being used to refer to Sufi affiliates. This is a direct implication of the *shahādah*, which intimates the unreality of everything other than God. Now the Platonic point of view, as we have seen, emphasizes participation, therefore analogy and continuity. Whereas the Sufi "exchange of qualities" is an immanent and mystical translation of the Islamic sense of transcendence—since it implies the exclusive Divine possession of qualities—the Platonic participation refers, in a sense, to the transcendent horizon of the qualities experienced within immanence. This is illustrated, for instance, by Plato's theme of educating the soul through an anagogic ascent from the love of physical beauty to that of the Beautiful

---

57. "The key to understanding the spiritual necessity of the virtues lies in the fact that metaphysical truths are also reflected in the will and not only in the intellect and reason. To a given principial truth there corresponds a particular volitional attitude. This is a necessary aspect—or a consequence—of the principle that 'to know is to be.'" Schuon, *Spiritual Perspectives and Human Facts* (Bloomington, IN: World Wisdom, 2007), 186.

58. *Al-Ghazālī's Path to Sufism and His Deliverance from Error: An Annotated Translation of Al-Munqidh min al-dalal*, by R. J. McCarthy (Louisville: Fons Vitae, 2000), 52.

in itself (*autò tò kalòn*).⁵⁹ This contrast has a significant bearing upon the distinction between ascetic and esoteric approaches to Sufism since the former consistently emphasizes the reduction of the human—identifying it with everything that entails its limitations and miseries—while the latter prefers to stress the God-given capacity of the human soul to realize its immanent divinity, so to speak.

As we have already noted, an overemphasis on physical and purgative asceticism is not only reductive, from the point of view of *ma'rifah*, it is also problematic from the perspective of the Prophetic *sunnah* or exemplary tradition. One of the charges often made against Sufism by Muslim exoterists—who either reject the idea of Islamic mysticism or criticize what they deem to be its excesses and deviations—relates to the incompatibility between the normative practices of Islam (which they rightfully see as being characterized by equilibrium, moderation, and even accommodation) and a sense that religion must not be difficult; for example, the ascetic feats of a number of Sufis, which are sometimes more attuned to the "holy disequilibrium" of Christian penitential asceticism than to the "holy equilibrium" of Islam.⁶⁰

The fifth pillar of Islam, the *hajj*, and a sixth one that is sometimes added to it, *jihād*, complete this survey of the spiritual perfections in Islam. They are both, however, of a less mandatory nature than the first four. *Hajj* is required only if the believer possesses the physical means to perform it. At any rate, Schuon, like Hallāj, understands the consummation of the *hajj* as being an inner pilgrimage to the Heart. He asserts that the spiritual archetype of the *hajj* is none other than an orientation toward the Heart as the center of spiritual consciousness. Hallāj, among the Sufis, was renowned for, most daringly, stressing the mystical meaning of the Ka'ba as the primary symbol of the Heart in Islam. He enjoined the believer to

---

59. "Beginning from obvious beauties he must for the sake of that highest beauty be ever climbing aloft, as on the rungs of a ladder, from one to two, and from two to all beautiful bodies; from personal beauty he proceeds to beautiful observances, from observance to beautiful learning, and from learning at last to that particular study which is concerned with the beautiful itself and that alone; so that in the end he comes to know the very essence of beauty." Plato, *Symposium* (211c–d), Volume 5, translated and edited by R. M. Lamb (Cambridge, MA: Harvard University Press, 1953), 207.

60. "We have said that Islam is the perspective of holy equilibrium and Christianity that of holy disequilibrium." Schuon, *Christianity/Islam: Perspectives on Esoteric Ecumenism*, 79.

"circumambulate the Ka'ba of heart seven times."[61] This analogy tends to relativize the significance of physically circumambulating the Ka'ba and was, for this very reason, condemned by the exoteric authorities. Hallāj, for his part, distinguishes between the collective religion of mankind and the personal religion of the Heart: "There is for men a pilgrimage, a *hajj*. As for me, I take a pilgrimage to the One who dwells within me."[62] Exoterically, the voluntary aspect of the *hajj* stems from the fact that making the pilgrimage may not be possible for many whereas, esoterically, it could be said that the Heart, representing esoterism subjectively, is only accessible to those who are endowed with the spiritual qualifications to search and approach it.

Finally, *jihād* is not always included among the pillars for reasons analogous to those related to the *hajj*. Exoterically, certain categories of believers are exempted from *jihād*, such as those who are sick, which can also be applied, analogically, to spiritual incapacity. Sufis have been inclined to understand *jihād* in spiritual terms, as spiritual exertion or *mujāhada*; that is, the fight against the tenebrous soul and its negative tendencies. Compared with other pillars, spiritual effort may be deemed to be relatively extrinsic. In other words, it facilitates and supports the virtues but has no direct meaning aside from them. In a sense, *hajj* and *jihād* reflect, each in its own way, the profoundly inclusive and realistic character of Muslim ascesis. The spirit of equilibrium and moderation that emanates from the practical prescriptions of Islam is also evidence of its specifically exoteric character and, therefore, of the implicit coexistence, within Islam, of an outer and an inner dimension.

These considerations, and the questions they raise with respect to the nature of Islamic spirituality, cannot be severed from the role of the Prophet as spiritual epitome of Islam and religious exemplar. The Prophet happened to behave as an ascetic but he did not impose, or even recommend, asceticism for the whole community. In fact, two characteristics of Islam, as taught in the Qur'ān, are equilibrium and moderation. Equilibrium results from a recognition that the hereafter does not invalidate, as it were, the rights of the here-below and that the spiritual does not, in principle, contradict the terrestrial. Moderation results from the fact that the negative tendencies of the human soul (*ghaflah*, negligence or

---

61. Alexander D. Knysh, *Islamic Mysticism: A Short History* (Leiden: Brill, 2000), 76.
62. Roger Arnaldez, *Hallāj ou la religion de La Croix* (Paris: Plon, 1964), 31.

forgetfulness) do not fundamentally disfigure the theomorphic nature of mankind. Accordingly, they do not call for an excessive penitential asceticism that emphasizes renunciation and suffering. The asceticism of Islam, or the religious discipline that shapes the life and character of Muslims, cannot be considered as vocational, individual, and sacrificial, since it is circumscribed by the stipulated limits of the *arkān* and the *sharīʿah*. On these grounds, Schuon calls our attention to the fact that there is an intrinsic duality in the Prophetic exemplar.[63] This duality allows us to distinguish, within the Prophet, two dimensions: an outer vocation that provides a mold for the normative practices of Islam and an inner, spiritual, reality that manifests a function of super-eminence rather than that of an exemplar, which cannot serve as a religious norm for all. In a sense, this dual consideration of the Prophet reproduces the generic distinction, found in classical Sufi works, between the prophet and the saint, the *rasūl* or the *nabī* and the *walī*.[64] In agreement with classical Sufi teachings, such as those of Ibn ʿAṭāʾ Allāh and Tirmidhī (which placed on the same spiritual level the three aforementioned categories, thus highlighting their inner commonality in *walāya* or sanctity),[65] Schuon distinguishes,

---

63. "Islamic spirituality presents an enigma in that its theoretical and practical expressions often seem to draw away from Islam as such, notwithstanding the efforts of the Sufi authors to emphasize the legality of their opinions and methods, even those most foreign to the overall perspective of Islam. The entire enigma lies in the fact that there is here a dimension which the Law has not articulated, or which it only suggests covertly; this enigma stems from the very person of the Prophet, who privately—if one may say so—practiced an ascesis which he doubtless recommended to some but did not make mandatory, and which moreover in his own case could not signify the 'purgative way' as it did with those who have emulated him. This ascesis, readily confused with Sufism—whereas it may merely be a preparatory trial at the threshold of the mysteries—is far from constituting the Substance itself of the Messenger; being a spiritual beatitude and thus a state of consciousness, the Prophetic Substance remains independent of all formal conditions, even though the formal practices can be rightly considered as paths towards participation in it." Schuon, *In the Face of the Absolute*, 123.

64. "Outwardly, the Prophet can readily be seen and understood in his role as Legislator; inwardly, in his Substance, he represents esoterism at every level, whence a duality that is at the source of certain antinomies and which in the last analysis determined the schism between Sunnites and Shiites." Schuon, *In the Face of the Absolute*, 122.

65. For a discussion of these distinctions, see Geneviève Gobillot, "Présence d'al-Hakīm al-Tirmidhī dans la pensée shādhilī," in Eric Geoffroy, *Une voie soufie dans le monde: la Shādhiliyya* (Paris: Maisonneuve et Larose, 2005), 32–35.

in the Prophet, a "form" associated with his function as *rasūl* (legislator or messenger), and a "substance" pertaining to his spiritual personality or inner "beatitude." Now the latter aspect is, by definition, more spiritually intimate and cannot be translated formally, as it were, since it pertains to a mode of being and consciousness. Schuon has devoted an entire essay to what he calls "The Mystery of the Prophetic Substance," providing therein a synthesis of the spiritual perfections of the soul of the Prophet, together with their ethical prolongations. As for the aspect of Messenger, this pertains, by contrast, to what Schuon sees as the "formal dimension" of the *Logos*. This refers to the law-giving function of the Prophet but also, more generally, to the outward example he provided in countless ways throughout his life. This is the outer *sunnah*, which encompasses an extremely wide array of actions and attitudes, from the most minutely practical to the loftiest ethico-spiritual aspects of life. This distinction has a very significant bearing upon the understanding of Sufism, in the sense that the latter has tended to manifest itself as a prolongation of the inner reality of the Prophet—understood as an emulation of his ascesis—beginning with vigils and fasting that are beyond the strict requirements of the religion. It is here that we find the distinction between a specifically ascetic understanding of Sufism and Schuon's esoteric emphasis. What makes his perspective remarkable is that it severs extreme asceticism from the spiritual core of the Prophetic substance and thus from the inner *sunnah*. Schuon does not see the Prophet's asceticism as purgative, in that viewing the prayerful vigils and rigorous fasts of the Prophet in this way would undermine the traditional account of the purification, by the angel Gabriel, of the Prophet's heart when he was a child.[66] Reza Shah-Kazemi has observed that the ascetic practices of the Prophet were primarily motivated by a sense of gratitude for the gifts received and not by any expectations or a sense of fear, as might be the case in purgative asceticism. This commentary is based on 'Alī's distinction between the

---

66. "Anas ibn Malik reported that Gabriel came to the Messenger of Allah (may peace be upon him) while he was playing with his playmates. He took hold of him and lay him prostrate on the ground and tore open his breast and took out the heart from it and then extracted a blood-clot out of it and said: 'That was the part of Satan in thee. And then he washed it with the water of Zamzam in a golden basin and then it was joined together and restored to its place.'" *Ṣaḥīḥ Muslim: Being Traditions of the Sayings and Doings of the Prophet Muhammad as Narrated by His Companions and Compiled Under the Title Al-Jāmiʻ-uṣ-ṣaḥīḥ*, Muslim ibn Ḥajjāj al-Qushayrī (New Delhi: Kitab Bhavan, 1971), 103.

worship of the "merchants" and the "slaves" in contrast to that of the "free" (*al-ahrār*), the spiritual motivations of which are, respectively, fear and gratitude.[67] Shah-Kazemi proposes, as illustrative of the latter, the Prophet's simple answer to the question of why he practiced long prayer vigils into the night: "Am I not a grateful servant?"[68] This answer epitomizes a sense of metaphysical debt for the gifts of the Spirit and also, no doubt, for all other gifts—including that of existence—this being a direct recognition of one's metaphysical consciousness of, and dependence on, the One. One may object that the language of gratitude does not take us beyond the scope of religious devotion and its ethical prolongations. However, it is important to understand that the asceticism of the Prophet, and the religious language in which he expresses its foundations, are a direct translation of an esoteric content that embodies *tawḥīd*, and which could hardly be manifested in any other way, given the inclusive nature of the Islamic religion as a whole. In other words, Schuon sees the innermost nature of the Prophet as a beatitude, that is, as a mode of inner union with God, which is expressed outwardly in ways that can be intelligible and spiritually edifying for the faithful. We thus return to the notion of *barzakh*, which, when perceived from the religious point of view, appears as the very essence of esoterism. Hence the need to refer to a quintessential esoterism that remains immune from the exoterizing tendencies of the tradition.

The decidedly esoteric character of Schuon's view of Sufism must raise the question of Sufi antinomianism, since the former appears to highlight the transcendence of the *ḥaqīqah* with respect to the *sharī'ah*. Given the emphasis Schuon places on the transcendence of esoterism vis-à-vis the exoteric, the discontinuity between the two is an invitation to a breaking of the shell, as Schuon often reminds his readers by quoting Meister Eckhart: "If you would have the kernel, you must break the shell."[69]

---

67. Reza Shah-Kazemi, *Spiritual Quest: Reflections on Qur'ānic Prayer According to the Teachings of Imam 'Alī* (London: I.B. Tauris, 2011), 32.

68. Shah-Kazemi, *Spiritual Quest*, 92.

69. "I have said before, the shell must be broken and what is inside must come out, for, if you want to get at the kernel you must break the shell." *The Complete Mystical Works of Meister Eckhart*, translated by Maurice O'C. Walshe (New York: Herder and Herder, 2009), 409. "Wan wiltû den kernen haben, sô muostû die scalen brechen" (102:25), *Deutsche Mystiker des Vierzehnten Jahrhunderts, 2, Meister Eckhart*, edited by Franz Pfeiffer (Leipzig: G.J. Göschen'sche Verlaghandlund, 1857), 333.

This appeal, by the German Dominican, to attain the essence appears in a discussion on the function of likeness, adequateness, or analogy, in the context of sapiential knowledge. Eckhart remarks that if knowledge of the essence is to be pursued, "all likeness must be shattered." This is an important remark in helping us to understand Schuon's emphasis on the discontinuity between essence and form, notwithstanding a complementary recognition, from another vantage point, of the essential continuity between the former and the latter.

In this respect, Schuon adopts a more balanced perspective, consistent with the metaphysical principle that requires a consideration, not only of Reality as such but also of its relative planes of manifestation. Schuon addresses the delicate question of the relationship between the practical consequences of the distinction between the *haqīqah* and the *sharī'ah* in a number of passages from his books. In particular, he is keen to affirm that the religion of the Heart—which is none other than the *haqīqah*—is independent of the Law. This independence, however, pertains more to the realm of principles than that of facts.[70] This means, in practice, that antinomian Sufism remains an exception that confirms the rule. This exception is a full manifestation of the principle, but its rarity reflects the overwhelming needs of human nature, both extrinsically and intrinsically. Extrinsically (with regard to the collective and institutional aspects of the matter), there is a sense in which the legal norm is a guarantee of objective conformity, without which the religious needs of the collectivity could not be met. Intrinsically, the reasons for the distinction between the principle and facts allow us to gain a deeper insight into the complexities of Schuon's view of Sufism and integral religion in general.

It is interesting and instructive to note that Schuon is far from absolute in his evaluation of the intrinsic reason for the normative adherence to the *sharī'ah* by Sufis. His evaluation of the matter is actually not explicit, and characterized by a significant degree of caution. Thus, in his own words, the reason for this phenomenon "results on the one hand from some facts of human nature and on the other from a spiritual opportuneness, or perhaps even a necessity."[71] In alluding to "facts of human nature," it is likely that Schuon echoes the principle enunciated by Christ when, recognizing implicitly both the need and the limits of religious law, he declared: "The

---

70. "The 'religion of the Heart' is independent from the religion of the Law, in principle if not in fact." Schuon, *Esoterism as Principle and as Way*, 231.
71. Schuon, *Esoterism as Principle and as Way*, 229.

Sabbath was made for man, not man for the Sabbath" (Mark 2:27). In other words, there is something in mankind that necessitates the existence of the Law, but the Law must not be turned into an absolute necessity independently of its intrinsically *relative* intentions and objectives. It is this paradoxical notion of "relative necessity" that lies at the core of Schuon's seeming hesitation regarding this matter. The opportuneness of the Law refers, no doubt, to the need to orient certain collectivities or individuals toward spiritual progress by addressing their specific predicaments and predispositions. This is the relative aspect of the Law that Islam, among other traditions, acknowledges (if only implicitly) by recognizing the diversity of the *sharā'ih*. As for "absolute" necessity, it is important to stress that it is envisaged by Schuon in terms of the radical—and irreducible—distinction between the human self and the Divine Immanence within the self. The *sharī'ah* refers, therefore, to that aspect of religious reality that addresses the individual, a dimension that remains, humanly speaking, essentially distinct from the Divine Self, irrespective of the degree of spiritual realization. It is important to note that Schuon refers to the necessity of the Law primarily in terms of worship, seeing the latter is the essence of the Law and because it best reflects the duality of servant and Lord. He mentions, in this connection, that Christ "prayed like everybody else" and that it is incumbent on the "delivered soul" (*jīvan-mukta*) that he maintain a *bhakti* "devoted to a given *ishta-devatā*." Thus, here, the Law does not necessarily mean the complex network of prohibitions that channel the human will, but the fundamental God-given forms that shape the relationship between the soul and the Divine. It might be possible, therefore, to distinguish between three interconnected but distinct dimensions of the Law, namely, the confessional way of access as a general adherence to the tradition, the integral Law that encompasses all legal requirements, and the devotional practices that constitute the operative core of the latter. The fact that this core cannot be rigidly distinguished from the other practices, and the recognition that the two extend along a continuum that spans from sacramental rites to external modes of social interaction, is evidence that the needs of mankind are both one, as a matter of principle, and diverse, as a matter of fact. It goes without saying that Islam tends to put more stress on the former, which reflects its self-perception as the last religion of mankind, one that therefore provides a response to, and a synthesis of, the needs of mankind in its entirety.

It is possible to conclude from these remarks that the quintessential Sufism propounded by Schuon is not antinomian but, rather, supranomian, in the sense that its principles lie beyond the realm of the Law. Moreover, this transcendence implies a tendency to distinguish, within the Law, that which refers to Divine intention, as approximated through a contemplation of the ultimate ends of religion, and that which primarily pertains to the relativity of forms. It cannot be ignored, however, that the supra-legal character of this quintessential esoterism raises the question of its historical reality and manifestations. Some might argue that Schuon's concept of a "quintessential esoterism of Islam" is an a posteriori theoretical reconstruction that finds little or no evidence in the historical development of Sufism. Yet Schuon, and others, would insist that it corresponds to an actual reality in the Islamic tradition, albeit one that is discontinuous and more or less hidden from sight. Schuon postulates that the historical reality of instances of quintessential esoterism must be assumed, given that the essence cannot but manifest itself through the form when opportunities arise, but he does acknowledge that there is relatively little evidence for this position. Nevertheless, the fact remains that the esoteric traditions of Islam (like other esoterisms the world over) have been maintained through an oral transmission. This would explain why there has been little evidence of a gnostic Sufism that is largely free from the exoteric emphasis on the *sharī'ah* and the exclusive confessional outlook of Islam. It is plausible that there may have existed uncommon forms and expressions within the tradition that have left little or no trace because their pronounced esoteric character made them difficult, or impossible, to assimilate and disseminate within a confessional context. This would also be a likely explanation for the fact that such esoteric teachings may have been rarely preserved in writing, since the written word was intended for the purposes of widespread promulgation.

Schuon's writings often make mention of 'Abd al-Jabbār al-Niffarī as a Sufi who embodies quintessential esoterism and gnosis. Schuon sees him as incarnating "esoterism in the truest sense of the word, and not a pre-esoterism still largely exoterist and conditioned by the will."[72] Schuon likes to quote the *mawqif* in which God reveals to Niffarī that Divine gnosis supersedes the outer *sunnah* and reveals its quintessence.[73] This

---

72. Schuon, *Understanding Islam* (Bloomington, IN: World Wisdom, 2011), 81.

73. "'Know'—God reveals to Niffari—'that I shall accept from thee nothing of the Sunnah, but only that which My Gnosis bringeth thee, for thou art one of those to whom I speak.'" Schuon, *Form and Substance in the Religions*, 246.

is, in Schuon's terms, the "innate and subjective religion" that transcends formal religion. In terms of spiritual typology and perspective, Schuon sketches a contrast between Ghazālī, whose work crystallizes an exotericization of esoterism, and Niffarī, whom he associates with the *Khadiriyyah* dimension of Islamic spirituality, the scriptural foundation of which lies with the story of Moses and al-Khidr.

It is significant that Schuon's reading of Ibn 'Arabī is much more ambivalent, even though it has been argued that the Shaykh al-Akbar's influence was central to Schuon's doctrinal development. This is due to the fact that although the Akbari *wujūdiyyah* perspective and Schuon's metaphysical position share a fundamental grounding in non-duality, the works of Ibn 'Arabī are also characterized by a wide array of speculative and mystical considerations that are not consonant with Schuon's understanding. This is why one should not analyze Schuon's writings as proceeding, in any direct way, from Ibn 'Arabī's perspective. By contrast, the metaphysicians that Schuon explicitly recognizes as being the most archetypal exemplars of gnosis are Shankara and Plato. It is no doubt with the former that Schuon shows most affinities, since the modes of exposition of the Advaitin sage are the most directly and exclusively focused on metaphysical discernment and interiorizing contemplation. Moreover, Shankara's metaphysical idiom is also more clearly independent of religious strictures, even though it is integrated within the Hindu tradition. Although this also holds true of Plato, Schuon sees Platonic dialectics as a more rationalizing modality that does not match the contemplative essentiality and focus of Shankara's. To return to Ibn 'Arabī: while Niffarī epitomizes pure esoterism, the Shaykh al-Akbar incarnates an esoterism that is implicated in mythological speculations and mystical inspirations, to an extent that some of his writing may, in Schuon's view, "produce vertigo rather than light."[74]

As for Ghazālī, Schuon perceives him as embodying both the virtues and the limitations of an esoterism insufficiently freed from its exoteric trappings. It would be inaccurate, though, to regard this assessment of Ghazālī in too negative a light. Schuon is far from being unaware of the important function played by Ghazālī in providing Sufism with legitimizing justifications in the eyes of Muslim society. Thus, in his important essay, "The Way of the Heart," we have seen that Schuon does not hesitate to

---

74. Schuon, *Sufism: Veil and Quintessence*, 20.

take Ghazālī as the starting point of his reflections on Islam, Sufism, and esoterism. What Schuon recognizes as the most fruitful dimension of Ghazālī's perspective is its orientation toward an inner revivification of religion, an orientation that is not simply an intensification of piety but a qualitative reflection on the degrees of spiritual sincerity. The revivification that Ghazālī has in mind can only be brought out by a spiritual refinement of the soul, *tazkiyyat an-nafs*, which is a way of saying that Islam must be fulfilled, beyond mere legal conformity, by reaching a depth of inner veracity that makes it a living spirituality and thus saves it from degenerating into hypocrisy and an ossified formalism. It is precisely this distinction between the inner and the outer—the consequences of which were not always discerned by Ghazālī—that lies at the core of Schuon's understanding of Sufism and Islam. It could be said that Ghazālī envisages the aforementioned distinction primarily from a subjective point of view, at least in the context of the *Ihyā 'ulūm ad-dīn*. However, he does refer, objectively, to a distinction between the "truth" and the "mould of the truth" in his *Alchemy of Happiness*,[75] whereas Schuon considers this notion both subjectively and objectively, in a way that goes beyond Ghazālī's focus on inner veracity. In order to understand this difference, it must be understood that Ghazālī is situated within a traditional Islamic context that strictly defines the formal perimeters of the spiritual path. As is true of most Sufi figures, it is unthinkable that Ghazālī would account for the *haqīqah* independently of the *sharī'ah*. Objectively, in order to understand the implications of this polarity between *haqīqah* and *sharī'ah*, the most helpful analogy is that of light and colors while, subjectively, the duality of Love and the Law comes to mind. For Schuon, "the formalist or exoteric point of view consists in affirming that such and such a colour is the light, and correlatively, that light is such and such a colour, as if substance were accident because the latter manifests the former."[76] By contrast, Schuon's quintessential Sufism is based on the principle that "form proceeds from essence, but the latter remains eminently free in regard to form."[77] Such

---

75. "It will never be possible for the truth of matters to be shown to him [the dogmatist]. That belief which the commonality of mankind learns is the mould of truth, not truth itself. Complete gnosis is that the truth be uncovered from that mould, as a kernel is taken out of the husk." Al-Ghazzālī, *On Knowing Yourself and God* (Chicago: Kazi, 2002), 195.

76. Schuon, *Esoterism as Principle and as Way*, 230.

77. Schuon, *Esoterism as Principle and as Way*, 230.

a radical freedom from what Schuon refers to as "confessional bias" was hardly available to classical Sufis for a variety of circumstantial, if not principial, reasons. On the one hand, there is a likely unavailability of serious information about other religions and, on the other, of intimate and psycho-spiritual solidarity with the Islamic ambience. Even those Sufis whom modern audiences have increasingly associated with a universalist outlook in religion—whether on a popular level with Rūmī or on a scholarly level with Ibn 'Arabī—cannot be expected, when situated in context, to draw all the consequences from the universalist bent of their metaphysics and spirituality. Schuon makes the point that, to the extent that they owe their degree of spiritual realization to the tradition in which they lived, such figures are unlikely to go beyond the scope of the latter to seek the truth. Indeed, it is likely that the sources on which they could have relied for furthering and deepening their information on foreign traditions were not conducive to an objective and integral representation of the latter. This is, by and large, analogous to the situation—frequent in Hinduism— that sees devotees of Śiva, Vishnu, Śakti, or other deities identify their *ishta-devatā* with the Ultimate itself, hence the references to Mahaśiva or Mahavishnu as equivalent to the supreme *Brahman*. For a Rūmī or an Ibn 'Arabī, to speak of Islam means speaking of the Religion, or religion as such, under which all authentic religions are ultimately subsumed. Similarly, when Shabistarī exhorts his reader to be "a Muslim,"[78] this is a summons to reach the heights and depths of Islam, thereby attaining to an inclusive totality of the Truth. In the same vein, Martin Lings has argued that the most "concentrated" understanding and realization of Islam, as exemplified by the greatest Sufis, is also the most universal in that it comes the closest to other paths and also, therefore, to the core of every creed.[79] This could be read as suggesting that access to this univer-

---

78. "Since our hidden selves are the real infidels,
   don't be satisfied with an outer worship of Islam.
   With every new moment turn to refresh your faith.
   Be a Muslim, be a Muslim, yes, be a Muslim!"

Garden of Mystery—The Gulshan-i rāz of Mahmūd Shabistarī, translated by Robert Abdul Hayy Darr (Cambridge: Archetype 2007), 166.

79. "Our image as a whole reveals clearly the truth that as each mystical path approaches its End, it is nearer to the other mysticisms than it was at the beginning. But there is a complementary and almost paradoxical truth which it cannot reveal, but which it implies by the idea of concentration which it evokes: increase of nearness does not

sality is contingent on attaining the perfection of particularity. While this suggestion is ostensibly compelling, it does not correspond to Schuon's expressed emphasis on essentiality, universality, and synthesis. In fact, the analogy of the light and the colors, used by Schuon in several contexts,[80] reveals, by contrast, the limits of the symbol of concentration in that no given color can provide access to pure light as such. Needless to say, the whole issue revolves around what meaning we give to the word concentration. It may refer to a kind of intensification and saturation within the specific outlook and forms of a given tradition, in which case it is hardly conceivable that this could possibly lead to a universal core. Another, more fruitful way of interpreting Martin Lings's image is by envisaging concentration as a pure archetypal substance or quintessence, rather than as the richest array of intensified formal expressions. It could be said, along such lines, that a concentration of Islam may refer to a measure of perfection or fullness in terms of realizing the Islamic archetype. Methodically speaking, this archetype is most directly and purely manifested by the Name of God, *Allāh*, which is the quintessence of the *shahādah*, and therefore the single most concentrated expression of *tawhīd*, that is, the principle Schuon would call the *idée-force* of Islam. As exclusive affirmation of Divine Unity and transcendence in Abrahamic and law-giving mode with a universal scope, the Islamic archetype is a Divine reality in its own right, one that is distinct from other religious archetypes, while being also identifiable at its core with the only religion, the *religio perennis* that is the Essence of all faiths. An analogy can be drawn, in this respect, to the relationship between Essence and Hypostases, or Qualities, whereby the distinctions that define the latter are resolved, as it were—or overwhelmed from another point of view—in and by the Essence. But there is also a

---

mean decrease of distinctness, for the nearer the centre, the greater the concentration, the stronger the 'dose.'" Martin Lings, *What Is Sufism* (Cambridge: Islamic Texts Society, 1993), 21–22.

80. "The antagonisms between these forms no more affect the one universal Truth than the antagonisms between opposing colours affect the transmission of the one uncoloured light (to return to the illustration used already). Just as every colour, by its negation of darkness and its affirmation of light, provides the possibility of discovering the ray which makes it visible and of tracing this ray back to its luminous source, so all forms, all symbols, all religions, all dogmas, by their negation of error and their affirmation of Truth, make it possible to follow the ray of Revelation, which is none other than the ray of the Intellect, back as far as its Divine Source." Schuon, *The Transcendent Unity of Religions*, xxxiv.

sense in which the archetype, as such, conveys the Essence even though it does so in a distinct way. In other words, there is in the archetype something that transcends its limitations and leaves it open to the universal. Considering this "something"—which is none other than the quintessence—one could say that it is independent of the archetype (as it is of other spiritual archetypes) while, at the same time, being "available" in it. One may, therefore, fulfill the archetype either by resting at its highest degree of perfection, or by piercing through it in order to reach the pure Essence. In the former case, access to the Essence will be possible only through a leap, a definite yet perplexing movement whose determining motivations and modalities appear difficult to fathom. Needless to say, this leap can ultimately be none other than the pure affirmation of the Self, which always remains a "miraculous" possibility and may be actualized, in principle, in any spiritual context. In the latter case, the continuum between the form, the archetype, and the Essence is apparent. Here, essentialization entails formal simplicity or synthesis—to various degrees— precisely because the form is not the archetype and the archetype is not the Essence. In keeping with the latter perspective, Schuon's approach begins and ends with a focus on the light as such, as it were, and not with a concentration on, or of, any particular color, notwithstanding the ability of this color to transmit the light or lead us to it.

Given that an objective approach to quintessential esoterism, from the point of view of Islam as a religious system, is necessarily constrained in some measure by the formal limitations of the religion, the search for this quintessence, within Islam, can only take place by considering matters from a subjective point of view, that is, from the perspective of a spiritual quest for the Divine and the interiorization of its requirements by the soul. This path is none other than the "Way of the Heart" or the "Religion of Love" to which—as we have seen in the discussion of Ghazālī's revivification of religion—an access to the core is opened by, and through, a purification of the knower. This serves to enlarge the scope of one's understanding, making one more keenly aware of the transparency of religious forms in light of the Essence. As we have suggested, it is precisely in the logic of this search for spiritual purity that Schuon takes Ghazālī's lesson a step further to unveil the universal horizon of Love. Thus, a spiritual reality is reached that, through a deepening of one's interiorization of the religion, relativizes the confessional way of access from within, so that the latter has no integral role once the goal has been reached. Such is the most profound reality of Love, the metaphysical substance of the "Religion of the Heart." In this fundamental sense, Love was "before" the world because it is the Essence of the Divine Itself, as its power of manifestation and reintegration. With this meaning in mind, "'the religion of the Heart' is independent of the religion of the Law, in principle if not in fact."[81] It is not, therefore, a coincidence that—in principle—the highest expressions of universalism in Islam have been conveyed in the language of Love, rather than through an emphasis on knowledge.

That the consummation of Love may result in an extinction of the lover before the Beloved raises the question of the *wahdat al-wujūd*, since after spiritual extinction, or *fanā'*, "only the Face of God remains." As we have seen, Schuon credits Ibn 'Arabī and his disciples with affirming the non-dual character of Reality in a most consistent and uncompromising way. The *wujūdiyyah* school has taken the metaphysical meaning of *tawhīd* to its summit. However, this does not mean that Schuon necessarily subscribes to the ecstatic and intoxicated expressions that have flowed from the mystical experience of Unity in Islam, or that he considers them as the supreme manifestations of metaphysical realization. One may even argue that Schuon's view of the spiritual path in Islam resonates more powerfully with the principles of sober Sufism, as exemplified by Junayd, than with those of mystical drunkenness. This affinity is no doubt in keeping with Schuon's emphasis on the sapiential excellence of objectivity. Toby Mayer's remark, that "Junayd's insistence on the subjectivity of the experience of annihilation and the imperative of passing beyond it to a reinstatement of the creature-creation distinction became a feature of so-called 'sober' (*sahwī*) Sufism, and was later enshrined in the doctrine of the *wahdat al-shuhūd* ('the unity of witnessing,' subjective theomonism),"[82] strikes a chord with the Schuonian outlook on the relationship between "the servant and Union."[83] For Schuon to speak of the "subjectivity of the experience of annihilation" can only mean that the subject that is in question is the Divine Selfhood Itself, as demonstrated by the theopathic statements of the kind that were uttered by Hallāj or Bistamī. In that sense, the passing beyond this annihilation is nothing else

---

81. Schuon, *Esoterism as Principle and as Way*, 231.

82. Toby Mayer, "Theology and Sufism," in Tim Winter, ed., *Classical Islamic Theology* (Cambridge: Cambridge University Press, 2008), 267.

83. On this question, see the enlightening chapter "The Servant and Union" in Schuon, *Logic and Transcendence* (Bloomington, IN: World Wisdom, 2009), 181–88.

than a return to the point of view of the creature, that is, a recovery of the distinction between a subject and an object, or between the human subject and the Divine Object of worship. This cannot be considered a "passing beyond" in a metaphysical sense, but only in a spiritual sense, or from the perspective of creaturely reality. Schuon's Sufism is certainly not ecstatic if by this term is meant an obliteration of the distinctions that are relatively, and therefore humanly, real. Wisdom is not fusional mysticism but a reintegration of the intellective nucleus of the soul into its divine prototype that is none other than the Divine Self. Needless to say, the distinctions to which wisdom gives its due are also real from God's point of view—if one may put it that way—without which God could not enter into a relationship with mankind or create the world to begin with. But this separative relationality only holds true on the level of God as Being, and not at the degree of the Essence as Beyond-Being which, as Divine Selfhood, lies beyond all distinctions while embracing them in its fold as being none other than Itself. Whereas the *wahdat al-wujūd* speaks to the Reality of Beyond-Being—the Essence of *al-dhāt al-ilāhiyyah*—*wahdat al-shuhūd* may be deemed to reflect the "relatively absoluteness" of God as Being and, therefore, the reality of the human soul in relation to Him. For Schuon, spiritual perfection demands that every degree of reality and consciousness be given its due, which amounts to saying that the Divine must be recognized as universally immanent and inclusive of degrees. It *is* the Manifestation given that nothing is outside of the undifferentiated Essence. It is also different from the Manifestation as Being, therefore as Principle of the former. It is, finally, encompassing it as universal Existence.

We conclude this chapter with three general observations that may capture the essence of Schuon's perspective on Sufism. First, Schuon's intellectual and spiritual perspective is not a Sufi perspective, in that it cannot be understood solely, nor even primarily, in terms derived from the Sufi traditions themselves. All that can be said, in this respect, is that one may indeed recognize—as has been noted—Sufi ideas and themes in Schuon's writings, as one may also find Hindu themes or Buddhist insights. Even though there may be a temptation to connect Schuon's views to those of a Ibn 'Arabī, it is quite clear that this can be done only laterally, as it were, and not generically. By this is meant that Schuon's perspective does not derive from Akbari speculations, although it parallels some of its intuitions, primarily in terms of the unicity of existence and, to some extent, the Divine roots of religious plurality. While some of Schuon's themes, such as the "transcendent unity of religions," may be deemed to meet with Ibn 'Arabī's view of religious diversity, the respective intellective roots of the two gnostics are significantly distinct. Schuon has made it clear that his intellectual starting point is not the Akbari doctrine or, for that matter, any other Sufi metaphysical exposition but, rather, the Advaita Vedānta as formulated by Shankara, with its adamantine metaphysical discernment, rigorously adequate dialectics, and freedom from any extrinsic religious limitations. Schuon's independence from a specifically Sufi idiom is not only apparent in his metaphysical exposition, but also from the ethico-spiritual perspective of his books. Thus, his writings do not reproduce traditional schemas of Sufi *maqāmat* and *ahwāl*, in all of their complexity and diversity, but proceed, rather, through a supra-confessional consideration of the dispositions of the contemplating soul in general, irrespective of any particular religious language. So it is, first and foremost, with regard to his exposition of the six "stations of wisdom" (developed in his book of the same title) that Schuon meditates on what he describes as the six fundamental stations of the soul in its relationship to the Divine. Far from being primarily rooted in Sufi concepts or experiences, these stations are actually considered by him as running through all contemplative traditions. In point of fact, the account of these stations that, in Schuon's work, comes closest to a confessional expression is to be found in his meditation on the six perfections of wisdom (*pāramitās*) in Mahāyana Buddhism.[84]

Second, Schuon' s exposition of Sufism is less a meditation on the Sufi tradition as such as it is an intellectual and spiritual interiorization of the pillars of Islam itself. In fact, as we have seen, Schuon is largely critical of a number of key characteristics of traditional Sufi metaphysics, hermeneutics, and hagiography.

Third, and consequently, this point of access and way of envisaging Islamic esoterism may be deemed to account for the specific features of its relationship with the *sharī'ah*. It bears stressing here that the term is not generally understood by Schuon in a strictly juridical sense but, primarily, as referring to the *arkān* or to Islam such as it is defined in the *hadīth* of Gabriel. By contrast with a number of neo-Sufi and Western Sufi movements that have become influential in the last decades, Schuon never severs the connection between *tarīqah* and *sharī'ah*, which means that he sees the basic practices of Islam as methodical foundations and

---

84. Schuon, *Treasures of Buddhism* (New Delhi: Smriti Books, 2003), 135.

symbolic supports of the Sufi path. On the other hand, his perspective is distinctly less sharaite than that of most *tasawwuf* authorities in Muslim lands today. This difference stems, mostly, from the fact that his perspective is primarily centered on what he considers to be the spiritual quintessence of the religious pillars.

In conclusion, in order to understand Schuon's complex position vis-à-vis Sufism, there is need to take account of four levels of consideration: the concept of the *religio perennis*; the tenets and system of Islam; Sufism as characteristic of an interiorization of the latter; and the Sufi tradition as an ambiguous blend of Islamic theological concepts, sentimental identifications, and mystical impulses. What Schuon refers to as the *religio perennis* constitutes the very foundation of his perspective.[85] This highest level of discernment regarding the Real and our attachment to it lies at the heart of the "religion of the sages." Schuon's insights into Islam and Sufism stem from—and only from—this "underlying religion," as he states, quite explicitly, in the opening lines of *Understanding Islam*.[86] Islam, as defined by the *hadīth* of Gabriel—that is, as consisting in the five pillars of the tradition—appears to Schuon as the "schema of all religions," which means that it provides direct access to the symbolic and practical keys to the *religio perennis*. Each of the pillars, to different degrees, provides a means of achieving the discernment and concentration that constitute religion as such. This is the meaning of quintessential Sufism. The broad historical manifestations of *tasawwuf* encompass instances of profound esoteric interiorization, including some that were conducive to bringing out the universal core of Sufism, as well as more ambiguous combinations of the mystical and the theological that have tended to confuse the sublime with the esoteric.

---

85. "The essential function of human intelligence is discernment between the Real and the illusory, or between the Permanent and the impermanent, and the essential function of the will is attachment to the Permanent or to the Real. This discernment and this attachment are the quintessence of all spirituality; carried to their highest level, or reduced to their purest substance, they constitute the underlying universality in every great spiritual patrimony of humanity, or what may be called the *religio perennis*; this is the religion to which the sages adhere, one which is always and necessarily founded upon formal elements of divine institution." Schuon, *Light on the Ancient Worlds*, 119–20.

86. "What we really have in mind in this as in previous works is the *scientia sacra* or *philosophia perennis*, that universal gnosis which always has existed and always will exist." Schuon, *Understanding Islam*, xvii.

Schuon's view of Sufism provides the means to resolve contradictions that distort the general perception and understanding of Sufism. In summary, the two main questions of concern are the nature of Sufism's relationship with Islam and the basis and extent of its universality. With the exception of some recent orders that have largely severed their ties with the Islamic tradition (in attempting to redefine Sufism in a Western context), Sufis have argued, through the centuries, for the intrinsically Islamic nature of Sufism. Yet a growing number of Muslims, over the past century, have highlighted what they consider as the extra-Islamic nature of many ideas and practices associated with *tasawwuf*. While Sufism had, previously, been attached to its many regional cultures, to the point of being indistinguishable from Islam, the rise of modernist, reformist, revivalist, and puritanical movements—together with the decline of traditional Islamic sciences and a growing politicization of Muslim identity—has led to a significant alienation of *tasawwuf* within the world of Islam. Schuon's presentation of Sufism may help alleviate the perplexity of those who, sometimes understandably, do not always recognize the worldview and ambience of Islam in some of the outer manifestations of contemporary Sufism. Furthermore, Schuon's insights help us to grasp the essential and universal elements of Sufi spirituality that continue to inspire and attract many seekers in the modern world today.

7

The Divine Feminine

Femininity occupies a central position in Schuon's work, representing a liberating reality that touches on virtually all his metaphysical and spiritual output. To ignore or belittle this dimension would amount to reducing the scope of his work, thus divesting it of its fundamental substance. This observation is justified to the extent that the Feminine, in its manifold aspects, is profoundly and intimately connected with the Divine Essence and the inner dimension of phenomena. Its association with esoterism, as illustrated by diverse traditions, is therefore in no way incidental and constitutes, on the contrary, a fundamental hermeneutic key.

To dispel any possible confusion, it is important to stress that the Feminine takes us, in a metaphysical context, radically beyond the realm of human sexes and genders. In keeping with the Platonic principle that sees in every earthly quality a distant reflection of an archetypical reality (along with the relative and imperfect manifestation of Divine Qualities radiating from the infinitude of the Essence), the male and the female are but one among many instances of the Masculine and the Feminine. As Jean Hani has observed: "Sex, in fact, is nothing but an adaptation to organic life of a polarity governing the whole of creation; it is but one of the things constituting the masculine or feminine genders, which in their turn, apply to levels of existence where sexual polarity has no role, except in a symbolic sense."[1] To be sure, the terms "feminine" and "masculine" cannot but be laden with human connotations, given their immediate

---

1. Jean Hani, *The Black Virgin: A Marian Mystery* (San Rafael, CA: Sophia Perennis, 2007), 72.

association with our experience of sexual differentiation and gender distinctions, but this is no less true, in a sense, for all the substantives and adjectives that are used to refer to the Divine, the linguistic implications of which are perforce rooted in human experience. To speak about God is to speak about Him humanly, which by no means signifies, however, that what is being spoken about is primarily human. While analogy lies at the core of any meditation on the Feminine (given the inclusive and integrative function of the latter), it bears stressing that "transcendence" and "abstraction" must also be applied to it in order not to subject the metaphysical substance of the discussion to any sort of human reductionism. In other words, while the terrestrial experience of the Feminine is a direct manifestation of Divine Femininity, the latter remains completely independent of the limitations inherent to human sexual differences.

At any rate, considering the profound significance of the polarity of feminine and masculine realities in the cosmic order, it should not come as a surprise that Schuon, in consonance with many traditional teachings, contemplates the metaphysics of this complementary dyad as integral to any intuition of the Divine. As for the Feminine specifically, it holds a particular significance when the religious dimension is envisaged from a point of view that transcends its merely formal aspects and touches upon metaphysical contemplation, spiritual inwardness, and the consideration of Divine intentions—all realities that, for Schuon as for a number of other spiritual authorities before him, involve a connection with the Feminine. In Schuon's writings, the Virgin (whom Christianity and Islam refer to as Mary or Maryam) is the epitome of the Feminine *in divinis*, to such an extent that the epithet of "Mother of God," or *Theotokos*, was applied to her. The way the Virgin is contemplated is, therefore, analogous to the Hindu consideration of the gods, from their avatāric manifestation in the flesh and the vicissitudes of their mythological careers to their ultimate identification with *Nirguna Brahman*. Analogously, the Virgin can be thought of as the one "chosen among all women" as well as the Divine Essence in its super-ontological Mystery. It is in light of his encompassing Mariology that Schuon's metaphysics of the Divine Femininity will be sketched out in this chapter, with a view to highlighting not only its profound coherence but also the way in which it challenges the strictly theological point of view. Moreover, the intrinsic and necessary connection of metaphysics to all domains of reality—beginning with religion and spirituality—means that the Feminine fulfills a specific role in the economy of inner emancipation and posthumous salvation. One of the primary objectives of this chapter is to bring to the fore the connection between the metaphysics of the Feminine and gnostic spirituality.

There is arguably no more important feminine figure in the Abrahamic world than the Virgin, whose presence, although relatively limited in terms of scriptural reference, provides essential keys to a deeper understanding of Schuon's perspective. Moreover, given the universalist scope of his work, Schuon's Mariology necessarily leads to a consideration of other feminine figures, particularly those regarded as manifestations of *Śakti* in the Hindu tradition. In addition to its metaphysical significance with regard to the Divine Essence, a meditation on the significance of these figures highlights the soteriological function of Mercy and its connection with transforming grace, the feminine foundations of Wisdom, the ambiguity of the onto-cosmogonic process (as expressed by the duality of Eve and Mary), and the spiritually interiorizing function of Manifestation in general, and Beauty in particular.

In a substantial study of Schuon's views on the Virgin, James Cutsinger notes that only two chapters in all of Schuon's books are devoted to the Virgin.[2] As Cutsinger points out, the relative paucity of references to Mariology in Schuon's written opus should not lead us to overlook its profound significance. In situating Schuon's Mariology in a normative Christian outlook, Cutsinger suggests that it may appear too "high" while his Christology is likely to be seen as being too "low."[3] This is directly connected to the way in which Schuon approaches the Logos, which he envisages as being differentiated according to a masculine and a feminine dimension. While the Logos constitutes the point of projection of the Divine within cosmic manifestation, or the zone of intersection between the two realms, its various aspects are characterized either as masculine

---

2. "As is often the case with Schuon's teaching on a given subject, however, these references are for the most part occasional in nature, and they are almost always rather brief; in fact, only two chapters in his published writings are specifically devoted to Marian topics." James Cutsinger, "Colorless Light and Pure Air: The Virgin in the Thought of Frithjof Schuon," *Sophia: The Journal of Traditional Studies* 6, no. 2 (Winter 2000), https://themathesontrust.org/library/colorless-light-and-pure-air, 2, http://themathesontrust.org/papers/christianity/colorless_light_and_pure_air.pdf.

3. "It is not surprising therefore if the Schuonian Mariology should be considered too 'high'—too high in where it places Mary in relation to God—even as his Christology is often considered too 'low' in what it says about the status of Jesus." James Cutsinger, "The Virgin," in *Ye Shall Know the Truth: Christianity and the Perennial Philosophy*, edited by Mateus Soares de Azevedo (Bloomington, IN: World Wisdom, 2005), 112.

or feminine. Whereas the former is associated with the formal dimension—including the ritual, theological, institutional, and legal domains—the latter pertains to the informal, or rather supra-formal, realm that may be understood metaphysically and spiritually. On the one hand, it means that the Feminine refers, at its highest level, to the Essence that transcends all relativities. It also signifies that it belongs to what lies beyond the various credal forms by which religious life is symbolized and mediated; hence, the characterization of the Feminine as an inward space of freedom vis-à-vis the theological crystallizations of a tradition. Issuing forth from this supra-formal and feminine dimension of the Logos, every masculine manifestation of this principle tends to embody the very form of the tradition that the Logos brings to the world. In the Abrahamic world, this mission appears most clearly in the cases of law-bringing prophets such as Moses and Muhammad, whose inward spiritual eminence is intrinsically coupled with their outer mission as bearers of sacred forms. The same can be said of Christ, although less so in some respects, since his function as the keystone of Christianity entails an intrinsic union with the very forms of the tradition he instituted, as clearly indicated by his words to Peter: "And I say also unto thee, That thou art Peter, and upon this rock I will build my church; and the gates of hell shall not prevail against it" (Matthew 16:18). The central status of Christ's formal function holds true even though his message points unambiguously toward the supra-formal heart of religion. By contrast with central manifestations of the masculine dimension of the Logos, whose spiritual eminence radiates outwardly into the domain of formal religion, the feminine dimension pertains to the supra-formal roots of prophecy and revelation. Schuon refers, on this point, to the "Logos under its feminine and maternal aspect," an aspect that appears most notably in the Virgin Mother, "the supra-formal Wisdom" from whose milk "all the Prophets have drunk."[4] This feminine eminence is also evident in the Buddhist *Prajñāpāramitā*, the Goddess of Wisdom who is revered and worshipped as "the mother of all buddhas."[5] From this

---

4. "The Virgin Mother personifies supraformal Wisdom; it is from her milk that all the Prophets have drunk. In this respect she is greater than the Child, who here represents formal wisdom, hence the particular revelation." Schuon, *Christianity/Islam: Essays on Esoteric Ecumenism* (Bloomington, IN: World Wisdom, 1985), 69.

5. "Prajñāpāramitā [is] depicted as a female goddess or bodhisattva. She is referred to as the mother of all the buddhas. Prajñāpāramitā Bodhisattva often sits cross-legged on a white lotus, appearing majestic and dignified with a golden yellow body.

vantage point, the Feminine occupies a super-eminent position precisely because it corresponds to that aspect of the Logos, the foundation of Wisdom and Revelation, which transmits blessings to the cosmic realm by virtue of its essentiality. This is conveyed either through the masculine messengers who have drunk the milk of her wisdom and transmitted it outwardly through religions, or more directly through intellective inspiration and therefore independently of the masculine aspect of the Logos.

The foregoing allows us to understand why and how Schuon's Mariology is not primarily or exclusively rooted in Christianity or in any particular confessional theology. In fact, the Marian perspective is, for Schuon, the very mark of supra-confessional universality and, even though the religious reality of the Virgin is situated *a priori* in the Abrahamic world, it remains essentially unconstrained by the exclusive framework of any formal universe. Moreover, the fact that Schuon's Mariology may be considered—from a Christian point of view—as too exalted points to the fact that its principles do not pertain to a dogmatic perspective but to a gnostic vantage point that transcends religious forms and which exceeds the purview of theology as such. The supra-ontological opening afforded by the Divine Feminine symbolizes, in a way, the transcendence of metaphysics over theology. Analogously, the supra-formal essentialization to which the Celestial Feminine invites us epitomizes the transcendence of esoterism over exoterism.

The essential mystery that the Marian Reality crystallizes is historically perceptible in the withdrawal, effacement, and occultation of Mary within the scriptural and theological framework of formal religion. On a most immediate level, Schuon notes that the outer effacement of the Virgin is the very sign of her inner elevation.[6] Thus, effacement is the human criterion of a sincere and consistent extinction before the Absolute,

---

In her radiance, Prajñāpāramitā dispels all darkness and distress. She also bestows wisdom upon those who venerate her." Taigen Dan Leighton, *Faces of Compassion: Classic Bodhisattva Archetypes and Their Modern Expression* (Somerville, MA: Wisdom Publications, 2012), 119.

6. "Awareness of one's existential naught before God, and effacement before men. The Virgin dwelt in effacement and refused to perform miracles; the near silence of the Gospel concerning her manifests this effacement, which is profoundly significant in more than one respect; Maryam is thus identified with the esoteric Truth (*Haqīqah*) in that she is a secret Revelation corresponding to the 'Wine' in the *Khamrīyah*." Schuon, *Form and Substance in the Religions* (Bloomington, IN: World Wisdom, 2002), nn. 21, 107.

which is one of the definitions of sanctity. In Christianity, as in Islam (albeit with different accentuations), the Virgin embodies sanctity as the personification of a perfect consent and receptivity to the Divine. In the Gospel, the Blessed Virgin is identified with the Divine *fiat*; she therefore embodies and symbolizes the perfect obedience of the soul emptied of all self-seeking and worldly traits. In the Qur'ān, Maryam, who is under the "protection" (*kafala*) of Zachary (in the way the inner is guarded by the outer), has withdrawn to an Eastern place—the heart oriented toward God—and is miraculously fed by her continuous contemplative prayer or *dhikr*. It must be noted that, in a way that is partially analogous to Mary, Fātima (the daughter of the Prophet) is hidden, sometimes ignored and even maligned in Islam.[7] These two saintly female characters are thereby identifiable with esoterism, which is either withdrawn and occulted or discarded and, at times, persecuted. Mary is associated with the "favorite disciple," John,[8] whom a number of Christian mystics have identified as having inspired the "spiritual Church." Analogously, some Shī'i speculations represent Fātima (wedded to 'Alī "the John of Islam") as the inner foundation of Islam at the "feminine" center of the Pleroma of the five figures of the People of the House (*ahl al-bayt*).[9]

The Virgin's effacement has its own prototype *in divinis* but in a transposed and, as it were, reversed manner. As the epitome of the "humble servant of the Lord," the Virgin is both most different from and most alike to the Divine Reality. This results from the distinctive characteristics of humility which she embodies among all virtues. Schuon observes: "Among the virtues, humility holds a special position—like that of the apex in a triangle—because it conforms to God, not by 'participation' but by 'opposition,' in the sense that the attitude of humility, poverty or self-effacement, is analogically opposed to the divine Majesty; this opposition is however a relative one, since it rejoins the direct analogy through its intrinsic perfection which is, *mutatis mutandis*, the simplicity of the Essence."[10] This appears in the way that other virtues, generosity for instance, can be conceived as

---

7. "It was the destiny of Fatimah to be deprived of the consolations of this lower world." Schuon, *Christianity/Islam: Essays on Esoteric Ecumenism*, 124.

8. "When Jesus therefore saw his mother, and the disciple standing by, whom he loved, he saith unto his mother, 'Woman, behold thy son!'" (John 19:26).

9. Henry Corbin, *Spiritual Body and Celestial Earth: From Mazdean Iran to Shī'ite Iran* (Princeton, NJ: Princeton University Press, 1989), 63.

10. Schuon, *Language of the Self* (Madras: Ganesh, 1959), 53–54.

modes of "participation"—in the Platonic sense of *methexis*—in the Divine Qualities. By contrast, what makes humility a quintessentially human virtue is that it is the "opposite" of Divine Majesty or Sovereignty. It is impossible, however, that this opposition between the human and the Divine can ever be absolute. Thus, there is also a way in which human humility is directly analogous to the Divine; namely, as simplicity. The Virgin is simple as the Essence is simple, in the sense of being without division. Her soul is undividedly consecrated to the Lord, which the Qur'ān expresses through the epithet of *batūl*, a word most often translated by "virgin" but which actually stems from the Arabic root meaning "to separate" and, therefore, connoting separation from the world and utter dedication or devotion to God.[11] If humility is distinguished, in its spiritual depth, by a recognition of one's nothingness before God, one may wonder whether there is a corresponding "nothingness" of God in relation to creation and mankind. Schuon suggests a possible response when he remarks that, aside from simplicity, there exists another mode of "humility" of the Essence, one he characterizes as intrinsic to the Divine Nature which "condescends" to grant His grace and respond to human prayer. In other words, God is "humbled" by whoever "constrains" Him to give His grace; that is, to the devotee who reflects His own simplicity. Meister Eckhart writes that God cannot but give Himself to one who is empty of himself.[12] This supernatural law of grace has both a direct and an indirect aspect: indirectly, it means that what is most "devoid" of God—meaning the most humbly and helplessly human—cannot but be filled by God; directly, it means that like attracts like. For the Divine "humility" to consent to respond to other-than-God reflects an aspect of His simplicity. If man actualizes humility by a full and consistent awareness of his nothingness before God, the Essence is "humble" by naughting Itself before that which is other-than-Itself. The highest "effacement" is, therefore, that of the Essence that "consents" not to be the only Reality, and to let the world be without compromising Its

---

11. The Qur'ān makes a significant use of words from this root in the verse: "And remember the Name of your Lord and devote yourself to it devotedly" [*wa-adhkuri isma rabbika wa tabattal ilayhi tabtīlān*] (Qur'ān 73:8).

12. "If there were anything empty under heaven, whatever it might be, great or small, the heavens would either draw it up to themselves or else, bending down, would have to fill it with themselves. God, the Lord of nature, does not allow that anything be empty or void." *The Complete Mystical Works of Meister Eckhart*, translated by Maurice O'C Walshe (New York: Crossroad Publishing, 2009), 59.

own simplicity.

Various metaphysical languages account for this Divine humility (if one may resort to such an ill-sounding expression) in different ways.[13] One can mention, for instance, the Lurianic Kabbalistic concept of Divine Self-withdrawal or contraction (*tsimtsum*), according to which the Divine Essence makes room for what is other-than-God, as well as the Christian Self-Emptying of God (*kénōsis*). The former accounts for the way in which the Divine Essence withdraws in order to leave space for the creation. This mystery allows for the existence of the finite by virtue of the Infinite's nature.[14] In other words, the Infinite would not be the Infinite were it not for the existence of the finite. *Kénōsis*, primarily, refers to Christ emptying himself through assuming human nature and the sacrifice that this entailed: "(He) emptied himself, taking the form of a servant, being made in the likeness of men, and in habit found as a man" (Philippians 2:7). Theologians have also extended this "emptying" to the Trinity itself. Indeed, the Thomistic definition of the Divine Persons (i.e., "relations as subsisting"), although not explicitly related to the notion of *kénōsis*, implies that each of the Persons is inherently emptying itself in relation to the others. In essence, *kénōsis* represents the initial phase of redemption, which is encapsulated by the Patristic formula that Schuon frequently quotes and paraphrases: "God has become man so that man may become God."[15] At any rate, this emptying out is first and foremost

---

13. "God is not 'humble' like man, because He could not abase Himself before someone external and superior to Himself, for such a one does not exist. The 'humility' of God, as we have said, is the simplicity of his essence, for He is without parts. There is, however, another aspect of the 'divine humility,' one that is both intrinsic and anthropomorphic: 'When the servant takes one step towards his Lord the Lord gets up from his throne and takes one hundred steps to meet his servant' (*Hadīth* of the Prophet). As for man, he is not a pure essence, but a mixture of spirit and earth; therefore he cannot in himself be 'good.'" Schuon, *Language of the Self*, nn. 16, 56.

14. "According to Isaac Luria, *Tsimtsum* is the idea of the 'original contraction' of the Divine that allowed the antinomy of the omnipresence of God and the being of the creature outside of God to be solved. If God is the totality, how can anything other than Him exist? The notion of *Tsimtsum* answers this question, stating that 'God contracted himself prior to the creation, to make a place, beside himself, for something other than himself.'" Marc-Alain Ouaknin, *The Burnt Book: Reading the Talmud* (Princeton, NJ: Princeton University Press, 1995), 226.

15. Schuon makes use of this formula as a key to understanding religion in general and he applies it—*mutatis mutandis*—to major world religions as illustrations of the *religio perennis*: "In Christianity, according to St. Irenaeus, God 'became man' so that

applicable to the Essence since it is from It that all other realities originate. This is why Buddhists consider the Ultimate as *Emptiness*, indicating thereby not only that the Absolute is a "Void" in light of the world's false plenitude but also by virtue of it "vacating" itself.[16]

It is this self-withdrawal of the Essence, *qua* Divine Femininity, that the perfect surrender and humility of Mary "reflects" in response to God's consent to let creatures be. While the Essence makes itself "receptive" in relation to what it lets be, the Virgin makes herself passive in relation to the Divine *fiat* by surrendering to its Will. Her "be it unto me according to your Word" is a response to "Let there be light!" Paraphrasing the Patristic formula mentioned above, it could be said that the Essence has made Itself "nothing" so that "nothing" could be made the Essence. Both statements are elliptical. The Essence cannot become or be made "anything" since it is already everything beyond anything. "Nothing" can mean either the lack of anything, which means it cannot become anything, or "not a thing" in that it is beyond determinations and thus already the Essence. So it is clear that "nothing" points to an illusory occultation of Reality, in the first case, and to a spiritual extinction—which the Virgin embodies as a paradigm of sanctity—in the second. As a whole, this formula is like an esoteric paraphrase of the Patristic statement. It can be understood as an exclusively metaphysical version of a Patristic assertion that, for its part, can be understood both theologically and metaphysically.

There is another way, however, in which the correspondence between the Essence and the Virgin may be contemplated. While the analogy that we have sketched above is founded on a consideration of the Essence as such, the latter can also be differentiated into a masculine and a feminine dimension. In Schuon's idiom, this refers to the distinction between the Absolute and the Infinite. These two dimensions are the highest modes of reality of the Masculine and the Feminine, from which all other degrees and aspects of existence are derived. Here absoluteness connotes

---

man might 'become God.' In Hindu terms one would say: *Ātmā* became *Māyā* so that *Māyā* might become *Ātmā*." Schuon, *Light on the Ancient Worlds* (London: Perennial Books, 1965), 122–23.

16. "This pure activity of emptying is the True Self. That is to say, the realization of this activity of emptying is the realization of one's True Self. If the activity of emptying is realized somewhat outside of the Self, it will again turn into something, because it is then looked at from outside and is objectified by the self." Masao Abe, *Zen and Comparative Studies* (Honolulu: University of Hawaii Press, 1997), 109.

transcendence and exclusion, whereas infinity represents immanence and inclusion: "The Absolute and the Infinite are complementary, the first being exclusive and the second inclusive: the Absolute excludes everything that is contingent; the Infinite includes everything that is."[17] These principial dimensions, which are but two sides of the same Reality, offer keys for understanding the complementary polarity of the masculine and feminine over the whole range of reality.

As the projection of the All-Possibility, the Infinite can be characterized as the "mirror" of the Absolute.[18] Schuon sees the Infinite as "the intrinsic dimension of plenitude inherent to the Absolute."[19] Based on Schuon's notion of the "Vertical Trinity" that regards Beyond-Being as Father and Being as Son, one may consider the Essence as Father under its masculine aspect of absoluteness and as Mother under its feminine aspect of infinity, with Divine Being corresponding to the Son Contemplated as the Infinite, the Divine Feminine is the boundless metaphysical space from and through which all of onto-cosmological Reality is unfolded. In the language of Śaivism, the supreme dyad of the two dimensions corresponds to the syzygy of Śiva-Śakti. Śiva is the pure Absolute, the main attribute of which is sovereign freedom, while Śakti is the creative power of the Absolute, the Infinite from which derive all the degrees and aspects of being. According to the Vijñānabhairava, "by means of Śakti is Śiva (who is one's own essential Self) cognized."[20] This means that Śiva and Śakti are one, and that the projection of the universe through Śakti is Śiva-knowledge both in the sense of Śiva's Self-knowledge and as the means of knowing Śiva. In the same text, Śakti is defined as visargātmā ("of the nature of visarga"), which means "letting go, projection or creation."[21] Śakti projects the nature of Śiva while being essentially not different from Him. At this

---

17. Schuon, *Form and Substance in the Religions*, n. 1, 44.

18. "The first triangle-symbol represents the Sovereign Good inasmuch as it comprises the two aspects of Absoluteness and Infinitude; this first bipolarity projects—so to speak—creative and personal Being thus 'engendering' the second triangle, which is upside-down because the duality is situated at the summit and the unity at the base." Schuon, *Survey of Metaphysics and Esoterism* (Bloomington, IN: World Wisdom, 2000), 61.

19. Schuon, *Survey of Metaphysics and Esoterism*, 15.

20. *Vijñānabhairava or Divine Consciousness: A Treasury of 112 Types of Yoga*, translated by Jaideva Singh (New Delhi: Motilal Banarsidass, 2014), 17.

21. *Vijñānabhairava*, 20.

degree, the Masculine and the Feminine are intrinsically interconnected and situated on the same level of Reality, of which they comprise two sides. This "equality in difference" appears, moreover, downstream on all levels of Reality, but in increasingly differentiating modes, by virtue of the segmenting function of relativity.

The possibility of a contemplation of the Essence as Divine Femininity—by contrast with what appears then as the masculine determination of Being—and its explicit identification with the Infinite by contrast with the Absolute[22]—manifests, albeit reflected on a lower level of Reality, in the metaphysical symbolism of the iconography of the Virgin Mother and the Child, on the one hand, and the adult Jesus and Mary, on the other. Schuon explains that, in the first case, the Virgin is "the formless and primordial essence" by contrast with the Child who represents the "formal wisdom" and "particular revelation":[23] transposed *in divinis*, this is the distinction between the super-ontological Essence and its first ontological Determination, namely Being. The Essence, as such, transcends all determinations and it can therefore never be an object of confessional faith, as it were. Being, on the other hand, through its various hypostatic faces, relates to the exoteric forms of revealed religion. Being is the "Child" of the Essence as the "formal" prophet is the "child" of supra-formal wisdom.

By way of corroborating, on the religious plane, this aspect of the relationship between the feminine and the masculine, one must note that not a single female figure ranks among the founders of religious traditions and the recipients of law-giving revelations. Modern interpretations of this phenomenon are most likely to be based on the historical and cultural assumption of a sociopolitical subservience of women. From this point of view, metaphysical categories such as the ones we have been exploring are seen as merely cultural and intellectual constructs, intended to justify and perpetuate social oppression. The traditionalist point of view diverges from such interpretations by virtue of its "essentialist" consideration of reality: anything that exists on the plane of phenomenal existence is the imperfect reflection, or the privation, of a divine reality. Accordingly, terrestrial realities (being only distant reflections of the archetypes) are subject to a host of imperfections and corruptions. While being a staunch essentialist in the Platonic sense of the word, Schuon fully acknowledges

---

22. It goes without saying that the Essence can also be contemplated as masculine, particularly when distinguishing it from the Manifestation, as in the pair *Ātman-Māyā*.
23. Schuon, *Christianity/Islam*, 69.

this discrepancy and takes into account the reality of sociocultural determinations and constraints that contribute to the construction of the type of femininity "needed" by traditional societies.[24]

Returning to the question of *Śakti*, Schuon notes the significance of representing Mary "next to the adult Jesus" in which—by contrast with the Mother and Child—"Mary is not the formless and primordial essence, but his feminine prolongation, the *śakti*: she is, then, not the Logos under its feminine and maternal aspect, but the virginal and passive complement of the masculine and active Logos, its mirror, made of purity and mercy."[25] Even though this passage refers specifically to the level of the Logos, it can also be applied to higher degrees of Reality, since at each of them we can differentiate between an active and a receptive principle. We have already mentioned this polarity on the level of Beyond-Being, with the Absolute and the Infinite, but it is also present on the level of Being, with its various traditional figures such as *Purusha* and *Prakriti*, which will be discussed later in this chapter. And yet, to refer to Mary as *Śakti* may be *prima facie* surprising since the latter literally means power and expresses, in an Indian context, an active exteriorization or manifestation that appears to differ sharply from the Virgin's contemplative receptivity. Receptivity and activity are, however, two sides of a same reality, the differences reflecting a matter of accent and, no doubt, particular mythological contexts. While being essentially understood as the efficient creative dimension of the Supreme, *Śakti* is also the mirror of the Absolute, or *Śiva*. The concept of *vimarśa*, crucial in Kashmiri Śaivism, is significant in this regard, as it refers to the emergence of a Self-awareness within Absolute Consciousness. It is quite noteworthy, in this respect, that *vimarśa* refers in dramatic art to the critical juncture in a plot between the dramatic "seed" and the cathartic resolution. This echoes the Śivaite universal dramaturgy since *vimarśa* refers to this critical unfolding within the Absolute that results in the distinction between *Śiva* and *Śakti*, and is a prelude to all further onto-cosmogonic uncoiling. Harsha Dehejia has suggestively compared *vimarśa* to the passage from "I" to "myself."[26]

---

24. "One could perhaps also make the point that social conventions, in the traditional surroundings in question here, tend to create—at least on the surface—the feminine type that suits them ideologically and practically." Schuon, *From the Divine to the Human* (Bloomington, IN: World Wisdom, 1982), 78.

25. Schuon, *Christianity/Islam*, 69.

26. Harsha V. Dehejia, *The Advaita of Art* (New Delhi: Motilal Banarsidass, 1996), 129.

Śakti is therefore comparable to "the mirror of Siva's awareness,"[27] being receptive in relation to Him and active with respect to her productions.

As we have seen, Schuon conceives of the Virgin's highest reality as being the unfathomable and supra-formal Essence. He also refers to Existence, which is none other than Divine Manifestation, as another metaphysical aspect of the Virgin. These are the two poles of the Virginal Reality: the super-ontological Essence that transcends all determinations and Existence as the extrinsic dimension of Divine Reality. The latter is, in that sense, the externalized dimension of the former. As meditations on these metaphysical degrees, Schuon's works prolong a tradition of mystical interpretations of the Feminine that finds one of its most celebrated representative in Ibn al-'Arabī. In the final chapter of his *Ringstones of Wisdom* (*Fuṣūṣ al-hikam*), Ibn 'Arabī comments on the Prophetic tradition in which the Prophet declares that three things of this world have been made "the coolness of his eyes": women, perfume, and prayer. The two main points one may draw from Ibn 'Arabī's speculative meditations on the topic lie, first, in his identification of the Divine Essence and Divine Cause as feminine,[28] and, second, in his remark that man is situated in between two feminine realities—the Divine Essence from which he originates and woman who, according to monotheistic traditions, is drawn from the human male.[29] Although Ibn 'Arabī relies primarily on linguistic speculations to buttress his views on the Feminine, it is quite clear that this is less a deductive method than a symbolic intimation. In other words, the grammatically feminine is just a mystical hermeneutic key, grounded in scriptures and the spiritual tradition, to open the door to profound meditations on the super-eminence of the Essence. As for the placement of the masculine between two feminine realities, this is discussed in the context of the contemplation of God in woman, which we consider later on in this work. At any rate, there is a clear parallel, *mutatis mutandis*, between this tripartite division and Schuon's reflections on the relationship

---

27. *Journal of Dharma* 20: 273.

28. "Follow any path you wish, you shall always find that the feminine comes first, even among the people of causation who consider the Real to be the cause of the existence of the world. 'Cause' is feminine." Ibn al-'Arabī, *The Ringstones of Wisdom*, translated by Caner K. Dagli (Chicago: Great Books of the Islamic World, 2004), 286.

29. "Indeed, man falls between the Essence, from which he manifests, and woman, who manifests from him. He is thus between two femininities: the femininity of the Essence and true femininity." Ibn al-'Arabī, *The Ringstones of Wisdom*, 286.

between the Divine hypostatic degrees: Essence or Beyond-Being, Being, and Existence. Beyond-Being, the Essence, is Feminine as limitless indetermination. Existence is feminine as the substance of all existing beings. In between the two lies Being, which is first determination, and also masculine as Creator, Revealer, and Judge.

Both Feminine hypostases are the Virgin at different degrees of Reality. First, the Virgin is the unfathomable Mystery of the Essence whose purity lies beyond all determinations, relationships, and relativities; second, as Substance of the manifested universe, she remains innocent and untouched by the imperfections and evils of cosmic relativity. She is like the vase of perfection that remains pure while the mixture of relativities is poured into it. As for God *qua* Being, He is passive in relation to the Essence and active in relation to Existence. It could be said, by way of analogy with Ibn 'Arabī's insight, i.e. "the contemplation of God through woman is the most perfect of contemplations,"[30] that Being's "contemplation" of the Essence is most perfect in Existence since He recognizes in It His own passivity in relation to the Essence (i.e., His relativity) and his activity as existentiating Principle (i.e., His absoluteness). This contemplation is operated, as it were, through the archetypes contained in Being itself and manifested in variegated ways by Existence.[31] Moreover, Relativity demarcates the Essence from Being and Existence in a way that prefigures the chasm of creation separating God from man and woman. Furthermore, in order to delve deeper into the implications of this analogy, one must meditate the oft-quoted *hadīth*: "I was a Hidden Treasure and I wanted to be known so I created the world." Schuon relates these two themes, the contemplation of God in woman and God's Self-contemplation through, and in, creation, which suggests a correlation between woman and Existence.[32] From this point of view, the Hidden Treasure is the Essence, the reality that is to

---

30. Ibn 'Arabī, *Fusus al-Hikam* 27 (Beirut: Dar al-Kitab al-Arabi, 1946), 217.

31. "The Good, which coincides with the Absolute, is thus prolonged in the direction of relativity and first gives rise to Being which contains the archetypes, and then to Existence which manifests them in indefinitely varied modes and according to the rhythms of the diverse cosmic cycles." Schuon, *Survey of Metaphysics and Esoterism*, 29.

32. "This too, *mutatis mutandis*, was the perspective of the Prophet who, according to Ibn Arabi, perceived God in woman, who 'was made lovable unto me' (*hubiba ilayya*) by Allāh, by reason of the very transparency of the feminine theophany; and in the same order of ideas, it is necessary to quote this *hadīth qudsī*: 'I was a hidden treasure and I wished to be known; therefore I created the world.'" Schuon, *Christianity/Islam*, 173–74.

be known through creation is Existence (the Essence known relatively), and the "I" who created the world is the Creator, or Being, the "relativization" of the Essence. Such an identification of the "I" with Divine Being may come as a surprise, since the Ultimate "I" is evidently the Essence itself, but it becomes quite plausible when considering that the "I" who "wants to be known" is already determined by this will to be known and, most obviously, by His creating the world. At any rate, this exteriorizing Self-knowledge that is the *raison d'être* of creation is itself reflected in the mode through which human beings gain access to the knowledge of the Essence within. The knowledge of God that man obtains through the contemplation of woman is none other than the knowledge of his own Essence in the mirror of this most direct theophany. Woman is so to the extent that she is both human—hence central—and feminine—hence "essential"—and it is in this way, therefore, that she is a theophany of man's Essence. This explains why man contemplates "the God within," the Essence, most perfectly in woman. As a central theophany, the primordial human male is a symbol of the Principle, including both Beyond-Being and Being, in relation to Manifestation in the manner of a causal power, while the archetypical human female is like a reflection of the Essence as envisaged from the point of view of Manifestation, that is, in the way of a "hidden" inwardness. It could not be stressed enough, however, that the Essence *qua* Essence is in itself beyond the polarity of the Masculine and the Feminine, while being eminently inclusive of both. Considering the cardinal dimensions of the Essence, one comes to understand how each of the genders can be identified with it in different ways according to a particular metaphysical perspective or emphasis. While woman is for man a manifestation of the Infinite, it could be said that, for woman, man is a symbol of the Absolute or, downstream, of Being as distinct from Existence. If, as Schuon asserts, the feminine mode of contemplating man is akin to a "centering"—given its connection to the Absolute that is the Center par excellence—the masculine mode of contemplating woman is "liberating" referring, as it does, to the Infinite that surpasses all limits. These profound and far-reaching differences in modalities are ultimately transcended, however, by the more fundamental principle that each gender is for the other a manifestation of its own essence.[33] This is so inasmuch

---

33. Hence we hear Dante, in the *Vita Nuova*, on first seeing Beatrice: "At that moment . . . the vital spirit, that which lives in the most secret chamber of the heart . . . uttered these words: *Ecce deus fortior me, qui veniens dominabitur michi*" ("Behold a god more powerful than I who, coming, will rule over me").

as the sexes are both the same with respect to being human and other as having a different gender, thereby mirroring the mysterious transcendent identity of the Self. In this sense the essence of man is feminine and the essence of woman is masculine, and each is for the other like a "rediscovered mirror of God."[34] The human theophany, whether male or female, may shine forth as "God" that is, from a human point of view, the central modality of Existence "revealing" the Essence.

Existence is the Virgin who remains immaculate in spite of the limitations and imperfections of the created order. The capitalization of the word indicates a fundamental distinction, on the one hand, between existence as the ontological status of all created beings or the world that Hindus would call *nāma-rūpa* (name-and-form or substance-and-accident), and, on the other, Existence as the degree of Divine Reality that is immanent in the created or manifested order. Existence is not, therefore, a synonym of Relativity since the latter also includes Being as its summit;[35] that is to say, the very Principle of Manifestation is Relative without being part of Existence.[36] On this ontological level, the Virgin is what Hindu speculative traditions refer to as *Prakriti*, which has its parallel with the *physis* of the Greeks.[37] It is, therefore, primordial nature or original matter that is antecedent to any informing "impression." As such, it is marked by simple, pure, primordial, and formless onto-cosmic Receptivity. The formlessness of *Prakriti* is the reflection, on the ontological level, of the supra-formal infinity of the Essence. *Prakriti* is defined by Schuon as the "divine femininity of *Māyā*,"[38] which implies that the latter also has

---

34. "[The person of another race is] a forgotten aspect of ourselves and thus also like a rediscovered mirror of God." Schuon, *Language of the Self*, 175.

35. "*Prakriti*, the ontological 'Substance,' is the divine 'femininity' of *Māyā*. The masculine aspect is represented by the divine Names which, in so far as they correspond to *Purusha*, determine and 'fertilize' Substance, in collaboration with the three fundamental tendencies comprised in Substance (the *gunas: sattva, rajas, tamas*)." Schuon, *Light on the Ancient Worlds*, nn. 9, 77.

36. "In its global reality, Existence is serene and not malefic: cosmic Wrath is re-absorbed in total and virginal Equilibrium. Existence in itself is the universal Virgin who vanquishes, by its purity as well as by its mercy, the sin of the demiurgic Eve, productive of creatures and passions; the Eve who produces, seduces and attaches is 'eternally' vanquished by the Virgin who purifies, forgives and liberates." Schuon, *Gnosis: Divine Wisdom*, 71.

37. Krishna Mohan Banerjee, *Dialogues on the Hindu Philosophy* (Calcutta: Thacker Spink and Co., 1861), 241.

38. Schuon, *Light on the Ancient Worlds*, nn. 9, 77.

a masculine aspect as *Purusha*, the determinative principle of Being. Essentially, Being is a reflection of the Absolute in the unfolding of the Infinite, so to speak, in the sense that it proceeds from the limitlessness of the latter while reflecting the former as the principle and summit of Relativity: "Supra-formal manifestation . . . is the direct and central reflection of the creative Principle, *Purusha*, in the cosmic Substance *Prakriti*." Schuon refers to this reflection as "Divine Intelligence manifested,"[39] which Hindus call *Buddhi* and the Abrahamic monotheisms contemplate as the Archangelic Realm, whereas Being, or its active aspect (*Purusha*), is the unmanifested dimension of Divine Intelligence. At any rate, the perfection of *Prakriti* is one of onto-cosmic receptivity vis-à-vis this Intelligence, but also one of projection of its potentialities into existence. As we have already intimated, the conjunction of receptivity and creativeness made possible by *Prakriti* is one of the hallmarks of the Feminine in general, irrespective of the degree of Reality.

In the mystical symbolism of the Abrahamic traditions, particularly as found in Sufism, the Essence is approached as *Laylā*, the impenetrable Night whose mystery attracts and liberates. The Algerian Sufi Shaykh 'Ahmad al-'Alawī, for instance, evokes Her irresistible power of attraction when he writes: "[She] raised the cloak that hid her from me, Made me marvel to distraction, Bewildered me with all her beauty."[40] At this highest level of contemplation, the Essence reveals Herself as being none other than the Self, *Ātman*,[41] that remains untouched by the objectification of relativity.[42] The Self remains pure in the sense that it cannot be affected

---

39. Schuon, *The Transcendent Unity of Religions*, 25.

40. "Lailā," in Martin Lings, *A Sufi Saint of the Twentieth Century—Shaykh Ahmad Al-'Alawī—His Spiritual Heritage and Legacy* (Cambridge: Islamic Texts Society, 1993), 225.

41. "[She] hid me in her inmost self, Until I thought that she was I." "Lailā," in Lings, *A Sufi Saint of the Twentieth Century*.

42. This is analogous, in another traditional language, to the Mahāyana concept of the "undefiled" Buddha nature as expressed, for instance, in Asvaghosa's *The Awakening of Faith*. From the point of view of Nirvānic consciousness, there has never been any samsāric defilement, since the latter is contingent upon ignorance which cannot sully the Buddha nature: "It is eternally abiding One Mind. All things appear in it because all things are real. And none of the defiled things are able to defile it, for the essence of wisdom [i.e., original enlightenment] is unaffected by defilements, being furnished with an unsoiled quality and influencing all men to advance toward enlightenment." Asvaghosa, *The Awakening of Faith*, translated by Yoshito S. Hakeda (Berkeley: Numata Center for Buddhist Translation and Research, 2005), 22.

by the limitations inherent to contingent consciousness, nor can it be objectified and therefore ensnared in the web of relativities. No relative mode of consciousness, as immersed in the imperfections and miseries of *Māyā* as it may be, can in any way make the Self other than what it is: absolute, infinite, and blissful. This unalterable purity results from the principle that "Essence is inaccessible to the existent as such, as was said by the inscription on the statue of Isis at Sais: 'I am all that has been, all that is, and all that will be; and no mortal has ever lifted my veil.' "[43] On the one hand, this rigorous aspect of Divine Femininity is untouched by profanation by any relative being *qua* relative. On the other hand, Isis's inaccessibility is also, paradoxically it seems, the pledge of a way to Liberation. The transcendent immanence of the Goddess has been, is, and will be what it is, irrespective of the vicissitudes of the relative order, which means that Deliverance is a virtual possibility at each and every point of the universe.[44] In this sense, Divine Mercy is present throughout the entire range of existence, including where this appears most distant from Reality. This is also what the Qur'ān tells us, in its own way, through the Divine declaration "My Mercy (*Rahmah*) encompasses everything."

The merciful and saving modalities of Divine Femininity span a range of symbolic expressions. Aside from the immaculate purity of the Feminine Essence, Schuon refers to Her "protectiveness" as Mother and her "attractiveness" as Virgin. Both of these attributes of Divine Femininity apply to the Self inasmuch as It is the Essence considered as Subject. Thus, the Virgin is the Self to the extent that she draws souls toward the source of their being, which is none other than our deepest Self and none other than Herself. What Schuon has written, in the tradition of the *Fedeli d'Amore*, about the worship of the Lady directly points to this mystery of the inner immanence of the Beloved. Attraction loses here all of its negative connotations—ordinarily connected to the centrifugal symbolism of Eve—and refers to a vertical emancipation through the power of grace as embodied by the Feminine, in the likeness of Mary: "The Divine *Māyā*—Femininity *in divinis*—is not only that which projects and creates; it is also that which attracts and liberates."[45] *Māyā* cannot be

---

43. Schuon, *Esoterism as Principle and as Way* (London: Perennial Books, 1981), 60.

44. This is probably this sense of the metaphysical omnipresence of Deliverance that leads Hindus to affirm, perhaps symbolically, that *Moksha* is bestowed upon any creature who dies in Benares.

45. Schuon, *In the Face of the Absolute*, 72.

only, or primarily, negative since it proceeds from the Essence and is not fundamentally different from It.

Furthermore, the Mother is the Self insofar as it encompasses every consciousness and therefore protects all, since there is none other than the Self. The Self is like an infinite space that surrounds us on all sides, like the mantle of the Virgin protecting the faithful under the folds of its grace. The Self is the Divine Mother, from whom everyone is born, and through whom everyone lives. In a sense—but not absolutely so, the symbolism of the Mother is more appropriate to express the Mystery of the Self than that of the Father. Indeed, the Father begets, but there is always a distinction, hence a duality, between Him and His begotten. Even in the context of Christian Trinitarianism, in which a consubstantiality of the Father and the Son is affirmed, the intrinsic relationship that is envisaged is still a distinction that, arguably, does not quite fully take us into the domain of non-duality. By contrast, the Mother has borne her child within herself—hence a sense of immanent integration—and his birth is, in a way, a severance from this blissful Unity, a fall from the non-dual Fullness of Reality.[46] From the point of view of this separation, however, or inasmuch as it is a reality, the Mother becomes a Divine Protectress[47] under a myriad of personal manifestations that are just so many facets of the Goddess.

On the plane of spiritual realization, the Virginity of the Essence is a spiritual allusion to the fact that only the Self can realize the Self. Schuon refers to *Māyā* as being the "Veil of Isis,"[48] hence the identification of Isis with the Self. Thus, commenting upon the Egyptian adage that "no human can lift this veil," Schuon sees this as affirming the impossibility for what

---

46. Needless to say, this maternal symbolism cannot be taken as an exclusive possibility. The Self can be conceived of as the Father inasmuch as it is identified with the Principle of everything. Ramana Maharshi, for instance, refers to the Self as his Father, Arunachala.

47. "Advaita Vedanta which has nothing individualistic and consequently nothing agitated about it, envisages only the second subjectivity [the transpersonal Self] and so to speak abandons the first [the individual subject] to its fate, by placing it in the hands of the Divine Mother." Schuon, *Sufism: Veil and Quintessence* (Bloomington, IN: World Wisdom, 1981), 56.

48. "In the final analysis, the Isis hidden behind her veil is none other than Divine Reality in which the objective and the subjective coincide; and the veil is none other than the cosmogonic projection by which this Reality is bipolarized and gives rise to that innumerable play of mirrors that is the Universe; Isis is *Ātmā*, the veil is *Māyā*." Schuon, *Roots of the Human Condition* (Bloomington, IN: World Wisdom, 1991), 24.

is other-than-the-Self to realize the Self. Nobody can lift the veil of *Māyā* except Isis Herself. How could That which is the Self of all selves be realized by anything other than Itself? Such a possibility would presuppose two selves, and would therefore run contrary to the ultimacy and non-duality of the Self. This statement is, therefore, another way of stating that the Self is not objectifiable: the immaculateness of the Self lies in its intrinsic resistance to being treated as an object. The first "sin"—indeed the source of all sins that is, in a certain sense, the only sin—is objectification, the source of the scission introduced into the Real. This sin of objectification can be illustrated, as Schuon has shown, by the eating of the fruit of the tree of good and evil by the first human couple.

The biblical account of the Fall from Eden signifies that mankind unduly appropriated the power of introducing duality into a view of reality that is the prerogative of the Divine, since the source of the distinction between good and evil lies ultimately in the Infinite, and the unfolding that flows from its All-Possibility. Mankind has no access to the All-Possibility, given its existential limitations. Therefore, within the strictures of these limitations, mankind has no right to a separative vision of reality, since the latter is like a superimposition, to use Advaitin language, or an association in Islamic parlance. Before the Fall, the first couple still lived within a non-separative consciousness, and spontaneously participated in the unitive aura of the Divine. The metaphysical key is that God can perceive separative multiplicity from the point of view of His Unity, without the former affecting the latter in any way.[49] By contrast, any attempt at such a vision and experience from a strictly human point of view is intrinsically transgressive and doomed to thicken the veil of relativity through an accumulation of hardening absolutizations, thereby producing a concatenation of negative karmic consequences. The misguided vision of the first couple following the transgression quickens, so to speak, what Schuon denotes as "the *Māyā* that moves downwards and disperses and, at the same time, gives rise to density and heaviness."[50] This is the negative

---

49. "We might also say that the Creator—through His unique and inimitable nature—essentially has the right to a separative and descending vision of possibilities, because this vision does not go outside the Divine Subject; for God is Unity and Totality, everything subsists in Him, and He cannot therefore sin by going outside Himself as does man, whose existence is limited to an individuality and whose actions affect existences other than his own." Schuon, *Esoterism as Principle and as Way*, 82.

50. "In this latter respect, the tree of the distinction between Good and Evil denotes 'impure' *Māyā*, the *Māyā* that moves downwards and disperses and at the same time

aspect of Femininity: an increasingly distant and centrifugal radiation of the Infinite. The demiurgic tendency has, moreover, a major impact on the way the opposite gender and sexual union is experienced. Prior to eating the fruit, the differentiation between man and woman, as well as their union, was not divorced from God-consciousness. It is only after the Fall that this becomes a principle of sin, hence, in the biblical narrative, the shame of the first couple at discovering their own nudity, a shame that reflects a moving away from "Divine Femininity" to "demiurgic Femininity."

In the same order of ideas, the attempts by modern science to "raise the Veil of Isis" in order to reveal the Mystery of the universe are founded on a failure to recognize the epistemological implications of there being a necessary correlation of subject and object in the realm of relativity. This ignorance, which undermines the claims of science as an objective enterprise, precludes a "scientific" knowledge of the Essence of the universe, since this can only ever be relative—given its premises—to its object and, therefore, external to it. Symbolically, modern scientific attempts at unveiling the mystery of the universe amount to forcing one's will over the Essence, as it were, from which ensue all manner of negative consequences with regard to the relationship between mankind and its environment. Traditionalist writers have referred to the Prometheism of modern science when highlighting its connection to an epistemological transgressiveness that carries in its wake a destruction of the anthropo-cosmic unity characteristic of premodern universes of meaning. By contrast with these scientistically disruptive forays, the implications of Femininity and Virginity can profoundly illuminate the spiritual and moral requirements for gnosis. These are encapsulated synthetically in the mystical notion of Love that entails an extinction of the lover in the Beloved and is beautifully suggested by Rūmī's admonition to the readers of the Book: "The Qur'an is like a bride. Although you pull the veil away from her face, she does not show herself to you."[51] The Essence, a fortiori, does not show Herself to anybody but to those who love Her and thereby die in Her: "And death in Love, of Love the essence is."[52]

---

gives rise to density and heaviness; this is cosmic Possibility, but in its inferior and centrifugal aspect." Schuon, *Esoterism as Principle and as Way*, 81.

51. William Chittick, *The Sufi Path of Love: The Spiritual Teachings of Rūmī* (Albany: State University of New York Press, 1983), 273.

52. *The Essential Frithjof Schuon*, ed. Seyyed Hossein Nasr (Bloomington, IN: World Wisdom, 2005), 527.

At the antipode of the activist exertion of scientific knowledge, Schuon extols a wisdom of the Feminine, as it were, that is founded on spiritual receptivity. One must be wary, however, of exaggerating or treating in a one-sided manner the relationship between genders and modes of knowledge. Intellection evidently lies beyond gender distinctions, and rationality, whether masculine or not, has an important role to play in the formal crystallization of wisdom. Nevertheless, esoteric wisdom is undoubtedly attuned to a receptivity to the inner dimension of Reality. Such a receptivity appears quite clearly in Schuon's treatment of the symbolism of the Virgin as "Seat of Wisdom"—*sedes sapientiae*—a medieval and liturgical epithet of the Virgin. The Virgin is the seat of Wisdom as Mother of the Word, and she therefore embodies the paradigm of the Heart that "is the predestined seat of immanent Wisdom."[53] On the one hand, the Virgin represents the perfection of receptivity; on the other, she is also the very content of this receptivity. For Schuon, her being the Throne or Seat of Wisdom cannot but mean that she is herself Wisdom; and this is by virtue of the Plotinian principle that "like is destined for like," the law of affinity being an indispensable component of any mystical receptivity.[54] This also appears in the fact that the Virgin has been, at times, considered as the spouse of the Holy Spirit—the immanent Wisdom of God—and even the Holy Spirit itself, or at least that aspect of it which pertains to the supra-formal dimension.[55] In other words, the Virgin embodies the essentially spiritual and ineffable content of Wisdom, in contrast to its masculine dimension (such as we find in the *Wisdom of Solomon*), the latter spanning the entire spectrum of reality, including cosmology and politics. Schuon points out, however, that the Virginal Wisdom, although synthetic and centered on metaphysics and spirituality—that is, on principles that are directly relevant to spiritual transmutation and salvation—contains virtually all other, more external modes of knowledge, as light contains all colors. This remark is important, not only because it suggests

---

53. Schuon, *In the Face of the Absolute*, 67.

54. George Joseph Seidel, *Knowledge as Sexual Metaphor* (London: Associated University Presses, 2000), 78.

55. Peter Schäfer has shown how the Wisdom of the Old Testament, being created before everything, and sometimes even identified as the daughter of God, enjoys a particularly privileged, and in a sense perplexing, status on the threshold of the Divinity. See his *Mirror of His Beauty: Feminine Images of God from the Bible to the Early Kabbalah* (Princeton, NJ: Princeton University Press, 2002).

a hierarchy in the modes of Wisdom, but also because it implies that the contemplative bypassing of the outermost expressions of sapience does not stem from an intrinsic incapacity, but from a vocational concentration on transcendence. In the religious domain, the Virgin personifies the Feminine dimension of the Holy Spirit, the informal aspect that "bloweth where it listeth" (John 3:8), in contrast to the masculine dimension of the Holy Spirit that inspires the crystallization of forms and presides, therefore, over the development of a tradition. In considering these perspectives, one can begin to fathom the meaning of theological remarks such as those by Nicolas Cabasilas, where he speaks of the Virgin as having unveiled "God's hypostatic Wisdom of God itself."[56] The term hypostatic is very striking here, since it is used in Eastern Christian theology to refer to the Persons of the Trinity.[57] In keeping with a similarly higher understanding of the Virgin, one of Schuon's most explicit statements concerning Her nature is that she "personifies both the universal *Shakti* and the *Sophia Perennis*."[58] She embodies, therefore, both Being and Knowing, the principle of the ontological unfolding and the perfection of God-knowledge. She is God's Self-Knowledge as Supreme Divine Object while being also, and as such, the very Principle of Being as Relativity. In a sense, she epitomizes the coincidence of Being and Knowing: as Self-Knowledge of God, she is the source of Being; as the very substance and ontological essence of knowledge, she is Universal Wisdom.[59]

While his metaphysical reflections on the Feminine, along with their esoteric and spiritual implications, may inspire a measure of interest in his work among some contemporary readers, Schuon's understanding is radically different to that of most recent religious advocates of the Feminine. The latter tend to proceed from past and present sociocultural grievances that they take as the starting point for an ideological and theoretical critique,

---

56. Nicolas Cabasilas, *La Mère de Dieu* (Lausanne: L'Âge d'Homme, 1992), 73.

57. This type of statement is, for Schuon, evidence that the Islamic view of the Christian Trinity, consisting of the Father, Son, and Mother, although theologically inaccurate, is symbolically meaningful.

58. Schuon, *Form and Substance in the Religions*, nn. 11, 115.

59. "The Blessed Virgin as *Sedes Sapientiae* personifies this merciful Wisdom which descends towards us and which we too, whether we know it or not, bear in our very essence; and it is precisely by virtue of this potentiality or virtuality that Wisdom comes down upon us. The immanent seat of Wisdom is the heart of man." Schuon, *In Face of the Absolute*, 72.

together with a call for sociopolitical activism. Schuon's metaphysics of the Divine Feminine belongs to a very different order: it is independent of any immediate contemporary concerns and proceeds from a meditation on the metaphysical principles of gender differentiation. As such, it is quite clearly essentialist and therefore at odds with modern forms of constructivism. However, it would be misleading to understand this essentialism as a sweeping reduction of individuals to generic and absolutized essences. Rather, it simply seeks to recognize primary essences over individualized manifestations that participate in them to various degrees.

In the wake of the growing impact of feminism, the question of the Feminine has tended to be couched either in terms of differentialism—which seeks to bring attention to issues that have been downplayed or repressed—or promoting gender equality. Schuon's metaphysics of the Feminine, which is consonant with a wide range of traditional sources from Hindu Tantrism to Christian Mariology, is essentialist in the sense that it adopts the principle that gender differences are grounded in ontology and not just in culture or biology. In fact, Schuon strongly criticizes modern trends that seek to erase or alter sexual distinctions on the level where they are existentially and spiritually relevant, cautioning against the pitfalls of a masculinization of women, and conversely.[60] Essentialism—which is the metaphysical perspective of traditional religions—must be complemented, however, by a discernment of the degrees of reality that allows one to take into account the increasingly determining weight of contingencies as we consider the full gamut of human phenomena. In other words, the recognition of transcendent essences cannot readily translate into a rigid categorization of human phenomena.

Indeed, Schuon's approach to the Feminine may allow one to parry the theological and religious consequences of such reductive absolutizations. In this regard, Schuon is keen to point out the ways in which a misogynistic bias has been inherent to some traditional streams of theology, or to some sociocultural features of religion. This is particularly evident in

---

60. Franklin Merell-Wolff echoes a similar concern when he writes that "too often, in these later days, womankind has been disposed to discredit her own natural glories and powers by becoming an imitator of man. This is really giving to man-power and man-function a greater tribute than they deserve. That essence the outer embodiment of which is woman in a peculiar sense constitutes a need of this world today that is especially poignant." *Experience and Philosophy: A Personal Record of Transformation* (Albany: State University of New York Press, 1994), 41.

Buddhism and Christianity on both a doctrinal and ethico-spiritual level, and in Islam on a sociocultural level. In traditional Christian theology, irrespective of more recent feminist developments that have been determined by contemporary ideological trends, Eve appears as the archetype of "centrifugal *Māyā*." The sin associated with the original transgression affects the way sexuality is envisaged in an essential manner and woman is, de facto, identified with its negative connotations. This is analogous to Buddhism, inasmuch as woman is considered—at least in early Buddhist teachings and sensibilities—to embody the samsāric principle of craving (*tanha*) and rebirth. The Marian redemption of Femininity and the Mahāyanic feminization of the Bodhisattva, both stressed by Schuon, provide a compensatory perspective in response to this bias, although they do so on a level that transcends the realm of natural life.

The key to Schuon's critique of religious misogyny may rest in the following passage: "Sages are the first to understand that femininity in itself is independent of earthly accidentality or of the samsarically contingent aspects of the carnal creature; if it is opportune to turn away from seductions and, in certain respects, from all attachments regardless of the nature of their supports, it is on the other hand neither possible nor desirable to escape from the feminine principle, which is nirvanic in essence, that is to say divine."[61] This statement presents us with a clear differentiation between principial realities and terrestrial contingencies. Under the moralistic spell through mesmerization by the latter, the error of too many traditional commentators has been to ignore or downplay the former. At any rate, the fundamental claim made by Schuon in this passage lies, by contrast, in a recognition of the beatific aspect of the Feminine. This does not only mean that the Divine Feminine is a metaphysical reality, but it also reminds us that this reality is essentially blissful: what it communicates, or rather awakens in us, is none other than beatitude itself. This is the main lesson to be drawn from Schuon's contemplation of the Feminine: there is an intrinsic correlation between the Feminine as manifestation of the Divine Reality and its ability to awaken the sanctifying grace and immanent wisdom that lies within us.

The Feminine informs Schuon's writings inasmuch as it is a symbol and manifestation of gnosis. While the perspective of esoterism transcends all relative differentiations, including gender, its primary emphasis on the

---

61. Schuon, *Treasures of Buddhism* (Bloomington, IN: World Wisdom, 1993), 149.

supra-formal and inward dimension of the spiritual life entails a profound affinity with the Feminine. From a certain point of view, form has a masculine aspect in that it defines and orders; the feminine, on the other hand, may relate to the inner grace of Essence that unites and delivers.[62] Conversely, the outer realm divides; it encompasses a wide array of human activities, including in the religious realm, that tend to be disconnected from the beatific unity of the Self. While Martha's excessive concern for the latter domain is gently scolded by Christ himself, Mary's contemplative silence, by contrast, represents our quest for "the one thing needful," "that good part which shall not be taken away from her" (Luke 10:42). Positively, religious outwardness is a principle of integration, because it includes a wide range of human realities within the compass of ultimate concerns. However, it is also a source of strife, if not destruction, as its limited emphasis on what to do and not to do (i.e., arguments about orthopraxy) is bound to impede the flowering of spiritual realization.

There is another way, finally, in which Schuon's view of esoterism presents us with an integration of the Feminine, and it is the sense of beauty. One may well wonder how esoterism relates to beauty, and why an equation between Femininity and beauty is warranted, given that beauty is obviously not a feminine privilege. With respect to the equation itself, it rests on Schuon's vision of beauty as a perfection of manifestation on which the Essence bestows its grace. While beauty has to do with form, it pertains to a domain in which the formal directly points to the essential; formal beauty must ultimately lead one beyond its own limited crystallizations. In this connection, Schuon writes quite suggestively that the most beautiful body is "like a congealed fragment of an ocean of inexpressible

---

62. "The human being is compounded of geometry and music, of spirit and soul, of virility and femininity: by geometry, he brings the chaos of existence back to order, that is, he brings blind substance back to its ontological meaning and thus constitutes a reference point between Earth and Heaven, a 'sign-post' pointing towards God; by music he brings the segmentation of form back to unitive life, reducing form, which is death, to Essence—at least symbolically and virtually—so that it vibrates with a joy which is at the same time a *nostalgia* for the Infinite. As symbols, the masculine body indicates a victory of the Spirit over chaos, and the feminine body, a deliverance of form by Essence; the first is like a magic sign which would subjugate the blind forces of the Universe, and the second like celestial music which would give back to fallen matter its paradisiac transparency, or which, to use the language of Taoism, would make trees flower beneath the snow." Schuon, *Stations of Wisdom* (London: John Murray, 1961), 80.

bliss."[63] This is, in a sense, the universal meaning of the Feminine: a manifestation of Divine Reality, penetrated with perfection and grace, that invites one to move beyond the frozen form and into the infinite Essence. Schuon's point of view lies, in this regard, at the intersection of Plato's path of transcendence toward the Beautiful and Abhinavagupta's alchemy of aesthetic awakening to our immanent Selfhood. From an objective point of view, the Feminine, given its musical orientation toward the Essence and its immanent streak of grace and Unity, is like an "open door" to higher degrees of Reality. From a subjective standpoint, the Feminine alludes to the deepest layer of Selfhood that the language of beauty, and the spiritual science of aesthetics, can contribute toward unveiling the internal vibrations of sensory experience. In this sense, Schuon sees the Feminine as a language of the Essence and as a quasi-necessary means of assimilating spiritual realities.

The Schuonian affinity with, and emphasis on, the Feminine dimension of Reality, from the metaphysics of the Essence to the alchemy of beauty, is not founded upon an attempt at developing a theology of the Feminine that would echo the growing interest in Goddess religions or feminist hermeneutics. Schuon's writings do not suggest in the least the advent of a new religious consciousness founded on the Feminine, nor any kind of theological and institutional revolution. They suggest, rather, the need for a harmonious balance between dimensions that have been either overly privileged because of one-sided social conditionings and others that have been neglected, or the deepest meaning of which has been occulted. The Feminine has no meaning except in relation to the Masculine, and vice versa, and this central duality itself has no ultimate significance but in view of realizing the non-dual Self, which is neither masculine nor feminine, and yet both.

---

63. "Although form has a positive function thanks to its power of expression, it limits at the same time that which it expresses, and which is an essence: the most beautiful body is like a congealed fragment of an ocean of inexpressible bliss." Schuon, *Gnosis: Divine Wisdom*, 90.

8

The *Yin-Yang* Perspective and Visual Metaphysics

The autochthonous Chinese traditions of Confucianism, Taoism, and indigenous shamanistic folk religion, as opposed to the traditions of India and the monotheistic Abrahamic religions, are not referenced very often by Schuon. There are several reasons for this relative marginality of Taoist and Confucian teachings in Schuon's opus, one of which is the profound specificity of the Chinese treatment of metaphysics, both in terms of outlook and symbolic language. Schuon's perspective, notwithstanding its supra-confessional and cross-religious universality, is couched in dialectical modes that are mostly tributaries of European and Indian doctrinal expression, which is what provides an initial explanation for his perspective on the Chinese tradition. This does not mean that Schuon's writings leave no room for Far Eastern forms, but it must be recognized that his intellectual and spiritual attention to East Asia is mostly focused on Japanese Buddhism and Shinto. This is no doubt both a matter of affinity and circumstance. The formal language of Japanese religious art exercised a very strong attraction on Schuon from his early youth, after which he began to maintain contacts with prominent Japanese spiritual figures, such as Shojun Bando. More generally, the forms of traditional Japanese culture, beginning with Shinto, resonated in Schuon's mind with what he considered to be the fundamental characteristics of primordial inspiration; namely, metaphysical simplicity, the sense of the sacred, and a keen sensibility regarding the spiritual message of nature. Needless to say, the Chinese world is far from being devoid of such primordial features, particularly in the Taoist tradition. However, it may well be that the intellectual and artistic treasures to which the Middle Kingdom gave rise brought about such a complex and sophisticated culture that its arguably overcivilized genius may have, sometimes, contributed to concealing the elemental and shamanistic substance of the ancestral tradition. Independently of these considerations, however, Schuon has himself recognized that Far Eastern dialectics are largely symbolic and allusive, rather than dialectical and systematic as found in Western and Indian metaphysics. These characters raise some formal challenges when one attempts to integrate Chinese insights into a contemporary European idiom; and this explains, in part—aside from the fact that Schuon was not extensively versed in the study of Chinese language and Taoist teachings—the incidental ways in which Chinese traditions come to participate in Schuon's cross-traditional lexicon. Among the symbolic and elliptical expressions of the Chinese traditions, we find a recurring concept that may be deemed to compensate for the relative paucity of textual dialectics, a far-ranging notion that belongs to the entire family of Chinese traditions and is already at work in the archaic and foundational cosmology of the *Book of Changes*, the *I-Ching*. This is none other than the *yin-yang* symbol, one that may be said to encapsulate the entire worldview of the Chinese.

The *yin-yang* concept (and its corresponding symbols) is probably the most famous Chinese contribution to metaphysics and cosmology. It has a very wide range of applications, from the highest principles of metaphysics to practical matters of divination.[1] The ideograms referring to *yin* and *yang* originate in the character for "hill," with *yin* being connected to "cloud" or the dark side of the hill, and *yang* to "sun" or its bright side. Other, simplified versions of these characters refer to the "moon" and "sun"; from these are derived associations such as North, dark, female, cold, and unmanifested for *yin* and South, bright, male, warm, and manifested for *yang*. The original symbolism of the two sides of a hill already suggests difference, in the sense that the two sides are exclusive of each other, but also mobility of perspective since brightness and darkness are dependent on the motions of the sun. Moreover, the original context of these concepts indicates that any change is none other than a transformation of one element into the other and vice versa: the *yin* and the *yang* do not exist in and of themselves, but only in relation to each other or in sequence. It also means that their degrees and modes of manifestation

---

1. The most recent and comprehensive academic study on the topic is Robin Wang's *Yinyang: The Way of Heaven and Earth in Chinese Thought and Culture* (Cambridge: Cambridge University Press, 2012).

are contingent on the sun that actualizes their respective predominance. It flows from this primordial symbolism that the unity of the hill is in no way affected by the polar complementarity, or opposition, of its two slopes. Unity, multiplicity, interdependent equilibrium, and transformation are, therefore, the key notions of the *yin-yang* worldview.

There are several graphic representations of *yin-yang*, two of which are prevalent in today's commentaries on the meaning of the two symbols. The first one is derived from the diagrams (*tu*) that were elaborated mostly during the Song Dynasty on the basis of the *I-Ching*. They are composed of trigrams or hexagrams comprising a number of full and broken lines. The standard way of depicting the universal range of cosmic manifestations to which *yin-yang* gives rise consists of sixty-four hexagrams that include all its possible combinations as classified in the *I-Ching*, the ancient cosmological and divinatory commentary. The totality of the combinations of six lines representing *yin* and *yang* provides a universal binary pattern of the universe. Each of the combinations of six lines manifests a particular cosmic quality that may be associated with divination or a cosmological application. In the *I-Ching*, *yin* is represented by a broken line and *yang* by a full line. The broken line suggests receptive and empty discontinuity, while the full line indicates active and full continuity. The sixty-four diagrams illustrate the extent to which the cosmos is conceived as being interwoven with these two principles. Thus, dualism could not be more foreign to Chinese metaphysics and cosmology. To wit, sixty-two of the hexagrams present us with the various permutations that are associated with *yin* and *yang*. Even the two first hexagrams, which combine respectively six *yang* lines and six *yin* lines, cannot be considered independently of each other: *qián* is pure initiative and active change, *kūn* is acceptance, receptivity, and flow. It would be misleading, however, to consider that activity excludes receptivity or the reverse. This appears clearly in the commentary of *qián* where we read: "Heaven, in its motion (gives the idea of) strength. The superior man, in accordance with this, nerves himself to ceaseless activity," which clearly implies that the superior man is receptive to Heaven. Conversely, "*Kūn*, in its largeness, supports and contains all things. Its excellent capacity matches the unlimited power (of *qián*). Its comprehension is wide and its brightness great,"[2] which obviously involves a non-active activity of great strength on the part of this *yin* hexagram.

---

2. *The Sacred Books of China*, translated by James Legge (Oxford: Clarendon Press, 1882), 214.

The arrangements of trigrams, hexagrams, or other symbolic forms, including visual onto-cosmological schemas, tend to give preponderance to spatial symbolism. By contrast, the second type of representation is the circular *yin-yang* symbol, which, through the flowing structure of its combination of black and white, and the interconnection of *yin* and *yang* suggested by a white dot in the black surface and vice versa, provides a sort of synthesis of temporal (or cyclical) and spatial representations. The prototype of this celebrated graphic representation appears with the *Tiandi Ziran hetu*, "The River Diagram of the Spontaneity of Heaven and Earth," included in a Ming Dynasty work by Zhao Huiqian.[3] The flowing and spontaneous image makes it clear that the *yin-yang* symbol is not static, as indicated by the formula *yi yin yi yang zhi wei tao*, "once *yin* once *yang* makes the Tao."[4] This can be understood to mean that the Tao is seized, if one say so, in the very space where change, *yi*, takes place, and without which it cannot take place, since the lack of such a "spaceless space" would be incompatible with the very possibility of change. In the same spirit, it has been read as meaning that *yi* is *wu* in the sense of the hidden unity underlying the two.[5] Moreover, Chung-ying Cheng has asserted that the term *zhi wei*, by contrast with *wei zhi* that refers to a more conventional definition, implies an insight into the nature of things. The *Tao* is, therefore, to be ontologically identified, through spiritual intuition, with the very alternation of *yin* and *yang*. This does not mean that the *Tao* is reducible to *yin* and *yang* but is perceived as the principle that makes this very alternation possible.

The graphic symbol also suggests the dynamic aspect of correlation, with its curved lines that evoke rotation. Moreover, as already indicated, the *hetu* synthetizes the interpenetration of the two principles through the presence of a white dot in the black surface, and vice versa. This makes unity manifest in difference, and difference manifest in unity, thereby accounting for the very possibility of transformation. Schuon focuses on this circular representation of *yin* and *yang* and does not consider the more static combinations of trigrams, the traditional hexagrams, or the sequential verbal expression *yi yin yi yang*. While the latter can be seen

---

3. Wang, *Yinyang*, 221.

4. Chung-ying Cheng, "Dao (Tao): The Way," in *Encyclopedia of Chinese Philosophy*, edited by Antonio S. Cua (New York: Routledge, 2003), 203.

5. Chung-ying Cheng, "The Yi-Jing and Yin-Yang Way of Thinking," in *History of Chinese Philosophy*, edited by Bo Mou (New York: Routledge, 2009), 72.

as situated in time—through an alternating sequence—and the former in space, through diagrammatic arrangements, the circular *hetu* provides a synthesis of both time and space, since it captures synthetically the universal interplay of *yin* and *yang* while suggesting their analytic and temporal alternations.

Any reader of Schuon will have not failed to notice his frequent references to the symbolism of the *yin-yang*. These are consistently very brief and allusive, which, in a way, is indicative of the fact that they serve a different purpose to the elaborate metaphysical developments that form the basis of Schuon's perspective generally. Sometimes the *yin-yang* is only implicit, while deeply informing the very style of his exposition. This is evident in some of his key statements that suggest cardinal interplays such as "the substance of knowledge is the Knowledge of the Substance."[6] At any rate, the presence of the *yin-yang* in Schuon's work epitomizes a mode of symbolic presentation that is to be found in most traditional metaphysical teachings. It fosters a specific mode of expression, assimilation, and meditation that offers a more synthetic way than merely through concepts, and provides an arguably more direct and existential means of actualizing metaphysical principles. Schuon has related a meeting he had with a venerable African Sufi who drew before him on the ground the circumference of a circle from which various rays joined the center, explaining that God was like this center and the circle like existence, with religions appearing as the various paths leading from the circumference to the center.[7] This was a simple and effective summary of the whole perspective developed by Schuon in his works, one that presupposes both a dimension of continuity between the Divine and the cosmic, expressed by the rays, and one of discontinuity, manifested by the circle. Furthermore, as a painter and a poet, Schuon was keenly aware of the spiritual power of graphic symbols and aesthetic supports for contemplation. The images of the concentric circles, the radii, and the spiral in Schuon's books could be taken as one of the most direct expressions of the metaphysical principles

---

6. Frithjof Schuon, *Logic and Transcendence* (Bloomington, IN: World Wisdom, 2009), 236.

7. "It was during my adolescent years. I went . . . to the Basle zoological garden where a Senegalese village was making a visit; they had brought their marabout with them—a venerable old man with a penetrating gaze, deep-black skin and short white beard—and I spoke to him. At the end of our conversation he bent down, drew a circle with radii in the sand, and said: 'God is in the center, all ways lead to Him.'"

that lie at the foundations of his work. He makes use of these symbolic representations not only to illustrate some key concepts of metaphysics, such as his doctrine of ontological radiation and reverberation, but also to buttress some of his considerations on the Christian Trinity. In fact, the specific symbolism of the spiral reveals, as we discuss later in this chapter, a profound affinity with the *yin-yang*, as it provides a functional equivalent to the highest applications of the Chinese symbol. At any rate, our argument is that Schuon's use of *yin-yang* is actualized at both the metaphysical and the cosmological levels, the latter including implications for the spiritual and ethical life. It is in this onto-cosmological context that the three concepts of immanent generation, harmonious interdependence, and existential transformation—which are all intimately connected to the traditional *yin-yang* and may be deemed central components of Chinese thought in general—inform Schuon's outlook in various ways. In this respect, his use of *yin-yang* may be approached as declining the various cases of non-duality, while providing a universal symbolic key for facilitating metaphysical intuition.

In contrast to monotheistic creationism, epitomized by the fundamental gap implied by the *ex nihilo*, the Taoist view of manifestation—and Chinese worldviews in general—appears to be much more inclined to emphasize presence and continuity when evoking the ways in which the Tao gives rise to the so-called "ten thousand things." It would be misleading, however, to understand this immanent tendency along pantheistic lines. This is because the Tao precedes the myriad of things as testified by Laozi and Zhuangzi's accounts of manifestation, and also because the Tao always remains independent, so to speak, of its manifestations in the cosmic order. It is indeed this transcendent freedom that gives it the power to act as the principle of an ever-fresh energy of creation within the cosmos. Thus, immanent generation simply means that the Principle is both transcendentally free and actively involved—albeit not in the usual sense of activity—in the onto-cosmological unfolding of things. This is powerfully expressed by one of Zhuangzi's evocations of the Tao: "Dark and hidden, [the Way] seems not to exist and yet it is there; lush and unbounded, it possesses no form but only spirit; the ten thousand things are shepherded by it, though they do not understand it—this is what is called the Source, the Root."[8] Although the presence of the Root may not

---

8. *The Complete Works of Zhuangzi*, translated by Burton Watson (New York: Columbia University Press, 2013), 178.

be evident outwardly, there is actually no real discontinuity between the Principle and its manifestation, and the latter is entirely shepherded by its hidden presence. As we will see, it is on this point that the *yin-yang* symbol reveals its deepest implications inasmuch as it mediates the passage from Unity to multiplicity. It lies at the heart of what Schuon refers to as the "relatively absolute." Immanent generation presupposes a domain of the relatively absolute, the transcendent source of relativity that, in turn, implies a kind of absoluteness of the relative order that is like the inverted reflection of the former, inverted in the sense that it is relative, but also reflective inasmuch as it mirrors the qualities of the Absolute.

As for interdependence and harmony, they refer respectively to unity in duality and duality in unity: the first makes duality one by virtue of an inherent ontological reciprocity, while the second expresses the equilibrium that characterizes the unfolding of the possibilities contained within Unity. Moreover, the first concept emphasizes necessity, whereas the second is more attuned to freedom. In the view of the universe that is consonant with the *yin-yang* dyad, interdependence means that duality is rooted in unity and cannot be severed from it. No term of any duality can remain on its own inasmuch as it is intrinsically relative to the other: this is the negative necessity of relativity, as it were, that bears witness to the positive necessity of the Tao. As for harmony, this implies freedom, inasmuch as these two terms function together without negating their respective identity, nor erasing their differences. This "dual unity" is none other than the reflection of the oneness of the Tao on the level of the ten thousand things. While the interdependence of manifested reality provides the model for an esoteric insight into the complexities and nuances inherent to relative existence, this sense of harmony reveals—in the form of beauty and equilibrium between different ontological and cosmic tendencies—the perfection of the Absolute on the level of relativity. These are two themes that are central to Schuon's onto-cosmology. The first informs, as we will see, the notions of aspects and points of view while the second relates to what Schuon likes to call the "metaphysical transparency of phenomena," whereby Unity shines through the diversity of symbolic forms.

Finally, transformation is inherent in a world that is both steeped in the Unity of the Tao and multiple in its manifestations. Transformation introduces the power of the One in the many by providing metaphysical evidence that the many cannot be considered as absolutely fixed monads, and that the flux of the Tao is constantly transmuting them by virtue of its immanence. Transformation does not mean the negation of essences but the negation of any absolutization of relative distinctions. In a sense, Asian non-dualistic teachings tend to relativize, or keep implicit, the reality of essences in the Platonic sense of the term. This holds true inasmuch as they emphasize the essential principle of continuity and unity between distinct realities rather than the ontological roots of their distinctions. Indeed, one would hardly find explicit equivalents of the Platonic Forms in East Asian metaphysics.[9] Toshihiko Izutsu has highlighted, in this connection, Zhuangzi's symbolic reference to "hollows" through which blows the existentiating "Wind" of the Tao, which could be considered a functional metaphysical equivalent of Ibn 'Arabī's "permanent entities"—the latter being analogous, but not identical, to the Platonic Forms. Izutsu has asserted, however, that Zhuangzi's emphasis is definitely anti-essentialist when considered from the point of view of spiritual awakening.[10] His view is that "the main difference between the two lies in the fact that in [Zhuangzi] the relation between Essence and Existence is merely symbolically suggested, whereas Ibn 'Arabī consciously takes up the problem as an ontological theme."[11] The Taoist perspective emphasizes mutability as a means of fostering a sense of the Unity of the cosmos as well as the availability of spiritual transmutation. It also affirms that only the Tao is fully and unconditionally what it is. Schuon refers to this kind of metaphysical transformation when mentioning the way in which some possibilities cannot but flow from relative impossibilities.[12] In other words, any distinction between two realities, and any exclusion resulting from it, opens the way to another manifestation that makes it possible for one to be the other, in the sense that grey is, as it were, the

---

9. This is not true, or less so, in non-dualistic forms of mysticism situated within religious monotheisms—intrinsically, because the a priori dualistic dimension of religion fosters distinctions and, extrinsically, insofar as monotheistic theology has been platonized.

10. "The 'things' ordinarily look as if they were distinct from each other in terms of 'essences,' simply because ordinary men are not 'awake'. If they were, they would 'chaotify' the things and see them in their original 'undifferentiation.'" Toshihiko Izutsu, *Sufism and Taoism: A Comparative Study of Key Philosophical Concepts* (Berkeley: University of California Press, 1983), 484.

11. Izutsu, *Sufism and Taoism*, 485.

12. "Thus, the impossibility of a round square entails the possibility of a quadrilateral with convex sides; the impossibility that black be white entails the possibility of grey; only the impossibility of All-Possibility is absolutely impossible." Schuon, *The Eye of the Heart*, nn. 2, 112.

possibility arising out of the impossibility of white being black. Although Schuon is far from being Taoist in his presentation of these matters, it can be asserted that the Taoist relative negation of essences, which is also in a sense parallel to the Buddhist rejection of substances, must be understood within the context of an emphasis on immanence. The immanent Unity of the Tao allows one thing to become another, so to speak, on the plane of cosmic existence. This is because it is already another in the sense that "in conformity with the principle of *yin-yang*—each of the two poles in its way contains the other."[13]

Thus, cosmically and humanly, Schuon's interpretation of *yin-yang* pertains to the principle of compensation whereby a given quality or reality cannot be totally absent from its opposite or complement. This recognition, which is symbolically horizontal, flows from the impossibility of the relative becoming absolute, hence the relativity—but not the unreality—of all distinctions within the cosmic realm. We see this, for example, in what Schuon calls "the theory of reciprocal compensation," whereby there is no lack or absence that is not compensated, on some level, by a manifestation of fullness or presence.[14] Moreover, metaphysically speaking, *yin-yang* crystallizes the principle of continuity in discontinuity which implies that the higher must be found within the lower, and vice versa. This vantage point relates to the paradoxical possibility, indeed necessity, of the Absolute becoming relative in its own absolute way. This paradox lies in the aforementioned notion of the relatively absolute and stems from absoluteness itself, since the latter excludes any metaphysical otherness lest the latter be viewed as a second absolute. It must embrace, therefore, and include within its own fold, its apparent negation, both as Being and as Existence. The same consideration of ontological reciprocity cannot but allow for a mode of presence of the Absolute in the relative order, without which the relative would be nothing. This is, as we shall see, the central application of *yin-yang* in Schuon's opus, which obviously lends to this Far Eastern symbol an inflexion of meaning that is both particular in its conceptual correspondences—when considered in relation

---

13. Schuon, *The Eye of the Heart*, 21.

14. "This appearance of inversion provides an illustration of the Taoist doctrine of Yin-Yang, which in short is the theory of reciprocal compensation; without this compensation, the dualities would be absolute and irreducible, which is an impossibility since Reality is one." Schuon, *Esoterism as Principle and as Way* (Pates Manor, Bedfont, Middlesex: Perennial Books, 1981), nn. 39, 51.

to its Chinese antecedents—and universal in its potential scope, when envisaged in terms of its metaphysical implications. As already noted, the binary of *yin-yang* does not merely amount to a static complementarity, nor does it refer to a contained totality (even though the integral range of cosmic and ontological reality falls under its polar dynamics). The starting point of Chinese meditation is change, *yi*, it being understood a priori as implying duality, the very principle of difference that is the precondition for transformation. In Chinese thought, *yin-yang* is a productive binary, as indicated by its association—in the *Tao Te Ching*, for instance—with the ideogram *sheng* ("to live," "to thrive," "to manifest," "to generate"), which is the law governing the Tao's self-transformation. The generative aspect of *yin-yang* can be effective on different levels of reality. Robin Wang notes that *yin-yang* can be considered "above forms" (*xingershang*) and "below forms" (*xingerxia*); that is, in the metaphysics of origination and in the cosmology of natural composition. From the former point of view, "the *qi* of *yinyang* is the generative force underlying all existence and serves an indispensable role in making an ontological link between a unitary source and the diversity of the myriad things, *wanwu* (literally, the 'ten thousands of things')."[15] It is quite clear, once again, that this *yin-yang* nexus corresponds functionally to Schuon's dyad of the "relatively Absolute" and the "reflection of the Absolute in the relative." As for the cosmogonic function assigned to *yin-yang*, it results from the fact that the endless reciprocal transformation, opposition, and harmonization between the two principles weave the very texture of cosmic existence. On the one hand, the dynamic polarity of *yin* and *yang* is in itself productive of creative energy; on the other, the free flow of energy emanating from the Tao, *qi*, calls for a balance between the two poles so that *qi* is not obstructed.[16] In a way that echoes the meaning of these productive dynamics, Schuon, for his part, refers to duality as to a kind of "creative explosion,"[17] while also repeatedly calling attention to the law of universal equilibrium that is the necessary context for any spiritual elevation and transcendence.

---

15. Wang, *Yinyang*, 19.

16. Interestingly, an early Chinese text, the *Yantie lun*, presents China as the cosmic epitome of this harmonization and balance, as the Empire of the Middle is said to be set in between heaven and earth and at the limit between *yin* and *yang*. "Chinese culture arises from the attempt to stay centered between Heaven and earth and to maintain the appropriate relations between *yin* and *yang*." Wang, *Yinyang*, 2.

17. Schuon, *The Eye of the Heart*, 25.

Hence, while the *yin-yang* must be understood cosmologically both as a principle of unity and diversity, sameness and difference, it also ought to be grasped metaphysically as an allusion to the immanent transcendence of the Tao that is at work throughout reality and translates, cosmically, into *qi*. In other words, the Tao cannot be tapped into except through the alternations and the changes that reveal its reality as a necessary metaphysical background. This means that Chinese thought sees *yin-yang* not only as a cosmic binary of interconnection but also as a metaphysical principle of generation. Hence, *yin-yang* is intrinsically metaphysical while being *prima facie* cosmological: its binary cosmology presupposes a non-dualistic metaphysics.

As we have suggested, the *yin-yang* dyad functions as an "alchemical" symbol of the interconnection and mobility between levels of reality. Even though reality includes degrees—without which the very notion of manifestation would be unintelligible—these are in no way totally discrete, which would amount to accepting the idea of absolute chasms, as it were, within the stuff of reality. Taoism maintains both a hierarchical understanding of the degrees of being—beginning with the Tao and ending with the ten thousand things—and a vision of the interconnectedness of cosmic principles as exemplified by the symbols of *yin* and *yang*. The organic status of *yin-yang* in the production of the ten thousand things appears in full light in Laozi's *Tao Te Ching*. There is, in fact, only one explicit reference to the *yin-yang* symbol in Laozi's classic (in chapter 42). This is one of the most directly metaphysical passages of the book, since it spells out the process of manifestation from the Tao to the world of multiplicity. Thus, the One is seen to be "manifested" (*sheng*) by the Tao, the Two by the One, the Three by the Two, and the ten thousand things by the Three. Moreover, Legge's translation of this passage is particularly interesting in that, following the genesis of the symbol, it associates *yin* with obscurity and *yang* with brightness in the context of the generation of things, indicating that it entails a passage from the obscurity of *yin* to the brightness of *yang*: "The Tao produced One; One produced Two; Two produced Three; Three produced All things. All things leave behind them the Obscurity (out of which they have come), and go forward to embrace the Brightness (into which they have emerged), while they are harmonised by the Breath of Vacancy."[18] The passage from darkness to brightness can

---

18. James Legge, *The Texts of Taoism, Part I* (New York: Dover, 1962), 85.

be taken either vertically, as implying a move from non-manifestation into manifestation, or horizontally, as an equilibration between the back and forth movement of *yin-yang*. Lin Yutang proposes a parallel translation while rendering the passage in a more concrete and literal manner: "The created universe carries the *yin* at its back and the *yang* in front."[19] The original reference to the dark and bright sides of the mountain is echoed by the reference to the back and the front, while suggesting two ontological modes, one symbolized by the "back" that connects to the origin, or returns to it, and the other by the "front," which points to the emergence of things in their full manifestation. The text confirms that the two poles are necessarily interconnected, with an expansion of one pole entailing a contraction of the other, or even their transformation into one another. At any rate, this insight is intrinsically rooted in the intuition of the Median Void, or Legge's "Breath of Vacancy," which, as we shall see later, is the element of emptiness that keeps the two poles both in motion and at rest. From another point of view, this third reality—that is both median and situated on a different ontological level than the two poles themselves—opens a space that keeps the duality from becoming an opposition. The harmonization of the Two involves and characterizes a third element, which is either their product or the space of their mutual encounter. In the first case, the Three is conceived as proceeding from the Two, and initiating the ontological chain of the "myriad things," whereas, in the second case, it appears to be the One itself from which the "non-dualistic duality" of *yin-yang* arises. There is, at any rate, an obvious correspondence between the One and the Three, both being in a position of fulfillment *vis-à-vis* the Two, either as its source or as its relational unfolding. Schuon expresses this paradox in his own way by stating that "duality is as if suspended between two Unities, one initial and principial and the other terminal and manifested."[20] This "suspension" of duality between two unities can be read either alchemically, from bottom up, as a way of return to the Tao, or, metaphysically, as an account of the downward procession of the creative energy of the Tao in and through *yin-yang*.[21]

Commentators on Laozi's forty-second chapter have been led to reflect further on the possibilities it suggests for a metaphysics of determination

---

19. Lin Yutang, *The Wisdom of Laotse* (New York: The Modern Library, 1948), 214.
20. Schuon, *The Eye of the Heart*, 24.
21. See the distinction between the *Taijitu* of Zhou Dunyi and the *Wujitu* of Chen Tuan in Wang, *Yinyang*, 218–19.

and indetermination. Thus, while the One is traditionally identified as *Taiji*, the Affirmative Ultimate, *Wuji* is the Negative Ultimate, or Non-Being, which is none other than the transcendent Tao. *Wuji* lies beyond the realm of *yin-yang*—where there is "no heaven nor earth: no *yin* nor *yang*"[22]—while *Taiji* initiates this realm considered as "the Grand Antecedence."[23] Thus, *Taiji* ("great pole"), the ontological Principle that lies at the foundation of the ten thousand things, emerges from *Wuji* (literally "no pole"). It is significant that the symbol of the pole expresses the prime affirmation of Unity and, thereby, its ontological "orientation"; it also comprises the link between heaven and earth and thus the very initiation of polarity. While "no pole" denotes an absence of limitations and a supra-relational infinity, "great pole" suggests ontological polarity, direction, and production. This is brought home by De Bary and Bloom's translation of *Taiji* as "Supreme Polarity" and *Wuji* as "Non-Polar." Furthermore, in a way that appears to join *Wu* and *Tai* as the two faces of the same Reality—and therefore perhaps the implicit metaphysical anticipation of *yin-yang*—we encounter, in the work of the neo-Confucian philosopher Zhou Dunyi (1017–1073), a marveling awe before the paradoxical mysteries of a Non-Polar Pole, a motion in stillness, and a stillness in motion: "Non-Polar (*wuji*) and yet Supreme Polarity (*taiji*)! The Supreme Polarity in activity generates *yang*; yet at the limit of activity it is still. In stillness it generates *yin*; yet at the limit of stillness it is also active. Activity and stillness alternate; each is the basis of the other."[24] Needless to say, this passage also evokes the visual representation of the *yin-yang* that crystallizes the interpenetration of polar opposites and the constant circular motion of their reciprocal transformation.

Connected to the binary of stillness and motion, Zhuangzi states that "perfect *yin* is stern and frigid; perfect *yang* is bright and glittering"[25] or "*yin* in its highest form is freezing, *yang* in its highest form is boiling."[26]

---

22. According to the Tang Dynasty, *Taishang laojun kaitian jing* (*'Scripture of How the Highest Venerable Lord Opens the Cosmos'*)." Cf. Livia Kohn, *The Taoist Experience* (Albany: State University of New York Press, 1993), 35.

23. Kohn, *The Taoist Experience*, 36.

24. *Sources of East Asian Tradition, Volume 1*, edited by Wm. Theodore de Bary (New York: Columbia University Press, 2008), 340.

25. Watson, *Zhuangzi*, 169.

26. Philip Ball, *The Water Kingdom: A Secret History of China* (Chicago: University of Chicago Press, 2016), 75.

Cold and freezing appear to convey the sense of a crystallization that results from a retraction, under the "fixing" influence of non-manifestation—or, symbolically, a lack of exposure to the sun—while boiling evokes a hyper-activation of the productive energy of heat, a "bubbling over" akin to an ontological multiplication. When not checked and balanced by each other, both freezing and boiling lead to death inasmuch as they involve an excessive and disintegrating excess of either *yin* or *yang*. Zhuangzi refers to the cold of *yin* as heavenly, and the heat of *yang* as earthy: "The chilliness comes from heaven while the warmness from the earth."[27] This appears to contradict other passages from Taoist texts in which earth lies on the side of *yin*, as a symbol of cosmic receptivity, and heaven on the side of *yang*, as a marker of determinative activity. The *Taishang laojun kaitian jing*, from the Tang dynasty, explains for instance that in the wake of the end of the Chaos (*huntun*) that sees the establishment of the cosmic order of the Nine Palaces, heaven has been henceforth associated with the pure energy of heaven, and *yin* with the "turbid energy" of earth. In this view of things, *yang* rises up to heaven while *yin* sinks down to earth. At any rate, *yang* is responsible for formation and structuration, whether it is a matter of the form of planets, natural shapes, or human physiology.[28] As for the turbidity of *yin*, it is obscure and cloudy, which may indicate the relative absence of delineation, a kind of receptive formlessness akin to darkness as indistinction. As a result of a difference in vantage point, Zhuangzi's outlook contrasts with Schuon's assessment that "there is in masculinity a danger of contraction and hardening, and in femininity a tendency to dissolving and indefinite exteriorization,"[29] the latter being implicitly connected to *yin* and the former to *yang*. The dissolution of *yin* is considered here from the point of view of its receptivity, which lacks form and cannot hold together in the absence of its complement, whereas the hardening of *yang* is considered from the perspective of its structuring activity, which can become overly defined and rigid to the point of hardness and death. Zhuangzi's symbolic perspective may be referring to a complementary view that is more vertical than Schuon's horizontal consideration of the aforementioned interplay of feminine and masculine,

---

27. Robin Wang, in *Riding the Wind with Liezi: New Perspectives on the Daoist Classic* edited by Ronnie Littlejohn and Jeffrey Dippmann (Albany: State University of New York Press, 2011), 211–12.

28. Kohn, *The Taoist Experience*, 39.

29. Schuon, *To Have a Center* (Bloomington, IN: World Wisdom, 2015), 67.

since it proceeds top-down from heaven to earth. It appears to suggest a link between the "chilliness" of heaven and the principle of non-manifestation, or retraction—the "back"—whereas the ebullient heat of *yang* refers to earth as active manifestation—the "front." Be that as it may, the very possibility of reversing this symbolism is, in itself, an illustration of the interconnectedness of *yin* and *yang*, and the need to remain keenly aware of the possibility of swift reversals in polarity.

Such a consideration leads to a discussion of the question of hierarchy with regard to *yin* and *yang*. When contemplating the matter in depth, one cannot but come to the conclusion that such a hierarchy is excluded because each of the terms, in whatever ontological or cosmic sector they may manifest, is intrinsically connected to the other. This also means, however, that there is necessarily a relative superiority of one or the other of these principles, as regards a given level of being in a particular cosmic sector, but never in any absolute manner.[30] Thus, the *Daoti lun*—a seventh-century commentary of the *Tao Te Ching*—teaches that once *yin* and *yang* have harmonized and thereby generated creative transformations, "*yang* comes to predominate, just as a ruler and minister jointly govern the world."[31] What is particularly striking about this passage of the *Daoti lun* is that it explicitly situates the predominance of *yang* within the strict outcomes of generative transformation. This implies that before the "establishment . . . of manifold transformations," there was no preeminence of the *yang*. In other words, *yang* is determinative in the domain of formal development but not upstream of this development, so to speak.

It follows that, when considering *yin* and *yang* as a dual principle that paradoxically undoes dualism constantly, the question of equality and superiority or hierarchy cannot possibly be approached in any exclusionary manner. Subordinating order must manifest in equality itself, and vice versa. This means that, although *yin* and *yang* are equally dependent on each other in cosmic existence, there is—necessarily—a "reciprocal superiority" of each over the other, depending on the vantage point that is envisaged. This is particularly true as we ascend the degrees of existence, since the higher the level the less exclusive and one-sided are the consequent relationships able to be. This is on account of a greater proximity to the "Breath of Vacancy" that dissolves distinctions, as it

---

30. Sachiko Murata has convincingly developed this point in *The Tao of Islam* (Albany: State University of New York Press, 1992).
31. Kohn, *The Taoist Experience*, 22.

were. Thus, for instance, Schuon remarks that a "reciprocal superiority" between the masculine and the feminine, implicitly connected to *yang* and *yin*, is most recognizable in the spiritual domain: "In the [spiritual] relationship there is, highly paradoxically, reciprocal superiority: in love, as we have said earlier, the woman assumes in regard to her husband a divine function, as does the man in regard to the woman."[32] Whereas it can be inferred that the distinction between the masculine and the feminine is quasi-absolute in the physical order, the psychic and spiritual dimensions manifest gradually higher degrees of compensatory interplays. Hence the spiritual principle that the feminine is "divine" in regard to the masculine and conversely, as testified by Dante's exclamation at the sight of Beatrice: "*Ecce deus fortior me.*"[33] This type of reciprocal relationship is the closest approximation of an equality that is never strictly attained since it is excluded in the world of difference.

While superiority and predominance cannot but manifest in some ways on the level of equality—or a reciprocal superiority that amounts to the latter—it is also true that a kind of equality cannot but be present in ontological hierarchies, and this is no doubt the most important conclusion to draw from Schuon's metaphysics of *yin-yang*. Interestingly, Schuon applies this paradoxical principle in the context of a discussion of "Dharmakara's Vow," which is the foundational story of Pure Land Buddhism. The *bodhisattva* Dharmakara is said to have vowed not to enter *Nirvāna* unless those who invoke his Name be saved and reborn in the Pure Land. Schuon highlights the fact that this situation presents *prima facie* a metaphysical problem in that it appears to give a human being power to constrain the Nirvānic Reality, whereas in actuality "it is metaphysically obvious that there is no common measure between man and the Absolute."[34] The application of the *yin-yang* symbol illustrates

---

32. Schuon, *Esoterism as Principle and as Way*, 136.

33. "Nine times, the heaven of the light had returned to where it was at my birth, almost to the very same point of its orbit, when the glorious lady of my mind first appeared before my eyes—she whom many called Beatrice without even knowing that was her name. . . . At that time, truly, I say, the vital spirit, which dwells in the innermost chamber of the heart, started to tremble so powerfully that its disturbance reached all the way to the slightest of my pulses. And trembling it spoke these words: '*Ecce deus fortior me, qui veniens dominabitur michi.*'" Dante Alighieri, *Vita Nuova*, translated by Andrew Frisardi (Evanston, IL: Northwestern University Press, 2012), 3.

34. Schuon, *Logic and Transcendence* (Bloomington, IN: World Wisdom, 2009), 219.

the compensatory relationship between subordinating and subordinated orders of reality: "Applying this symbol here we may say that *Nirvāna* comprises a sector of relativity that is open to the cosmos whereas the Bodhisattva possesses an element of absoluteness that integrates him in a certain respect in the absolute and metacosmic nature of *Nirvāna*."[35] While "*Nirvāna* comprises a sector of relativity," the *bodhisattva* embodies the presence of Nirvānic reality in *samsāra*. Indeed, the "relatively absolute" dimension of *Nirvāna*, which is—in the "dynamic" context of salvation—its receptive aspect (which Schuon contemplates as *yin*), can be characterized as Compassion. As for the "element of absoluteness that integrates" the *Bodhisattva* in the Absolute, the *yang* principle, it can be considered to be Grace, that is, the essential content of Nirvānic Reality. In other words, Compassion is the "extrinsic *Nirvāna*" whereas saving Grace is the "intrinsic Bodhisattva," if one may put it this way. This amounts to saying that the Bodhisattva is equal—and, in a way, even superior—to *Nirvāna* from the point of view of his integration in the latter, and his active function vis-à-vis its receptive dimension. Here, we can see how the *yin-yang* functions in a manner that not only relates the higher and lower degrees of being—illustrating a necessary relationship and continuity between them—but also equalizes them by virtue of there being different dimensions of the same Reality. While totally equal principles simply cancel each other out, exclusively unequal ones simply cannot interact.

As previously mentioned, the receptive aspect of Nirvānic Reality and the Bodhisattva corresponding to the second and third moments could therefore be summarized as *yang yin yang yin*, with the first *yin* corresponding to the receptive dimension of *Nirvāna* and the second *yang* to the Bodhisattva. However, since the *yin-yang* cannot be fixed in a single pattern of sequence and meaning, an alternative sequence of the type *yin yang yin yang* suggests itself. In Schuon's parlance, it could be said that the Nirvānic Reality is *yang* as Absolute and *yin* as Infinite. In the alternative *yin-yang*, it is the latter dimension that is the highest prototype of receptivity and "darkness" in the sense of an all-encompassing mystery of limitless depth. As for samsāric existence, it can be considered as *yang* inasmuch as it determines the very conditions of life as suffering in terms of "active" craving. The latter is therefore demiurgic and productive, albeit in an illusory way. As for the Buddha, being essentially identified with

---

35. Schuon, *Treasures of Buddhism* (Bloomington, IN: World Wisdom, 1993), 158.

Nirvāna and having passed on to the Other Shore, he is like the *yang* or active aspect of *Nirvāna* that draws existence to it through the *Dharma*. Within samsāric existence itself, it is the *Sangha* that embodies the *yin* element by being drawn in by the Buddha-Dharma, and thereby constituting—within existence—the only sector of receptivity to emptiness as active or determinative pole. While the Bodhisattva constrains *Nirvāna*, if one may use such an ill-sounding term, the Buddha constrains *samsāra*, or rather that region of *samsāra* that takes refuge in Him. Irrespective of their differences, these two ways of understanding the *yin-yang* at play in the relationship between *Nirvāna* and *samsāra* are dynamic, in the sense that they involve a passively active pole and its actively passive counterpart. Needless to say, this is not the only manner of envisaging the relationship between those terms; in fact, Schuon himself proposes another *yin-yang* application that is its complementary opposite, albeit in static mode: "if *Nirvāna* is the Real and *Samsāra* is illusion, the Buddha is the Real in the illusory and the *Bodhisattva* is the illusory in the Real; this suggests the symbolism of the *Yin-Yang*."[36] This presentation views the interconnection between *Nirvāna* and *samsāra* as a sequence of metaphysical interplays that largely replicates the great chain of Being, from the Absolute as such to the relative as such. While the Bodhisattva is the Real in its aspect of relationship to the illusory, the Buddha is the Real in the illusory, or as the "realized" summit of the latter.

As we have mentioned earlier, Schuon makes use of applications of the *yin-yang* that are akin to the principle of horizontal complementariness, in keeping with cosmological symbolism, as well as drawing analogies that involve a vertical relationship, within a metaphysical perspective. In both cases, it is a matter of suggesting the unity of being, and the absence of gaps, as it were, within creation. It is clear, however, that it is the vertical axis that is highlighted in his work, given the metaphysical emphasis of his perspective. Considering metaphysics as the science of eternal and unchanging principles, one may see it, at least from a Western point of view, as being immune to the type of modification through interrelatedness that is inherent to the *yin-yang Weltanschauung*. In her book, Robin Wang alludes to a contrast between a Western philosophical emphasis on "dualism, transcendence and eternal principles" and Chinese

---

36. Schuon, *Lights on the Ancient Worlds* (Bloomington, IN: World Wisdom, 2006), 124.

affinities with "interconnection, immanence and cyclical changes."[37] Wang acknowledges that this is too broad a contrast to do justice to the two intellectual universes, but it does indicate fundamental leanings within each of the two spiritual worlds. As a qualification to this contrast, however, it can be argued that it may result from a partial and reductive view of metaphysics that overly emphasizes the rational, or even rationalist, bent of its modalities. In a way, this fixation, with its dualistic bent, may have been the relatively recent outcome of a growing European alienation from the anthropo-cosmic and symbolic vision whose influence had remained prevalent in China until the Cultural Revolution. As a response to this reductive tendency, Schuon makes it plain that the eternity of transcendent principles does not exclude—quite the contrary—fluidity and transformation (both vertically and horizontally). In a way, his pervasive use of the *yin-yang* symbol bears witness to this observation. As illustrations of this point, one must note the importance of the two notions of Beyond-Being and Intellect in Schuon's work, and the way in which they give rise to a contemplation of different applications of *yin-yang*. These two notions define most characteristically, according to Schuon, the point of view of esoterism, as they lie at the foundation of the gnostic ability to contemplate the wealth of infinite transformations of the All-Possibility within the receptive and fluid "mobility" of the mirror of the Intellect. Many Taoist teachings resonate with such a sense of limitless Possibility, and a similar receptivity to an indefinite number of shifts in subjective perspective. By contrast, theological expressions—in the West—have largely been tied to a one-sided and anthropomorphic concept of the Supreme Being and, epistemologically, to an exclusive reliance on reason as the major instrument of dogmatic elaboration.

The most significant evidence of this appears in the fact that Schuon does not hesitate to apply the *yin-yang* to what he characterizes as the most central component of his metaphysical exposition. Indeed, Schuon explicitly asserts that the "profoundest meaning of the Far Eastern *yin-yang*" manifests in the reciprocal relationship between *Ātman* and *Māyā*, or *Ātman* as *Māyā* and *Māyā* as *Ātman*. The first refers to Being or the Personal Divinity, while the second corresponds to Existence, *Vaishvānara*, the Universal Man, or Cosmic Intelligence, *Virāj*, the "Shining forth" that

---

37. Wang, *Yinyang*, 5.

is the primordial division of unity into a prototypical Cosmic Being.[38] If the Absolute is to be represented by the black half of the circle, and the relative by the white half, then the white dot in the black surface is none other than the relatively Absolute or the Personal God; in other words, that degree of the Divine which is relative to the world of creation, with the black dot in the white half being the uncreated dimension of the relative, or the relative inasmuch as it is "uncreated." This means that the Absolute and the relative must somehow participate in each other, without that negating the radical distinction between them. Such is the crucial significance of the notion of the relatively Absolute on the one hand and that of the "relative as Absolute"[39] on the other. This relationship is fundamentally vertical, inasmuch as it ranges from the absolutely Absolute—*Ātman*—to the relative as relative—*Māyā*—inasmuch as it is not *Ātman*, through the metaphysical mediations, as it were, of the Personal Divinity; that is, the degree of the Ultimate that relates to the Manifestation as its Principle, or the Divine Root of *Māyā* in the Principle. Thus, the Divine has to become relative in order to existentiate relativity and relate to it, if one may say so, hence the level of Divine Being—Creator, Revealer, and Judge—as distinct from that of the Divine in and of itself or the Essence as Beyond-Being. Moreover, when Schuon writes, in an elliptical and paradoxical manner, that "God has to 'create Himself' *in divinis*," one may infer from it that Manifestation has to be prefigured in the Principle so that the Manifestation may be projected by the Principle into existence, which means that Existence must be Divine, otherwise it simply could not be. Existence is an "uncreated creation" if one may resort to a dissonant expression. By contrast, to say that the Absolute is in no way relative—thereby equating de facto the Creator with the Absolute as such—and that the relative is in no way absolute would amount to asserting that there cannot be any relationship between God and creation, and to claiming that the world is pure nothingness.

---

38. "In other terms: there is *Ātmā* and there is *Māyā*; but there is also *Ātmā* as *Māyā*, and this is the personal Divinity, manifesting and acting; and conversely, there is also *Māyā* as *Ātmā*, and this is the total Universe under its aspect of reality both one and polyvalent reality. In this case, the world will be the Divine aspect of 'Universal Man' (*Vaishvānara*) or, in Sufism, the aspect 'the Outward' (*Zāhir*); this moreover is the profoundest meaning of the Far Eastern *Yin-Yang*." Schuon, *Form and Substance in the Religions* (Bloomington, IN: World Wisdom, 2002), 208.

39. The first expression is consistently used by Schuon throughout his work, and the second refers to aspects or degrees of the relative realm that "participate" in the Absolute, in other words, that are reflections of the latter within the former.

Now, it must be noted that, in the passage that we have just quoted, Schuon does not explicitly provide a one-to-one correspondence between the various degrees of Reality that he highlights and the *yin-yang* elements. Given the traditional Hindu association between *Māyā* and the "feminine" dimension of Reality, one can infer that *Ātman* and *Māyā* would correspond to *yang* and *yin*, respectively. According to such an interpretation, the personal Divinity would be *yin* in *yang* and the Universal Man *yang* in *yin*. In other words, the personal God would be contemplated as receptive vis-à-vis the Essence and also, in a different way, with regard to Universal Man as illustrated, among other possible modes, by the relationship between the Bodhisattva and the receptive dimension of Nirvānic Reality that we have discussed above.

It lies in the very texture of *yin-yang*, however, that it precludes any exclusionary application, as it were, which means that another correspondence can, and must, be propounded. In this alternative consideration, *Ātman* should be considered as the All-Possibility or the Infinite—therefore as *yin*—while *Māyā* would be *yang* from the point of view of its formal coagulation and segmented "evaporation." Such a symbolic meditation would lead one to conceive of Being, or the personal God, as *yang* and Universal Man as *yin*. In keeping with a view of Being as "first determination of the Principle,"[40] the latter is *yang* in relation to the dimension of *Māyā* that reflects the infinity of *Ātman*; that is, "Universal Man" as pure receptivity to the various theophanic manifestations, as exemplified in Sufism by Ibn 'Arabī's famous reference to the heart of the gnostic as "capable of every form."[41]

This interpretation of the *yin-yang* is in accordance with a number of Taoist insights. This is true, both with respect to Laozi's vision of the Ultimate as the "Great Female" or the "Spirit of the Valley," but also with regard to Laozi and Zhuangzi's vision of the Perfect Man as pure receptivity. In regard to the former, verse 6 of the *Tao Te Ching* is particularly instructive in its reference to the parallel concepts of *ku shen* and *hüan*

---

40. "The 'Personal God' or Being is simply the first determination from which flow all the secondary determinations which make up cosmic Existence." Schuon, *The Transcendent Unity of Religions* (Wheaton, IL: Theosophical Publishing House, 1984), 38.

41. "My heart has become capable of every form: it is a pasture for gazelles and a convent for Christian monks, and a temple for idols and the pilgrim's Ka'ba and the tables of the Tora and the book of the Koran." Muhyiddīn Ibn al-'Arabī, *The Tarjumān al-Ashwāq—A Collection of Mystical Odes*, edited and translated by Reynold A. Nicholson (London: Theosophical Publishing House, 1978), 67.

p'in, the "Spirit of the Valley" and the "Mysterious Feminine." Arthur Waley renders this verse thus: "The Valley Spirit never dies. . . . It is named the Mysterious Female . . . and the Doorway of the Mysterious Female is the base from which Heaven and Earth sprang."[42] This is probably the best example of a Taoist contemplation of the Ultimate as *yin*. In terms of the human and cosmic implications of this metaphysics of *yin*, Toshihiko Izutsu has emphasized how the Perfect Man of Taoism is characterized by "the virtue of Negativity," that is, the qualities encapsulated by the "symbols for 'flexibility,' 'softness,' 'being low,' 'being simple.' " This is also associated with the notion of "infancy" and the central principle of *wu wei* ("non-active action") whereby "the Perfect Man is in every respect a Perfect image of Heaven and Earth, i.e. the Way as it manifests itself as the world of Being."[43] Most significantly for our current focus, Laozi also mentions that the Perfect Man "knows the 'male,' yet keeps to the role of the 'female.' "[44] This is a very direct manner of emphasizing the *yin* dimension of spiritual perfection as pure receptivity, which is itself a reflection of the highest metaphysical *yin*.

In the domain of sexual symbolism, an extremely interesting development of the *yin-yang* appears in the relationship between the Divine Feminine and the Cosmic Masculine. Schuon develops one of the most paradoxical aspects of this relationship by making use of the Hindu terminology of *Purusha* and *Prakriti*. The first corresponds to the active essence, whereas the second refers to the receptive substance. In the ordinary ontological hierarchy, *Purusha* denotes the Divine and the celestial, while *Prakriti* means the cosmic and the terrestrial. There is a way, however, in which the Divine appears as *Prakriti* and the cosmos as *Purusha* by virtue of a metaphysical *yin-yang* of the most significant kind. Hence, the Divine takes on the nature of *Prakriti* when it is envisaged in its receptive aspect as "facing the cosmos." Any such relation implies by necessity an aspect of receptivity. Conversely, the cosmic may be considered as *Purusha* by virtue of its identification with the Divine. The latter, which

---

42. Lao Tzu, *Tao Te Ching*, translated by Arthur Waley (Ware, Hertfordshire: Wordsworth Editions, 1997), 6. D. C. Lau's translation runs parallel to Waley's: "The spirit of the valley never dies. This is called the mysterious female. The gateway of the mysterious female is called the root of heaven and earth." *Tao Te Ching*, translated by D. C. Lau (Hong Kong: Chinese University Press, 1989), 9.

43. Izutsu, *Sufism and Taoism*, 448.

44. Izutsu, *Sufism and Taoism*, 447.

Schuon relates to grace and *gnosis*, is like the black dot of the Divine in the white surface of the cosmos. This reciprocity allows one to understand the very possibility of spiritual deliverance by virtue of the mercy of the Divine Feminine: "The feminine Divinity, who loves the masculine God, also loves the reflected image of God in the cosmos and seeks to deliver this image by appropriating it to herself, hence absorbing it and rendering it divine." *Yin-yang* lies here at the very heart of the mystery of spiritual realization by divine grace or immanent wisdom.[45]

One of the most striking among Schuon's interpretations of the *yin-yang* is his application of the Chinese symbol to the Islamic *shahādah* or profession of faith. In his esoteric exegesis, the four words of the first half of the Muslim profession of faith are associated, respectively, with the four components of the Chinese graphic symbol. Although the analytic terms of Schuon's symbolic correspondence remain implicit in this passage, reflection on his writings allows us to delve further into the implications of his metaphysical allusion. Thus, considering the four words that form the *shahādah*, that is, *lā* (no), *ilāha* (divinity), *illā* (if not, or except), and *Allāh* (the Divinity), one infers that the first word of the *shahādah*, the negation *lā*—or the pure negation—refers to the black section of the *yin yang* symbol, whereas the last word, *Allāh*—the pure affirmation—relates to its white half. This binary cannot, however, be the last word in the metaphysical doctrine of Unity since it would be tantamount to a duality that is incompatible with the all-encompassing Unity of the Divine Principle. The second word, *ilāha*—which literally means "divinity"—represents, therefore, the white dot in the black surface, whereas the third word, *illā*—the analytically explicit meaning of which is "if not"—corresponds to the black dot in the white surface. The word divinity opens, as it were, on the Divine affirmation of the Name *Allāh*, in the sense that it represents— within the world of negation—a reflection of the affirmation. As for the word *illā*, it carries the negative *lā* (which it includes) within the domain of pure affirmation. The two words *ilāhun* and *illā*, under their appearance of unequivocalness, entail an ambiguity of meaning, since they can be taken in two different ways. The divinity must be taken to mean, within the negative context of the first statement, or *nafy*, the false deity or the idol that the word *lā* is negating; but it can also mean, esoterically this time, the object of worship that can be no other than God since, as Ibn

---

45. Schuon, *Logic and Transcendence*, 220.

'Arabī asserts, there is only the Real and all worship is thus, essentially, a worship of God which is why all are on "the straight path."[46] As for the word *illā*, it also carries a measure of ambivalence since, even though its immediate and literal meaning is affirmative—it initiates the *ithbāt* or affirmation of *Allāh*—it is, in fact, a compound of an affirmation and a negation, since it incorporates the negation *lā*. Thus, the four words of the formula refer, in Schuon's metaphysical idiom, to the respective terms of the *yin yang yin yang* sequence: *lā* symbolizes the manifestation, *ilāha* represents the Principle in the manifestation, *illā* relates to the manifestation in the Principle, and *Allāh* is the Principle.[47]

This is a very significant application of the *yin-yang* inasmuch as it provides one with an understanding of the Islamic *Weltanschauung* that does not freeze, so to speak, the various terms of the metaphysical statement. The ordinary (and exoteric) understanding of the first *shahādah* can be taken to set the terms of the enunciation in a binary pattern of "exclusive exclusion" that is both the direct strength and the indirect pitfall of the Muslim creed. Its intrinsic strength lies in establishing an unambiguous discernment between *ilāhun* and *Allāh*, asserting the transcendence of the latter and the vanity of the former. It is also a virtual pitfall, however, in that it may give rise—against the grain of its own tawḥīdic intent—to an unconscious dualistic petrification when the negative half of the formula, which is in principle utterly contingent upon the affirmative half that crowns it, becomes in practice a kind of symmetrical opposition to the latter. This happens when the spiritual intuition of the encompassing and inclusive Unity of the Real has been weakened to the point of giving rise to an exclusively "vengeful" assertion of the conceptual and legal dimension of its exclusive aspect. This fateful assertion of dualism from within the strictest doctrine of Unity echoes Schuon's several references, throughout his works, to the Taoist principle enunciated by Zhuangzi that "only error

---

46. "Anything that walks is on the straight path of its Lord. . . . Just as misguidance is an accident, so too is the Divine Wrath an accident. The final end is Mercy, which encompasses everything and outstrips [others]." Ibn al-'Arabī, *The Ringstones of Wisdom*, 105.

47. Let us note that Schuon also applies the *yin-yang* principle of compensation to the relationship between the two Islamic professions of faith: "Joined to the mystery of incommensurability (Islam: *Lā ilāha illā 'Llāh*) is adjoined the compensatory mystery of reciprocity (Islam: *Muhammadun Rasūlu 'Llāh*). . . . Once again, we rejoin here the Taoist symbolism of the *Yin-Yang*: the white part contains a black dot, and the black part has a white center." Schuon, *Form and Substance in the Religions*, 252.

is transmitted."[48] Against the possible, and in a sense unavoidable, inversion of the symbol of faith, the *yin-yang* symbol reveals a deeper sense of the Unity of the Real whereby each word of the *shahādah* takes up an onto-cosmological meaning in relationship to the three others. So we can see, through this example, how the *yin-yang* symbol may be used as a hermeneutical tool in order to cast light on some of the most important metaphysical statements of traditions that are historically unrelated to Chinese cosmology.

As we have suggested earlier, immanence, interconnectedness, and transformation are none other than three aspects of the Unity of Being. An exclusive emphasis on transcendence cannot but lead to some form of dualism since it tends to absolutize, at least subjectively, the separation between the transcending and the transcended, while the *yin-yang*, by contrast, presupposes an immanent and underlying Unity that makes it possible for the two to relate with each other in the way of a fluid complementarity. Schuon asserts that Two cannot but open onto Three lest it become an opposition.[49] This sense of immanence, that Taoism stresses through its focus on the creative pervasiveness of the Tao, is mostly the prerogative of esoterism since it presupposes an ability to see through the "transparency of phenomena" instead of considering them as distractions or "idols." The interconnected complementarity of beings and phenomena that this immanence makes possible—since there would not be, without it, a universal uniting bond inherent to the texture of the universe—expresses the presence of a totality of segmentation and unity in diversity. Schuon

---

48. "If a Taoist master could say that 'only error is transmitted,' it is because there is an inverse relationship between 'idea' and 'reality,' the 'thought' and the 'lived,' the 'conceived' and the 'realized'; . . . seen from above the symbol is darkness, but seen from below, it is light. This inversion, however, is not everything, for there is also direct analogy, essential identity, otherwise there would be no symbolism to provide a framework for the wisdom of the sages; to show the earthly or human side—an inevitable side—of tradition is by no means to destroy tradition." Schuon, *The Stations of Wisdom* (Bloomington, IN: World Wisdom, 1995), 20.

49. This appears, for instance, in the conjugal relationship: "In a permanent confrontation of two beings, there must be two equilibrium-producing openings, one towards Heaven and the other on earth itself: there must be an opening towards God, who is the third element above the two spouses, without which the duality would become opposition; and there must be an opening or a void—a ventilation, so to speak—on the immediate human plane, and this is abstinence." Schuon, *Esoterism as Principle and as Way*, 134.

is particularly sensitive to the numerous pairs and interplays that characterize the world of relativity—from the Divine to the human—such as appear in the Islamic notions of *jalāl* and *jamāl*, majesty and beauty, to the complementarity of geometry and music. He refers to the duality of necessity and grace, the inexorable rigor of the law and the liberating freedom of grace and compassion, or else to the human perfections of the feminine and the masculine. Such complementarities and interrelated polarities are always considered by Schuon in the spirit of the *yin-yang*, as conducive to reaching a harmonious equilibrium between distinct, and complementary, tendencies. Schuon conceives of wisdom as a middle ground between various ontological qualities, as an ability to situate one in relation to the other, or a balance that is not an end in itself but an approximation of "relative perfection," that is, a facilitating precondition for any serious spiritual foray into transcendence. Thus, Zhuangzi's assertion that "there are no enemies greater than the *yin* and *yang*—because nowhere between heaven and earth can you escape from them. It is not that the *yin* and *yang* deliberately do you evil—it is your own mind that makes them act so."[50] The wisdom of *yin yang* is a way to align oneself with their constant interplay.

Schuon's view of the *yin-yang* is principial and synthetic. As we have seen, it does not enter the specific connotations of the symbol within a Chinese context but it does extract from it a metaphysical and epistemological pattern that crystallizes an intuition of what is arguably the most important principle of non-dual metaphysics, Unity-in-diversity and diversity-in-Unity. As such, this perspective is primarily centered on the meaning of the reciprocal interpenetration of degrees of reality, and it is only secondarily relevant to other cosmological and alchemical phenomena, such as are developed in various streams of the Taoist tradition. Schuon's main thrust is the assertion that there is no metaphysical insularity, as it were, and that the infinity of the absolute Principle must translate, on all levels of reality, in interplays that reflect both the transcendence and, therefore, separativity of the Ultimate, as well as its immanent Unity and connectivity. Thus, it is clear that, for Schuon, the *yin-yang* reciprocity of the Absolute and the relative is the foundational principle on which all other compensatory and interdependent realities are based. This perspective is, a priori, quite distinct from the Chinese onto-cosmological view of

---

50. *Zhuangzi*, translated by Burton Watson, chapter 23, part 8B, https://terebess.hu/english/chuangtzu2.html.

change that comprises the core Taoist teachings and the various graphic symbols that illustrate and, in a sense, "enact" it. What Schuon suggests, however, through his universalization and metaphysical application of *yin-yang* is profoundly consonant with the spirit of the Chinese tradition, or traditions, since the latter do converge in not excluding *yin-yang* from any particular mapping out of Reality. *Yin-yang* is, by definition, "available" for any metaphysical or cosmological teaching that highlights the interplay of realities and forces, on any level and in any realm of reality to which it may be applied. Moreover, and no doubt more importantly, the primary metaphysical application of *yin-yang* articulated by Schuon, and modulated in contexts as different as the Islamic confession of faith and the Pure Land view of the Bodhisattva's function, is intrinsically connected to a non-dualistic metaphysics that is the quintessential core of his view of the *Sophia Perennis*. A thorough understanding of the non-dual essence of Reality provides a principle of universal Relativity that gives us a way to understand its innumerable modulations. Thus, Schuon is able to assert that his entire doctrine of *Māyā* is contained in the *yin-yang* symbol: "Herein lies the whole play of *Māyā* with its modes, degrees, cycles, diversity and alternations."[51] *Yin-yang* is, in a sense, none other than Relativity, which presupposes the Absolute, and implies the presence of the relative in the Absolute and, in a way, that of the Absolute in the relative. Understood in this light, the *yin-yang* symbol encapsulates what may be the most important contribution of Schuon to metaphysical and religious understanding—and its most central key—and that is the sense of the relative in the Absolute and that of the Absolute in the relative. The first consideration is connected to what could be called a "wisdom of aspects," while the second could be considered a "wisdom of perspectives." The Absolute is like an infinite crystal the innumerable sides of which are as many ontological aspects: these aspects are relative in relation to the Infinite Essence while being indissociable from it. The relationship between these aspects, particularly those which present a polarity, is akin to that of *yin* and *yang*, as their distinction points to the Essence that makes them both different and one. On the other hand, the domain of relativity is not homogeneous to the extent that it contains realities that are manifestations of the Absolute each in its own right. Here again the *yin-yang* functions as a symbol of the intrinsic relativity of perspectives,

---

51. Schuon, *From the Divine to the Human* (Bloomington, IN: World Wisdom, 2013), 130.

as epitomized by Zhuangzi's dream of being a butterfly and wondering whether it might not be, rather, the butterfly that was dreaming that it was Zhuangzi.[52]

The *yin-yang*, however, cannot be considered—as Robin Wang has indicated—as a graphic representation of a doctrinal statement. It is rather a symbol, meaning a basis for meditation on reality or realities. Wang makes the important point that its meaning is not to be deciphered but used as a means to decipher the world in ways that "depend on where one draws the boundaries among things and events."[53] It appears to us that Schuon's use of the *yin-yang* is in keeping with such an understanding of the Chinese symbol. In his work, *yin-yang* does not denote a given reality but facilitates the understanding of the various ways in which Reality, and realities, unfold and relate. It is also most significant that *yin-yang* be connected to "visual thinking."[54] Schuon's works have sometimes acquired the reputation of being conceptually dense and arduous or even "abstract"—in an age when principles tend to be reduced to "abstractions"—but one should observe that some of his most central insights are actually couched in the language of graphic symbols that are both direct and synthetic. We have mentioned earlier the symbols of the concentric circles and the radii, as well as the spiral, that virtually summarize Schuon's whole metaphysical perspective. The recognition of transcendence—akin to the concentric circles of the onto-cosmic unfolding and the discrete degrees of being that they highlight—and the intimation of immanence—similar to the rays or radii that extends the Unity into the multiplicity—are

---

52. "Once Chuang Chou dreamt he was a butterfly, a butterfly flitting and fluttering around, happy with himself and doing as he pleased. He didn't know he was Chuang Chou. Suddenly he woke up and there he was, solid and unmistakable Chuang Chou. But he didn't know if he was Chuang Chou who had dreamt he was a butterfly, or a butterfly dreaming he was Chuang Chou. Between Chuang Chou and a butterfly there must be some distinction! This is called the Transformation of Things." *Zhuangzi*, Section 2, https://terebess.hu/english/chuangtzu2.html.

53. "The *yinyang* symbol . . . is only an invitation for perceivers to think and meditate, to contemplate human beings and the world. It cannot be simply defined through the question 'what does it mean?' because the *yinyang* symbol denotes nothing in terms of fixed human abstraction." Wang, *Yinyang*, 225.

54. "The efforts of making different *tu* [diagrams] disclose a tacit insight that thinking is not simply a mental process above or beyond perception, but rather it is an essential ingredient of perception itself. Visual perception is visual thinking." Wang, *Yinyang*, 222.

synthesized in the spiral[55] that is like a ray "transformed" into concentric circles or a set of concentric circles "assuming" the form of a ray.[56] Put simply, the spiral is like a circular ray or a radial circle, and the graphic *yin-yang* evokes a double spiral, motionless in its constant motion. It is a deep analogue of the *yin-yang* in the way it suggests the dynamics of metaphysical immovability and the stillness of cosmogonic production, echoing Laozi's symbol of a wheel's axle.[57] Thus, the presence of the *yin-yang* symbol is too pervasive in Schuon's writings not to accentuate the centrality of visual intuition in his doctrinal expositions, but also in the modes of spiritual assimilation that they foster.

---

55. "We may specify the structure of this metaphysical 'vision' by having recourse to the following symbol: the spider's web, formed of warp and weft threads—or of radii and concentric circles—represents the Universe under the twofold relationship of essential identity and existential separation; the synthesis of these two relationships will be indicated by the spiral." Schuon, *Treasures of Buddhism*, 34.

56. "Indirect union . . . is pre-existent; in other words, it is realized in advance through the Divine homogeneity of the Universe, which pantheism would account for if it had the complementary and crucial notion of transcendence. The geometric symbol of this homogeneity, which is not 'material' but transcendent, is the spiral, for it combines the perspective of the concentric circles with that of the rays." Schuon, *Form and Substance in the Religions*, nn. 15, 255.

57. "We put thirty spokes together and call it a wheel, but it is on the space where there is nothing that the usefulness of the wheels depends." *Tao Te Ching*, translated by Arthur Waley (Ware, Hertforshire: Wordsworth Editions, 1997), 11.

9

The "Tantric" Spiritualization of Sexuality

A reader of Schuon's works will notice that two terms, related to the sacralization of human love and sexuality, frequently occur in his vocabulary. These are "Tantrism" (or "Tantric") and "Krishnaite," which Schuon uses very broadly but with enough consistency to reveal the significance they assume in his perspective on the spiritualization of human sexuality.

It is in light of these broad categories of experience that we propose to delve into the complex question of the meaning and spiritual integration of sexuality in the widest sense of the word. By this is meant not only the physical dimension of sexuality to which the latter is often reduced in our day, but also—and above all—to the psychic and spiritual dimensions of sexual polarity and the transcendent significance of eros.[1] Needless to say, this question involves many considerations and numerous ramifications on account of the diversity of human needs and qualifications, and the divergences of religious perspectives. Schuon was a Westerner deeply cognizant of the defining characteristics of the Christian sensibility that has shaped the spiritual identity of Europe and its historical extensions, while also having been exposed very early to the quite distinct perspectives and modalities of Asian wisdom traditions. Understandably, his starting point was based in a meditation on the deep divergences between the Christian outlook on sexuality and other perspectives with a less exclu-

---

1. On the manifold dimensions of this question, it is worth mentioning Julius Evola's *Metafisica del sesso* (Rome: Atanòr, 1958), published in English under the title *Eros and the Mysteries of Love* (Rochester, NY: Inner Traditions, 1991), which, in spite of a few idiosyncratic and questionable considerations (particularly with respect to *magia sexualis*), remains an unsurpassed synthesis and source of information on the topic.

295

sive character. In order to begin addressing this question, it is important, following Schuon's reflections, to recognize that in the West the particular civilizational and cultural experiences that have marked the development of the Christian and "post-Christian" vision have had significant consequences on the ways sexuality is approached in its religion dimension, and even outside of religion. In this respect, Schuon highlights the significant role of what he refers to as a "theology of Augustinian inspiration" in shaping the Christian outlook and, indirectly, more recent responses to it in the context of secularization in the West. This theological apprehension of sexuality is based on the centrality of sin and its de facto identification with sexuality as transgression par excellence.[2] Thus, in his *Confessions*—in the context of a discussion of the "chain of lust" that had "shackled" him and hampered "the new will that had come to life" in the form of his conversion—Saint Augustine refers to the perception of sexuality as sinful when highlighting the duality of his own will: "These two wills within me, one old, one new, one the servant of the flesh, the other of the spirit, were in conflict and between them they tore my soul apart."[3] Now, it is important to note that Saint Augustine places the problem in the will on the one hand, and in the conflicting nature of its tendencies on the other. Sexuality, or rather sexual passion with which it is identified, becomes the symbol of the two postulations of the soul: one toward concupiscence and sin, the other toward God. Moreover, the example of Christ, who lived as an ascetic celibate, and the teachings of Saint Paul on marriage, which attached to sexuality "a maximum of penance,"[4] oriented further the Christian imagination toward a vision of sexuality as being intrinsically at odds with the otherworldly vocation of mankind. There is no question that

---

2. "Traditionally, the West is marked by a theology of Augustinian inspiration, which explains marriage from a more or less utilitarianist angle, while neglecting the intrinsic reality of the thing. According to this perspective—leaving aside every apologetic euphemism—sexual union in itself is sin; consequently the child is born in sin, but the Church compensates, or rather more than compensates, for this evil with a greater good, namely baptism, faith, sacramental life." Schuon, *Esoterism as Principle and as Way* (Pates Manor, Bedfont, Middlesex: Perennial Books, 1981), 129.

3. Saint Augustine, *Confessions*, VIII.5.1 (London: Penguin Books, 1961), 164.

4. "Since Christianity sees in sexuality a maximum of concupiscence—sexuality is almost the 'ontological sin,' the sin par excellence—and therefore exalts chastity and recommends celibacy, it is logical in wishing to combine with marriage a maximum of penance, and consequently in being opposed to all eroticism and forbidding divorce and polygamy." Schuon, *Christianity/Islam* (Bloomington, IN: World Wisdom, 2008), 59.

this overall negative vision has left traces in the Western imagination and that it has contributed both to "desexualizing" religion, if one may say so, and consequently to rendering sexuality more "worldly." The consequences of this separation have been numerous, including a frequent incapacity to integrate the sexual dimension, as such, within religious life, and an underlying and unresolved collective complex crystallized around sexuality. The most recent backlash against the constraints inherent in this reductionist and negative Christian vision has come in the guise of the concept and practices of so-called "sexual liberation."

In contrast to the tensions inherent in the traditional Christian outlook, it is interesting to note, in what Schuon refers to as "the Judeo-Islamic perspective," a greater measure of integration of sexuality within the religious domain. When commenting on these "confessional divergences," Schuon notes that they are related to the very outlook and structure of the respective religions. In other words, Judaism and Islam are aiming at a goal that is both "natural" and "realistic." This realism does not amount, however, to a reduction of sexuality to its instinctive and animal dimensions. Even though humans share with animals the physical aspects of sexuality, they alone can elevate or degrade them by either transcending their limitations or falling below the purely natural instinct. In other words, these religious perspectives do not oppose a priori the natural and the supernatural, as illustrated, for instance, by the rich and profound Kabbalistic symbolism of sexual union. In Moshe Idel's words, "In Sefirotic Kabbalah: the supernal union is a hidden process, which is reflected in human sexual union without our being able to understand its exact nature."[5] It is clear, in this view of things, that the natural order—and sexuality as the very symbol of this order—is a reflection of the content of the Divine Essence. From another more limited but nonetheless significant point of view, Islam and Judaism provide their faithful—through their respective sacred laws—with the most accessible ways of integrating sexuality within religion. This means giving a Divine sanction to human limitations—not to say at times weaknesses—in a way that is not without ambiguities and, therefore, not without risking its own negative consequences and abuses, humans being what they are. This may mean at times, from the point of view of a Christian sensibility, a quasi-distasteful religious accommodation to the lowest common denominators of sexuality.

---

5. Moshe Idel, *Mystical Experience in Abraham Abulafia* (Albany: State University of New York Press, 1988), 204.

On the other hand, a Muslim sensibility will tend to assess the traditional Christian outlook as being contrary to nature and thus, in that sense, contrary to Divine law and intent. This profound difference appears most explicitly in the ways in which Christianity and Islam represent the reality of celestial bliss. Pascal, for instance, in his apologia of the Christian religion—the *Pensées*—revealingly referred to the Qur'ānic vision of the afterlife (most specifically its sexual components) as a sign of the "ridiculousness" of the Muslim faith.[6] This view finds its scriptural basis in Qur'ānic accounts of the celestial delights associated with eroticism. Among several verses referring to heavenly unions, one can quote verse 44:54: "And We shall wed them unto fair ones with wide, lovely eyes" (trans. M. Pickthall). Schuon connects this perspective to the Platonic metaphysical *anamnesis*, in conformity with the verse "as often as they are regaled with food of the fruit thereof, they say: this is what was given us aforetime; and it is given to them in resemblance" (2:25). The Arabic term *mutashābihan*, rendered by Pickthall as resemblance, is significantly akin to *mutashābihāt*, a word that also refers to the Qur'ānic verses that are deemed ambiguous in the sense of allowing for various interpretations, and which some Sufi commentators consider to be addressed to a spiritual elite.[7] This word is also akin to *tashbīh*, often rendered in translations of Sufi texts as *analogy*, a term that fittingly conveys the sense of "continuity in discontinuity" that is inherent in the Qur'ānic outlook on sexual pleasure.

The paradoxical indication involved in the expression of this continuity in discontinuity offers a key to understanding the divergence between the Christian and Judeo-Islamic points of view. As Schuon observes, the whole matter lies in whether one emphasizes the discontinuity, the transcendent gap, between the archetype and the phenomenon, or whether one stresses, on the contrary, the continuity that links them together. By and large, the former perspective is more attuned to the needs and capacity of the majority—indeed the totality—of mankind, inasmuch as all people can conceive, in one way or another, of Divine transcendence. The latter

---

6. "It is not by that which is obscure in Mahomet, and which may be interpreted in a mysterious sense, that I would have him judged, but by what is clear, as his paradise and the rest. In that he is ridiculous. And since what is clear is ridiculous, it is not right to take his obscurities for mysteries." Blaise Pascal, *Pensées*, translated by W. F. Trotter (Mineola, NY: Dover, 2003), 164.

7. "The *muhkamāt* verses constitute the basic message necessary for salvation addressed to all mankind while the *mutashābihāt* are addressed to an elect group of individuals." Kristin Zahra Sands, *Sūfī Commentaries on the Qur'ān in Classical Islam* (New York: Routledge, 2006), 15.

point of view is more delicate, in the sense that it is more likely to give rise to misunderstandings and abuse. Schuon is not unaware of these negative possibilities, and he actually does not neglect to remark that the principle of analogy that is at work in the "metaphysical transparency of phenomena" presupposes a contemplative point of view and a distance or freedom from the opacity of the passions. In the absence of this, such analogy cannot but be experienced as idolatrous, which may give rise to hedonism or, in the case of its transposition to the thereafter, to a gross materialization of the celestial reality that opens the way to all kinds of corruptions and misguided delusions. This is why it appears unlikely that such verses should be taken literally, since they pertain—by definition—to the domain of analogy, unless it is understood that the content of the celestial experience is literally equivalent, in its essence, to the terrestrial experience of pleasure, this being weighed according to the principle, mentioned by Schuon, that God never gives less than He promises. Moreover, a strictly literal interpretation of such verses—in the sense that would espouse all the modalities of terrestrial sexual pleasure—would then necessarily involve the limitations of the latter, including the various modes of physical and ritual impurities that they entail. However, this would lead to absurdity—a need for purification in paradise, for instance—and annul the very distinction between the two realms of reality. What becomes apparent, therefore, is that the analogy of terrestrial pleasures and celestial pleasures may take us in three very different directions. Exoterically, and normatively or traditionally, it causes and stimulates a desire for paradisal bliss, and it is thereby, on a collective and average level, a powerful means of persuasion and motivation in the "arsenal" of the Islamic *upāya*. The reality of sexual pleasure becomes a springboard toward a higher level of aspiration. Esoterically, the same experience of sexual pleasure is a way to direct the human self toward the essence of beatitude, what Hindus refer to as *ānanda* and the Qur'ān connotes, with a different emphasis, as *rahmah*. Negatively, or heterodoxically, the hereafter is brought down to the level of the herebelow, thus debasing religion into gross idolatry.

While addressing the implications of the above divergences and issues, Schuon's writings emphasize the fundamental ambiguity inherent in the experience of sexual pleasure. In one of his most striking passages, we read: "Man oscillates between sacraments and idols, objectively and subjectively."[8] This evaluation is, in a sense, a particular illustration of the ambiguity of *Māyā*, one that is predicated on the scission of the subject

---

8. Schuon, *Christianity/Islam*, 60.

and the object. To the extent that *Māyā* is a superimposition upon *Ātman*, or a veil over the Absolute, it is objectively the seed of idols but, insofar as it is transparent to *Ātman*—that is, from an Advaitin point of view—it is recognized as appearance and can thus be considered a sacrament, that is, a phenomenon that conveys the Reality of *Brahman*. Schuon acknowledges that the same phenomenon may be experienced by people in markedly different ways, or even by the same person in different circumstances. His point is two-fold in this respect: first, he wishes to stress that contemplativeness is a requirement for realizing the "transparency of phenomena." In other words, the capacity to recognize the Divine in theophanic forms—particularly in aesthetic and erotic instances—is dependent on one's degree of spiritual maturity, whether the latter be understood karmically, that is to say in terms of one's terrestrial state of being and consciousness, or in terms of one's advancement along the spiritual path. This is precisely why religions, as social and ethical realities, do not ordinarily foster such spiritual apprehensions of the Divine through the erotic, given the very ambiguity that it involves. When they do so, incidentally but never in a way that would make sexuality central to the religious experience as such, it is in the terms of what Schuon would call a "mysticism of gratitude" rather than from a strictly unitive point of view. In such a perspective, sexual pleasure, like other forms of sensory satisfaction, must be responded to gratefully and lived as an opportunity to increase one's awareness of God's gifts. Furthermore, Schuon also recognizes that every person, independently of the spiritual degree with which they have been bestowed, is necessarily exposed to the vicissitudes that are part and parcel of cosmic relativity. This is an important point to stress inasmuch as it alludes to the dual nature of mankind or what Meister Eckhart refers to as the duality of the "outer man" and the "inner man." The outer man is, by definition, confronted with outwardness, meaning that he is apt to experience the world without being aware of its dependence on God's Reality. Outwardness, in Schuon's spiritual vocabulary, means the world—both within and without—inasmuch as it takes one away from the remembrance and consciousness of God. The latter is inward because "the Kingdom of Heaven is within you"; in other words, there is no direct access to God but through the point at which the human "touches" the Divine, this being a more than human and thus purely spiritual reality. The deeper the contact with this inward dimension, the more penetrating one's ability to read phenomena of beauty as manifestations of God. By contrast, the outward dimension of existence is a phenomenal surface that fails to disclose the inner ontological depth of terrestrial experiences, that Divine source from which they emerge and draw their meaning *sub specie aeternitatis*. With regard to outwardness, the human soul is passive inasmuch as it receives the influence of the outer realm and is determined by it. It is active to the extent that it actualizes its capacity to master, situate, and orient the perception of phenomena. It is precisely in this connection that Schuon makes the point that time is most likely to rob human subjects of their active and determinative powers. This is so because activity needs to be actualized in the present; it is a mode of vigilant wakefulness that time, as duration, tends to erode or weaken. The present is, from this point of view, akin to the Absolute whereas time—as the sequence of the anterior and the posterior—represents manifestation as diversity under its aspect of illusion. There is a profound correspondence, therefore, between the inner man and the present on the one hand, and the outer man and duration on the other. The sacramental aspect of sexuality is connected, precisely, to its ability to actualize a consciousness of the Absolute in the present through erotic or ecstatic experiences, thus dispelling the outer and revealing the inner.

The foregoing considerations furnish an insight into what Schuon refers to as "Tantrism," which leads us to assess the extent to which his usage of this term coincides with what is usually understood by it. It is difficult, if not impossible, to provide a synthetic definition of the tantric path, as it manifests in very diverse ways within the Hindu and Buddhist traditions.[9] The adjective *tantric* is used—in its broadest sense—to refer to spiritual perspectives as varied as Tibetan Vajrayāna and some schools of Indian Śaivism. The etymology of the word *tantra* has been connected by traditional commentators to the ideas of continuity, weaving and mutual dependence.[10] It may be inferred, from this etymology, that tantric teachings

---

9. An eminent scholar of Tantrism, André Padoux, makes the point that a definition of "Tantrism" is quite problematic, and goes so far as to wish it would possible to "be rid of the difficult notion of Tantrism" altogether. He proposes two approaches: one refers to a "way of making use of this world for supramundane ends [through] the ritual and soteriological use of things that are normally forbidden, that is the transgression of norms," while another "would underline the particular and proliferating nature of the ritual, and its conjunction with speculations and practices concerning the power of the word (*mantras*, etc.)." *The Roots of Tantra*, ed. Katherine Anne Harper and Roberet L. Brown (Albany: State University of New York Press, 2002), 20, 23–24.

10. "From the viewpoint of its etymology, the word *tantra* is used to refer to a continuum of sound (*sgra rgyud*), to a web or weaving (*thags*), and to things that depend on other things." José Ignacio Cabezón, *The Buddha's Doctrine and the Nine Vehicles—Rog Bande Sherab's Lamp of the Teachings* (Oxford: Oxford University Press, 2013), nn. 27, 113.

emphasize the connection between the various aspects and orders of reality, and make use of this principle of connection as a spiritual resource. What constitutes their common core is a focus on converting various forms of celestial and cosmic energy into the means for attaining enlightenment. They do not proceed, therefore, through intellectual or contemplative abstraction or discrimination but by identifying with particular forms or forces that quicken the process of spiritual realization. When applied more specifically, or restrictively, to paths connected to aesthetics or eroticism, Tantrism is considered to rely on that which, in ordinary circumstances, would be a cause of degeneration, in order to foster, by contrast, spiritual elevation and integration. In this respect, tantric paths are based on the principle that the objects of our desires are like crystallizations of supernal bliss that contain within themselves the seeds of a transcendence from their own limitations. Schuon applies this general principle in a way that is perhaps more metaphysical than strictly theurgic or methodical when referring to the notion of a "metaphysical transparency of phenomena."[11] The principle of transparency pertains, here, to the intuition that the world of outer manifestation, in spite of its peripheral character and its consequent veiling of the central Reality, remains in principle transparent to what it veils inasmuch as the Center is everywhere. This holds true objectively inasmuch as the periphery is none other than the Divine Center and, therefore, cannot but convey the latter's qualities or modes of being, but also subjectively insofar as human contemplation may pierce through the veil of appearances to perceive Reality in, and through, its manifestations. It may be seen, following a first insight into the notion of the transparency of phenomena, that while providing orientations that are in profound consonance with the spirit of *tantra*, Schuon's Tantric leanings are also characterized by an aesthetic inflection. In other words, they have perhaps more to do with perception and contemplation than with transformational energy and rituals as such, to the extent of course that the two can be distinguished for beauty is productive of its own modes of energy and sacredness while a kind of sacred energy is necessarily immanent to the unfolding of beauty. It may be necessary to specify that by aesthetic is

---

11. "The sense of the Sacred likewise implies a sense of the metaphysical transparency of things, the capacity to grasp the uncreated in the created; or to perceive the vertical ray—a messenger from the Archetype—independently of the horizontal plane of refraction, the latter determining the existential degree but not the divine content." Schuon, *Esoterism as Principle and as Way*, 239.

not meant a mere appreciation of beauty, and even less so an attraction toward beauty for its own sake, but rather a perception—from the Greek word *aisthēsis*—in beautiful phenomena of the beauty inherent to Reality as such. By contrast, *tantra* would probably be more in conformity with concepts such as "cosmic availability" or "energetic wherewithal" than with references to transparency and beauty. Thus, it may be argued that Hindu and Buddhist tantric paths are primarily concerned with cosmic power, productive vibration, and energetic pulsation, the aesthetic dimensions of which constitute only some of their modalities.

Different in some respects, but not entirely unrelated to the foregoing discussion, is the traditional Indian distinction between right-hand *tantra*, which is normative in relation to traditional expectations and practices, and left-hand *tantra*, which is predicated on the principle of formal transgression. Both Hindu and Buddhist traditions distinguish between left-handed and right-handed *tantra*, the first "taking the repudiation of conventional morality literally and the latter figuratively."[12] Left-handed *tantra* may be based on what Schuon would call the "nature of things," or it could pertain to the way of the contrarian, the path of inner freedom vis-à-vis conventional strictures (although the two types of motivation are not necessarily exclusive of one another). The second possibility—which appears, for instance, in Śivaite *Paśupati* spirituality—may entail some deeply esoteric intentions, but it does not seem to correspond to what Schuon primarily has in mind when referring to Tantrism. This is, no doubt, because this type of *tantra* is intentionally transgressive, and not only so de facto, as it may occur in the context of the first possibility. In other words, transgressive left-hand *tantra* presupposes (a) a traditional order and civilization, and (b) that the intentional transgression of its norms is undertaken with a spiritual intention. On the one hand, this type of intention is based on the esoteric intuition that traditional forms are not absolute and that "he who wants the kernel must break the shell." It is also founded—and it is at this juncture that it differs from Schuon's understanding of Tantrism—on an ascesis of antinomian behavior, the purpose of which is to free the inner self from social expectations that confine it to factitious identifications. Schuon shows little affinity with this type of mystical subjectivism—without, however, questioning its validity in some contexts—because it is more vocational than primordial. Schuon's

---

12. Masao Abe, in *Our Religions*, edited by Arvind Sharma (New York: HarperOne, 1995), 99.

concept of Tantrism, by contrast, refers to the primordial as normative and universal, and it is connected to the idea that some ways of acting can be in conformity with divine intentions and natural laws while being contrary to particular religious codes and civilizational norms.[13] This distinction lies at the core of what is entailed by the esoteric; namely, an awareness of the core reality of things, a contemplation of their objective integrity and archetypical referent independently of the function and meaning they may accrue in a particular traditional context: "The tantric or shaktic perspective is based, not on rules dictated by a given social opportuneness, but on the nature of things."[14] It is more than likely, therefore, that Schuon's general concept of Tantrism agrees more explicitly with the right-hand variety, inasmuch as he considered aesthetics integral to traditional religious forms. This being said, the transgressive tantric perspective can be seen to have implications for Schuon's distinction between esoterism and exoterism, at least inasmuch as esoterism challenges the formal emphasis of exoterism. However, in contrast to typical left-hand *tantra*, his esoteric leanings do not purposely transgress a formal order with a view to liberating a specific type of inner energy or crystallizing a specific mode of awareness. For one thing, such left-hand tantric methods presuppose traditional formal constraints and conventional norms that are strongly anchored both within the human psyche and in the society that shapes its ways of thinking. It is precisely this anchoring that gives the transgressive impulses and actions their spiritual effectiveness as a kind of shock therapy. To free oneself from these norms through symbolic or actual transgression is like experiencing a social death that may provoke a spiritual breakthrough. As a consequence, the very notion of transgression takes an altogether different meaning depending on whether it is defined within the strict formal constraints of a traditional universe or by a culture that questions the very notion of norms; in the latter case, it could be argued that the reality and meaning of transgression loses most, if not all, of its significance and power. Schuon does not consider

---

13. "There are even cases, in Tantrism for example and in certain cults of antiquity, where acts which in themselves would count as sins, not only according to a particular religious morality but also according to the legislation of the civilization in which they occur, serve as a support for intellection, a fact which presupposes a strong predominance of the contemplative element over the passionate." Schuon, *The Transcendent Unity of Religions* (Wheaton, IL: The Theosophical Publishing House, 1984), 50.

14. Schuon, *Roots of the Human Condition* (Bloomington, IN: World Wisdom, 2002), 35.

these matters from a specific traditional context such as this, since his work provides a means of access to the traditional outlook and spiritual consciousness from within the ambience of secular modernity, and in a language that is appropriate to the realities of modern thought, as well as being independent of any specific cultural identity. In a sense, the traditional spirit of his work lies in the conviction that what is most needed for modern mentalities is, generally, not an inner motion of transgression but a conscious and deliberate conformity to formal norms through which the heart and mind may be disciplined and "rehabilitated."

With respect to the term "Krishnaism," it ought to be noted that Schuon refers to it by the adjectival form "Krishnaite." Moreover, Schuon's use of this adjective is consistently accompanied by quotation marks in order to suggest, not any particular devotion to the god Krishna but, in a much broader sense, an allusion to a certain way of apprehending manifestations of femininity and eroticism within a religious and spiritual framework, one that Krishna manifests in a paradigmatic manner. As we will see, this universalized use of the term Krishnaite by Schuon is applicable to a number of major prophetic figures from various traditions. In other words, the Schuonian use of the adjective Krishnaite proceeds from a universalization of an understanding of certain characteristics of the god Krishna, specifically in his relationship to women, and in connection to the episodes of his divine play with the cowherd girls (*gopis*). The interpretation of these narratives is not so much focused on the *gopis*' amorous modes of worshipping the god as it is on the quality of consciousness that presides over the god's erotic play that may also, by extension, characterize analogous ways of being on the part of other deified beings.

In writing about this Krishnaite aspect, Schuon draws, more symbolically than literally, on the Hindu accounts (from the *Purana Śrīmad Bhāgavatam* to Jayadeva's *Gita Govinda*) of Krishna's amorous *līlā* with the *gopis*. In doing so, he applies the symbolism of Krishna's *līlā* to a wide range of realities, from the highest metaphysics to concrete modalities of the spiritual life. In other words, while Schuon refers to Krishnaism as a particular path of devotion within the Hindu tradition, he reserves the adjective Krishnaite to a state of being or consciousness, irrespective of the tradition within which it may manifest. For Schuon, this term applies to a number of *avatāras* and spiritual luminaries, and refers to a capacity to experience the Divine in and through manifestations of femininity, as well as conferring a mode of spiritual presence actualized in the context of a devotional relationship. One must therefore distinguish, in Schuon's works, between references to the story of Krishna and the *gopis*—together with the associated devotion to Krishna—and considerations pertaining to Krishnaite manifestations. Regarding the former, Schuon provides metaphysical and spiritual insights into the meaning of *rasā-līlā*, the loving play of Krishna with the cowherd girls. His meditations flow from the Hindu concepts of *Māyā* and *līlā*, delving as they do into the interplay of Unity and multiplicity or the mystical hide and seek that flows from this spiritual reciprocity. What is most significant in these narratives and meditations is not so much the feminine identity of the *gopis* as the symbolic feminization of the devotee in relation to God. Schuon notes that "masculine adepts consider themselves as *gopis*, lovers of Krishna, which is all the more plausible in that in relation to the Divinity every creature has something feminine about it."[15] By feminine is meant here receptive since it is the god who actively confers the blessings of his grace to the devotees.

This sexualized consideration of the relationship between the Divine and the human goes even further in pointing to the ways in which the Krishna-*līlā* contains the whole metaphysics of deliverance. In one of his poems, Schuon proposes an intriguing interpretation of Krishna's alluring play of the flute from the darkness of the woods of Vrindavan:

> The wheel of the world turns, and it mocks thee—
> It does not wish that thy heart aspire to peace.
> Didst thou not see Krishna, who stood in the dark
> And whose flute-play laughed at this illusion?
> In the dark, in Vrindavan, the holy wood;
> May it be the refuge of thy soul.
> For Vrindavan is far more than the cosmic wheel—
> It is what thou thyself art before all beginning.[16]

Here, the erotic scene that has been illustrated, in many Hindu miniatures, reveals some of its deepest metaphysical and spiritual implications. The Divine *līlā* is envisaged from two vantage points, which are both connected to mocking laughter. There is, first of all, the *līlā* as onto-cosmic unfold-

---

15. Schuon, *From the Divine to the Human* (Bloomington, IN: World Wisdom, 2013), nn. 22, 100.

16. Schuon, *Songs without Names—Volumes I–VI* (Bloomington, IN: World Wisdom, 2006), 215.

ing, which is none other than the wheel of *samsāra*. This is the domain of relativity from which the "Divine in the human" aspires to be freed. We must remember, however, that the non-dualistic perspective excludes any absolute gap between degrees of Reality. This means, among other consequences, that there exists a zone of "onto-cosmological ambiguity" where the lowest point of the demiurgic order—which can appear as divine from a human point of view—corresponds to the highest point in the tenebrous or subversive realm.[17] Such is, properly considered, the range of demiurgic production. It is on this lowest level of dynamic creation that the mocking aspect of Reality can, and does indeed, appear. Mocking mankind amounts, according to this demiurgic tendency, to making the world turn inasmuch as the worldly wheel entails a flight from the metaphysical Center and, therefore, surrender to a constant psychic agitation that precludes Peace. The playfulness of Krishna can be interpreted, in this context, as both celebratory of the cosmic dance and, no doubt more profoundly, as symbolizing an amused detachment from the play of illusion. Divine play presupposes both a creative joy and a transcendent distance, for play is both enjoyable and not quite serious. Krishna's flute is both singing the cosmic comedy of existence and laughing at it from behind a tree. The darkness of the forest is imbued with a sense of mystery and security that evokes the Divine Self: the play can only be known to be a play from the hiding place of the Self that the god objectifies. This is not without implications for the way in which human love may be approached from a spiritual point of view. There is a sense in which love—any love—is none other than a quest for the Self and a limited, most often unconscious identification with it as taught by Yājñavalkya in the *Brhad Āranyaka Upanishad*: "Verily it is not for the love of the husband that the husband is dear but for the love of the *Ātman* that is in him" (1, 3, 28). Love is nothing but a play of hide and seek in which the Self is both the seeker and the one who is sought. The detachment that is inherent to the one who is identified with the Self is neither the result of an ascetic effort nor an indifference to beings. It results quasi-spontaneously from a

---

17. "Be that as it may, there is some ambiguity, traditionally speaking, concerning certain negative functions of the Logos-Demiurge on the one hand, and particular aspects of satanic personification on the other, so much so that one could say that the lowest point of the demiurgic domain and the highest point of the satanic domain can coincide, as is shown by certain terrifying images of divinities, in the Mahayanic as well as in the Hindu pantheon." Schuon, *To Have a Center* (Bloomington, IN: World Wisdom, 2015), 84.

consciousness of the fact that what is loved is infinitely contained in the Self and cannot, therefore, be possessed as an object or lost.[18] It is this consciousness that lends to the experience of human love both its depth and its contemplative background.

In the story of Krishna, it is the incarnation that is, in a way, the most determining factor in terms of the devotion itself.[19] Krishnaite devotion is characterized by a sense of intimacy and the modes of this particular *bhakti* tend to be physically expressive. There is, however, a fundamental ambivalence in the love of Krishna in that it presupposes distance while being perfected in proximity. *Vaishnava* Krishnaite theology takes account of this ambivalence in ways that outline the paradoxes of the highs and lows of terrestrial love. Thus, Krishnaite devotion appears to be focused on three fundamental moments or realities that have been variously highlighted or favored by different theological interpreters and devotees. These three moments can be considered as inherent to all manifestations of love, on whatever level the latter may be contemplated. In order to understand what is at stake, it is important to begin with the consideration that devotional love necessarily involves an aspiration toward union that is predicated on a sense of separation, without which it has no meaning. The search for union that lies at the core of *bhakti* begins with a sense of separation and alienation, often if not always colored with feelings of pain and suffering, which form the spiritual springboard of devotion. Like the *gopis* experiencing the pangs of separation from their beloved Krishna, the soul left to itself cannot but feel bereft of fullness away from the Principle of its being. From a human point of view, love is, a priori, a search for union, thereby a quest for totality. As for union itself, it is contemplated—in this perspective—as the blissful fruition of the search for the Beloved. This fulfillment of love is none other than a return to one's

---

18. "He who knows that all he loves here below is lovable only in virtue of the Essences—and therefore preexists infinitely in the Divinity—becomes detached from the earthly shadows almost without wishing to; he knows that nothing is ever lost, the perfections of this world being no more than fleeting reflections of the eternal Perfections. In other words, the thing or the being that is loved is to be found infinitely more in God than in this world; God is, in infinite measure, every beloved thing and every beloved being." Schuon, *The Eye of the Heart* (Bloomington, IN: World Wisdom, 1997), 171.

19. "Krishna is the supreme deity; his form is not something which is accepted by him temporarily but is identical with his self." Jan Brzezinski, "Does Krishna Marry the *Gopis* in the End?," *Journal of Vaisnava Studies* 5, no. 4 (Fall 1997): 50.

true ontological reality since Love is the Divine Essence of everything. This amounts to saying that, in addition to separation and union—which are like co-dependent sequential moments of the *bhakti* path—Krishnaite *bhakti*, like most other forms of devotion, presupposes that, essentially, God is never truly separated from the devotee or that, in the transcendent realm of Reality, the two are forever united. The Krishnaite *līlā* is characterized by an alternation of these three different points of view that necessarily enter, in one way or another, in the very constitution of the *bhakti* way. The Krishnaite tradition, in its historical development and theological diversity, presents us with a variety of outlooks and practices with respect to these three moments. Such theological perspectives place spiritual perfection in either one of the aforementioned moments, with different intents and emphases.[20] Irrespective of the various devotional postures and theological crystallizations, each of the three moments that have been mentioned corresponds, phenomenologically, to a particular aspect of the path of *bhakti*, even though the last perspective is arguably less typically Krishnaite than the others, given its implicit non-dualistic leanings. The excellence of separation is apparent in at least two ways: first as the fuel of devotional intensity and, second, as the paradoxical means whereby the omnipresence of God may be achieved. This becomes apparent when considering that, in order to send his *gopis* back to their homes, the dharmic duties of which they had left without any hesitation or delay to come and be with him, Krishna himself declares—in the *Srīmad Bhāgavatam*—that "it is not necessary that my devotee should be physically close to me."[21] The concept of the "man-center"—which Schuon uses at times to refer to a human being whose consciousness of the Absolute is central in the world of his spiritual jurisdiction—is clearly illustrated by the *gopis*'s response to Krishna's dharmic admonition to them: "You have taught us that service to our husbands is our foremost duty. Let that be so. But are you not the very self of all beings, hence the very self of our husbands? So by serving you we are serving them."[22] We can read in these nimble remarks a reversal of the god's argument that amounts to a subordination of all relative *dharmas* to the absolute *dharma* of spiritual

---

20. Brzezinski, "Does Krishna Marry the *Gopis* in the End?," 52.

21. Swami Venkatesananda, *The Concise Srīmad Bhāgavatam* (Albany: State University of New York Press, 1989), 264.

22. Swami Venkatesananda, *The Concise Srīmad Bhāgavatam*, 265.

liberation and worshipping the Absolute. In other words, the highest possibility contains all other possibilities.

The Krishnaite character of a particular figure, whether of the Indic or Abrahamic world, is also related to divine or prophetic individuals who assume human nature in all of its aspects, including amorous love and sexuality. This type of person is sometimes referred to by Schuon as one in whom the crystalline simplicity of the Logos appears under a human complexity that both veils its inner perfection and manifests it extrinsically within the realm of imperfection. By contrast with this latter type, the two geometrically perfect symbols of the cross and the circle can be applied paradigmatically to Jesus and the Buddha, for instance, by suggesting a Divine formal perfection that is consonant with an otherworldly mode of manifestation. Thus, the human dimension of these characters is as if effaced before the Divine substance that radiates through them. Such instances of a "Logos-crystal," while exercising an obviously strong influence among humankind, do not engage in the ordinary vicissitudes of everyday life such as raising families and undertaking social responsibilities. They show the path of renunciation and exclusive transcendence and are not inclined to embrace the human condition as a whole. A sure sign of this type of vocation lies in the absence of involvement with human sexual love, marriage, and procreation, an exclusiveness that carries into the general spirit and forms of the tradition itself, including some of its institutions like monasticism.

In sharp contrast to this exclusive spiritual modality, we find examples of spiritual perfection characterized by a full and complex engagement with all aspects of human existence, as an indication of a more general assumption of immanence and manifestation in the totality of their aspects. Such symbols as the cross and the circle could not be used when referring to the complex figures that we are now considering. The symbol of the star would be, no doubt, more appropriate in this case, as it evokes a mode of radiation that extends from the center to the wider and most peripheral aspects of existence. It is within the context of such an assumption of the full scale of human destiny that the Krishnaite vocation and function may manifest itself. In spiritual perspectives of this kind, the question of sexual polarity is not envisaged from the point of view of its latent or patent opposition to the spiritual vocation, but as a natural component of the human condition. As such, sexuality—broadly considered—must not only be integrated with any endeavor toward transcendence but may even be the hallmark of a heightened sensibility to the Divine, one that finds its most powerful support in immanence itself. It is in this sense that Schuon can refer to the Krishnaite quality of the Prophet of Islam, for instance, as a mark of his spiritual vocation. The Krishnaite possibility, with its strong emphasis on terrestrial immanence, is specifically superimposed on the generic spiritual framework of transcendence that is the defining characteristic of divine and prophetic beings.[23] The former is therefore less of a spiritual imperative than a functional vocation that may respond to particular collective needs, or facilitate appropriate teachings and ways of being.[24] However, when considered from the strict point of view of exclusive transcendence, and within the context of mentalities that have been shaped by an ascetic severance of religion from sexuality, such Krishnaite manifestations tend to be considered as either weaknesses or evidence of straying and error. It is enough to consider the ways in which Christian apologetics have been unable to evaluate Muhammad's Krishnaite aspect without portraying it as a symptom of the falseness or incompleteness of Islam, to realize how profoundly divergent religious sensibilities can be in this regard. There are spiritual and religious points of view that can barely apprehend the manifestations of sexuality in the spiritual domain other than as deviations and turpitudes or, at the very least, as complacencies and self-indulgence. Such limitations are partially derived from the very ambiguity of sexuality itself, and the inherent tensions that it involves, but it may be deemed that they do not do justice to the full scope of the phenomenon, not to mention their failing to account for its highest spiritual potentialities.

Aside from rare references to the same reality through the use of terms such as Solomonian, the most frequent use of Krishnaite appears, in Schuon's work, with regard to the Prophet of Islam. This may come as a surprise, considering the profound differences between the playful god

---

23. This is what Schuon implies when he writes, in one of his German poems, "The sage has two poles in his nature, but he is not split. Shankara he must be; Krishna he may be. Truth is everything and Beauty is its radiation. The sage is Truth overtly, and Beauty gently." *Songs Without Names*, 9th Collection, Volume 14, http://www.frithjofschuon.info/uploads/pdfs/poems/didactic_poems.pdf.

24. This is, in a way, connected to the other distinction, drawn by Schuon, between paths of inwardness and paths of interiorizing outwardness: "There are sages whose sole duty is to attract souls towards the 'within,' and this is the rule; there are others who add to this function that of creating sensible supports, and this is the exception." Schuon, *The Play of Masks* (Bloomington, IN: World Wisdom, 2003), 32.

and the Prophet of Divine Unity and the Law. The similarity is obviously not situated on the level of the respective traditional economies, nor is it to be found in the ontological and functional characters of Krishna and Muhammad; rather, it is reflected in the analogies pertaining to their spiritual substance as regards the way it relates to femininity. Thus we find the following characterization of the Prophet: "It is within this context that one must situate that feature of the Muhammadan Substance which could be called 'Solomonian' or Krishnaite, namely its spiritual capacity to find concretely in woman all the aspects of the Divine Femininity, from immanent Mercy to the infinitude of universal Possibility. The sensorial experience that produces in the ordinary man an inflation of the ego, actualizes in the 'deified' man an extinction in the Divine Self."[25] We note, first of all, a clear distinction between the ordinary experience of sexuality, which intensifies an illusory sense of individual selfhood—independently of the remembrance of God—and the spiritual disappearance into the bliss of God-consciousness. This allows one to understand why sexuality is rigorously regulated, in one way or another, in all traditional societies. There is, here, the potential danger of inflating the individual who runs the risk of divinizing himself given the ecstatic intensity of amorous and sexual experiences. Erotic inebriation may amount to a kind of self-absolutization that results both in the forgetfulness or rejection of the vertical link to transcendence and a neglect of the horizontal connection to one's social duties. By contrast, the spiritual experience of sexual pleasure is characterized by a sort of extinction in the Self by virtue of the analogy, and essential identity, between physical ecstasy and contemplative union. Furthermore, this distinction is connected to the fact that what is sought by most human beings (in that it reflects a lack) is given to the Krishnaite consciousness as sexual totality and completeness. Schuon quotes, in this respect, the famous tradition in which the Prophet declares that three things of this world have been made lovable to him: perfumes, women and prayer.[26] The love of women is therefore not a choice on the part of the Prophet but is, rather, a reality inherent to his God-given vocation. In following this love, he does not follow an instinctive or natural incli-

---

25. Schuon, *In the Face of the Absolute* (Bloomington, IN: World Wisdom Books, 1989), 130.

26. "According to a *hadīth* as enigmatic as it is famous, 'women, perfumes, and prayer' were 'made lovable' (*hubbiba ilayya*) to the Prophet." Schuon, *In the Face of the Absolute* (Bloomington, IN: World Wisdom, 2014), 135.

nation—for in this case there would be no need to highlight the love of women as an eminently prophetic gift—as it is an essential component of his prophetic mission. In other words, the love of women is the very criterion of a spiritual eminence.

One of the keys to understanding Schuon's view of Śaktic Tantrism and Krishnaism lies in the way he conceives of the spiritual relationship between the feminine and the masculine within and beyond the confines of human experience. The general orientation of this conception is encapsulated in the following remark from a chapter he devotes to the problem of sexuality: "Man is prolonged towards the periphery, which liberates, just as woman is rooted in the center, which protects."[27] It is important to stress, first of all, that this general statement needs be understood as being founded in metaphysical realities. It could not be reduced, therefore, to the plane of psychological considerations. Moreover, before elaborating the connection that binds sexual phenomena and metaphysical principles, it is advisable not to draw from these principles overstated or excessive conclusions. While metaphysical principles do provide necessary keys for understanding a wide array of phenomena, their application to any relative field necessarily entails qualifications and exceptions. The realms of relativity and multiplicity are inherently characterized by alternations, compensations, exceptions, and paradoxes. Notwithstanding these important qualifications, it goes without saying that Schuon's point of view is likely to be dismissed as an outmoded manner of essentializing realities that postmodern thinking can only apprehend as mere social constructs. Schuon's perspective, in this respect, lies at the antipode of contemporary deconstruction and has its source in the tradition of Platonic intellectuality. The core insight rests on the principle that the greater cannot come from the lesser and that the latter is but the reflection of the former. Platonic essentialism does not reduce phenomena *qua* phenomena to essences but understands them as ontologically rooted in essences that they manifest in imperfect and sometimes ambiguous ways. Finally, it bears stressing that the symbol of the center and the periphery—which Schuon applies to the relationship of the masculine and the feminine—is not the last word on the matter as other symbolic approaches may mitigate, or even reverse, some of the implications of this symbolism that implies both complementarity and alternation. The center lacks—not literally, but symbolically—what the

---

27. Schuon, *Esoterism as Principle and as Way*, 132.

periphery possesses and, conversely, the periphery is none other than the center and the center none other than the periphery. The center is the periphery unmanifested and the periphery the manifested center.

Be that as it may, we have highlighted, in other chapters of this work, how Schuon's characterization of the Ultimate begins with the two dimensions of absoluteness and infinitude. These constitute the highest principles of what manifests—on a much lower degree of reality—as the masculine and the feminine, being understood that *in divinis* these two dimensions belong to the same Reality. What is Unity at the top—the dyad Absolute-Infinite—is reflected at the bottom as the relativity of the distinction of the masculine and the feminine. From another point of view, it is the very distinction of absoluteness and infinitude that, flowing downstream, lends to the differentiation of the masculine and the feminine its core relevance. At any rate, when applied to the Absolute and the Infinite, the notion of being liberated through the periphery and rooted in the center reveals its fullest and most elevated meaning. Needless to say, the terms liberated and rooted can only be considered symbolically with reference to the Ultimate since the latter is, by definition, unconditioned freedom and intrinsic center. While the Absolute provides centering and protection by virtue of being the necessary and independent Reality in and of itself, the Infinite offers freedom on account of its expansive limitlessness. The Absolute is "freed" by the Infinite from being only itself, as it were, while the Infinite is "rooted" in the Absolute that "centers" its limitlessness. It is on the basis of these metaphysical premises that one may best understand how the perspective of Tantrism or Śaktism is that of the periphery that liberates. Śaktism presupposes a periphery, since it implies that the power inherent in the supreme *Śakti* is productive of concentric circles through an indefinite series of Śaktic centers. The unfolding of *Śakti* creates the world through vibrations. The world can be likened to a dynamic periphery that manifests the Divine creativeness in an utterly free manner. Conceiving and experiencing this ontological periphery as liberating amounts to living it as a manifestation of the center that returns to the center. In this connection, Krishnaism could be characterized as a manifestation of the "center that roots." Krishna attracts the *gopis* because he radiates a central quality of being. In fact, Schuon mentions in this connection the charisma of a physical irradiation of spiritual consciousness. Vaishnava *bhakti* is entirely founded on this structure of a center radiating with a periphery. Everything and everybody revolves around Krishna, who is ultimately the Lord, the Supreme, and the Absolute itself.

It has become apparent that Schuon approaches the Krishnaite reality with regard to the grace inherent in the Krishnaite being rather than in reference to the devotional love of the *gopis* for Krishna. In other words, Krishnaism, in the Schuonian sense, is intrinsically connected to the metaphysics of femininity on the one hand and to spiritual consciousness on the other; Krishnaism recognizes the whole range of meaning and reality found in femininity, instead of reducing it to its merely physical periphery. In fact, Krishnaism entails an apprehension of the unity and continuity encompassed by femininity. It is neither a physical reduction, as we have mentioned, nor an abstraction that would sever the Divine archetype from its terrestrial reflections. As Schuon has often asserted, the immanent reality of femininity is a vehicle of Divine Reality and, therefore, a means of realizing its essence and various aspects. One may wonder why this privilege is attached to femininity and not to other terrestrial realities while considering that this vision hypostatizes, in a way, a subjective masculine experience. A prelude to any consideration of the first question must include an obvious recognition that the feminine is not the only manifestation of the Divine in the domain of relativity. In fact, everything—in one way or another—manifests the Principle and every conditioned reality bears witness to what Schuon calls "the miracle of existence" and, beyond that, to the Absolute Essence itself. As for the feminine, it is only one among many theophanies while being, in some respects, the most complete. This stems from the fact that it is one of the modalities of human theophany in general, the latter being—according to Schuon—the most central and integral in our universe. What makes the feminine eminently total, in addition to sharing in the centrality of the human state, is the way in which it involves an informal and fluid quality that specifically reflects the supra-formal reality of the Essence. It is to this dimension that Krishnaism is characteristically attuned by virtue of being itself spiritually identified with the Essence. What this means, concretely, is that "alike attracts alike"; in other words, that which is recognized and loved in a woman is that which the self identifies in its deepest core. It is because Krishna is beautiful, generous, and free in his inward reality that he can experience these qualities in the *gopis* to the fullest extent. This also means that the dimensions of Divine Beauty, Mercy, and All-Possibility are eminently made present in the cosmos through the feminine and, in the human realm, by women.

With respect to beauty—particularly feminine beauty as a paramount means of contemplating the Divine—it has been a cardinal theme in the thought of certain Sufi thinkers, among whom Ibn ʿArabī and Rūzbehān Baqlī are particularly remarkable. The former has taught that the contemplation of God in and through woman is the most perfect.[28] Such contemplation can only be a witnessing through forms since the human being is a formal being. According to the Qurʾān, God has created man "in the most beautiful form" (*ahsana taqwīm*), which means that he cannot contemplate God in a better way than through His most beautiful creation and, at the same time, as other, that is, as female. This is also why man's contemplation of God in woman is both active and receptive. It is active with respect to woman as "object of witnessing" and passive or receptive as extinction in the other—who is none other than God—in sexual union. This means that the contemplation of God through woman offers a totality that is a direct reflection of the Divine Reality. Henry Corbin has shown how Rūzbihān, for his part, has propounded a theophanic vision of feminine beauty that resonates with Schuon's theme of the "metaphysical transparency of phenomena." The notion of *iltibās*—a term that Carl Ernst has translated as "clothing with divinity"[29]—implies that feminine beauty is the garb in which the Divine Beauty manifests itself.[30] One can also mention Rūmī, who has referred to the feminine as creative, thereby endowing it with a divine and inspiring function.[31] On the one hand, woman represents creation as the work of God; on the other, she is the very substance of the act of creation as projection of the Essence into manifestation. When referring to Mercy and All-Possibility as two principal dimensions of the contemplation of God in the feminine, Schuon continues a long tradition that approaches the feminine—

---

28. Cf. *The Bezels of Wisdom*, translated by R.W. J. Austin, "The Wisdom of Singularity in the Word of Muhammad" (Marwah, NJ: Paulist Press, 1980), 274–75.

29. Carl Ernst, *Ruzbihan Baqli: Mysticism and the Rhetoric of Sainthood in Persian Sufism* (New York: Routledge, 1996), 35.

30. Kazuyo Murata, *Beauty in Sufism: The Teachings of Ruzbihan Baqli* (Albany: State University of New York Press, 2017), 90.

31. "If you rule your wife outwardly, yet inwardly you are ruled by her whom you desire. This is characteristic of Man: in other animals love is lacking, and that shows their inferiority. The Prophet said that woman prevails over the wise, while ignorant men prevail over her; for in them the fierceness of the animal is immanent. Love and tenderness are human qualities, anger and lust are animal qualities. Woman is a ray of God: she is not the earthly beloved. She is creative: you might say she is not created." Rūmī, *Mathnavi* I, 2431. *A Rūmī Anthology*, translated by Reynold A. Nicholson (London: Oneworld, 2000), 44.

and woman as the human embodiments thereof—as pertaining to the mystery, the *ghayb*, of the Divine Essence. This Essence of God is also equated with Mercy inasmuch as the tradition refers to the latter as the most fundamental aspect of Divine Reality. Thus, in Islam, as in some other traditions, one can observe a sort of bifurcation within the tradition between an outer formal layer that is, by and large, the prerogative of men as a manifestation of rigor, and an inner layer—sometimes hidden and always synonymous with spiritual inwardness and inner prayer—which is contemplated as the particular, but not exclusive, province of the feminine. It has been observed, in this connection, that the Names of God used in the consecrating formula of the *Basmalah* are *ar-Rahmān* and *ar-Rahīm*, often translated as the Compassionate and the Merciful, which implies that the essential reality of the Divine is Mercy. The experience of the feminine in our relative world of forms—whether through women in the context of maternal or erotic love, for instance, or independently from women as manifestations of cosmic qualities—is therefore ultimately a more or less direct participation in the dimension of Divine Mercy. As for All-Possibility, it must be referred to as the reality of Infinite freedom, which means that it excludes any constraints and limitations and thus manifests as a sense of limitless expansion. The Krishnaite inspiration is characterized, in this respect, as a capacity to transcend the limitations of feminine manifestations to plunge, as it were, into the depth of their reality, which is, literally, unlimited. If sexuality is, among all aspects of human existence, the most likely to give rise to a mistaken absolutization of phenomena—given the centrality and therefore intensity of the reality that it involves—it is also, and for the same reasons, an open door onto the unlimited horizon of Reality. The profane experience of sexuality and human love itself, in its most diverse forms, bears witness to intimations of a sense of the Absolute, as evidenced in the language of lovers and the depth and intensity that they associate with their love. There is in every paradigmatic love story a religious, and even spiritual, dimension.

The receptive centering inherent to the spiritual experience of human love—as epitomized by the *gopis*—is equivalent, in a methodically reverse manner, to what Śaivite and Tantric practices aim at in developing their techniques of reconnection between the pulsation of the emotions and their absolute source, which is none other than the beatific freedom of *Śiva*. By contrast, the idolatrous potential of sexuality results from its ability—itself a function of its centrality and power—to divert awareness from present God-consciousness, thus leading it into the blind alleys of dissipated consciousness and its submission to the lures of sequential time. As we have touched on earlier, time erodes the spiritual resolve of the soul and reveals the measure of its failing to identify with the Spirit; moreover, outwardness is productive of the illusions of time, with its dual pitfalls of attachment to the past and alienation through an inordinate consideration of the future.

Tantrism has become popularized, in the West, as a type of Asian spirituality, whether Hindu or Buddhist, that conceives of sexuality—more specifically sexual energy—as a means of realizing the Unconditioned. However, the context of Tantrism is "invariably one of cultic ritual or meditation."[32] Sexuality may or may not play a central role in such practices, but when it does it is in a context that excludes both hedonism and sentimentality. The major ambiguity, if not peril, of the current popular concept of Tantrism is that it takes a contemporary predicament as a starting point for something that is quite deeply foreign to the cultural presuppositions of modernity. A fundamental misunderstanding arises whereby popularized forms of Tantrism are deemed to echo the mood of the so-called sexual revolution when, in fact, these types of discipline are actually among the most constraining and demanding, being subject to the strictest spiritual guidance. Tantrism is therefore less a sexual liberation than a liberation through sexuality, if one may put it this way.

When considering Schuon's references to Tantrism, it is important to stress that his use of the term is not technical. Although he explicitly refers to the energy that is inherent to Śaktic realities, his perspective on the matter cannot be equated with *kundalinī yoga*. It is both more gnostic and bhaktic—in the non-restrictive sense of the term—than strictly methodical. Even when commenting upon the more technical dimensions of sexual yoga, Schuon situates the latter within a metaphysical and religious context. This clearly appears, for instance, in an important passage devoted to *Mahashakti*: "As immanent and latent liberating power—or as potentiality of liberation—the *Shakti* is called *Kundalinī*, 'Coiled-up,' because it is compared to a sleeping snake; its awakening in the human microcosm is effected thanks to the yogic practices of Tantrism. This means, from the standpoint of the nature of things or of universal spirituality, that the cosmic energy which liberates us is part of our very being, notwithstanding the graces that the *Shakti* confers upon us, through mercy, 'from without' and

---

32. Arvind Sharma, ed., *Our Religions* (New York: HarperOne, 1995), 31.

but for which there can be no Path."[33] It is significant that Schuon would move from a specific technical consideration of *kundalinī* as a field of energetic locations to a broader, more metaphysically grounded, view of it as "part of our being," thus implicitly identifying it with spiritual Selfhood. It is no less meaningful that the same reference to Śaktic energy tends to be couched in terms of spiritual grace rather than as a technical method of awakening of energy centers, such as *chakras*. This is an important point to stress, inasmuch as it highlights that Schuon's view of spirituality suggests an equilibrium between spiritual method and divine grace. For him, there is no conflict between technique and grace, since the two are necessarily involved in any spiritual path corresponding, as they do, to different accentuations and vantage points.[34]

In this respect, the case of Ramakrishna reveals a fundamental concordance with Schuon's "Tantrism" both with respect to the centrality of the Goddess and to the general principle of the "metaphysical transparency" of earthly femininity and beauty.[35] It is worth noting, however, a somewhat different accentuation in each of their perspectives. Ramakrishna is more exclusive than Schuon regarding the possibility of integrating sexuality into spirituality in our day and age. Thus, he declares to his disciples: "Although *Tantra* prescribes spiritual discipline in the company of woman, that is not desirable. It is a very difficult path and often causes the aspirant's downfall. There are three such kinds of discipline. One may regard woman as one's mistress or look on oneself as her handmaid or as her child. I look on woman as my mother. To look on oneself as her handmaid is also good; but it is extremely difficult to practice spiritual discipline looking on woman as one's mistress. To regard oneself as Her child is a very pure attitude."[36] It is quite clear that Ramakrishna is keenly aware that the path of "worshipping" woman—under her erotic aspect—presents particular challenges, and it is quite apparent that these are virtually insurmountable for most. Elsewhere, in the same passage, he characterizes the erotic path as that of the "hero" who "pleases *Śakti*

---

33. Schuon, *Roots of the Human Condition*, 31.

34. On this matter, see "A View of Yoga" in *Language of the Self*, 43–61.

35. Schuon notes that "the Paramahamsa adored his wife without touching her; which is of infinitely greater worth than touching her without adoring her." *Esoterism as Principle and as Way*, 134.

36. *The Gospel of Sri Ramakrishna* (New York: Ramakrishna-Vivekananda Center, 1942), 123.

even as a man pleases a woman through intercourse," adding that "the worship of *Śakti* is extremely difficult." This difficulty is also present in the path of service to woman (i.e., as the "handmaid" of *Śakti*), which is an interesting reminder of the modalities found in the *service d'amor* of the medieval troubadours addressed to high-ranking ladies.

In a sense, Ramakrishna's triplicity corresponds to Schuon's consideration of the Eternal Feminine as Virgin, Mother, and Betrothed or Fiancée. It is to the Virgin that corresponds the service of the handmaid's love, and it is this quality that predominates in the devotion to Kālī. Purity, Mercy, and Beauty are therefore prominent, and Ramakrishna's choice of the "child" vocation obviously relates to the fact that the second of these divine feminine qualities presents mankind with a more accessible path, one that is characterized by grace rather than by ascetic efforts. Even though Ramakrishna is not explicit about the reasons for his caution concerning the third path, it appears quite likely that this implies a reference to the Hindu eschatological concept of the Dark Age (*Kali-Yuga*), which is marked by the domination of passions and disorders. In such an age, any attempt at a technical integration of sexuality into the spiritual path is likely to be fraught with grave perils. Our day and age intensifies, in all likelihood, such dangers, due both to the centrifugal predispositions of contemporary mankind and to the qualitative influence of the cultural ambience, the two being in fact inextricably linked. The first consideration relates to the fact that modern mentalities are unlikely to be trained to deal with sexuality in a way that would be independent of hedonistic desires, while the second takes account of the desacralization of sexuality within a contemporary context. On the one hand, Schuon's nontechnical and traditionally sanctioned envisioning of Tantrism echoes Ramakrishna's concerns. On the other, Schuon suggests the possibility of integrating sexuality in a way that does not necessarily entail abstinence.

Schuon's universalizing extension of the term "Tantrism" may be deemed as preferable in view of the more profound understanding of the relationship between spirituality and sexuality that his perspective offers. Contemporary sensibilities, especially in the West, appear to be determined by extremely polarized positions that can hardly be reconciled and that lie at the source of many tensions and confusions. The trivialization of sexuality, in both secular and some legally sanctioned religious contexts, has made it very difficult to write about the matter without raising moral suspicions or inviting fanciful and perilous responses. In the West, such reactions may be considered a backlash against one-sided Augustinian or puritanical views of sexuality, leading to the widely held view that hedonistic license and moralistic rigorism are but two sides of the same predicament. Contemporary Islamic perspectives, by contrast, reflect a kind of religious formalization of sexuality that can easily degenerate into self-serving practices and their own form of unconscious profanation. A universal and principial consideration of Tantrism can open the way, in such contexts, to a rehabilitation of human love and sexuality informed by a renewed sense of the sacred. The fact that Schuon, in contrast to many other writers on the subject, does not approach Tantrism from a technical point of view—but rather as a general category—makes it all the more amenable to a wider spiritual application. This broader interpretation of *tantra* invites faithful seekers from various traditions to consider more inclusively the ways in which the Divine Presence manifests itself with a view to inviting a deeper reintegration of sexuality. More specifically, and considering that sexuality is most likely to give rise to a subjective divinisation of the object contemplated,[37] it is important to discern the sacred dimension of that domain and its inherent connection with transcendence. This does not amount to embracing any form of sexual yoga but simply to situating a fundamental dimension of human life within a context that is focused on its most elevated and beautiful manifestations. As such, this is an invitation to sacralize human love without losing sight of the ambiguities and inferior possibilities that sexuality carries in its wake. As for the specifically tantric path, it normally presupposes or requires a number of objective and subjective conditions, in terms of social ambience, traditional guidance, and vocational qualifications that are most likely to remain unfulfilled in a contemporary context. Its power is also the measure of the depth of its virtual pitfalls. Taking stock of both the need for bringing out the sacred dimension of sexuality and the limitations of the context in which this need arises, Schuon proposes to extract the spiritual quintessence of erotic emotions and aesthetic awe, while pointing out that it cannot bear fruits aside from the imperatives of the contemplative life, which itself requires the protection of a religious and traditional framework.

The Krishnaite quality that Schuon recognizes in some prophetic and sapiential luminaries may help one to look beyond the conventional suspicions that are attached to the conjunction of spirituality and sexuality,

---

37. "Beauty—sexual beauty above all—invites to 'let go of the prey for its shadow,' that is, to forget the transcendent content through being attached to the earthly husk." Schuon, *From the Divine to the Human*, 86.

even though these reductions are not without extenuating circumstances given the abuses that this domain invites, particularly in the modern world. To the extent that such examples are a model for spiritual seekers, they also bring to their understanding of sexuality a contemplative sense of the sacred. That which tends to draw most people away from a sense of transcendence may thus be reconsidered in a new light, thus contributing to a resacralization of existence above and beyond the unconscious profanations of secularized sexuality and their backlash of puritanical suspicions and negations. Thus the ascetic ideal of abstinence and the contemplative potentialities of eroticism may not necessarily be mutually exclusive or incompatible. This important point is clearly brought out in Schuon's remark that "abstinence does not necessarily signify that the sexual act is sinful by nature; it may signify on the contrary that sinners profane it; for in sexual union sinners rob God of enjoyment which belongs to Him."[38] Whether considered from the point of view of the Krishnaite vocation or in the perspective of methodical Tantrism, the point that needs to be stressed is that sacralized sexuality, whatever its modes and scope, is a way to give back to the Absolute what truly belongs to it. Contemplated in this way sin is less a transgression than a benighted limitation and a misguided appropriation of a reality that is in itself free from the curse it has too often incurred. As for the sacramental quality and transformative power of human love and sexuality, this emerges from a heightened sense of the Absolute and the Infinite. By advocating a deeper connection, Krishnaite contemplatives do not necessarily invite others to follow literally in their footsteps, for this is doubtlessly more a question of spiritual function and karmic constitution than one of spiritual striving. One may not thus be induced to imitate that which, surely, demands more than most individuals can attain, let alone fathom, but one may draw from the Krishnaite exemplar lessons that evoke—at the very least—the horizon of what lies beyond the ordinary human frailties and confusions associated with sexuality. A consideration of the Krishnaite paradigm may well help us to maintain a healthy balance between a realistic awareness of the ambivalence of human sexuality and its pitfalls, and a liberating sense of the ultimate Object of our longings and desires. Krishna is indeed one of a kind, surrounded as he is by the many *gopis* in love with him, but he is also, in reality, none other than the Self of all selves, the one who awakens each lover to the hidden, deepest secret of Love.

---

38. Schuon, *Esoterism as Principle and as Way*, 131.

10

Esoteric Ecumenism

The two notions of ecumenism and esoterism are rarely combined. In the contemporary world, the two concepts most often appear within radically distinct contexts. The first one tends to refer either, in the most limited sense, to efforts at promoting convergences and unity among the various Churches professing the Christian creed or, more generally, to any attempt at bridging gaps between various religious communities. It may be, therefore, depending on the context, a mostly theological, pastoral, or sociocultural undertaking. Whatever form it may take, ecumenism has been brought to the fore by increased social and cultural mobility and communication, and the overall ambience of religious globalization. By contrast, the term esoterism has become gradually disconnected from any religious anchoring, increasingly referring to various principles and disciplines that entail arcane meaning and occult practices. Indeed, the popular referents of the word esoterism would exclusively fall under the broad heading of occult sciences, foremost among which are popularized forms of astrology, alchemy, and kindred disciplines and practices reformulated in the context of neo-spiritualism. Even though the word esoterism has a long and rich history of denoting inner philosophical circles and teachings as well as spiritual hermeneutics, among other phenomena, it has unfortunately accrued connotations of fantasy or vain abstruseness that have led many, especially in academia, to use it as a dismissive term, if not a derisory one. Needless to say, the way Schuon approaches and defines esoterism is radically different from the neo-spiritualist understanding of the term. Without entering the detail of his extensive characterization of the term, and the particular emphases that it may involve within different contexts, it suffices to say that Schuon takes the concept of esoterism back to its denotations of an inner, spiritual knowledge that may be reached through intellectual and contemplative means, and is therefore accessible only to the relatively small number of those who are both aspiring to, and qualified for, its reception and cultivation. Schuon defines esoterism in terms of metaphysics and spirituality. In other words, there are esoteric doctrines and esoteric contemplative methods, and integral esoterism combines both. Doctrinally speaking, as we have indicated in another chapter, esoterism is characterized by its focus on three key concepts: Beyond Being, *Māyā*, and the Intellect, all of which are relevant to the definition of an "esoteric ecumenism." This means, in a nutshell, that esoterism holds the notion of the "absolutely Absolute" and not simply that of the Divine Principle while identifying everything but the Absolute to Relativity, including the Personal Divine Being, and postulating the immanence of Divine Intelligence as a kind of prolongation of the Absolute within all of creatures, and eminently so within human beings. Operatively, esoterism is practically synonymous with spiritual inwardness, and more comprehensively so with objectivity or the path of transcending egoic delusions, both dispositions providing the foundations for an encounter between contemplative and spiritual traditions.

As already intimated, whereas ecumenism refers to a religious reality, esoterism is considered to pertain to a spiritual domain, either in the proper sense of a life centered on the transcendent or with the mere contemporary connotations of a diffuse aspiration toward a subjective realm of personal experience. While ecumenical endeavors are primarily prompted by a need to build social and cultural bridges between communities, esoterism, with the wide spectrum of meaning and deep ambiguities that the term entails, tends to be the province of individual quests for meaning and inner fulfillment. Hence the rarity of the association of the two terms, hence also the particular significance of Schuon's use of them, one that differs profoundly from ordinary concepts and practices of ecumenism.

The name of Frithjof Schuon has been largely associated with his celebrated book *The Transcendent Unity of Religions*, first published in French in 1948. Cursory references to this work take stock of the implications of its title, and identify Schuon as a representative of the so-called perennialist school, which most academic and popular accounts characterize, often within the context of a discussion of contemporary pluralism, as propounding a convergence of world religions. In the wake of such a hasty assessment, some analysts understand the perennialist outlook as amounting to a negation of differences among religious faiths, whether they applaud this negation or not.[1] A careful reading of Schuon's work shows, however, that his perspective on religious diversity cannot be equated with the ideological or sentimental types of pluralism or ordinary ecumenical perspectives of modernity. Although it opens the way, as the latter may also, to a potentially greater and deeper reciprocal understanding among religious faiths and communities, it is profoundly different from most manifestations of modern pluralism in its unflinching and consistent opposition to any kind of relativism, and because it is not determined or motivated by social and political factors consistent with the contemporary ethos of multiculturalism.

In order to buttress this point, there is probably no better way than to compare Schuon's perspective with what is arguably the most influential form of religious pluralism in Western academia, articulated by John Hick in his book *An Interpretation of Religion: Human Responses to the Transcendent*.[2] The type of pluralism that has been theorized by Hick, and widely discussed in academic circles, deserves to be situated in contrast with Schuon's "esoteric ecumenism" in order to bring to the fore what may escape a superficial reading. Let us note, first of all, that Hick's pluralism, like Schuon's esoteric ecumenism, cannot be fairly considered as dismissing religious differences a priori in the name of ecumenical unity.[3] Both accounts recognize the irreducible diversity of religious

---

1. See, for example, Stephen Prothero's *God Is Not One* (Melbourne: Black Ink, 2010), in which the author criticizes what he calls the "pretend pluralism" of perennialist scholar Huston Smith on various counts, including the fact that Smith exclusively focuses on "religions at their best," therefore ignoring the "dirty laundry" of religious controversies and conflicts (*God Is Not One*, x–xi). The least one can say is that Schuon, for his part, does not bypass these issues, tensions, and oppositions. At any rate, Prothero's remarks might illustrate Henry Corbin's penetrating insight that "the mode of understanding is conditioned by the mode of being of the one *who understands* [Le mode de comprendre est conditionné par le mode d'être de celui qui comprend]." Henry Corbin, *Histoire de la philosophie islamique* (Paris: Gallimard, 1964), 14.

2. John Hick, *An Interpretation of Religion: Human Responses to the Transcendent* (1989; New Haven, CT: Yale University Press, 2004).

3. "Contrary to common misperception, the perennial philosophy does not claim that all religions are the same." Andrew Noel Blakeslee, "The Great Chain of Pluralism: Religious Diversity According to John Hick and the Perennial Philosophy," in *The World's Religions after September 11*, vol. 3, edited by Arvind Sharma (Westport, CT: Praeger, 2009), 51.

paths, while also asserting for them a common goal, which Hick characterizes as the "transformation of human existence from self-centredness to Reality-centredness"[4] and Schuon as religion's "unanimous function of detaching man from the here-below and from the ego in order to lead him toward the hereafter and toward the Divine."[5] Like Schuon's, Hick's approach is indeed quite circumstantiated, but its specificity rests upon a distinction between two levels of consideration that are conceived as allowing for the validity of both religious plurality and pluralism, or else the fact of religious diversity and its theological legitimization. Thus, Hick makes use of his own version of the fundamental Kantian epistemological distinction between the "noumenal" and the "phenomenal" to account for his argument in favor of religious pluralism. As we will see, these two concepts function in a way that is formally analogous, but essentially different, from Schuon's dyad of the esoteric and the exoteric. In other words, Hick's whole theological development begins with the philosophical distinction between "an entity as it is in itself and as it appears in perception."[6] Whether understood theistically or not, or to use Hick's own expressions whether referring to *personae* or to *impersonae*[7] of the Real, it is clear that what is related to generically as the Real,[8] that is the ultimate and non-subratable Reality, pertains to the domain of the unknowable. Only the "phenomenal" dimensions of religious traditions are accessible to mankind, as they define the contours of the various objects of faith, as it were. This distinction between the "unknown" and the "known" as "intentional objects" of the human knower allows Hick to provide the theoretical foundation for a pluralistic outlook that preserves both the legitimacy of religious diversity inasmuch as it relates to a diversity of

---

4. Hick, *An Interpretation of Religion*, 36.
5. Schuon, *From the Divine to the Human* (Bloomington, IN: World Wisdom, 2013), 100.
6. Hick, *An Interpretation of Religion*, 241.
7. "The environing divine reality is brought to consciousness in terms of certain basic concepts or categories. These are, first the concept of God, or of the real as personal, which presides over the various theistic forms of religious experience; and second, the concept of the Absolute, or of the Real as non-personal, which presides over its various non-theistic forms." Hick, *An Interpretation of Religion*, 245.
8. "'The Real' is then, I suggest, as good a generic name as we have for that which is affirmed in the varying forms of transcendent religious belief. For it is used within the major theistic and non-theistic traditions and yet is neutral as between their very different ways of conceiving, experiencing and responding to that which they affirm in these diverse ways." Hick, *An Interpretation of Religion*, 11.

human phenomena, and the unity of a common, albeit unknown and unknowable, horizon. Several points deserve consideration here to sharply contrast Hick's perspective with Schuon's.

The first point to highlight refers to the theistic and non-theistic concepts of the Principle in relation to the latter's noumenal reality. For Hick, these are two basic ways of representing and experiencing the Real, as it were, while keeping in mind that these expressions are inadequate since the Real lies ultimately beyond all representations and experiences. These two ways involve personal divine figures on the one hand and impersonal realities on the other hand; *personae* and *impersonae* of the Real. It must be understood, however, that there is clearly no subordination of one way to the other, nor any ontological hierarchy with respect to their respective objects, since both the *personae* and *impersonae* of the Real are situated on the same level of human "imaginal" and conceptual crystallizations that shape and nurture religious experiences. Moreover, there does not appear to be any relationship between the *personae* and the *impersonae*, with no intimations, for instance, that the first might be manifestations of the second. The two are simply different ways of envisioning the Real, such as the *personae* of Jehowah and Allāh and the *impersonae* of the Tao and the Buddha-nature. In fact, the *personae* and *impersonae* belong to different religious universes of meaning, whether in different religious traditions or, as is more rarely the case, in different schools belonging to the same tradition; and their only relationship, if one may call it so provisionally, is the one they respectively enjoy with the Real, leaving aside for now the thorny question of the modes of this relation.

Any reader of Schuon will recognize that Hick's hypothesis of religious pluralism is radically different from the perennialist metaphysics of the transcendent unity of religions.[9] By contrast with what Hick refers to as the Real, that which Schuon diversely denotes by terms such as Beyond-Being and Essence is not only an epistemological assumption, so to speak, but an ontological, or rather supra-ontological, Principle to which all traditions refer more or less explicitly in different ways. This Ultimate Reality is not relational since it is intrinsically absolute, that is, utterly free and independent, and therefore cannot be personal in and of itself, inasmuch as the concept of *persona*, at least as understood by

---

9. For an analysis of these major differences, see the already quoted essay by Andrew Noel Blakeslee, "The Great Chain of Pluralism: Religious Diversity According to John Hick and the Perennial Philosophy," in Sharma, *The World's Religions after September 11*, vol. 3, 49–69.

Hick, necessarily entails relationality. By contrast, Schuon's Essence, often referred to as Beyond-Being to highlight its transcending all determinations, including Personal Being, is "impersonal," not in the sense of any privation, but inasmuch as it lies beyond delimitations of persons and aspects. Now one of Schuon's most important metaphysical intuitions is that the Divine Essence, which is none other than the Absolute, gives rise, by virtue of the Absolute's very dimension of Infinitude, to the ontological degree of Relativity *in divinis*, which Schuon refers to as "relatively Absolute." This is the first Determination or Delimitation of the Principle *qua* Being, which assumes a personal aspect in relation to mankind. Theistic faiths are based on Being as personal determination of the Essence, and they therefore necessarily entail a kind of "phenomenality" of the Divine, if one may say so, the term being taken here in the etymological sense of an appearance of Reality, or in regard to Reality as determining and manifesting Itself within the context of a relationship. Therefore, it is plain that Schuon's metaphysical account does not treat "the *impersonae* and *personae* of the Real" as different aspects, but considers them, rather, as distinct degrees. Far from being simply Schuon's personal view of the matter, several metaphysical traditions, within distinct religious universes, provide similar accounts of a hierarchization of the "absolutely Absolute" and the "relatively Absolute" within the Great Chain of Being. Thus, the Divine Essence of Sufi theosophy (*adh-dhāt al-ilāhiyyah*) transcends any relationship with creation, mankind, and any relativity whatsoever, and is therefore non-personal,[10] as is the Hindu Non-Qualified Ultimate or *Nirguna Brahman*.[11]

---

10. "Know that the Essence of God The Supreme is the mystery *(ghayb)* of the Unity*(al-ahadiyah)* which every symbol expresses in a certain respect, without it being able to express It under many other respects. One conceives It then not by some rational idea, any more than one understands It by some conventional allusion *(ishārah)*; for one understands a thing only by virtue of a relation, which assigns to it a position, or by a negation, hence by its contrary; but, there is not, in all existence, a single relation which 'situates' the Essence, nor a single assignation which applies to It, consequently nothing that can deny It and nothing which is contrary to It. It is, for language, as if It did not exist, and in this respect It refuses human understanding." Abd al-Karīm al-Jīlī, *Universal Man*, translated by Titus Burckhardt (Roxburgh, Scotland: Beshara Publications, 1983), 4.

11. "It is *Saguna Brahman* who is in relation to human beings as well as the world. *Nirguna Brahman* cannot be worshipped because it is pure consciousness and completely transcends the empirical world." Kiseong Shin, *The Concept of Self in Hinduism, Buddhism, and Christianity* (Eugene, OR: Pickwick, 2017), 33.

The second main difference between Schuon and Hick lies in their respective approaches to the relation between the Real *qua* Real and the human experience of it, or the noumenal and the phenomenal. In Hick's account, the nature of this relation remains largely elusive, both in its teleology and modalities. Here is what Hick has to say about the way the Real relates to human religious experience: "The 'presence' of the Real consists in the availability, from a transcendent source, of information that the human mind/brain is capable of transforming into what we call religious experience."[12] The key words herein are, no doubt, "availability" and "information." The nature and modes of both this availability and this information remain relatively unspecific. Is the information intrinsically contained, as it were, within the Real, and if so, what makes it susceptible of becoming available and in what ways? Hick all too easily gives the impression that the Real is like a transcendent and virtual library of data that are somehow accessed by mankind and translated into largely mythological accounts shaped by the very limitations of the human brain. The very use of terms such as "availability," "information," and "mind-brain" may already betray, for many metaphysicians, a somewhat scientistic perspective that reduces religious phenomena to a manner of Divine information technology. While the Abrahamic notion of Revelation—to take only one example—refers, in a way, to the transmission of some information from a transcendent source, it also entails a providential intentionality on the part of the latter, as well as a theophanic and transformative reality to which a mere reference to availability and information may be deemed to fail to do justice. Indeed, in traditional religions, the mode of the presence of the Real is thought to extend well beyond instances of theological information. Religion not only provides one with epistemic facts, if one may say so, but also, and above all, with sacred and transformative means, the virtues of which are thought to derive both from their transcendent origin and their ontological texture, as it were. The institution of rites and sacraments is particularly central in this respect, since it is believed to flow from a transcendent source.

The distinction between revelation—a word that Hick rarely uses—and information has profound implications in terms of the Schuonian delineation between orthodox traditions and those religious movements that fall beyond the pale of orthodoxy. For Schuon, as for all perennialists, the main virtue of religious traditions is not, in a sense, the conceptual

---

12. Hick, *An Interpretation of Religion*, 244.

framework that they provide through their theology—for such a framework could be conceivably recognized and conceptualized outside of religion—but the intrinsic power of transmutation of forms that is inherent in what transcends the formal realm. Considering Hick's pluralistic hypothesis with regard to the relationship between the supra-formal Real and the forms in which it is couched, the question remains of understanding how the Real, which is intrinsically noumenal and unknowable, may make itself present within forms. Such an understanding would demand a differentiated metaphysical survey that could provide insights into the paradox of the unknowableness of the Real and its capacity to make Itself known through "information." In other words, it is not enough to refer to the Real and to the formal accounts of the Real, but one must also provide some doctrine of the ways the Real is mediated or the ways in which it manifests through degrees of reality that entail both continuity and discontinuity.

Now, in Schuon's view, the human relatability of the Absolute and its information flows both from the essence of the Real Itself and from the nature of mankind. As do most diverse metaphysical traditions, Schuon sees the Ultimate as both unrelatable in itself and necessarily relatable in relation to other-than-Itself. This is the distinction between the Absolute and the relatively Absolute that we sketched above. In a sense, this distinction provides the paradigm for all further ontological distinctions, so that the line that separates the Absolute from the Relative is reproduced, relatively speaking, on all lower degrees of reality. The gap between the Real and human reality, that Hick contemplates primarily as epistemological, is actually bridged ontologically through the degrees of the Real. It is the same Reality that manifests Itself, delimits Itself, through the entire range of being. This is the way in which the Real becomes knowable extrinsically so to speak. But there is also a way in which the Real is known as Self, and therefore by Itself, within or through the human subject. Among all spiritual traditions, *Advaita Vedānta* is probably the one that has brought out this teaching of the realization of the Divine Self in the most explicit way, with the notion of *Ātman*. This Self-realization is in itself not mediated, for the very notion of mediation presupposes an objectification that is contrary to Self-recognition. The means of Self-realization can be conceived as mediations, and the human awareness of Self-realization is necessarily mediated by psychic and cultural factors, but that does not prevent Self-realization itself from being unmediated and utterly independent from representations.[13] However, this Self-realization, which transcends human knowledge as such, is connected to the theomorphic aspect of mankind. In other words, there is in man a Divine spark that is the seed of God-knowledge. Such an understanding highlights a major difference between Schuon's gnostic point of view and Hick's Kantian epistemology. For Hick, the Real, to the extent that it can be equated with the Ultimate Essence, is deemed to be unknowable: it is a pure noumemon. Religious phenomena are only human responses to this transcendent noumenon. Andrew Noel Blakesleee encapsulated the difference between this view and the perennialist outlook when he writes that "from the perennialist perspective, each of the great tradition of the world is a manifestation of a divine archetype" whereas "from Hick's perspective, each religion is a very human creation and culturally conditioned response to the one ineffable Real."[14] This epistemological situation raises, obviously, the question of the adequacy of the various religious ways of knowledge of the Real, and of the criteria that allow one to assess their adequacy, or lack thereof. It is interesting to note, in this respect, that Hick includes Marxism and numerous recent religious movements among religions, and that he does not provide, more generally, any criteria that would allow one to separate the grain from the chaff.

By contrast with Hick's overly inclusive concept of religion, Schuon's ecumenism does not embrace just any religious realities. It is founded on a rigorous notion of orthodoxy; and this is another respect in which it parts company with Hick's pluralism and many other forms of contemporary ecumenism. As we have mentioned, John Hick goes so far as to include within his pluralistic span, albeit with some hesitation, not only new religious movements, but even ideologies such as Marxism on the

---

13. When Hick claims that "there is a transcendent reality which is the ultimate focus of religious concern but it can only become an object of human awareness in the range of forms made possible by our conceptual repertoire" (*An Interpretation of Religion*, xxii), he is both right and wrong depending on the meaning one gives to "human awareness." *Advaita Vedānta*, for instance, claims that the recognition of the Self is both supra-human and immanent to human consciousness, defying thereby the categories of ordinary experience.

14. Andrew Noel Blakeslee, "The Great Chain of Pluralism: Religious Diversity According to John Hick and the Perennial Philosophy," in *The World's Religions after September 11*, 64.

basis that "there is no inherent incompatibility between a basically Marxist analysis of the development of capitalist society and belief in the Transcendent."[15] By contrast, Schuon's definition of orthodoxy is based, first of all, on a distinction between "intrinsic" and "extrinsic" orthodoxy, and, second, on the consideration of a series of objective criteria of intrinsic orthodoxy. For him, the adjective extrinsic means, in this context, that the standard of reference for orthodoxy is not the nature of things as such, but rather the dogmatic crystallization of a particular religious standpoint. A particular metaphysical point of view may be intrinsically orthodox without being necessarily extrinsically orthodox in any religious context. In other words, any religion needs be in some ways extrinsically heterodox in relation to the tenets of another one. However, this does not preclude both of those traditions being intrinsically orthodox—which must lead to the question of the determination of the criteria of intrinsic orthodoxy. It is significant that these criteria are of two different types, conceptual on the one hand and operative on the other hand. The first condition for the intrinsic orthodoxy of a religion lies, for Schuon, in its offering "a sufficient, if not always exhaustive, idea of the absolute and the relative, and therewith an idea of their reciprocal relationships."[16] Now the concept of the Absolute is characterized by unity, exclusive transcendence, and inclusive immanence. In his *Understanding Islam*, Schuon further specifies that metaphysical error dwells "in holding that the Absolute is not, or that it is relative, or that there are two Absolutes, or that the relative is absolute."[17] This statement provides us with keys for identifying the various kinds of metaphysical hererodoxy from a Schuonian point of view. The negation of the Absolute, whether explicit or implicit, excludes from the circle of orthodoxy atheistic, relativist, dualist, and pantheistic concepts. Thus ideologies such as Marxism, but also nihilistic interpretations of Buddhism, for instance, lie beyond the pale of an orthodox "pluralism." As for the second misconception of the Absolute, it can be asserted that many neo-spiritualist movements, particularly in the New Age constellation, fall into the category of relativistic spirituality, as they see spirituality as being founded on individual needs and preferences and

---

15. Hick, *An Interpretation of Religion*, 379.
16. Schuon, *Light on the Ancient Worlds* (Bloomington, IN: World Wisdom, 2006), 121.
17. Schuon, *Understanding Islam* (Bloomington, IN: World Wisdom, 2011), 1.

geared toward a greater peace of mind, ease, and effectiveness in the world of relative concerns. Some forms of extreme Christian incarnationism would also be characterized, albeit in a very different way, by an abusive relativization, if not in some extreme cases a gross materialization, of the Absolute. Moreover, forms of religious dualism that posit two supreme metaphysical forces are also incompatible with an orthodox concept of the Absolute, since the very concept of the Absolute entails an utter freedom that dualism precludes. It must be noted, moreover, that some forms of religious faith that tend to absolutize the reality of evil end up making the latter into a second Absolute, if not theoretically at least subjectively or practically. They forget that evil is only a privation of the Good and not a substance on its own. Moreover, a religious perspective that would not make room for any reciprocal relationship between the Absolute and the relative, would be, analogously, fundamentally lacking in orthodox foundations in the sense that it would also amount to the affirmation of two Absolutes: the Absolute on the one hand, and the relative as a kind of independent, and therefore absolute, substance on the other hand. As for the fourth anti-absolutist position, according to which "the relative is the absolute," it corresponds to forms of pantheism and paganism that divinize creation, here again either objectively or subjectively, making a true god out of it, or worshipping it as if it were a god.

These metaphysical misconceptions can be contrasted with any intrinsically orthodox concept of the Absolute, including the dogmatic tenets of the major world religions. However, a sufficient idea of the Absolute is not enough to guarantee the orthodoxy of a religious movement. The second component of intrinsic orthodoxy is the *operative* complement, in a sense the practical proof of the validity of the metaphysical inspiration of the religion, and this means "a spiritual activity that is contemplative in its nature and effectual as concerns our ultimate destiny."[18] This pertains to the rites, spiritual practices, and contemplative disciplines without which the metaphysical content of the religion remains abstract. The criteria of effectualness of those spiritual means are not specified in the aforementioned passage, but Schuon explains elsewhere that the operative effectiveness of an orthodox religion is demonstrated by its teachings about the summits of human sanctity or wisdom, and its actual capacity to produce

---

18. Schuon, *Light on the Ancient World*, 121.

saints and sages—in other words, to be spiritually transformative.[19] This is another way of saying that the source of the religion is not human but Divine, since only a transcendent source could endow formal and ritual supports with the power to transmute the human soul. The understanding and modalities of sanctity may differ from one religion to another, but they always involve some modes and degrees of transparence of the human receptacle vis-à-vis the Transcendent. What Schuon implies here is that one would hardly find the equivalents of the contemplative summits of Christianity or Hinduism, for instance, in the quasi-religious movements that have appeared in the twentieth century. Moreover, the traditional seal of this orthodox capacity lies in the development of a sacred art that crystallizes the principles and values of a given religion. Here again, the language of artistic forms is a highly revealing standard of evaluation of orthodoxy that excludes the trivial, the chaotic, and the individualistic and testifies, above all, to a homogeneous formal style flowing from the very principles and spirit of the tradition.[20] Needless to say, a discussion of these criteria in a contemporary context may raise all manner of questions and objections. Perhaps the simplest and most direct way to address those questions in a general manner is to stress that the substance of the Schuonian standards of orthodoxy all derive from a reference to the sense of the sacred, which he defines as the human receptivity to the emergence of the Center within the periphery.[21] This is true as much in the domain of metaphysics, where the Center must manifest on the mental periphery in the manner of a rigorous intellectual sense of the Absolute, as in the

---

19. "For a religion to be considered as intrinsically orthodox it must be founded upon a fully adequate doctrine of the Absolute (extrinsic orthodoxy depending upon particular formal elements which cannot be applied literally outside the perspective to which they refer); it must also advocate and realize a spirituality that is adequate to this doctrine, which means that it must comprise both the notion and the fact of sanctity. The religion must therefore be of Divine, and not philosophical, origin, and in virtue of this origin it must be the vehicle of a sacramental or theurgic presence which manifests itself especially in miracles and also—though this may seem surprising to some—in sacred art." Schuon, *Form and Substance in the Religions* (Bloomington, IN: World Wisdom, 2002), 13.

20. "The formal language of the sacred, whether it be the language of sanctuaries or of nature, is like the complement or prolongation of sapience." Schuon, *Form and Substance in the Religions*, 214.

21. "The sacred is the presence of the center in the periphery." Schuon, *Understanding Islam*, 38.

domain of sanctity, where the grace of the Divine must be experienced in and through the human crystallizations of the religious message.

Besides those fundamental criteria that pertain to the presence of the sacred, there is another, more extrinsic,[22] criterion of orthodoxy, or rather heterodoxy, which is of a cyclical character. In this respect, Schuon's claim is that the time for the appearance of orthodox dispensations has passed, a consideration that also reflects, extrinsically, the claims of the three Abrahamic traditions, if not those of other living traditions. Although Schuon does not elaborate on the reasons for such a claim, it is not too difficult to infer them from a meditation of his works. Like other proponents of the perennial philosophy, he sees our day and age as being characterized by an unprecedented onslaught on spiritual and civilizational principles, and therefore ill disposed to become the recipient of a major sacred dispensation. Even if one agrees with this diagnosis, one may still wonder whether the specific and acute crisis of the modern world does not require, precisely, a compensation in the form of new religious movements that would bring responses to the intellectual and spiritual disorders of the age. After all, the historical appearance of religions like Christianity and Islam can be understood as corresponding to specific needs having arisen from the state of spiritual and moral crisis of the Ancient Mediterranean world and the Arab pagan culture. Notwithstanding the validity of those remarks, Schuon's point is that the appearance of a given religion presupposes a human and cultural context of a type that he deems utterly lacking in the modern world. Such pre-revelatory contexts are characterized by a state of traditional corruption, rather than by one of post-traditional confusion. What is at stake in religious revelations is the restoration of a mode of consciousness that has been either forgotten or neglected. The modern world, and even more so in its post-modern phase, is characterized, by contrast, by a deliberate and active rejection of transcendence and a quasi-exclusive emphasis on worldly values and objectives. Moreover, from the point of view of traditionalist writers such as Schuon, the cultural and psychological ambience induced by modern trends and lifestyle is not conducive to the reception of a message of transcendence, if only because of the individualistic atomization of culture and the psychic disintegration

---

22. "And this provides us with yet another criterion of orthodoxy—or of heterodoxy—for it is certain that in our times, that is for the last few centuries, the cyclic moment for the manifestation of the great perspectives (*darshanas*) is past." Schuon, *Stations of Wisdom* (Bloomington, IN: World Wisdom, 1995), 5.

that is generally prevalent. In fact, it could be argued that, by and large, what characterizes contemporary new religious movements is a deficit in their sense of transcendence, which amounts also to a lack of sense of the sacred. Psychological and ideological forms of reductionism are a rampant feature of contemporary religious life, and such trends inform and produce types of human make-up and predispositions that cannot provide an appropriate receptive substance for a direct reception of revelation. Schuon's view amounts to recognizing that there comes a time when it is too late for providence to offer ways of spiritual restoration on a collective level. Needless to say, the possibilities of individual redemption and spiritual realization cannot but remain open, even in the absence of traditional institutions and transmissions, but they become all the rarer and more precarious as the disintegrating wheel spins faster and faster. Similarly, it must be said that forms of spiritual renewal may take place in some relatively limited religious circles through various modalities of reconnection with the inspiring spirit of a tradition. Such circumscribed spiritual reinvigorations are quite different in modalities and scope from the appearance of major world religions. They actualize, from within the latter, latent possibilities that are awakened in accord with various historical needs. In fact, such actualizations are likely to be connected to the influence of esoterism in the context of a decay of religious forms. Here is the way Schuon articulates this paradoxical coincidence: "When the religious phenomenon, hard-pressed as it were by a badly interpreted experience, appears to be at the end of its resources, esoterism springs forth from the very depths of this phenomenon to show that Heaven cannot contradict itself."[23] The "badly interpreted experiences" most likely refer, here, both to the human vicissitudes of the religions themselves and to the extrinsic conflict between the various religious truth-claims. This allows one to fathom why only esoterism, which constitutes the uniting core-essence of all religious phenomena, can be the principle of restoration of each and every tradition while unveiling their unanimity. The "victory" of religions "on every level" can only occur on the basis of their essence, which is another way of saying that it occurs in consideration of the Essence.[24] Does it mean that Schuon contemplates the likelihood

---

23. Schuon, *From the Divine to the Human*, 115–16.

24. "The divine origin and the majesty of the religions implies that they must contain all truth and all answers; and there, precisely, lies the mystery and the role of esoterism. When the religious phenomenon, hard-pressed as it were by a badly interpreted

of an actual and external reassertion of religion on the level of forms? It is highly unlikely, since—as we have seen—the forms of religion have already been largely destroyed, or corrupted, by formalistic abuses and secularized compromises. What is affirmed by the Essence, therefore, through the means of esoterism, is the legitimacy, necessity, and validity of forms as such, but not their historical restoration or reassertion. In that sense, esoterism provides ways for religions to reconnect with their foundational principles, and to regain an intellectual position that may allow them to confront and engage other faiths both respectfully and fruitfully, and without compromising any element of their identity. The apparent paradox, however, is that the esoteric outlook is able to reestablish the inner authority of religions precisely to the extent that their outer authority has collapsed. It must be noted, moreover, that this intellectual reestablishment, to the extent that it flows from a consideration of the essence, and not from a sentimental or conventional attachment to the forms, envisions the existence of the latter in a non-formalistic manner and, therefore, in a way that cannot but entail some measure of synthetic essentialization. What all this means is that the esoteric outlook is the only essential and permanent foundation of orthodoxy.

Although the important and complex question of the nature of orthodoxy may *prima facie* seem peripheral to a consideration of esoterism and ecumenism, it is in point of fact crucial to an esoteric approach of religious plurality since it keeps ecumenism from being merely founded on social or sentimental considerations. What differentiates most clearly Schuon's esoteric ecumenism from most contemporary forms of ecumenism and interfaith initiatives is that it is vertical rather than horizontal. While most interreligious efforts in the modern world are motivated by external factors that are extrinsic to the spiritual reality of religion, Schuon's ecumenism proceeds from a point of view that transcends the very forms

---

experience, appears to be at the end of its resources, esoterism springs forth from the very depths of this phenomenon to show that Heaven cannot contradict itself; that a given religion in reality sums up all religions and that all religion is to be found in a given religion, because Truth is one. In other words: the contrast between the absolute character of Revelation and its aspect of relativity constitutes indirectly one more proof—along with the direct and historical proofs—both of the reality and the necessity of the esoteric dimension proper to all religion; so much so that the religions, at the very moment when they seem to be defeated by experience, affirm themselves victoriously on every level by their very essence." Schuon, *From the Divine to the Human*, 115–16.

that it mediates and considers them from the point of view of the Essence and their ultimate intentionality. On the one hand, such an ecumenism accounts for the legitimacy of religious diversity, since it proceeds from a source that illuminates differences in light of unity. On the other hand, it must be recognized that it also relativizes the very basis of ecumenism as a way of addressing religious diversity, since this diversity is shown to be non-ultimate. From the former point of view, esoteric ecumenism may provide keys to a dialogue among religions, first in highlighting the organizing logic of each religious perspective, and second in pointing to zones of metaphysical and spiritual commonalities. This can allow one to situate religious phenomena within their appropriate context, instead of drawing mere formal parallels between traditions. A case in point is that of comparisons between Christ and the Prophet Muhammad: parallels between the two are bound to remain superficial as long as they do not take into account the functional aspects of the two figures. When considering the latter, by contrast, one can realize that the function of the Prophet in Islam reveals striking analogies with that of the Virgin Mary in Christianity. This correspondence, which Louis Massignon had noted in his time, is developed by Schuon, who highlights the analogies between the virginity of Mary and the "illiteracy" of Muhammad, while stressing the similarities between the reception of the Word made flesh and the Quran through the angelic annunciation. Moreover, from the vantage point of what lies beyond traditional forms and pertains to the transcendent unity of religions, Schuon's ecumenism opens the way to esoteric and mystical forays into the highest reaches of the various religious traditions, each contribution confirming or complementing the others in terms of giving access to the supra-formal Essence.

As has been intimated above, the esoteric ecumenism propounded by Schuon is, as a compensatory phenomenon, the positive side of a recognition of the state of decay, or even subversion, of contemporary world religions, or rather of their visible, public, and institutional aspects. This also means, however, that the state of degeneracy of religions calls into question the validity and effectiveness of many interreligious encounters, since the latter would seem to presuppose that the participants are integrally representative of their respective traditions. Schuon would opine that such a condition is unfortunately rarely fulfilled. Although Schuon does not fully elaborate his critique of contemporary religions and the corrupting effect of modernity on their manifestations, we can identify, in his published works, a number of allusions to the "apocalyptic" situation of

ESOTERIC ECUMENISM | 339

most sectors of contemporary religious life. In point of fact, we can trace these incidental critiques in the treatment of all major religions, albeit in different ways. We find them, for instance, in references to neo-Hinduism and some modern interpretations of Zen, as well as in marginal references to the post-conciliar crisis of the Roman Catholic Church and the contemporary predicaments of Islam. These criticisms are generally made by way of asides in Schuon's discussions of metaphysical and spiritual principles, but they also shed light *a contrario* on what Schuon considers as normative in terms of orthodoxy. The cases of Christianity and Islam are the most apparent in this respect, no doubt because they are the largest and fastest-growing religious communities in our day and age. It is instructive, in this regard, to see how Schuon articulates traditional excesses and modern influence to account for the contemporary disorders within the Roman Church. Thus, for instance, he asserts that a certain ecclesiastical narrowness and rigidity has opened the way, theologically and institutionally, to modernist influences, either by reaction or as a kind of Trojan horse.[25] With respect to the content of these influences Schuon is particularly intent on highlighting their humanizing tendencies[26] and the manner in which they move away from the primacy of transcendence and an integral sense of the sacred.[27] This is, for example, plainly illustrated in what Schuon refers to as the "liturgical improvisations" that took place

---

25. "The disorders—of a gravity without precedent—with which the Roman Church is now beset prove that the Latin conception of the Church is theologically narrow and judicially excessive; if it were not, these disorders would be inconceivable." Schuon, *Form and Substance in the Religions*, 203.

26. "It seems that the new 'pastoralism' seeks specifically to speak the 'language' of the 'world' which has become an honourable entity, without there being any discernible reason for this unexpected promotion; to wish to speak the language of the 'world,' or that of 'our time'—another empty argument which carefully avoids proving anything whatsoever—is to make truth speak the language of error and virtue the language of vice." Schuon, *Esoterism as Principle and as Way* (Pates Manor, Bedfont, Middlesex: Perennial Books, 1981), 161.

27. "The connection—enunciated in the Magnificat—between fear and Mercy is of capital importance; this doctrine cuts short the illusion of a superficial and easy religiosity—very much in vogue among today's 'believers'—that confuses Divine Goodness with the weaknesses of humanism and psychologism, and even of democracy, and that fits right in with modern narcissism and the desecration it entails." Schuon, *Form and Substance in the Religions*, 112.

in the wake of the Second Vatican Council.[28] The same kind of remark would hold true, in a somewhat reversed way, in Islam, in the sense that the modernizing influences are deemed to affect herein the spirit of the tradition, rather than its forms, since the latter are fixed in an unchanging canonical way. This is the case, more evidently, in the growing ideologization of the Islamic identity, but also in terms of a religious legitimation, if not banalization, of human flaws such as narrow intolerance, inordinate brutality and passionate lack of magnanimity, or even in a substitution of political fanaticism for godly mercy.

The critiques of some trends in Hindu and Buddhist spirituality are of a different order, but they involve similar concerns. Here, Schuon's considerations are more focused on the directly spiritual dimensions of the traditions. Given the strong attraction exercised by Hinduism and Buddhism among contemporary Western seekers, what is at stake is the intellectual and aesthetic integrity of Asian traditions, particularly in terms of their transmission to Europe and America. Schuon is particularly intent on debunking the psychologization of Eastern spirituality, its disconnection from any sense of intellectual orthodoxy, and the trivialization of some of its formal supports. Thus, in "Self-Knowledge and the Western Seeker," published in the first edition of *Language of the Self*, Schuon highlights the dangers lurking in any ill-prepared encounter between the neo-Hindu underestimation of intellectual orthodoxy characteristic of many new paths and neo-gurus, and the psychology of Western spiritual seekers, often unable to assimilate Hindu teachings because of their repressed but indelible Abrahamic genealogy.[29] Schuon goes so far as to criticize

---

28. "One of the major errors of our time, at least on the religious plane, is to believe that a liturgy can be invented, that the ancient liturgies are inventions or that elements added in a spirit of piety are such; this is to confuse inspiration with invention, the sacred with the profane, saintly souls with bureaus and committees." Schuon, *Christianity/Islam: Perspectives on Esoteric Ecumenism* (Bloomington, IN: World Wisdom, 2008), 5.

29. "[Some Western seekers] Being Europeans, they think too much, which gives them an appearance of intelligence; in reality their thought, more often than not, is basically passionate, and has no contemplative serenity whatsoever; the idea that 'I am *Brahman*' may easily fill them with pride and contempt, because their ancestors have always thought: 'I am a mortal, a sinner,' and because their minds, unless they have been purified by severe disciplines, are not accustomed to bear *jñanic* formulas. The conviction that one is not the mind but the Self can perfectly well be situated in a secret fold of the mind and not outside it; one who considers God more or less as a creature of man prevents the Divine Grace from coming to his aid and freeing

many Hindu authorities' lack of awareness and due consideration of the particular make-up, cultural conditioning, and subjective limitations of Western seekers who come to them. Analogously, Schuon alerts his readers to some of the pitfalls of modern Zen, particularly with respect to Zen's alleged transcendence of rational thought and formal supports in general. In a chapter on the Zen *koan*, he cautions that this type of riddle-like meditation is not to be understood as a repudiation of rationality and metaphysics, as it is sometimes assumed among anti-intellectualist and anti-dogmatist spiritual seekers,[30] but rather as a means of accessing the intuition of a specific spiritual perspective on reality—of which a given Zen master may be the embodiment, one that necessitates a removal of some ordinary or conventional veils. He also criticizes the frequent tendency to reduce Zen to a mere psychology, thereby depriving it of its anchorage in transcendence and its rigorous cultivation of a sense of form. What Schuon criticizes in all these cases is the flattening down of theological dogmas and metaphysical principles but also, and above all, all modes of unconscious profanation of religion resulting from a disconnection from the imperatives of transcendence and the sacred. For him, these tendencies betray an atrophy of the instinct of Divine Majesty, and a deep erosion of the religious sensibility to the sacramental and aesthetic vibrations of the sacred and the Divine Presence. In such contexts interreligious dialogues are likely to amount to no more than psychological, sentimental, and sociocultural exercises. Ecumenism, when not inspired by a spiritual perspective that alone can elevate its participants, through a sort of emulation, toward transcendence, can unfortunately all too often play into the hands of dissolving agencies that adulterate or neutralize religious realities.[31] It can contribute, therefore, to a relativization of all

---

him from the mind." Schuon, *Language of the Self* (Madras: Ganesh, 1959), 48–55.

30. "Followers of Zen in the course of their scholastic and academic contacts with the West find it hard not to capitalize on what is, in a sense, the adogmatic character of their tradition, as if the absence of dogmas bore the same meaning and color for a contemplative Asiatic as for a Western agnostic." Schuon, *Treasures of Buddhism* (Bloomington, IN: World Wisdom, 1993), 68.

31. "All of this should serve to make it clear that we are as far as can be from approving a gratuitous and sentimentalist 'ecumenism,' which does not distinguish between truth and error and which results in religious indifference and the cult of man. What in reality one has to understand, is that the undeniable presence of transcendent truth, of the sacred and the supernatural, in religions other than that of our birth, ought to lead us, not in the least to doubt the Absolute character proper to our religion,

values that erases the transcendent character of religion, and makes it into a mere component of the humanist or humanitarian ethos that prevails as a kind of pseudo-spirituality. This "profanation" of religion is but one of the shadows that the "apocalypse" of religions projects onto human history.

As foreign and shocking as it may be to the sensibility of the faithful, one cannot stress enough the fact that, in Schuon's perspective, religion itself is a kind of "desecration." Thus, in *The Transcendent Unity of Religions*, Schuon goes so far as to write:

> In order to save one of the 'sick' parts of humanity, or rather 'a humanity,' God consents to be profaned; but on the other hand—and this is a manifestation of His Impersonality, which by definition lies beyond the exoteric point of view [the French original is "*point de vue religieux*" or "religious point of view"], He makes use of this profanation, since 'it must needs be that offences come' in order to bring about the final decadence of the present cycle of humanity, this decadence being necessary for the exhausting of all the possibilities included in this cycle, necessary therefore for the equilibrium of the cycle and the fulfillment of the glorious and universal radiation of God.[32]

What is most striking in this passage is the characterization of religion as a kind of profanation of the Divine. The Christian "Word made flesh" is probably the most direct expression of this profanation: "Light has shone in darkness and darkness comprehended it not." The positive side of God's consent to be profaned entails a negative corruption of the sacred, and this is in a sense the whole history of religion, one that is often mentioned in critiques of religion as the most powerful argument against it. It is this history, and its most ambivalent external outcomes, that is one

---

but simply to acknowledge the inherence of the Absolute in other doctrinal and sacramental symbols which manifest and communicate It by definition, but which also by definition—since they belong to the formal order—are relative and limited, despite their quality of uniqueness. This latter quality is necessary, as we have said, inasmuch as it testifies to the Absolute, but is merely indicative from the point of view of the Absolute in itself, which manifests Itself necessarily by uniqueness, yet just as necessarily—in virtue of Its Infinitude—by the diversity of forms." Schuon, *From the Divine to the Human*, 114–15.

32. Schuon, *The Transcendent Unity of Religions* (Wheaton, IL: Theosophical Publishing House, 1984), 137.

of the major causes of the gradual decline of religious civilization and as a result, in the modern world, the loss of religion's cultural preeminence. On the other hand, the negative corruption that is at work in the history of religions is also, and ultimately so, the positive means whereby what Guénon called the "partial disorders" are called to realize the "total order," that is, the manifestation of all possibilities included in the Infinite.[33] Let us note, however, that contrary to the consenting to profanation, this use of disorder in view of order does not regard the Personal Divinity, but only the Impersonal Essence. If God "misguides" religions it is not obviously as a Creator, a Law Giver, and a Savior, but as a consequence of the infinitude of His Essence, the Impersonality of which transcends all vicissitudes and relativities and bring them back to the universal order of the All-Possibility.

While the plurality of religions is one of the factors that compromises the power of persuasion among the exoteric majority, and therefore contributes to the exhaustion of all the possibilities, there are also ways in which this plurality could be a positive factor for religion as a whole. For Schuon the most important objective of any kind of interreligious dialogue and cooperation has to be situated within the context of an opposition between religion and the secular worldview. If there is a domain in which Schuon sees ecumenism playing a positive role, it is in forming a common front of traditional religions against scientistic ideology and "organized irreligion." In other words, while religions cannot, and should not, compromise what constitutes their respective dogmatic and ritual specificities, they should be able to recognize their common affirmation of transcendence and their shared faith in the existence of spiritual realities as a basis for a collaborative effort to counter the pervasive influence of secularism in the modern world. There are three issues to distinguish in this respect: the integrity of exoteric dogmatic orthodoxy, the opposition to atheism, and the extent and means of affirmation of exclusivism. From the first point of view, religions have not only a right but also a duty to affirm and defend what is their very *raison d'être*, that is, the integrity of their dogmatic claims as expressions of their particular perspective on Reality. Schuon's position is not pluralist in this respect, at least not in

---

33. "Partial disorders are completely effaced in the presence of the total order into which they are finally merged, constituting, when stripped of their 'negative' aspects, elements in that order comparable to all others." Guénon, *The Reign of Quantity and the Signs of the Times* (Hillsdale, NY: Sophia Perennis et Universalis, 2001), 279.

the usual sense of the term. He actually defends the right of religions to be "intolerant," if by this is simply meant not recognizing the full validity of other faiths and claiming the superiority of one's own. Each tradition is invested with a sense of the Absolute that is de facto identified with its own perspective. Inasmuch as religion is about forms, which is a necessity since it must attract souls from within the formal domain, it cannot but be exclusive and even intolerant. However, it also contains a principle of tolerance inasmuch as it is the vehicle of a unitive grace emanating from its Divine source. A poem by Schuon epitomizes the complexities of the question of religious tolerance:

> Intolerant or tolerant?
> I am intolerant if it is a question of truth;
> But I am tolerant, because the brilliance of the Divine Truth,
> Shines, like the sun, in every direction.[34]

These lines crystallize the point of view of Schuonian esoteric ecumenism. They express the paradoxical coincidence of transcendence and immanence, or exclusiveness and inclusiveness. It is possible to consider that these two perspectives reflect, in a sense, the two poles of truth and presence. This distinction is cardinal in Schuon's spiritual vocabulary. Truth is associated with discernment. It is distinguished from error that it rejects and extinguishes, as it were. It has to do with adequation to reality. In the absence of such an adequation, nothing is truly possible in the spiritual domain. While many modern spiritual seekers would deem intellectual principles to be foreign to spiritual endeavors, and largely inoperative or useless when it comes to realization, Schuon, like most gnostics from the past, sees the intellectual discernment of Reality as a prerequisite for any grounded and sustainable spiritual life. Why is it so? First of all, the intellectual perception of the truth is a sort of virtual realization of its content. The truth that is understood theoretically is the same truth that must be realized. In point of fact, it can even be said that a theoretical assimilation of the truth is already something of its realization. While it

---

34. *Songs without Names—Volumes VII–XII* (Bloomington, IN: World Wisdom, 2006), 197. "*Unduldsam oder duldsam? Unduldsam/ Bin ich, wenn es sich um die Wahrheit handelt;/ Doch duldsam, weil der Gotteswahrheit Strahl/ Wie Sonnenschein in jeder Richtung wandelt.*" *Lieder ohne Namen XI, XII* (Sottens, Switzerland: Les Sept Flèches, 2004), 22.

is true that a purely theoretical contemplation of metaphysics may have the fragility of merely mental notions, "realizationism"—that is, the disdain or rejection of doctrine in the name of spiritual experience—may be given to inspirationism and phenomenal or psychological delusions. In a passage from his work, Schuon compares theoretical vision to a planimetric perception, while the actual realization of the truth is analogous to a three-dimensional apprehension.[35] The former lacks the volume of an actual and existential assimilation, but it is also true that it contains volume virtually in the same way as the visual representation of a landscape undoubtedly shares in some limited way with the content of this landscape. To the extent that it offers one with a limited, but fully valid, adequation to reality, intellectual recognition, and the discernment that is its bedrock, provides the spiritual seeker with a rigorous framework that is objectively grounded and therefore immune from subjective and individualistic illusions. Without this intellectual guarantee, spiritual life lacks objectivity and is therefore prone to be limited to, or confused with, subjective perceptions and emotions. This is all the more true in the post-traditional world, when the dogmatic guardrails of the various religious traditions have largely collapsed, and have left a vacuum that is likely to be filled with ideological or psychological contents. To sum up, therefore, intolerance can be the concomitance of discernment and, as such, it must be considered as providing religions with a necessary protection. What clearly distinguishes Schuon's perspective from mainstream ecumenical sensibilities and movements is his defense of a margin of religious intolerance as an expedient and inevitable dimension of religious exoterism.[36]

The point of view of presence, by contrast, entails an emphasis on the radiance of Reality, a radiance that nothing can limit since it is inherent to Reality itself. This is the point of view of metaphysical Unity, a Unity that is present in everything, without which everything would fall into

---

35. "Transposed to other orders, the difference between planimetric and three-dimensional geometry is equivalent to that between the abstract and the concrete, theory and practice, program and realization, truth and reality, doctrine and sanctity." Schuon, *To Have a Center* Bloomington, IN: World Wisdom, 2015), nn. 10, 67.

36. "If a religion is intolerant, it will no doubt exclude many foreign values, but since it offers everything that man has needs to reach his final ends, the harm is in practice quite relative; if it is tolerant, however, it opens the door to the lethal poison of pseudo-spiritualisms without the values of the foreign religions offering the slightest help." Schuon, *Sufism: Veil and Quintessence*, 39.

nothingness. From the point of view of the pole "thinking," intolerance is nothing else than the negation of error. In the perspective of the pole "being," tolerance is a recognition that nothing lies "outside" of the Real. This explains why it is possible to judge and love at the same time. One must judge evil for what it is while loving the human receptacle of this evil, to the extent at least that the two can be disassociated. God does not forgive heresy, but He may forgive heretics in so far as their circumstances and intentions may warrant it, therefore from the point of view of the existential totality. On a human level, the relative indifference to formal orthodoxy that may characterize some saintly figures, particularly in a bhaktic context, stems from this perspective of existential unity. One point of view must balance the other, without which intolerance turns into narrowness and fanaticism, and tolerance into infra-formal and sentimentalist relativism.

The foundational substance of Schuon's esoteric ecumenism is contained in his concept of the hypostatic faces of the Divine Essence. The use of the term hypostasis clearly suggests that Schuon conceives of the Divine roots of religious diversity as personal modes of Being, each of them being in a way God for the particular religious collective subjectivity that it addresses. Moreover, the reference to a Divine face means here both a Divine aspect and a basis for a relationship between the Divinity and mankind. While the Divine Essence has no face, inasmuch as it transcends all modes and relations, each "confessional Divinity" is the "face of God" for those who relate to it as Divine Reality. It could be said, therefore, that the God of Christians is, in a way, the same as the God of Muslims, while adding that, in another way, the Christian God is not the Islamic God. The term God refers, in the first sense, to the Essence that lies beyond determinations and hypostatic delimitation. Thus, what Christians and Muslims share, most of the time unknowingly, lies beyond any determinations and, therefore, beyond formal sharing. The common God of Christianity and Islam is the Mystery that has no face and knows of no Christianity and no Islam, if one may put it this way. As for the God of Christians, who is different from the God of Muslims, He is intrinsically determined by the Incarnation and the Redemption. For Christians, therefore, any "God" who does not partake in the latter is not, and cannot be, the true and living God, but only—at best—an abstraction. Similarly, the God of Muslims is absolutely transcendent and incomparable. Therefore, He cannot take flesh without ceasing to be God, or without becoming an idol. From an exoteric point of view, the

Christian God is different from the Islamic God, but from an esoteric point of view He is both different and the same: being none other than the Essence, each "God" is God and therefore none other than the other "God." However, considered as a distinct hypostatic face, each "God" is evidently different from the other. As we can infer from the previous remarks, such a differentiation presupposes the concept of Divine Relativity. It implies, therefore, that the Absolute includes a diversity of degrees and aspects, which are themselves the prefigurations of Manifestation as such. The Absolute is, in this sense, both unknowable and the principle of all knowability. It is unknowable because it transcends all determinations, insofar as knowledge is understood as being relative to delimitations and definitions. However, the Absolute is also, and more fundamentally, the principle of all knowledge inasmuch as it is the very Subject from which all knowledge flows. Within its own epistemological framework of reference, Hick's pluralistic hypothesis emphasizes the former dimension, or in a sense the transcendence of the Real, but it is less clear as to the ways in which the nature of the Real contains, as it were, the diversity of aspects that give rise to religious plurality. Stating that the Real as such is unknowable means opening the way to a plurality of apprehensions of this unknowableness, and this is the gist of Hick's pluralistic hypothesis. However, it tells us very little, or nothing, about Divine intentionality as well as about the adequacy, or lack thereof, of the plural apprehensions of this unknowable. This is where Schuon's esoteric ecumenism greatly differs from Hick's pluralism: it highlights the Divine foundations of religious plurality, and provides criteria of assessment of the effectiveness of religious knowledge that are strictly dependent upon those foundations. Esoterism not only recognizes the unfathomability of the Essence, but also affirms its modes of manifestation and revelation.

Among those manifestations, there is a type of revelation that bears a particular affinity with esoterism, namely virgin nature.[37] When Schuon writes that virgin nature is the "art of God"[38] and the sacred

---

37. "On the outward and therefore contingent plane, which however inevitably has its importance in the human order, there is a concordance between the *religio perennis* and virgin nature, and by the same token between it and primordial nudity, the nudity of creation, of birth, of resurrection, or that of the High Priest in the Holy of Holies, of a hermit in the desert, of a Hindu *sādhu* or *sannyāsin*, of a Red Indian in silent prayer on a mountain." Schuon, *Light on the Ancient Worlds*, 125.
38. Schuon, *Logic and Transcendence* (Bloomington, IN: World Wisdom, 2009), 166.

book of esoterism, he alludes to the fact that Shamanistic traditions, to the extent that they remain monotheistic in their metaphysical scope, present a major point of convergence with the esoteric outlook. First of all, their strong sense of the presence of Divine Reality in nature reveals a significant consonance with esoteric gnosis, which is also characterized, although with different inflections, by a strong integration of the dimension of immanence. The absence of a revealed Book means there is no need for scriptural hermeneutics, which precludes the appearance of polemics pertaining to the interpretation of the Word of God, while preventing the development of overly complex and contentious theological concepts. The spiritual theme of sacred nudity is also relevant here. Like Shamanism, it refers to nature, in this case the human body, as a direct manifestation of the Divine, prior to the religious and civilizational "clothing" of the truth. Thus, Shamanism, like the esoteric perspective, is primordial in that it does not presuppose any scriptural and authoritative or institutional mediations. It begins, and ends, with the metaphysical fact of the human vocation for the Absolute, as reflected in mankind's meaningful position in nature, the latter being experienced as the mirror of God's Qualities. The primordial directness of the Shamanistic relationship with the Divine manifests also in the absence of institutionalized hierarchies: the sacred function of mankind is extended to all. It includes, however, particular vocations for the technicians of the sacred, as it were, as evidenced by the central role of the shaman. Notwithstanding the presence of the shaman, spiritual contacts with the sacred are open to all members of the group. Schuon has mentioned, in this regard, that in the Shamanism of the American Indians of the Plains, for instance, each and every human being is his own "prophet."[39] This is in keeping with the idea that, in principle, human beings bear within themselves all that they need spiritually. Mankind is innately equipped with the "supernaturally natural" resources that make it witness of the Absolute. In a sense the primordialist dimension of Shamanism, as expressed for instance among the Natives of the North American Plains (whom Schuon took as a reference-point in this regard), lends to this principle a more individual translation, in

---

39. "In a certain sense, however surprising as it may seem, each man is his own prophet having received his own revelation, though naturally within the framework of the tradition in general, which strictly regulates the outward and even inward modalities of this collective prophethood." Schuon, *The Feathered Sun* (Bloomington, IN: World Wisdom, 1990), 19.

that each and every human being is potentially endowed with a "vision," therefore with a "mission." Esoterism presents us with an analogous perspective, since the realization of the Self that is its goal is at the same time the unveiling on the true nature of the soul in God. Moreover, esoteric schools have tended to emphasize that the multiplicity of paths is a direct consequence of the diversity of mankind. Sufis, for instance, like to quote the saying that "there are as many paths to God as there are children of Adam."[40] Similarly, both because of their generally strong identifications with a land and a people, and their emphasis on the relationship of each soul with the Mystery, Shamanistic traditions do not extend beyond the confines of a particular group. In a sense, this is also in consonance with the esoteric perspective, since the latter focuses on the inner connection with the Divine, recognizes the diversity of qualifications and vocations, and normally refrains from proselytizing.

The esoteric character of Schuon's ecumenism can be seen as functioning on different levels, since it is multilayered and qualified. While spiritual unity lies above and religious diversity reigns below, the two degrees must not be confused, and neither annuls the other in the realm in which they are respectively operative. In some ways, esoterism may be deemed to transcend the very notion of any ecumenism since it invalidates the ultimacy of exclusiveness, thereby postulating a point where all religious divergences are reconciled. But this holds true only on the highest level, and from the highest point of view. When considered from this transcendent vantage point, each form is absolute as intrinsic manifestation of the Essence, but relative in its extrinsic limitations. In this perspective, one cannot speak of relativism, however, since it is the Absolute that is contemplated in and as relative form, and within the range of manifestation of the Absolute itself. As for the level of confessional identifications and limitations, there is obviously no room for relativism therein, in the sense that the religious relativity is considered as absolute. This is a legitimate, and in a sense necessary, perspective, since the religious outlook is the horizon of most believers. Between these two poles, Schuon's quintessential esoterism and confessional partiality, lies a wide spectrum of intermediate positions that reflect various degrees of intuition of the Essence and a plurality of levels of identification with religious forms. In fact, the scope of Schuon's esoteric ecumenism is

---

40. Mohammed Rustom, *The Triumph of Mercy: Philosophy and Scripture in Mullā Sadrā* (Albany: State University of New York Press, 2012), 204.

analogous to the multistratified metaphysics of Unity, of which it is, in a sense, but an application. The non-duality of the *Brahman*, which lies above all multiplicity, does not invalidate the ontological differences that are experienced on the level of relativity, or within the domain of *Māyā*. Within its range of relevance, *Māyā* domain is intrinsically dualistic since it is predicated on the distinction between a subject and an object. This is why the notion of "religious *Māyā*"[41] is not only quite justifiable but also in some ways illuminating. The ultimate reality of non-duality does not exclude the multiplicity of existents on the level on which this multiplicity is experienced as real, or at least not unreal. Whether as a mode of realized consciousness or as a theoretical doctrine, the affirmation of the non-dual Absolute is not incompatible with the perception of diversity. Analogously, a religious experience lived within a particular formal universe is obviously quite compatible with an affirmation of the transcendent unity of religions. By contrast, the religious point of view, which is predicated on dualism, sentimental identification with forms, and necessary exclusiveness—without which it has no legitimacy and no effectiveness as a distinctive system—cannot possibly coexist in a same consciousness with the supra-confessional outlook of gnosis. From the point of view of those who perceive, or assent to, the transcendent unity, there is no more hypocrisy in practicing a particular religion than there is contradiction for a *jivan-mukta* in living in a body and a soul. Evidently, the way a given religion is lived within the context of esoteric ecumenism is profoundly different from the manner it is experienced from the point of view of ordinary religious faith. The esoteric outlook remains inwardly independent from the forms through which it must perforce manifest in the formal universe of relative existence. As regard the world of religions and the various competing truth claims that it presents, esoteric ecumenism provides a powerful antidote against the relativistic tendencies of de facto pluralism while giving access to a recognition of religious plurality. Through a vision of plurality within Unity and differences in Identity, the gnostic contemplation of the Divine hypostatic faces brings back relative aspects and points of view to the universal foundation of the Absolute.

---

41. See Patricia Reynaud, "Religious *Māyā*," in Sharma, *The World's Religions after September 11*, vol. 3.

Conclusion

Schuon never claimed to be a comparatist, and his approach can hardly be considered to fulfill the normative requirements of the academic study of religion. As we have mentioned, even the concept of a "transcendent unity of religions"—the title of one of his most celebrated books—was considered by him to be relatively extrinsic with respect to the core of his teachings, which he defined as a reformulation of the *Sophia perennis*, or *Religio perennis*, conceived as the conjunction of a metaphysical doctrine and means of spiritual realization. Hence the comparative dimension of his work arises only as a consequence of the position of a universal gnosis present at the heart of all spiritual traditions. It is the unity of this essence, as manifested through the diversity of traditional outlooks, that informs Schuon's meditations on religious parallels and contrasts. Given the profound differences of perspective that distinguish Schuon's oeuvre from the contributions of most scholars of comparative religion, it might appear misplaced to bring Schuon into the fold of academic discourse. On closer examination, however, one cannot brush aside the pertinence of his works to the domain of scholarship, if only because his extra-academic approach presents the discipline with challenges that it can hardly ignore without risk of falling into its own brand of methodological dogmatism.

In keeping with the teachings of most gnostics and mystics, Schuon rarely misses an opportunity to remind his readers that the unconditioned Real lies beyond words and that all terminology is but an approximation in the way of characterizing, but not exhaustively defining, the Ultimate. Even conceptual and methodical paths of access to the latter are characterized by a measure of variation in their expressions, precisely because of the transcendence and infinitude of their object. This is a principle that the academic study of religion may all too easily overlook, given its methodological presuppositions and the analytic focus of most of its inquiries. Notwithstanding the need to emphasize this gap between expression and reality, the symbolic character of metaphysical and spiritual terms does involve an epistemological adequacy of the symbolizer in relation to the symbolized. This is largely contingent upon intuitive and contemplative conditions that may lie outside the scope of the specifically academic outlook, although this phenomenological reality ought to be recognized as fundamental in any spiritual context. In Schuon's idiom, this dual aspect of spiritual expression is but one instance of the more encompassing question of the relationship between form and essence, the former being a distant reflection of the latter. One may therefore insist on the aspect of "distance" or that of "reflection" depending on one's particular doctrinal or methodical intention. At any rate, regardless of how refined they may be when applied to transcendent realities, conceptual terms can never be unambiguously adequate; nor can they ever exhaust the wealth of being and meaning comprising Reality. There is, therefore, a certain degree of contingency in any metaphysical or spiritual expression. To insist on the contrary would amount to missing a crucial aspect of how symbolic formulations function. This indeterminacy, which is in no way contrary to religious and spiritual efficacy, stems both from the nature of Reality and the limitations of human language. For Schuon, Reality encompasses an unlimited number of aspects while language necessarily involves particular points of view. This principle is particularly relevant when undertaking a comparative approach to diverse religious traditions in that it may help prevent the reductionism that is prominent among certain scholars. Needless to say, this way of contemplating symbolic terms is also grounded in an ontology that can only be considered as dogmatic from an exclusively critical academic point of view.

It is precisely from a consideration of their symbolic function in relation to metaphysical realities that a case can be made for the legitimate semantic expansion of certain traditional terms. Thus, a term borrowed from one tradition may serve to enlighten some aspects of another. Schuon's application of the *yin yang* symbol is an example of this kind. Moreover, a term chosen for its symbolic function may shed light on particular tensions or difficulties in a particular theological framework. This is, for instance, according to Schuon, the symbolic function of *Māyā*, the absence of which—in Abrahamic monotheism—can account for some of the most serious theological conundrums, starting with the problem of theodicy. This might be construed as theological reductionism were it not for the fact that the term in question can be contemplated in a symbolic manner rather than in a purely literal fashion. The integrity and effectiveness of this approach can only be assessed on the basis of a speculative intuition that, while not fulfilling conventional "scientific" requirements per se, can, nevertheless, reveal its relevance by virtue of its hermeneutic fruits. When considering what may appear to be an extra-scientific reliance on a type of intuition for which no external epistemological guarantee can be provided, it is important to note that comparative methodologies themselves do not escape, at their very basis, a certain measure of intuitive recognition. The methodology of comparative religion sets out with the very act of selecting what is to be compared, along with the corresponding *tertium comparationis*. It can hardly be denied that the basis for choosing the *comparanda* and *tertium comparationis* is a subtle and elusive matter. Any comparative study is preceded by a prior estimation that the comparison to be undertaken can be fruitful. There lies, therefore, at the heart of comparative religion an insight or intuition that cannot merely be reduced to the bareness of objective data.[1] In a sense, this observation is nothing new in the study of religion, but it can often be obscured by descriptive complexity and implicit theoretical biases. Taking stock of the intuitive premises of religious studies, Anders Nygren—in his classical *Agape and Eros*—has claimed that "the underlying idea or fundamental motif of a religion may be intuitively discerned."[2] This means that the multiplicity of phenomena pertaining to a particular religion can actually be reduced to some fundamental elements without which it would, in fact, be impossible to hold a coherent discourse about it, or even to recognize it as a distinct religion from others. Nygren proposed that this conception is fundamental

---

1. "A closer look reveals that the process of *selecting* both the comparands and the *tertium comparationis* is extremely complex. Multiple factors are at play in the selection process, from the researcher's training and personal interests to cultural, academic, and disciplinary frameworks and paradigms. In addition, thorough reflection shows that the comparands and the *tertium* that eventually get chosen have been in a complex relationship—in the mind of the scholar and possibly also in academic discourse—long before they were put forward for comparison in an actual study. The selection of two comparands presupposes a prior act of comparison in which a productive comparability of the two was established. In other words, the assertion that two items deserve to be compared implies that they have already been compared." Oliver Freiberger, "Elements of a Comparative Methodology in the Study of Religion," *Religions* 9, no. 2 (2018): 38.
2. Anders Nygren, *Agape and Eros* (London: SPCK, 1953), 37.

to the extent that "a religion deprived of [it] . . . would lose all coherence and meaning; and therefore we cannot rightly regard anything as a fundamental motif unless its removal would have such an effect." Nygren's underlying notion is clearly consonant with what Schuon refers to as the "*idée-force*" of a given religion, which he identifies further as deriving from a religious archetype; that is, in the last analysis, a Divine intention. This archetype is an ontological and epistemological reality that antecedes the vicissitudes of history and constitutes nothing less than the transcendent *raison d'être* of a particular religious tradition. Academic comparatists may be critical or impatient when such archetypes or fundamental postulates are confidently asserted but they cannot avoid basing their own scholarly endeavors upon perceptions or intuitions that are not a priori reducible to the mere description and analysis of data.

Another important dimension in the study of religion is the methodological duality that it shares with anthropology and other social sciences. The latter tend to be divided between what is sometimes known as the *emic* and the *etic* approaches to human and social phenomena. These terms, which originated in the work of the linguist Kenneth Lee Pike (1912–2000), are derived from the distinction between *phonemics*, as the science of phonemes applied within a single language (hence the word *emic*), and *phonetics* as the science of phonemes in general (hence *etic*). Roughly speaking, the emic approach refers to the immanent or subjective apprehension of religious phenomena, while the etic refers to the objective study of the same phenomena from the vantage point of an external observer. When applied to the study of religion, the first type of methodology emphasizes the experiential particularity of religious life, whereas the second, by contrast, moves toward theoretical generalizations. Needless to say, this distinction reflects the tension often found between the immediate vitality of religious belief and the detached protocols of scholarly inquiry. For the believers, no profound knowledge of the religious object is possible without an apperception of what this means for their spiritual life. However, for many academic students of religion, only the detachment of the impartial analyst can afford proper "scientific" access to the religious object. The title of one of Schuon's later works, *Approaches to the Religious Phenomenon*, provides insights into his perspective on this question, since it suggests the importance of having both a sense of subjective apprehension—conveyed by the word "approaches"—and a disinterested perspective, implied by "phenomena." Conversely, the word "approach" could also indicate an "objective" methodology, whereas "phenomenon" might be taken (consistent with its etymology) in the *phenomenological* sense of that which appears to one's consciousness, which could include an object of belief. At any rate, Schuon's perspective integrates both emic and etic dimensions. On the one hand, it considers the Divine Object and religious phenomena as they are envisaged from within a particular religion. In doing so, he manifests a rare ability to penetrate a given confessional outlook in ways that have been lauded by representatives of various traditions.[3] A good example of this appears in the chapter "The Sense of the Absolute in Religions." Schuon shows therein how the Absolute is not only a metaphysical reality but also the object of a subjective "sense" that is determined by the perspectival emphases of a particular religion.[4] For a Christian, the sense of the Absolute is entirely concentrated on the reality of the Man-God, whereas, for a Muslim, it is integrally informed by the affirmation of an exclusive and transcendent Divine Unity. Such considerations from within—which could also be deemed akin to a phenomenological approach—contemplates religious objects in the very terms that the tradition itself apprehends and embodies them. Here, it is pertinent to keep in mind that the word "term" refers, in its Latin etymology, to the idea of limit or a boundary. In this sense, a term is that which limits a particular religious outlook and defines its formal contours. At the same time, Schuon considers the various traditions from an etic point of view, in the sense that he provides typologies and patterns that are applicable beyond the boundaries of a particular tradition. Thus the chapter "Outline of Religious Typologies" provides a cross-traditional classification of spiritual and religious paths, by observing a distinction between ways centered on "God as such" and those focused on "God as the Logos."[5]

While comparative religion might find it difficult to keep the emic and etic in balance, given the aforementioned tension between belief

---

3. For instance, Christopher Bamford considers that "Schuon the metaphysician was also a Christian theologian of exceptional depth and understanding, one who was able to penetrate Christian dogma and mystery brilliantly from within." Quoted in *The Fullness of God—Frithjof Schuon on Christianity*, edited by James S. Cutsinger (Bloomington, IN: World Wisdom, 2), 254.

4. "Religions are separated from each other by barriers of mutual incomprehension, and one of the principal reasons for this seems to be that the sense of the absolute is situated in each case on a different plane, so that points of comparison often prove illusory." Schuon, *Gnosis: Divine Wisdom* (Bloomington, IN: World Wisdom, 2006), 3.

5. Schuon, *Survey of Metaphysics and Esoterism* (Bloomington, IN: World Wisdom Books, 2000), 103–13.

and "scientific" analysis, Schuon's perspective integrates them as two complementary dimensions of the Real. The emic corresponds, by and large, to various points of view on Reality, while the etic derives from a consideration of its aspects. Whereas points of view are exclusive of each other, the same aspect might be considered from a variety of perspectives. Any aspect of the Real participates in the latter's totality and is therefore none other than the Unity itself. Thus, the term *qua* term—as related to the aspect—is not separated from the whole, and can thus be considered from the vantage point of totality. To illustrate this, Schuon refers to the well-known story of the elephant and the blind men, a Jain apologue that Ghazālī and Ramakrishna, among others, have used in different contexts.[6] The elephant represents the Real, which has a limitless number of aspects, while each of the blind men holds firmly to one part of the animal by identifying it in ignorance—hence dogmatically—with the Real itself. Likewise, the use of certain terms may entail an absolutization of limiting relativities, in the way the statements of the blind men do; but they may also be contemplated as crystallizations of Divine messages or intents; symbolic articulations, as it were, of the Absolute insofar as the various members of the elephant belong to the animal and are indeed, in a certain sense, the elephant itself. Schuon's esoteric perspective on religions, far from ignoring theological differences or disdaining traditional terms of reference—a charge that is all too often leveled against it—embraces both immanent religious particularities and the transcendent totality that situates and measures the limitations of the latter by giving due consideration to the Ultimate and its diversified modes of manifestation. Therefore, Schuon's integrative approach cannot merely be equated with a simplistic non-dualistic reduction of religious multiplicity to an undifferentiated metaphysical unity.

As indicated earlier in this essay, Schuon's work is generally associated with the perennialist theme of the transcendent unity of religions. Whether one agrees or not with Schuon's premises and conclusions in this regard, we have noted that the concept of a transcendent unity of religions is, in fact, relatively extrinsic to his perspective. This aspect of

---

6. "By this parable Al-Ghazzālī seeks to show the error involved in trying to enclose the universal within a fragmentary notion of it, or within isolated and exclusive aspects or points of view." Schuon, *The Transcendent Unity of Religions* (Wheaton, IL: Theosophical Publishing House, 1984), 5.

his work is largely a response to a contemporary Western context in which the question of religious plurality raises unprecedented challenges to a God-centered vision of the universe. One of the main arguments of contemporary atheism and agnosticism lies in the contradictions that pit religions against each other, which makes their truth claims all the more precarious. Schuon provides responses to these claims on a level of conceptual refinement and sophistication that evidently transcends ordinary irenic feelings and pluralistic platitudes. He does so primarily by distinguishing a spiritual and supra-formal "stratosphere"—which is the purview of esoterism—from a human and formal "atmosphere," this being the province of exoterism.[7] Needless to say, this is a highly schematic way of characterizing what are, in fact, much more nuanced affirmations. At any rate, the main thrust of Schuon's argument is more focused on the needs of religion as such than on comparative considerations. What may remain of traditional religion, particularly in the higher realms of metaphysics and spirituality, is arguably not in urgent need of an esoterically founded pluralism. To wit, there is generally little interest in interreligious engagement on the part of traditionally orthodox schools of thought and practice; in fact, it is from the side of reformed or modernized religious movements that the greatest enthusiasm for such engagement is more readily discernible. As suggested earlier, this development is not without its own difficulties. The lessons one may draw from the transcendent unity of religions are more likely to amount to recognizing commonalities than resolving differences. The former provides a shared foundation, one upon which religions may form a common front to withstand the onslaught of atheistic ideologies and their materialistic ambience. As for differences, they can only be resolved on a non-dual level that is de facto inaccessible to most faithful and that only the deepest metaphysical forays and mystical insights can fathom. Paradoxically, though, it is on this level that the need for an affirmation of interreligious unity is the least pressing, as has been recognized by major representatives of the contemplative traditions, particularly in regions characterized by a history of interreligious contacts, such as the Indian subcontinent.

---

7. "It follows from these considerations that God is the same for all the religions only in the Divine 'stratosphere' and not in the human 'atmosphere'; in this 'atmosphere,' each religion has its own God for all practical purposes, and there are as many Gods as there are religions." Schuon, *Sufism: Veil and Quintessence* (Bloomington, IN: World Wisdom, 2006), 41.

One of the most striking features of Schuon's doctrinal vocabulary is that it comprises terms that suggest the presence, within religious realities, of various degrees of relativity. These include such notions as the "relatively absolute," the "human margin," *upāya* and *yin-yang*, to mention but a few. One of the objectives of the present study has been to bring out the import of these notions and to give them their due weight in any adequate assessment of Schuon's perspective. It must be added, moreover, that the significance of this acute awareness of religious relativities is all the more remarkable in that the main metaphysical thrust of Schuon's writings lies in its uncompromisingly consistent emphasis on the primacy of the Absolute and, therefore, on the spiritual, ethical, and aesthetic demands that this entails.

These two fundamental features of Schuon's work, a strict definition of the Absolute and a keen sense of relativities, arguably address the central religious predicaments of our times. For example, acknowledging religious relativities does not entail embracing relativism. Modern sensibilities are profoundly shaped by the idea that perceptions of reality are necessarily relative, as they are increasingly thought to derive from sociocultural conditionings. The modern world is fundamentally wary of objective absolutes while at the same time unconsciously, and often feverishly, impelled by subjective motivations. This suggests that the sense of the Absolute is in the nature of things and that no ambient relativism can extinguish this inherent thirst in mankind, which, if unsatisfied on the spiritual level, is bound to manifest in countless other ways and, therefore, precisely as an absolutization of relativities. Schuon's supra-confessional metaphysics consists primarily of a meditation on the Absolute and the ways it determines the definition and requirements of human nature. This adamantine metaphysical keystone is the most fundamental gauge of readers' responses to his works. Indeed, Schuon's "absolutism" is not the least of obstacles for many contemporary readers of his works. In this regard, Schuon's emphasis on the contradictions of relativism is a sure way to clear the ground for any further consideration of his output.[8] This task is particularly needed in religious worlds that are more and more inclined to de-absolutize their claims as a result of a loss of metaphysical and spiritual acumen,

---

8. The core of Schuon's argument lies in the very first sentence of *Logic and Transcendence* (6): "Relativism reduces every element of absoluteness to relativity while making a completely illogical exception in favor of this reduction itself."

accentuated by the pressures of a relativistic ambience (not to mention the bugbear of modern fundamentalism). On the other hand, the hardening of the religious crust of identities calls for a need to sift the contingent accidents through a clear and profound contemplation of the substance. This cannot be achieved without cultivating an acute sense of religious relativities. While, for Schuon, a deep-seated consciousness of the Absolute must extend to the sacred vehicles of emancipating absoluteness, this cannot but entail a heightened perception of how these very same vehicles reflect a contingent aspect. This means understanding the limitations and, therefore, pitfalls of religious language. Thus, Schuon's works can be read on three levels. The first is an exposition of the universal metaphysics of the Absolute, together with its spiritual and moral correlates. This is the most fundamental, and the only intrinsic, dimension of his work. By intrinsic we mean that this layer touches on the "one thing needful" from which, in principle, everything else can be drawn. However, far from any alleged intellectualism or abstraction, Schuon asserts time and time again that a consistent understanding of the Absolute gives rise to imperative spiritual and moral consequences. One of the leitmotives of his work, "the oneness of the object demands the totality of the subject,"[9] resonates with the deepest implications of our consciousness of the Absolute. The exclusive reality of the Absolute requires from us all that we are.

The second level of Schuon's discourse pertains to the Absolute in religions, or religions, inasmuch as they are the vehicles of the sense of the Absolute. In this realm, Schuon is fundamentally "essentialist": he sees religions as archetypes and religious archetypes as *"idées-force."* On this level, Schuon's critics are likely to charge him with idealism and oversimplification, not to say abusive essentialization. To postulate an archetype of religions appears to many contemporary minds as a reduction of the historical and cultural complexities of religious universes. By contrast with analytic considerations of religions, Schuon understands the religious archetype as being the crystallization of Divine intention. The totality of the religious universe can only be grasped from the point of view of this synthetic soteriological intent. While most scholars of religion would contend that such a perspective is inaccessible, it being impossible to claim a Divine vantage point, Schuon argues that human intelligence,

---

9. Schuon, *To Have a Center* (Bloomington, IN: World Wisdom, 2015), 55.

inasmuch as it is a transcendent dispensation, can—in principle—be adequate to the recognition of the archetype of any given religion. This capacity presupposes, however, a penetrating contemplative intuition and an unbiased receptivity to its spiritual radiation.

There is, finally, a third layer, that corresponds to the dimension of relativity inherent in any religion. It is worth stressing that, in Schuon's view, the fundamental rationale for any consideration of this contingent realm lies in a need to prevent any confusion of the relative with the Absolute or any conflation of the specifically human with the Divine. In other words, it must be recognized that, as mediating realities, religions are unavoidably encumbered with approximative and problematic phenomena that may hinder the recognition the Absolute. There is therefore, to some extent, a need to clear the religious ground to make the metaphysical path more accessible.

It is clear that Schuon's "metalanguage" is determined by his exposition of fundamental metaphysical axioms, hence its capacity to function as a cross-religious conceptual idiom that points to a universal perspective. Extrinsic, limitative, and centrifugal phenomena in religions should not be casually dismissed but be seen as indirect modes of discerning the transcendent reality of the Essence.[10] At a time when orthodoxy (in the extrinsic sense deployed by Schuon) becomes more and more fragile and compromised, there is arguably a need to emphasize "intrinsic orthodoxy." The latter is independent of a particular traditional language, since it is not specifically and exclusively associated with any. While religious language is being eroded by worldly concerns, or taken in an exclusively literal sense, it has to be taken back to its roots as referring to the Absolute. This requires, in a sense, that concepts and terms be freed from their most constraining and exclusive acceptations.

In the modern world, one is confronted with some measure of the hardening and freezing of religious language, whereby theological and metaphysical terms become sclerotic and petrified into simplistic systems and ideological agendas. Beyond this largely unavoidable but gradually mortiferous "solidification" lies the even deadlier "dissolution" of meaning that is all too often a response to the calcifying limitations of extrinsic

---

10. "Only the infinite, eternal and formless Essence is absolutely pure and inviolable, and (because) Its transcendence must be made manifest by the dissolution of forms as well as by Its radiation through them." Schuon, *The Transcendent Unity of Religions*, 104–5.

orthodoxy. Thus, words like "Charity," "Divine Unity," or "Emptiness" have largely been depleted of the deepest meanings they hold when related to the Absolute. Such terms have been not uncommonly reduced to sentimental, quantitative, or merely mental notions. The concept of charity as a theological virtue, for instance, which entails the principle of Love as a divine gift or *Agape*, appears to be very distant from the mostly philanthropic nature of many contemporary Christian concerns. Similarly, the Islamic notion of Divine Unity rarely exceeds the status of an objectifying understanding of the Divine Being as a kind of numerical idol, if one may say so. As for Buddhist emptiness, it can all too often be turned into a mere psychological void that is bereft of any qualitative spiritual content. In this context it is crucial that the esoteric relativization of traditional language, if it is to provide unambiguous signposts, should not to be confused with its postmodern parodies.

The allegorical tale of the frozen and thawed words in Rabelais's *Fourth Book* might be a good hermeneutic key here.[11] In the context of our discussion, this may mean that terms can be frozen by theology, and it may even be that theology is mostly a freezing of words, so that collective mankind may keep a needful, albeit indirect, grip on spiritual realities. Schuon often criticizes what he sees as theology's pedantic "dotting of the i's." Needless to say, this is not a dismissal of doctrines and teachings as such, but a way to caution against an excessive concern with formalizing the truth that can lead to an overemphasis on what might have been better left in parenthesis as mere *theologoumena*. From the point of view of non-dual metaphysics, terms refer—in principle or intrinsically—to the Essence or to that which, directly or indirectly, points to the Essence, even though there lies an ever-widening gap between a term and its referent as one emerges from the level of contingent and merely instrumental notions to that of direct symbols. It is only by reference to the Absolute that terms may be "thawed" and used as keys to the beyond. In the absence of a rigorous sense of the Absolute and a keen awareness of its

---

11. "Antiphanes said that Plato's philosophy was like words, which, being spoken in some country during a hard winter are immediately congealed, frozen up, and not heard: for what Plato taught young lads, could hardly be understood by them when they were grown old. Now, continued he, we should philosophise and search whether this be not the place where those words are thawed." *The Works of François Rabelais, Volume 4*, translated by Sir Thomas Urquhart (London: Gibbings, 1897), 246.

demands, thawed meanings can only result in a mere dissolution leading to arbitrary formlessness. The decay of traditional universes of meaning and the formal ossification of doctrine that it entails also provokes—by way of reaction—a growing questioning, if not rejection, of formal orthodoxy. It means, as a consequence, either the fall into an infra-formal, relativistic, and subjectivist slough or an intuition of an Essence enduring beyond the collapsing forms. In other words, we can once again refer to Schuon's point that if "limitations are necessary for the vitality of a religion, they remain nonetheless limitations with the consequences that that implies."[12]

It goes without saying that Schuon's conceptual idiom cannot escape the destiny that afflicts all terminology: as any language, it can be reduced to a literal and planimetric, if not scholastic, system. As he puts it himself: "The ideas formulated in esoterism and in metaphysical doctrines generally may in their turn be understood according to the dogmatic or theoristic tendency."[13] However, as with other forms of esoteric discourse, Schuon's "metalanguage" refers to its own limitations both through the implied recognition of its own relativity, and—which amounts to the same—by its explicit recognition of "the limits of the expressible"; hence its eminent receptivity to the supremely signifying powers of the Transcendent, beginning and ending with Silence.

---

12. Schuon, *The Transcendent Unity of Religions*, 104–5.
13. Schuon, *The Transcendent Unity of Religions*, 2.

Bibliography of the Works of Frithjof Schuon

First editions in French and German, and first editions of English translations.

Leitgedanken zur Urbesinnung. Zurich and Leipzig: Orell Füssli Verlag, 1935.
Urbesinnung—Das Denken des Eigentlichen, Freiburg im Breisgau: Aurum Verlag, 1989.
De L'Unité transcendante des religions. Paris: Gallimard, 1948.
The Transcendent Unity of Religions. London, Faber & Faber, 1953; New York: Harper & Row, 1975; Wheaton, IL: Theosophical Publishing House, 1993.
L'Oeil du coeur. Paris: Gallimard, 1950.
The Eye of the Heart. Bloomington, IN: World Wisdom Books, 1997.
Perspectives spirituelles et faits humains. Paris: Les Cahiers du Sud, 1953.
Spiritual Perspectives and Human Facts. London: Faber & Faber, 1954
Sentiers de gnose. Paris: La Colombe, 1957; Paris: La Place Royale, 1987, 1996.
Gnosis—Divine Wisdom. London: John Murray, 1959.
Castes et races. Lyon: Paul Derain, 1957.
Castes and Races. London: Perennial Books, 1959.
Les Stations de la Sagesse. Paris: Buchet/Chastel, 1958.
Stations of Wisdom. London: John Murray, 1961.
Language of the Self. Madras: Ganesh, 1959.
Images de l'esprit. Paris: Flammarion, 1961.
Comprendre l'Islam. Paris: Gallimard, 1961.
Understanding Islam. London: Allen & Unwin, 1963.
Regards sur les mondes anciens. Paris: Editions Traditionnelles, 1968.
Light on the Ancient Worlds. London: Perennial Books, 1965.
In the Tracks of Buddhism. London: Allen & Unwin, 1968.
Dimensions of Islam. London: Allen & Unwin, 1969.
Logique et transcendance. Paris: Editions Traditionnelles, 1970.

Logic and Transcendence. New York: Harper & Row, 1975.
Forme et substance dans les religions. Paris: Dervy-Livres, 1975.
Form and Substance in the Religions. Bloomington, IN: World Wisdom, 2002.
Islam and the Perennial Philosophy. London: World of Islam Publishing Co., 1976.
L'Esotérisme comme principe et comme voie. Paris: Dervy-Livres, 1978.
Esoterism as Principle and as Way. London: Perennial Books, 1981.
Le Soufisme voile et quintessence. Paris: Dervy-Livres, 1980.
Sufism, Veil and Quintessence. Bloomington, IN: World Wisdom Books, 1981.
Du Divin à l'humain. Paris: Le Courrier du Livre, 1981.
From the Divine to the Human. Bloomington, IN: World Wisdom Books, 1982.
Christianisme/Islam: visions d'oecuménisme ésotérique. Milano: Archè, 1981.
Christianity/Islam—Essays on Esoteric Ecumenism. Bloomington, IN: World Wisdom Books, 1985.
Sur les traces de la Religion pérenne. Paris: Le Courrier du Livre, 1982.
Approches du phénomène religieux. Paris: Le Courrier du Livre, 1982.
In the Face of the Absolute. Bloomington, IN: World Wisdom Books, 1989.
Resumé de métaphysique intégrale. Paris: Le Courrier du Livre, 1985.
Survey of Metaphysics and Esoterism. Bloomington, IN: World Wisdom Books, 1986.
Avoir un centre. Paris: Maisonneuve, 1988.
To Have a Center. Bloomington, IN: World Wisdom Books, 1990.
Racines de la condition humaine. Paris: La Table Ronde, 1990.
Roots of the Human Condition. Bloomington, IN: World Wisdom Books, 1991.
The Feathered Sun—Plains Indians in Art and Philosophy. Bloomington, IN: World Wisdom Books, 1990.
Les Perles du pèlerin. Paris: Le Seuil, 1991.
Echoes of Perennial Wisdom. Bloomington, IN: World Wisdom Books, 1992.
Images of Primordial and Mystic Beauty. Bloomington, IN: Abodes, 1992.
Le Jeu des Masques. Lausanne: L'Âge d'Homme, 1992.
The Play of Masks. Bloomington, IN: World Wisdom Books, 1992.
Treasures of Buddhism. Bloomington, IN: World Wisdom Books, 1993.
Trésors du Bouddhisme. Falicon: Nataraj, 1997.
Road to the Heart. Bloomington, IN: World Wisdom Books, 1995.
La Transfiguration de l' Homme. Paris: Maisonneuve Larose, 1995.
The Transfiguration of Man. Bloomington, IN: World Wisdom Books, 1995.
Liebe. Freiburg im Breisgau: Verlag Herder, 1997.
Leben. Freiburg im Breisgau: Verlag Herder, 1997.
Glück. Freiburg im Breisgau: Verlag Herder, 1997.
Sinn. Freiburg im Breisgau: Verlag Herder, 1997.
Poésies didactiques (Vol 1–10). Sottens: Les Sept Flèches, 2001.
Songs for a Spiritual Traveler: Selected Poems. Bloomington, IN: World Wisdom, 2002.

Adastra & Stella Maris: Poems by Frithjof Schuon. Bloomington, IN: World Wisdom, 2003.
René Guénon: Some Observations. Hillsdale, New York: Sophia Perennis, 2004.
Songs without Names—Volumes VII–XII. Bloomington: World Wisdom, 2006.

Bibliography

Abe, Masao. *Our Religions*. Edited by Arvind Sharma. New York: HarperOne, 1995.
Abe, Masao. *Zen and Comparative Studies*. Honolulu: University of Hawaii Press, 1997.
Abhinavagupta, *Parā-trīśikā-Vivarana: The Secret of Tantric Mysticism*. Translated by Jaideva Singh. New Delhi: Motilal Banarsidass, 1996.
Addas, Claude. *Ibn 'Arabī—The Voyage of No Return*. Cambridge: Islamic Texts Society, 2000.
Al-Ghazālī, Abu Hamid. *Ninety-Nine Names of God in Islam*. Translated by Robert Charles Stade. Ibadan: Daystar Press, 1970.
Al-Ghazālī, Abu Hamid. *On Knowing Yourself and God*. Translated by Muhammad Nur Abdus Salam. Chicago: Great Books of the Islamic World, 2002.
Al-Jīlī, 'Abd al-Karīm. *Universal Man*. Translated by Titus Burckhardt. Roxburgh: Beshara Publications, 1983.
Al-Qushayrī, Muslim ibn Ḥajjāj. *Ṣaḥīḥ Muslim: Being Traditions of the Sayings and Doings of the Prophet Muhammad as Narrated by His Companions and Compiled under the Title Al-Jāmi'-uṣ-ṣaḥīḥ*. New Delhi: Kitab Bhavan, 1971.
Alighieri, Dante. *Vita Nuova*. Translated by Andrew Frisardi. Evanston, IL: Northwestern University Press, 2012.
Anton C. Pegis, ed. *Basic Writings of Saint Thomas Aquinas*. Volume 1. Indianapolis: Hackett Publishing, 1997.
Arnaldez, Roger. *Hallāj ou la religion de La Croix*. Paris: Plon, 1964.
Asvaghosa. *The Awakening of Faith*. Translated by Yoshito S. Hakeda. Berkeley: Numata Center for Buddhist Translation and Research, 2005.
'Atā Allāh, Ibn. *Sufi Aphorisms—Kitab Al-Hikam*. Translated by V. Danner. Leiden: Brill Academic Publishing, 1997.
Augustine, Saint. *Confessions*. London: Penguin Books, 1961.
Aymard, Jean-Baptiste, and Patrick Laude. *Frithjof Schuon: Life and Teachings*. Albany: State University of New York, 2001.
Ball, Philip. *The Water Kingdom: A Secret History of China*. Chicago: University of Chicago Press, 2016.

Banerjee, Krishna Mohan. *Dialogues on the Hindu Philosophy*. Calcutta: Thacker Spink and Co., 1861.
Barth, Karl. *Church Dogmatics Study Edition 2: The Doctrine of the Word of God.* I.1 A§ 8–12. London: T&T Clark, 2010.
Barth, Karl. *Church Dogmatics, Vol 1.1 Doctrine of the Word of God.* Volume 2. London: T&T Clark, 2010.
Barthes, Roland. *Critical Essays*. Evanston, IL: Northwestern University Press, 1972.
Basavanna. *Speaking of Śiva*. Translated by A. K. Ramanujan. Baltimore: Penguin Books, 1973.
Blakeslee, Andrew Noel. "The Great Chain of Pluralism: Religious Diversity According to John Hick and the Perennial Philosophy." In *The World's Religions after September 11*. Volume 3. Edited by Arvind Sharma. Westport, CT: Praeger, 2009.
Burckhardt, Titus. *Introduction to Sufi Doctrine*. Bloomington, IN: World Wisdom, 2008.
Burckhardt, Titus. *Mirror of the Intellect*. Albany: State University of New York Press, 1987.
Cabasilas, Nicolas. *La Mère de Dieu*. Lausanne: L'Âge d'Homme, 1992.
Cabezón, José Ignacio. *The Buddha's Doctrine and the Nine Vehicles—Rog Bande Sherab's Lamp of the Teachings*. Oxford: Oxford University Press, 2013.
Campo, Juan E., ed. *Encyclopedia of Islam*. New York: Facts on File, Inc., 2009.
Carus, Paul. *The Gospel of Buddha according to Old Records*. Chicago: Open Court, 2004.
Cheng, Chung-ying. "Dao (Tao): The Way." In *Encyclopedia of Chinese Philosophy*, edited by Antonio S. Cua. New York: Routledge, 2003.
Cheng, Chung-ying. "The Yi-Jing and Yin-Yang Way of Thinking." In *History of Chinese Philosophy*, edited by Bo Mou. New York: Routledge, 2009.
Chittick, William. *The Sufi Path of Knowledge*. Albany: State University of New York Press, 1989.
Chittick, William. *The Sufi Path of Love: The Spiritual Teachings of Rūmī*. Albany: State University of New York Press, 1983.
Chodhkiewicz, Michel. *Spiritual Writings of Amir 'Abd al-Kader*. Translated by James Chrestensen and Tom Manning. Albany: State University of New York Press, 1995.
Chouiref, Tayeb, ed. *Spiritual Teachings of the Prophet*. Louisville: Fons Vitae, 2011.
Chouiref, Tayeb. *Spiritual Teachings of the Prophet: Hadith with Commentaries by Saints and Sages of Islam*. Louisville: Fons Vitae, 2011.
Colledge, Edmund, and Bernard McGinn. *Meister Eckhart: The Essential Sermons, Commentaries, Treatises, and Defense*. Mahwah, NJ: Paulist Press, 1981.
Corbin, Henry. *Histoire de la philosophie islamique*. Paris: Gallimar, 1964.
Corbin, Henry. *Spiritual Body and Celestial Earth: From Mazdean Iran to Shī'ite Iran*. Princeton, NJ: Princeton University Press, 1989.

BIBLIOGRAPHY | 369

Cutsinger, James, ed. *The Fullness of God—Frithjof Schuon on Christianity*. Bloomington, IN: World Wisdom, 2004.
Cutsinger, James. "The Mystery of the Two Natures." In *Every Branch in Me: Essays on the Meaning of Man*, edited by Barry McDonald, 87-120. Bloomington, IN: World Wisdom, 2002.
Cutsinger, James. *Advice to the Serious Seeker: Meditation on the Teaching of Frithjof Schuon*. Albany: State University of New York Press, 1997.
Cutsinger, James. *The Splendor of Truth*. Albany: State University of New York Press, 2012.
Cutsinger, James. "The Virgin." In *Ye Shall Know the Truth: Christianity and the Perennial Philosophy*, edited by Mateus Soares de Azevedo. Bloomington, IN: World Wisdom, 2005.
De Bary, William Theodore. *Sources of East Asian Tradition*. Volume 1. New York: Columbia University Press, 2008.
Dehejia, Harsha V. *The Advaita of Art*. New Delhi: Motilal Banarsidass, 1996.
Deutsch, Eliot. *Advaita Vedānta: A Philosophical Reconstruction*. Honolulu: University of Hawaii Press, 1973.
Dupré, Louis, and James A. Wiseman, eds. *Light from Light: An Anthology of Christian Mysticism*. New York: Paulist Press, 2001.
Durand, Gilbert. *L'imagination symbolique*. Paris: Quadrige/PUF, 1964.
Eck, Diana. *Banaras, City of Light*. Princeton, NJ: Princeton University Press, 1982.
Eckhart, Meister. *Die deutschen und lateinischen Werke III*. Stuttgart: W. Kohlhammer, 1936.
Eckhart, Meister. *The Essential Sermons, Commentaries, Treatises and Defense*. Mahwah, NJ: Paulist Press, 1981.
Ernst, Carl. *Ruzbihan Baqli: Mysticism and the Rhetoric of Sainthood in Persian Sufism*. New York: Routledge, 1996.
Fitzgerald, Michael. *Frithjof Schuon: Messenger of the Sophia Perennis*. Bloomington, IN: World Wisdom, 2010.
Fitzgerald, Michael Oren, ed. *Letters of Frithjof Schuon: Reflections on the Perennial Philosophy*. Bloomington, IN: World Wisdom, 2019.
Garrigou-Lagrange, Reginald. *Reality: A Synthesis of Thomistic Thought*. London: Aeterna Press, 2016.
Geoffroy, Eric. *Introduction to Sufism*. Bloomington, IN: World Wisdom, 2010.
Guénon, René. *The Reign of Quantity and the Signs of the Times*. Hillsdale, NY: Sophia Perennis et Universalis, 2001.
Guénon, René. *Studies in Hinduism*. Hillsdale, NY: Sophia Perennis, 2001.
Guénon, René. *Symbols of Sacred Science*. Hillsdale, NY: Sophia Perennis, 2004.
Hadot, Pierre. *Philosophy as a Way of Life: Spiritual Exercises from Socrates to Foucault*. New York: Wiley, 1995.
Hallāj, Al-Husayn ibn Mansūr. *Kitāb al-Tawāsīn*. Berkeley, CA: Diwan Press, 1974.

Hani, Jean. *The Black Virgin: A Marian Mystery*. San Rafael, CA: Sophia Perennis, 2007.
Hegel, G. W. F. *The Phenomenology of Mind*. Volume 1. Translated by J. B. Baillie. New York: Routledge, 2014.
Hick, John. *Disputed Questions in Theology and the Philosophy of Religion*. London: Palgrave Macmillan, 1997.
Hick, John. *An Interpretation of Religion: Human Responses to the Transcendent*. London: Palgrave Macmillan, 1989; New Haven, CT: Yale University Press, 2004.
Hossein Nasr, Seyyed. *Knowledge and the Sacred*. Albany: State University of New York Press, 1989.
Houman, Setareh. *From the Philosophia Perennis to American Perennialism*. Chicago: Kazi Publications, 2014.
Huxley, Aldous. *The Perennial Philosophy: An Interpretation of the Great Mystics, East and West*. New York: HarperCollins, 2009.
Ibn Al-'Arabī. *The Bezels of Wisdom*. Translated by R. W. J Austin. Mahwah, NJ: Paulist Press, 1980.
Ibn Al-'Arabī. *The Four Pillars of Spiritual Transformation: The Adornment of the Spiritually Transformed (Hilyat al-abdāl)*. Translated by Stephen Hirtenstein. Oxford: Anqa Publications, 2008.
Ibn Al-'Arabī. *Fusus al-Hikam XXVII*. Beirut: Dar al-Kitab al-Arabi, 1946.
Ibn Al-'Arabī. *The Ringstones of Wisdom*. Translated by Caner K. Dagli. Chicago: Great Books of the Islamic World, 2004.
Ibn Al-'Arabī. *The Secrets of Voyaging*. Translated by Angela Jaffray. Oxford: Anqa Publishing, 2015.
Idel, Moshe. *Mystical Experience in Abraham Abulafia*. Albany: State University of New York Press, 1988.
Izutsu, Toshihiko. *Sufism and Taoism: A Comparative Study of Key Philosophical Concepts*. Berkeley: University of California Press, 1983.
Kohn, Livia. *The Taoist Experience*. Albany: State University of New York Press, 1993.
Ksemarāja. *The Doctrine of Recognition: A Translation of Prathyabhijñāhrdayam*. Translated by Jaideva Singh. Albany: State University of New York Press, 1990.
Lao, Tzu. *Tao Te Ching*. Translated by Arthur Waley. Ware: Wordsworth Editions Ltd., 1997.
Lao, Tzu. *Tao Te Ching*. Translated by D. C. Lau. Hong Kong: Chinese University Press, 1989.
Legge, James. *The Texts of Taoism Part I*. New York: Dover, 1962.
Leighton, Taigen Dan. *Faces of Compassion: Classic Bodhisattva Archetypes and Their Modern Expression*. Somerville: Wisdom Publications, 2012.
Lings, Martin. *A Sufi Saint of the Twentieth Century*. Cambridge: Islamic Texts Society, 1993.

BIBLIOGRAPHY | 371

Lings, Martin. *A Sufi Saint of the Twentieth Century—Shaykh Ahmad Al-'Alawī— His Spiritual Heritage and Legacy*. Cambridge: Islamic Texts Society, 1993.
Lings, Martin. *What Is Sufism?* Cambridge: Islamic Texts Society, 1993.
Littlejohn, Ronnie, and Jeffrey Dippmann, eds. *Riding the Wind with Liezi: New Perspectives on the Daoist Classic*. Albany: State University of New York Press, 2011.
Madhavananda, Swami. *Vivekachudamani of Shri Shankaracharya*. Kolkata: Advaita Ashrama, 1966.
Maharshi, Ramana. *Talks with Ramana Maharshi*. Carlsbad, NM: Inner Directions, 2001.
Massignon, Louis. *Essay on the Origins of the Technical Language of Islamic Mysticism*. Notre Dame, IN: University of Notre Dame Press, 2003.
Mayer, Toby. "Theology and Sufism." In *Classical Islamic Theology*, edited by Tim Winter. Cambridge: Cambridge University Press, 2008.
McCarthy, R. J. *Al-Ghazālī's Path to Sufism and His Deliverance from Error: An Annotated Translation of Al-Munqidh min al-dalal*. Louisville: Fons Vitae, 2000.
Merell-Wolff, Franklin. *Experience and Philosophy: A Personal Record of Transformation*. Albany: State University of New York Press, 1994.
Meyendorff, John. *Byzantine Theology: Historical Trends and Doctrinal Themes*. New York: Fordham University Press, 1979.
Moltmann, Jürgen. *The Trinity and the Kingdom: The Doctrine of God*. Minneapolis: Fortress, 1993.
Moule, Handley C. G. *Outlines of Christian Doctrine*. Eugene, OR: Wipf & Stock, 2007.
Murata, Kazuyo. *Beauty in Sufism: The Teachings of Ruzbihan Baqli*. Albany: State University of New York Press, 2017.
Murata, Sachiko. *The Tao of Islam*. Albany: State University of New York Press, 1992.
Nagamma, Suri. *Letters from Sri Ramanasramam*. Tiruvannamalai: Sri Ramanasramam, 2014.
Nagarjuna. *Nagarjuna's Mūlamadhyamakakārika: Fundamental Wisdom of the Middle Way*. Translated by Jay L. Garfield. Oxford: Oxford University Press, 1995.
Narang, G. Ch. *Message of the Vedas*. Lahore: New Book Society, 1946.
Nasr, Seyyed Hossein, ed. *The Essential Frithjof Schuon*. Bloomington, IN: World Wisdom, 2005.
Nygren, Anders. *Agape and Eros*. London: SPCK, 1953.
Oldmeadow, Kenneth (Harry). *Frithjof Schuon and the Perennial Philosophy*. Bloomington, IN: World Wisdom, 2010.
Oldmeadow, Kenneth (Harry). *Traditionalism—Religion in the Light of the Perennial Philosophy*. Colombo: Sri Lanka Institute of Traditional Studies, 2000.
O'Neil, L. Thomas. *Māyā in Śankara: Measuring the Immeasurable*. New Delhi: Motilal Banarsidass, 1980.

Ouaknin, Marc-Alain. *The Burnt Book: Reading the Talmud.* Princeton, NJ: Princeton University Press, 1995.
Padoux, André. *The Roots of Tantra.* Edited by Katherine Anne Harper and Robert L. Brown. Albany: State University of New York Press, 2002.
Panikkar, Raimon. *Hinduism, Part 1: The Vedic Experience.* New York: Orbis Books, 2016.
Paraskevopoulos, John. *The Unhindered Path: Ruminations on Shin Buddhism.* Kettering, OH: Sophia Perennis, 2016.
Pascal, Blaise. *Pensées.* Translated by W. F. Trotter. Mineola, NY: Dover, 2003.
Pérez, Ángel Cordovilla. "The Trinitarian Concept of Person." In *Rethinking Trinitarian theology*, edited by Giulio Maspero and Robert J. Wozniak. New York: T&T Clark International, 2012.
Pfeiffer, Franz, ed. *Deutsche Mystiker des Vierzehnten Jahrhunderts.* Leipzig: G.J. Göschen'sche Verlaghandlund, 1857.
Plato. *Symposium.* Volume 5. Edited and translated by W. R. M. Lamb. Cambridge, MA: Harvard University Press, 1953.
Prothero, Stephen. *God Is Not One.* Melbourne: Black Ink, 2010.
Pseudo-Dionysius. *The Complete Works.* Translated by Colm Luibhead. New York: Paulist Press, 1987.
Qutbi, Muhammad Mahmood Ali. *Fragrance of Sufism.* Karachi: Royal Book Co., 1993.
Rabelais, François. *The Works of François Rabelais, Volume 4.* Translated by Sir Thomas Urquhart. London: Gibbings, 1897.
Rawlisson, Andrew. *The Book of Enlightened Masters: Western Teachers in Eastern Tradition.* Chicago: Open Court, 1998.
Reynaud, Patricia. "Religious Māyā." In *The World's Religions after September 11.* Volume 3. Edited by Arvind Sharma. Westport: Praeger, 2009.
Ricoeur, Paul. *Freud and Philosophy: An Essay on Interpretation.* New Haven, CT: Yale University Press, 1970.
Ringgenberg, Patrick. *Diversité et unité des religions chez René Guénon et Frithjof Schuon.* Paris: L'Harmattan, 2010.
Rūmī, Jalāl-ad-Dīn. *Music of a Distant Drum: Classical Arabic, Persian, Turkish, and Hebrew Poems.* Edited and translated by Bernard Lewis. Princeton, NJ: Princeton University Press, 2001.
Rumi, Jelaluddin. *A Rūmī Anthology.* Translated by Reynold A. Nicholson. London: Oneworld, 2000.
Rustom, Mohammed. *The Triumph of Mercy: Philosophy and Scripture in Mullā Sadrā.* Albany: State University of New York Press, 2012.
Sands, Kristin Zahra. *Sūfī Commentaries on the Qur'ān in Classical Islam.* New York: Routledge, 2006.
Śaṅkarācārya, Sri. *Saundaryalaharī.* Translated by V. K. Subramanian. New Delhi: Motilal Banarsidass, 2011.

Śankarācārya, Sri. *Vivekachudamani*. Mayavati: Advaita Ashrama, 1921.
Saraswati, Swami Satchidanandendra. *The Method of the Vedanta: A Critical Account of the Advaita Tradition*. Delhi: Motilal Banarsidass, 1997.
Schäfer, Peter. *Mirror of His Beauty: Feminine Images of God from the Bible to the Early Kabbalah*. Princeton, NJ: Princeton University Press, 2002.
Scholem, Gershom. *On the Kabbalah and Its Symbolism*. New York: Schocken Books, 1969.
Sedgwick, Mark. *Against the Modern World*. Oxford: Oxford University Press, 2009.
Seidel, George Joseph. *Knowledge as Sexual Metaphor*. London: Associated University Presses, 2000.
Shabistarī, Mahmud. *Garden of Mystery—The Gulshan-i rāz of Mahmūd Shabistarī*. Translated by Robert Abdul Hayy Darr. Cambridge: Archetype, 2007.
Shah-Kazemi, Reza. *Spiritual Quest: Reflections on Qur'ānic Prayer according to the Teachings of Imam 'Alī*. London: I.B. Tauris, 2011.
Shankara Source Book, Volume 1: Shankara on the Absolute. Translated by A. J. Alston. London: Shanti Sadan, 2004.
Sharma, B. N. Khrishnamurti. *History of the Dvaita School of Vedānta and Its Literature*. New Delhi: Motilal Barnarsidass, 1960.
Shin, Kiseong. *The Concept of Self in Hinduism, Buddhism, and Christianity*. Eugene, OR: Pickwick, 2017.
Shulman, Eviatar. *Rethinking the Buddha: Early Buddhist Philosophy as Meditative Perception*. Cambridge: Cambridge University Press, 2014.
Smith, Huston. *Forgotten Truth—The Common Vision of the World's Religions*. New York: HarperCollins, 1992.
Smith, Huston, and Jeffrey Paine. *Tales of Wonder—Adventures Chasing the Divine*. New York: HarperOne, 2009.
Smith, Wilfred Cantwell. *The Meaning and End of Religion*. Minneapolis: Fortress Press, 1991.
Sopa, Gheze Lhundub. *Steps on the Path to Enlightenment: A Commentary on Tsongkhapa's Lamrim Chenmo—Volume 3: The Way of the Bodhisattva*. Edited by Beth Newman. Boston: Wisdom Publications, 2008.
Stinissen, Wilfrid. *The Holy Spirit, Fire of Divine Love*. San Francisco: Ignatius Press, 1989.
Suzuki, D. T. "Religion and Drugs." In *Selected Works of D. T. Suzuki Volume III*. Berkeley: University of California Press, 2016.
Suzuki, Daisetz Teitaro. *The Zen Koan as a Means of Attaining Enlightenment*. Boston: Charles E. Tuttle Co., 1994.
Thera, Nārada Maha. *The Buddha and His Teachings*. Bangkok: Buddhadhamma Foundation, 1980.
Tsong Khapa, Rje. *Ocean of Reasoning: A Great Commentary on Nāgārjuna's Mūlamadhyamakakārikā*. Translated by Geshe Ngawang Samten and Jay L. Garfield. Oxford: Oxford University Press, 2006.

Venkatesananda, Swami. *The Concise Srīmad Bhāgavatam*. Albany: State University of New York Press, 1989.
Versluis, Arthur. *American Gurus: From Transcendentalism to New Age Religion*. Oxford: Oxford University Press, 2014.
Wang, Robin. *Yinyang—The Way of Heaven and Earth in Chinese Thought and Culture*. Cambridge: Cambridge University Press, 2012.
Watson, Burton. *The Zen Teachings of Master Lin-chi*. Boston: Shambhala Publications, 1993.
Weil, Simone. *Gravity and Grace*. New York: Routledge, 2003.
Weil, Simone. *Notebooks of Simone Weil*. Translated by Arthur Wills. New York: Routledge, 2004.
Xing, Guang. *The Concept of the Buddha: Its Evolution from Early Buddhism to the Trikāya Theory*. London: Routledge, 2005.

Index

'Abd al-Karīm al-Jīlī, on knowing that the Essence of God The Supreme is the mystery (*ghayb*) of the Unity (*al-ahadiyah*), 328n10

'Abd al-Qādir al-Jazā'irī, Emir, 91, 91n65

Abe, Masao, on the realization of one's True Self, 255n16

abheda (non-difference), and Abhinavagupta's *MahāMāyā tattva* as characterized by the its shrinkage and appearance of *bheda* (difference), 45n30

Abhinavagupta:
  MahāMāyā tattva characterized by the "shrinkage of *abheda* (non-difference) and appearance of *bheda* (difference)," 45n30
  Parā-triśikā-Vivarana, 45n30
  and Schuon's thought, 13n24, 263

Absolute, the:
  and the distinction between *Saguna Brahman* and *Nirguna Brahman*, 328n11
  and the Infinite as complementary (according to Schuon), 245-246
  in light of the frozen and thawed words in Rabelais's *Fourth Book*, 361-362, 361n11
  misconceptions of (identified by Schuon), 332-333
  and the reality of the Man-God for Christians, 355
  and the realization of Buddhahood, 70
  and Schuon's insight that "the oneness of the object demands the totality of the subject," 359
  Schuon's strict definition of, in light of his keen sense of relativities, 358-359
  and Schuon's understanding of orthodoxy, 333-334, 334n19
  See also Divine Unity (*tawhīd*); Man-God

Advaita:
  inclusivity and gradualness of Kashmir Śaivism contrasted with, 45
  and the onto-cosmological why of Māyā, 36
  perspective on the Name, 214
  See also Shankara

Advaita Vedānta:
  distinction between *Saguna Brahman* and *Nirguna Brahman*, 44
  and *Māyā*. See *Māyā*—and Advaita Vedānta

375

Advaita Vedānta *(continued)*
  and Schuon's perspective on Sufism, 232–233
  as the summit of *philosophia perennis* according to Schuon, 27
ahadīth:
  hadīth qudsī: "I was a Hidden Treasure and I wanted to be known so I created the world," 250, 250n32
  on women, perfumes, and prayer made lovable' (*hubbiba ilayya*) to the Prophet, 312n26
Al-'Alawī, Shaykh Aḥmad ibn Muṣṭafā, on *Laylā*, 253
'Ali, Imam, 221–222
Aquinas, Thomas, Trinitarian theology of:
  the Divine Person ("relation as subsisting") criticized by Schuon, 179–180, 244
  and the integral concept of the Unity of God, 171–172, 178
  and stating that the Trinity is in the Essence entitatively but not intentionally, 166
  and the term *formaliter eminenter*, 172, 182, 182n56
Ash'arite theology, 204, 206, 212n48
Augustine, Saint:
  and the Christian perception of sexuality as sinful, 296, 296n2
  felix culpa of, 39
  Trinity of "Memory, Understanding and Will," 166n20
avatāras:
  Alexander and Caesar attributed with an *avatāric* function by Schuon, 57n7
  and Buddhism:
    and physical representation of the Buddha, 72–73
    and the realization of Buddhahood, 69–71
    tathāgatas compared with, 59
  and the concept of Divine manifestation, 57–58
  and Hindu religious sensibility, 55–59
  major and minor types distinguished by Schuon, 57n7
  Mary as a feminine *avatāra* explained by Schuon, 85, 85n49
  Muhammad's *avatāric* nature, 92n67, 238
  See also Man-God

Bamford, Christopher, 355n3
Barth, Karl, on modes of being, 176–177, 183
Beyond-Being. *See* supra-ontological Principle—Beyond-Being defined by Schuon as the unity of
Bhaghavad Gītā:
  the illusion (*Māyā*) associated with the eternity of the cycle of *samsāra*, 37n19
  Krishna's appearance to Arjuna as *viśvarūpa*, 65, 65n17
  and Visnuite *avatāras*, 57n7
Bible:
  2 Corinthians 13:13, on "the Wisdom of the Father," 166
  Caesar mentioned in, 57n7
  Fall from Eden, 256
  Genesis, God's Self-characterization as *I am*, 177
  John 3:8, "The Spirit bloweth where it listeth," 167
  John 19:26, 242n8
  Philippians 2:7, 244
Blakeslee, Andrew Noel, 325, 331
Borella, Jean, Schuon's approach and mode of expression as characterized as "spherical" by, 11

Brzezinski, Jan, 308n19
Buddhism:
  and Buddha-nature, 42n42, 68–69, 111, 327
  Divine formal perfection of the Buddha, 310
  doctrine of skillful means. See *upāya*
  doctrine of the three bodies of the Buddha (*trikāya*), 68–71
  feminization of the Bodhisattva, 261
  four aspects of Buddha, 72–73
  and *Nirvāna*, 104–105, 112
  and Dharmakara's Vow, 280–281
  and the Englightenment of the Buddha, 70, 70n29
  pāramitās (six perfections of wisdom), 233
  Prajñapāramitā:
    and the inner-most layers of the human heart, 87, 87n55
    and the super-eminent position of the Feminine, 240–241, 240–241n5
  rejection of substances compared with Taoist negation of essences, 273
  Schuon on the saving function of the *avatāra* as a characteristic shared by the Buddha and Christ, 68
  solution to the problem of fundamentalism, 120n29
  tathāgatas compared with *avatāras*, 59
  Zen *koans*, 67, 241
  See also Nāgārjuna

Cabasilas, Nicolas, 259
Cabezón, José Ignacio, 301n10
Chiodkiewicz, Michel, 212n47
Chittick, William, on "creative command" (*al-amr al-kawnī*)
  and "religious command" (*al-amr al-dīnī*), 206
Christian theology. See Bible; Trinity and Trinitarian interpretation
Coomaraswamy, Ananda K.:
  Māyā translated as "Divine Art" by, 33
  perennialist worldview articulated by, 2, 4, 188
Corbin, Henry:
  insight that "the mode of understanding is conditioned by the mode of being of the one who understands, 325n1
  notion of "dialogue in meta-history," 1
  on Rūzbihān's theophanic vision of feminine beauty, 316
Cutsinger, James, 8n18
  esotericism, traditionalism, and universalism associated with Schuon's articulation of perennialism by, 188, 188n3
  on Schuon's views on the Virgin, 239, 239nn2–3
  on the Trinity, 81–82n43

Dante Alighieri, 53
  exclamation at the sight of Beatrice, 251n33, 280, 280n33
Dehejia, Harsha V., 248
Deutsch, Eliot, 27–28n2, 33
  Sat, Cit, and *Ānanda* identified with Brahman, 160n10
Dickson, William Rory, 187n1
Dionysius, on the Trinity, 172–173, 180
Divine Unity (*tawhīd*):
  and God's capacity to perceive separative multiplicity from the point of view of his Unity, 256, 256n49

Divine Unity *(continued)*
  the Incarnation of the Word and
    Christ's crucifixion as a challenge
    to, 130–131
  and the metaphysical meaning of
    the *shahādah*, 213
  and the point of encounter between
    Islam and Christianity (according
    to Schuon), 209
  and the Pythagorean tetradic
    triangle *Tetraktys*, 54
  and Schuon's understanding of
    "religion," "heart," "way," and
    "oneness," 207–210
Durand, Gilbert, the sign, the
  allegory, and the symbol
  distinguished by, 21

Eaton, Gai, 2
Eck, Diana, 58–59, 58–59
Eckhart, Meister:
  on atheists, 50
  on the duality of the "outer man"
    and the "inner man," 300
  and the equality of images of all
    things in God, 174n40
  on the mysticism of the Essence, 172–
    175, 180, 222–223, 243, 243n12
  and the term *bullitio*, 175
emic and the *etic* approaches to
  human and social phenomena:
  and the distinction between
    phonemics and *phonetics* by Pike
    (Kenneth Lee), 354
  Schuon's integration of both
    dimensions in his perspective,
    354–355
Ernst, Carl, on *iltibās* ("clothing with
  divinity," 316
esotericism:
  barzakh (isthmus) dividing the
    esoteric from the exoteric, 76,
    89–90, 203nn27–28, 214, 222

  and the decay of religious forms,
    336
  as the foundation of orthodoxy, 337
  and the "nature of things," 124
  and Shamanism, 27, 348, 348n39
  See also Islam—esoteric core
    (*haqīqah*) of
esotericism—Schuon's definiton of:
  and the Feminine, 259–263
  manifold perspectives of, 123,
    123n1
  and perennialism, 188, 188n3
  and Tantrism, 319–322
  See also Schuon, Frithjof—
    works—*Esoterism as Principle
    and as Way*; supra-ontological
    Principle—Beyond-Being defined
    by Schuon as the unity of
esotericism—Schuon's view of esoteric
  ecumenism, 323–350passim
  multilayered aspects of, 349–350
  and religious tolerance, 344
Evola, Julius, 295n1

Fātima (the daughter of the Prophet),
  86, 242, 242n7
Francis, Saint, 57n7
Freiberger, Oliver, 353n1

Garrigou-Lagrange, Reginald, 182n56
Al-Ghazālī:
  on Divine Presence, 65
    manifestation in human
    intelligence, 64
  on the "mould of truth," 125, 125n4
  on *mutasawwifūn* and the
    excellence of Sufism, 217
  Niffarī's spirituality contrasted with
    (by Schuon), 226
  and the parable of the elephant and
    the blind men, 356, 356n6
  on the polarity between *sharī'ah*
    and *haqīqah*, 227

and Schuon's understanding of
Sufism and Islam:
and Ghazālī's equation of Sufism
as *ihsān* ("perfect practice"), 208
and Ghazālī's orientation toward
an inner revivification of
religion by means of a
spiritual refinement of the soul
(*tazkiyyat an-nafs*), 226–227,
227n75
Unicity of Essence expressed by
"there is none in existence save
God" (*laysa fi'l wujūd ill'Allāh*),
207
gnosis—Schuonian understanding of,
16
and asceticism (*zuhd*), 202
the Feminine as a symbol and
manifestation of gnosis, 261–262
the Heart identified as the
Śakti (actualizing power) of
intelligence, 199n20
the individualism of religious zeal
as incompatible with, 198–199,
199n20, 215–216
and *tasawwuf*, 189–190, 209, 214,
234–235
and Trinitarian interpretation,
88–89, 93
Gregory of Nazianzus (Gregory the
Theologian), 81n43, 180
Guénon, René:
on the *avatara* as "downward
crossing," 59
the *avatara*'s place of birth located
in the cave of the heart by, 92n66
on the cosmology and
metacosmology of numbers, 55
on defining Metaphysics, 15n289
the opposition between the
East and West traced to the
materialism of the modern West,
142–143, 143n27

on partial disorders, 343, 343n33
perennialist worldview articulated
by, 2, 4, 188
Sufism associated with Shadhilism
by, 191n6
Sufism defined as "Islamic esoterism"
by, 189
Schuon's understanding of
esoterism contrasted with, 210

hadīth. See *ahadīth*
Hadot, Pierre, 104
Hallāj, Al-Husayn ibn Mansūr, 78,
189, 206, 211, 218–219, 231
Hani, Jean, 237
haqīqah (esoteric Truth):
and Mary's outer effacement, 241,
241n6
sharī'ah in relation to, 212, 212n47,
222–223, 227
Hegel, G.W.F., 54, 54n2, 102
Hick, John:
pluralism theorized by (contrasted
with Schuon's ecumenism),
325–332, 347
on the Real, the Ultimate, Ultimate
Reality, 95, 95n1, 329–331
religious pluralism articulated by,
325–327, 331–332
Hinduism:
concept of the *avatāra*, 92n67, 238
cosmological triad of *sattva, rajas,*
and *tamas,* 158
karma-yoga (way of action through
adherence to prescriptions), 154,
212
and the difference between
"average" and "quintessential"
Sufism distinguished in terms
of, 202–205, 203n28
nāma-rūpa (name-and-form or
substance-and-accident), 252
pendantic formalism of, 141n25

Hinduism *(continued)*
  Purusha and *Prakriti*, 252–253, 286–287
  Trimūrti 'Triple Manifestation', 54, 81–82, 89, 91, 166–167n21
  ultimate identification with *Nirguna Brahman*, 238, 328
  See also Advaita Vedānta; Krishna and Krishnaism; *Māyā*; *Sat, Cit,* and *Ānanda* (Being, Consciousness, and Bliss); Shankara
Houle, Handley, on the distinction between the immanent and the economical Trinity, 167–168
human margin:
  as a Divine condescension to human limitations and weaknesses, 131–133
  and the balance between inwardness and outwardness, 147, 147n36, 295
  and racial factors in religion (according to Schuon), 133–135, 134nn22-12, 135n17
Huxley, Aldous:
  perennialist worldview articulate by, 2–4, 2n4
  and Smith (Huston), 5–6, 6n13

Ibn al-'Arabī, Muhyī-al-Dīn:
  assertion that there is only the Real, 288, 288n46
  contemplation of God through woman, 250, 250n32, 316
  enunciation of the metaphysics of Unity, 212, 212n47
  on the Feminine, 249, 249nn28–29
  hermeneutic speculations of, 202
  on hunger resulting from fasting, 215n54

Izutsu on the multi-stratified structure of his metaphysics, 54n3
  non-duality of his *wujūdiyyah* perspective shared with Schuon's metaphysical position, 226, 232–233
  "permanent entities," 272
  sharī'ah equated with *haqīqah* by, 212, 212n47
  on "station of no station" (*maqām lā maqām* or *maqām la muqām*) as the summit of human perfection, 17
Ibn 'Atā Allāh, Ahmad ibn Muhammad:
  distinction between *rasūl* or the *nabī* and the *walī*, 220
  Hikam, 65
Idel, Moseh, 297
Islam:
  Divine manifestation in and through human agency excluded from, 58, 62
  doctrine of *tawhīd*. *See* Divine Unity
  See also Prophet, the; *sharī'ah*; *shirk* ("sin" of "association")
Islam—doctrine of the Trinity of *al-'Arsh* ("the Throne"), *ar-Rūh* ("the Spirit"), and *an-Nūr* ("the light"):
  and the Hindu *Trimūrti*, 167, 167nn21–22
  Jesus as *Rūh Allāh*, 82
  and onto-cosmological reality, 89–90
Islam—esoteric core (*haqīqah*) of:
  and the highlighting of the transcendence of (in Sufi antinomiansim), 222–223

its polarity to *sharī'ah* (explained by Ghazāli), 227
Maryam identified with (by Schuon), 241, 241n6
sharī'ah equated with (by Ibn 'Arabī), 212, 212n47
sharī'ah viewed as the "symbolic" of (by Schuon), 212
veiling of criticized by Schuon, 197-198
See also Sufi theosophy
Islam—pillars of (*arkān al-Islām*):
1. *shahādah* (profession of faith), 0 and the metaphysical meaning of the name of the Prophet, 82-83
2. *salāt* (canonical prayer), 213-215
3. (fasting during Ramada) and 4. (giving alms), 215-216
5. *Hajj*, 218-219
and the essential principles of Sufism (according to Schuon), 211-212
as gateways to the esoteric meaning of Sufi doctrine and method, 212-213
and *jihād*, 218-219
Izutsu, Toshihiko:
on the 'multi-stratified' structure of Taoist and Sufi metaphysics, 54n3
philosophia perennis called for, 1, 6-7
on Zhuangzi, 272, 272n10

Jīlī. See 'Abd al-Karīm al-Jīlī
Judaism:
Divine manifestation in and through human agency excluded from, 58, 62, 64
integration of sexuality within religion, 297

Jewish *upāya*, 115
See also Kabbalah

Kabbalah, and the *Shekhinah*, 55, 55n5
Kantian epistemology:
and Hick's distinction between "noumenal" and the "phenomenal," 326, 331
Schuon's epistemology distinguished from, 19-20
Kashmir Śaivism:
Abhinavagupta's outlook compared with, 28
and the concept of *vimarsa*, 46, 248
exclusivity and immediacy of Advaita contrasted with, 45
and the syzygy of Śiva-Śakti, 25, 28, 45, 246
Krishna and Krishnaism:
amorous *līlā* with the *gopis*, 305-309, 314-315, 317, 322
and the Krishanaite quality of the Prophet, 311-313
Schuon's use of the adjective Krishnaite, 305-306

Laozi (or Lao Tzu). See *under* Taoism
Leighton, Taigen Dan, 240-241n5
Lings, Martin, 126n5, 228-229, 228-229n79, 253n41
Lin Yutang, 276
Luria, Isaac, on *tsimtsum* (Divine Self-withdrawl or contraction), 244, 244

McGinn, Bernard, 174
Maharshi, Ramana:
the Self referred to as his Father, 255n46

Maharshi, Ramana *(continued)*
    the sign, the allegory, and the
    symbol distinguished by, 22–23,
    23n41
Mahoney, Timothy, 180n54, 181n55,
    184–185
Man-God:
    and the image of descent, 58–59,
        65–66
    and the Hindu archetype of the
        avatāra, 62, 65
    as the Luminous Centre of the
        cosmos, 81–82
    and the notion of *barzakh*, 89
    the sense of the Absolute
        concentrated on its reality for
        Christians, 355
    and the three Islamic concepts of
        al-'Arsh ("the Throne"), *ar-Rūh*
        ("the Spirit"), and *an-Nūr* ("the
        light"), 89–90
    Unity and multiplicity that is
        inherent to it, 55
    See also *avatāras*
Marian Reality, her outer effacement
    identified with esoteric Truth
    (*haqīqah*), 241, 241n6
Mariology. *See* Virgin Mary (or
    Maryam)
Massignon, Louis, 187, 338
Māyā:
    and the contemplation of the
        Essence as masculine, 247n22
    identification as Revelation, 36,
        39–40
    the illusion (*Māyā*) associated
        with the eternity of the cycle of
        samsāra, 37, 37n19
    Prakriti defined as "the divine
        femininity of *Māyā*" (by Schuon),
        252n35, 252–253

and "saving mirages" (*upāya*), 102
Upanishads on, 33–35, 38, 43
Māyā—and Advaita Vedānta, 29n4
    and the range of relativity that
        forms the realm of qualified
        reality, 44
    the provisional nature of *upāya*
        compared with, 112–113
    relative silence on the onto-
        cosmological why of, 36
    transition from Ātman to, 40, 43,
        299–300
Merell-Wolff, Franklin, 260n60
Meyendorff, John, 180
Moltmann, Jürgen, on Barth's modes
    of being, 177–178
Moses, 226, 240
Muhammad, *See also* Prophet, the
Murata, Sachiko, 279n30
mutashābihāt:
    distinguished from *muhkamāt*
        verses, 298n7
    and the term *mutashābihan*, 298

Nāgārjuna:
    critique of substantial causality, 28
    statement that there "has never
        been ever any Dharma taught,"
        70, 111
    on the two truths of Buddha's
        teaching of the Dharma, 113,
        119
Nasr, Seyyed Hossein, 2n2, 53, 190n5,
    191n6
nature of things:
    and left-handed *tantra*, 303
    religious or traditional norms and
        practices contrasted with (by
        Schuon), 128–129
    and Tantrism, 303–304
    and *upaya*, 130

INDEX | 383

Niffarī, Muḥammad ibn 'Abd
al-Jabbar, 225–226
Nygren, Anders, 353–354

Oldmeadow, Harry, *Frithjof Schuon and the Perennial Philosophy,*
8–9n18, 10n20
Oldmeadow, Kenneth, 2
O'Neil, L. Thomas, 29n4, 34, 34n15
orthodoxy:
  and the Absolute (according to
    Schuon), 333–334, 334n19
  esoterism as the foundation of, 337
  Schuon's perspective assessed by
    scholars, 9n18
  and Schuon's criticisms of
    contemporary religious life, 141–
    142, 142n26, 332, 335, 335n22,
    339–340, 360–362
  and Schuon's notion of "intrinsic
    orthodoxy," 140–141, 141n24,
    196n14, 332–335, 360

Padoux, André, 301n9
Panikkar, Raimon, 34n16
Paraskevopoulos, John, 120n29
Pascal, Blaise, on Qur'anic vision of
  the afterlife, 298, 298n6
pendantic formalism of Hinduism,
  141n25
perennialism. See *philosophia perennis*
philosophia perennis:
  Advaita Vedānta as the summit of
    (according to Schuon), 27
  popularization in the English-
    speaking world, 2–6, 188
  and religious differences, 325n3,
    327–328, 331
  Schuon on *Religio perennis,* 12, 196,
    229, 234, 234n85, 244–245n15,
    347n37

and Schuon's insights into Islam
  and Sufism. *See* Schuon,
  Frithjof—and perennialism
  and Sufism, 188–189, 195–196
and the theme of the transcendent
  unity of religions, and Schuon's
  response to the challenges raised
  by religious plurality, 357
Pickthall, Marmaduke, *mutashābihan*
  rendered as resemblance by,
  298
Plato and Platonic philosophy:
  Abinavagupta's awakening to
    our immanent Selfhood
    compared with Platonic path
    of transcendence toward the
    Beautiful, 263
  and the allegory of frozen and
    thawed words in Rabelais's
    Fourth Book, 361n11
  archetypal realism and noetic
    adaequatio, 237
  and the main metaphysical
    streams of Sufism, 197
  and Schuon's epistemology,
    19–20, 100–101, 108, 197
  Ash'arite reductions adopted
    by Sufis contrasted with the
    intellective transparency of, 204
  and connection and unity with the
    Supreme Good, 205
  the contemplative essentiality and
    focus of Shankara contrasted
    with (by Schuon), 226
  and East Asian metaphysics, 272,
    272n9
  on educating the soul beginning
    with the love of physical beauty
    (*autò tò kalòn*), 217–218, 218n59
  and *methexis* (participation),
    216–217, 217n57, 242

philosophia perennis (continued)
  "immanentist" bent of Sufi metaphysics compared with, 217–218
  Platonic Good (*to agathón*) characterized as *epekeina tēs ousias* (beyond being), 162–163
Plato and Platonic philosophy—Neo Platonism, and realized gnosis (according to Schuon), 126
Plotinus, principle that "like is destined for like," 258
Prajñapāramitā. *See under* Buddhism
Prophet, the:
  Christ compared with, 338
  daughter of. *See* Fātima
  and the Hindu concept of the *avatāra*, 92n67
  identified as a greater *avatāra* by Schuon, 63
  and Schuon's commentary on the second testimony of faith of Islam, 82–83
  Krishanaite quality of, 311–313
  Muhammadun Rasūl Allāh, 82
  on the Pillars of Islam as keys to Islamic spirituality, 211, 211n45
  purification by the angel Gabriel when he was a child, 221, 221n66
  Schuon on the duality of, 220, 220nn63–64
Prothero, Stephen, 325n1

Qur'ān:
  3:54, on *Allāh* as the best of schemers, 102n8
  28:88 "Everything perishes but the Face of God," 60
  33:13 admonition to not turn back, 17
  55:66, "the stars and the trees prostrate," 213
  73:8, on the epithet of *batūl*, 243, 243n11
  Alexander mentioned in, 57n7
  bātini interpretation of, 188
  as a descent (*tanzīl*), 64, 92
  on equilibrium and moderation, 219–220
  Maryam under the "protection" (*kafala*) of Zachary in, 242
  notion of *barzakh*. *See under* esotericism
  on *rahmah*, 299
  on the relationship between God, creation, and mankind, 36
  the relationship between the Divine and the human interpreted by, 204
  Rumi's statement that "The Qur'an is like a bride," 257
  on the "unmixable" Essence of the Divine Reality that does not "descend" and does not "incarnate," 78
  vision of the afterlife and sexual pleasure, 298

Rabelais, François, frozen and thawed words in his *Fourth Book*, 361–362, 361n11
Rahner, Karl, immanent Trinity identified with the economical Trinity, 168
Ramakrishna:
  assertion that "God and His Name are one," 214
  Christian and Islamic devotional occurrences of, 192
  and the parable of the elephant and the blind men, 356
  and Schuon's "Tantrism," 319–320

Ricoeur, Paul, "hermeneutic of suspicion" coined as a term by, 13
Ringgenberg, Patrick, the validity of Schuon's concepts of universality and objectivity questioned by, 12n13
Rūmī, Jalāl ad-Dīn Muhammad:
  on the feminine as creative, 316, 316n31
  and perennialism, 189
  the power of Love to transcend all dualities and all forms, 96, 96n15
  statement that "The Qur'an is like a bride," 257
Rūzbihān, Corbin on his theophanic vision of feminine beauty, 316

Sands, Kristin Zahra, *muhkamāt* verses distinguished from the *mutashābihāt*, 298n7
Sat, Cit, and Ānanda (Being, Consciousness, and Bliss):
  and Beyond-Being (the supraontological and undifferentiated Essence), 175
  Brahman identified with, 79, 160, 160n10
  and the primacy of *Ātman* as the hallmark of Advaita Vedānta, 29, 50
  and Schuon's two types of ternaries, 158
  Vendantic triad related to Christian trinitarianism by Schuon, 168-170
Schäfer, Peter, 258n55
Scholem, Gershom, 55n5
Schuon's gnosis. *See* gnosis—Schuonian understanding of
Schuon, Frithjof:
  and Abhinavagupta, 13n24, 263

Beyond-Being. *See* supraontological Principle
letter to Martin Lings, vi
—and esoteric ecumenism, 323-350passim
  pluralism theorized by Hick (John) contrasted with, 325-332, 347
—and perennialism, 187-236passim
  esotericism, traditionalism, and universalism associated with, 188
  philosophia perennis articulated by, 6-7, 27, 234, 234n86
  the transcendent source of tradition emphasized by, 194
  and universality, 195-196
—and the Divine Feminine, 237-264passim
  and the traditional association of the feminine with *ghayb* (mystery) of the Divine Essence, 316-317
—on Sufism:
  and the absence of the term Sufism from his writing, 195
  and the Islamic character of Schuon's work and life, 189-194
—works—*Christianity/Islam*:
  on archetypes that determine religion, 197n16
  on ascesis that consists simply of sobriety, 216, 216n55
  on Christian perception of sexuality as sinful, 296n4
  on Christian trinitarianism from Schuon's "absolutist" point of view, 170, 171
  on the contemplation of God through woman by Ibn Arabī, 250n32
  on contemplation of the Essence through archetypes contained in Being, 250n32

Schuon, Frithjof *(continued)*
  on the dogmatic premises and sacramental means of each religion, 106–107, 107n15
  on Fatimah, 242n7
  on the fundamental ambiguity inherent in the experience of sexual pleasure, 299n8
  holy equilibrium of Islam compared with the holy disequlibrium of Christianity, 218, 218n60
  on the mainstream and Esoteric currents of religions originating in the biblical world, 193–194, 193n11
  Muhammad indentified as a greater *avatāra* in, 63n13
  on pedantry among theologians, 140
  on the Virgin as the "formless and primordial essence" in contrast to the Child as "formal wisdom," 247
  on the Virgin Mother as supraformal Wisdom, 240, 240n4
  —works—*Dimensions of Islam*:
    on *al-'Arsh* ("the Throne"), *ar-Rūh* ("the Spirit"), and *an-Nūr* ("the light"), 167n22
    on *an-Nūr* and *Ar-Rūh*, 89–90, 90n64
  —works—*From the Divine to the Human*:
    on the femininization of the devotee in relation to God, 306
    on gratuitous and sentimentalist forms of ecumenism, 341–342n31
    on the influence of esotericism on the decay of relgious forms, 336
    on sexuality giving rise to a subjective divinisation of the object contemplated, 321n37
    on the construction of femininity by traditional societies, 248n24
    the "victory" of religions that is affirmed by their Essence, 336–337n24
  —works—*Esoterism as Principle and as Way*:
    on abstinence, 319n35, 322
    on ascesis that brings us closer to gnosis, 216
    on Augustinian influence on the Christian perception of sexuality as sinful, 296n2
    on contemplative concentration, 199n19
    on God's capacity to perceive separative multiplicity from the point of view of his Unity, 256n49
    on the humanizing tendencies of modernist influences, 339n26
    on the incompatibility of the individualism of religious zeal with gnosis, 199n20
    on the metaphysical transparency of phenomena, 302n11
    on the nature of the soul with respect to zeal and disinterested contemplation, 201n23
    on necessary Sufism, 207
    on objectivity and de-humanization, 16n28
    the principle that form precedes from essence underlying quintessential Sufism asserted in, 227
    on the "reciprocal superiority" between the masculine and the feminine, 280
    on the relationship between essence and form, 208
    on the religion of the Heart, 223, 223n70

on "religious nationalism," 192,
  192n8
on the saving power of Islam,
  208n28
and Schuon's understanding of
  "religion," "heart," "way," and
  "oneness," 209
on the spiritual relationship
  between the feminine and the
  masculine, 313
on the theological limitations of
  some trends of Sufi theosophy,
  204
—works—*The Eye of the Heart*:
on duality as kind of "creative
  explosion," 274n17
on God in every beloved thing and
  being, 308n18
on *philosophia perennis* in India, 27
on relative impossibilities, 272n12
response to Guénon's idea of a
  reform of the West, 143n28
on the "suspension" of duality
  between two unities in the Tao,
  276n21
on *upāya* as a "saving stratagem,"
  101n7
—works—*Face of the Absolute*:
on the *barzakh* (isthmus) dividing
  the esoteric from the exoteric,
  203n27
on the danger of excessive
  emotivity, 200n22
on the duality of the Prophet,
  220nn63–64
on "formalist zeal," 198
Prajñāpāramitā and *Sophia*
  associated with the inner-most
  layers of the human heart, 87n55
on women, perfumes, and prayer
  made lovable' (*hubbiba ilayya*) to
  the Prophet, 312n26

—works—*The Feathered Sun*, 348n39
—works—*Forgotten Truth*, and the
  perennialist worldview, 4
—works—*Form and Substance in the
  Religions*:
on the Absolute and the Infinite as
  complementary, 246
on concentric circles and radii
  that summarize his metaphysical
  perspective, 293n56
on falling upward into knowledge,
  200, 200n21
on the human margin as a Divine
  condescension to human
  limitations and weaknesses,
  132
Maryam identified with esoteric
  Truth (*Ḥaqīqah*) in, 241n6
on *Māyā*, 37, 38, 39n24
and Schuon's notion of "intrinsic
  orthodoxy," 141n24
on semitic religions as gifts
  descended from Heaven,
  194n12
theological trinitarianism
  distinguished from the Trinity in,
  168
on Virgin Mary as *Shakti* and
  Sophia Perrennis, 259
yin-yang applied by Schuon to
  explain Islamic professions of
  faith, 288n47
—works—*Gnosis: Divine Wisdom*:
chapter "The Sense of the Absolute
  in Religions" in, 355, 355n4
on Existence as the universal
  Virgin who purifies, forgives and
  liberates, 252n36
Hindu terms related to Christian
  terms of the Trinity, 169–170
on the positive function of form,
  263n63

Schuon, Frithjof *(continued)*
—works—*Islam and the Perennial Philosophy*:
  Taoist tradition used to illustrate the concept of *upāya*, 115, 115n23
  on totalitarian obedientialism, 116n14
—works—*Language of the Self*:
  on "divine humility," 244n13
  on *Māyā*, 37
  on the other as like a "rediscovered mirror of God," 252n34
  on racial factors in religion, 114n22, 133
  on "Self-Knowledge and the Western Seeker," 340, 340–341n29
  Smith's (Huston) appreciation of, 4
  "A View of Yoga," 319n34
  on the Virgin as the epitome of "the humble servant of the Lord," 242
—works—*Light on the Ancient World*:
  on *Māyā*, 36
  on *Prakriti* as the "divine femininity of, 252
  Prakriti defined as "the divine femininity of *Māya*" (by Schuon), 252n35
  on *religio perennis*, 234, 234n85, 244–245n15, 347n37
  on "sacred facts" and the nature of things, 128
  on the universal intellective principle of Truth, 198–199, 199n18
Schuon, Frithjof
  assertion of the inherent self-contradiction of relativism, 13
  critique of Christian trinitarianism, 168
  on the lack of a common measure between man and the Absolute, 280
  on the relationship between the Divine Feminine and the Cosmic Masculine, 287
  and Schuon's emphasis on the contradictions of relativism, 358n8
  statement that "the substance of knowledge is the Knowledge of the Substance," 269
  on the third plane that is the Luminous Centre of the cosmos, 81, 166–167n21
—works—*Play of Masks*, on paths of inwardness and of interiorizing outwardness, 147n36, 311n24
—works—*Roots of the Human Condition*:
  on the rapid expansion of Islam, 210–211, 211n44
  in *Shakti* as *Kundalinī*, 318–319
  on Tantrism and the nature of things, 304
—works—*Songs without Names*:
  on Krishna-*līlā*, 306, 311n23
  poem the epitomized the complexities of religious tolerance, 344
—works—*Spiritual Perspectives and Human Facts*, on ascesis that brings us closer to gnosis, 217n57
—works—*Stations of Wisdom*:
  on the human form, 262n62
  major and minor types of *avatāras* distinguished in, 57n7
  on "Modes of Prayer," 214–215
  on orthodoxy, 335n22
  Zhuangzi's "only error is transmitted" interpreted by, 131, 131n7, 288–289, 289n48

—works—*Sufism: Veil and Quintessence*:
on asceticism (*zuhd*) in Sufism, 202
distinction between a Divine "stratosphere" of esoterism and a human and formal "atmosphere" of exoterism, 357, 357n7
and the Divine "stratosphere" distinguished from the human "atmosphere," 201n24
on the Essence of God and of the human being, 204n30
on the four quasi-transcendent elements, 201n25
on Ibn 'Arabī's enunciation of the metaphysics of Unity, 212, 212n47
metaphysics in Sufism, 207
on necessary Sufism, 207
on the pendantic formalism of Hinduism, 141n25
on racial factors in religion, 135, 135n17
on the resemblance of the word *lā* to a pair of scissors, 213
on *salāt* (canonical prayer), 213
and Schuon's understanding of "religion," "heart," "way," and "oneness," 210
on *siyām* (fasting) as detachment, 215
on *upāya* as a "saving mirage," 101n7, 102n9
—works—*Survey of Metaphysics and Esoterism*:
chapter "Outline of Religious Typologies" in, 355
on contemplation of the Essence through archetypes contained in Being, 250n31
illustrations of a legalistic sense of fear that borders on the absurd provided by, 205–206n31
the Infinite characterized as the "mirror" of the Absolute by, 246n18
—works—*To Have a Center*:
on "confessional bias," 192, 192n8
dangers of masculinity and femininity assessed in, 278
leitmotif of his work that "the oneness of the object demands the totality of the subject," 359
Mary as a feminine *avatāra* explained in, 85, 85n49
on the negative functions of the Logos-Demiurge, 307n17
on racial factors in religion, 134nn11–12
on the unlimited aspects of the Real, 16n29
—works—*The Transcendent Unity of Religion*:
analogy of light and colors, 229n80
on the consequences implied in limitations considered necessary for the vitality of a religion, 362
and critique from the perspective of modern pluralism, 324–325, 325n1
dogmatic conception contrasted with the metaphysical outlook, 17
on Al-Ghazālī and the parable of the elephant and the blind men, 356, 356n6
on religion as a kind of "desecration," 342
and Schuon's criticisms of contemporary religious life, 142n26
on Tantrism as normative and universal, 304n13
on the transcendent reality of the Essence, 360n10

Schuon, Frithjof *(continued)*
—works—*Treasures of Buddhism,*
6n15
on the adogmatic character of Zen,
341n30
on the doctrine of the three bodies
of the Buddha (*trikāya*), 68
on the *pāramitā*s (six perfections of
wisdom), 233
on religious misogyny, 261
on the saving function of the
avatāra as a characteristic shared
by the Buddha and Christ, 68
on the structure of metaphysical
'vision' as like a spiral, 293n55
on the view of *upāya* as mere
illusion, 112
—works—*Understanding Islam*:
chapter "The Way" on Sufism, 195
the epistemological and cultural
norms of modern mankind
addressed by, 5
on the metaphysical meaning of
Muhammadun Rasūl Allāh, 82
on misconceptions of the Absolure,
332–333
Muhammad discussed in light
of the Hindu concept of the
avatāra, 92n67
and Schuon's commentary on the
second testimony of faith of
Islam, 82–83
Smith's (Huston) praise of, 4n8
the Unity as an essence hidden
with the Trinity explained in,
166, 169
—works—*World's Religions,* and the
perennialist worldview, 4
Shah-Kazemi, Reza, 222
Shankara:
Plato's rationalizing modality
contrasted with (by Schuon), 226

on the relationship between *Ātman*
and *Māya,* 37–38
and the Goddess, 38n21
the illusion (*Māyā*) associated
with the eternity of the cycle
of *samsāra,* 37, 37n19
See also Advaita Vedānta
sharī'ah, 134
and *haqīqah,* 212, 212n47, 222–223,
227
and *tarīqah,* 233
Shaykh 'Ahmad al-'Alawī, 253,
253n41
Shaykh al-Akbar. See Ibn al-'Arabī,
Muhyī-al-Dīn
Shin, Kiseong, 328n11
shirk ("sin" of "association"):
of idolatry, 59, 224
and polytheism, 78
Shulman, Eviatar, 104n12
Singh, Jaideva, 45n30
Śiva-Śakti, and the Kashmir Śaivite
account of metaphysical
unfolding, 28
Smith, Huston:
and the critique of the scientistic
outlook, 5
and Huxley (Aldous), 5–6, 6n13
perennialist worldview articulated
by, 2, 4, 325n1
Smith, Wilfred Cantwell, on the
intellectualization of faith,
139–149, 139n22
Steuco, Agustino, 1–2
Sufism:
ascetic feats of Sufis, 218
and Ash'arite theology, 204, 206,
212n48
emphasis on tradition and lineage,
188–189
limitations of voluntaristic
perspective of classical Sufism

(according to Schuon), 198–201,
205–206, 215–216
and *philosophia perennis*, 188–189,
195–196
and the Qurʾānic perspective on
the relationship between God,
creation, and mankind, 36
and Schuon's understanding of
Reality, 196, 196n15
and Schuon's understanding of
"religion," "heart," "way," and
"oneness," 207–209
Schuon's views contrasted with
Guénon's association of it with
Shadhilism, 191n6
See also Rūmī, Jalāl ad-Dīn
Muhammad
Sufism—"quintessential Sufism":
"average" and "quintessential"
Sufism distinguished in terms
of exoterism and esoterism,
202–205, 203n28
and "fifth essence" (*quinta essentia*),
201
and the principle that form
precedes from essence, 227
—"quintessential Sufism" and the
pillars of Islam, 211–213
viewed as quintessential esoterism
(according to Schuon), 209–210,
233
Sufi theosophy—Divine Essence of
(*adh-dhāt al-ilāhiyyah*), 328,
328n10
"immanentist" bent of Sufi
metaphysics compared with
the Platonic emphasis on
participation, 217–218
supra-ontological Principle:
and Christian trinitarianism from
Schuon's "absolutist" point of
view, 170

Mary as the Divine Essence in its
super-ontological Mystery,
238
supra-ontological Principle—Beyond-
Being defined by Schuon as the
unity of, 74–75, 154
and the Buddhist doctrine of the
three bodies of the Buddha
(*trikāya*), 67–71
and the supreme and horizontal
view of the Essence, 79
Suzuki, Daisetz Teitaro:
on four aspects of Buddha, 72–73
statement that "the world induced
by LSD is false or unreal," 6,
6n14
Suzuki, Shunryu, on "the way things
is," 124

Tantrism:
and the aesthetic inflection of
Schuon's leanings, 302–303
definition of, 301–302, 301nn9–10
and Krishnaite qualities. See
Krishna and Krishnaism
left-handed and right-handed
tantra, 303–304
and the nature of things (according
to Schuon), 303–304
popularization of, 318
and the primordial as normative
and universal, 304, 304n13
Tao-ch'o (Jp. Doshaku), on four
aspects of Buddha, 72–73
Taoism:
Laozi on "The Name that can be
named is not the true Name,"
115, 115n23
Laozi's metaphysical account, 55,
270
Laozi's symbol of a wheel's axle,
293, 293n57

Taoism *(continued)*
  Laozi's vision of the Ultimate as the "Great Female" or the "Spirit of the Valley," 285–286, 286n42
  Zhuangzi's dream of being a butterfly, 292, 292n52
  Zhuangzi's statement that "only error is transmitted," 131, 131n7, 288–289, 289n48
  Zhuangzi's Taoist view of manifestation, 270
  Zhuangzi's vision of the Perfect Man as pure receptivity, 285–286
Taoism—*yin-yang* symbolism:
  and hierarchy with regard to *yin* and *yang*, 279
  and Laozi's *Tao Te Ching*, 275
  and Schuon on "visual thinking," 292, 292n54
  and the symbolic presentation found in traditional metaphysical teachings, 269–270
  and Schuon's dyad of "relatively Absolute" and the "reflection of the Absolute in the relative," 274
  and Schuon's explanation of Islamic *shahādah* (profession of faith), 287–288, 288n47
  and Schuon's explanation of the relationship between the Divine Feminine and the Cosmic Masculine, 286–287
  and terms suggesting degrees of relativity in Schuon's doctrinal vocabulary, 358
  Wang (Robin) on *yin-yang* as a graphic representation of a doctrinal statement, 292, 292nn54-54
  Zhuangzi on the cold of *yin* and the heat of *yang*, 277–278

tasawwuf. See under gnosis—Schuonian understanding of
Trinity and Trinitarian interpretation:
  Buddhist doctrine of the three bodies of the Buddha (*trikāya*) contrasted with, 67–71
  and the conflation of the super-ontological and the ontological, 172
  and the identification of each of the Persons with the "entirety" of the Essence by the Fourth Lateran Council (1215), 181–182
  Dionysius on, 172–173, 180
  and Eckhart (Meister). *See* Eckhart, Meister
  and the Hindu tradition. *See Sat, Cit,* and *Ānanda*
  immanent and economical Trinity distinguished, 167–168
  and incarnation as anathema from an Islamic perspective, 78–80, 91–93, 92n67
  Schuonian gnosis, 88–89, 93
  theological trinitarianism distinguished from the Trinity (by Schuon), 168–169
  Trinitarian Thomism. *See* Aquinas, Thomas, Trinitarian theology of
  See also Islam—doctrine of the Trinity of *al-'Arsh* ("the Throne"), *ar-Rūh* ("the Spirit"), and *an-Nūr* ("the light")
  —and Schuon's geometric symbolism of "horizontal" integrity and "vertical" begetting, 79–80, 164–168, 175
  "supreme" and "horizontal" view of the Essence, 79–80, 92–93
  "horizontal" view of three aspects of God, 80–81

"vertical" understanding of the three hypostases as different degrees of the Real, 81, 92
"horizontal" view from the level of Existence, 81–83
and the Hindu cosmological triad of sattva, rajas, and tamas, 158
and the Hindu triplicity of *Sat*, *Cit*, and *Ānanda*, 158, 160, 163, 169, 175
on the Man-God is the Luminous Centre of the cosmos, 81–82
Trinity—Father (first Person), as *aita* (the cause of the Son and the Spirit), 80–81n43
Trinity—Son or Logos (second Person), incarnation as Jesus, 80n43
Trinity—Holy Spirit (third Person), the Infinite associated with, 80

Upanishads:
on love as a quest for Self, 307
on *Māyā*, 33–35, 38, 43
the religious and spiritual climate of the Bible, the Talmud, and the Islamic *sharī'ah* distinguished from, 134
upāya:
Buddhist view of the conventional nature of, 101, 118–119, 120–121, 120n29
and the view of *upāya* as mere illusion, 112
and the Mahāyana differentiation between conventional truth (*samvriti*) and the ultimate truth (*paramārtha*), 119–120
Schuon on Christian *upāya*, 102, 102n9, 113–117
Schuon on Islamic *upāya*, 102, 102n9, 113, 115–117, 299

and Schuon on the nature of things, 114, 130
Schuon's rendering as "saving mirages" and "saving stratagems," 101–102, 101n7
and terms suggesting degrees of relativity in Schuon's doctrinal vocabulary, 358

Virgin Mary (or Maryam):
as the epitome of the Feminine *in divinis*, 25
and the epithet of "Mother of God" or *Theotokos*, 238
as the epitome of "the humble servant of the Lord," 242
Islam—esoteric core (*haqīqah*) of, 241, 241n6
John (the "favorite disciple") associated with, 242, 242n8
Mary as a feminine *avatāra* explained by Schuon, 85, 85n49
Schuonian Mariology critiqued by Cutsinger (James), 239, 239nn2–3
the Virgin as the "formless and primordial essence" in contrast to the Child as "formal wisdom" (according to Schuon), 247
and Wisdom, 240, 240n4, 258–259, 259n59
Shakti and *Sophia Perrennis* associated with her by Schuon, 259

Wang, Robin, 274n16
on *yin-yang* as a graphic representation of a doctrinal statement, 292, 292nn54–54
Weil, Simone, 17–18

Xing, Guang, 68

yin-yang symbolism. *See* Taoism—*yin-yang* symbolism

Zhou Dunyi (1017–1073), 277
Zhuangzi. *See under* Taoism

www.ingramcontent.com/pod-product-compliance
Lightning Source LLC
Chambersburg PA
CBHW020258240426
43673CB00039B/634